Fruits Basket

Volume 21

Ow!

Even Ren-san might try to get up too fast and crush her hair with her elbow.

snag

Natsuki Takaya

Fruits Basket Volume 21
Created by Natsuki Takaya

Translation - Alethea & Athena Nibley
English Adaptation - Lianne Sentar
Copy Editor - Stephanie Duchin
Retouch and Lettering - Star Print Brokers
Production Artist - Michael Paolilli
Graphic Designer - Tina Corrales

Editor - Alexis Kirsch
Pre-Production Supervisor - Vicente Rivera, Jr.
Print-Production Specialist - Lucas Rivera
Managing Editor - Vy Nguyen
Senior Designer - Louis Csontos
Senior Designer - James Lee
Senior Editor - Bryce P. Coleman
Senior Editor - Jenna Winterberg
Associate Publisher - Marco F. Pavia
President and C.O.O. - John Parker
C.E.O. and Chief Creative Officer - Stu Levy

A  **TOKYOPOP** Manga

TOKYOPOP Inc.
5900 Wilshire Blvd. Suite 2000
Los Angeles, CA 90036

E-mail: info@TOKYOPOP.com
Come visit us online at www.TOKYOPOP.com

ISBN: 978-1-4278-0682-6

First TOKYOPOP printing: November 2008

10 9 8 7 6 5 4 3 2 1

Printed in the USA

Fruits Basket ™

Volume 21

By
Natsuki Takaya

HAMBURG // LONDON // LOS ANGELES // TOKYO

Fruits Basket

Table of Contents

STORY SO FAR...

Hello, I'm Tohru Honda, and I have come to know a terrible secret. After the death of my mother, I was living by myself in a tent, when the Sohma family took me in. I soon learned that the Sohma family lives with a curse! Each family member is possessed by the vengeful spirit of an animal from the Chinese Zodiac. Whenever one of them becomes weak or is hugged by a member of the opposite sex, that person changes into his or her Zodiac animal!

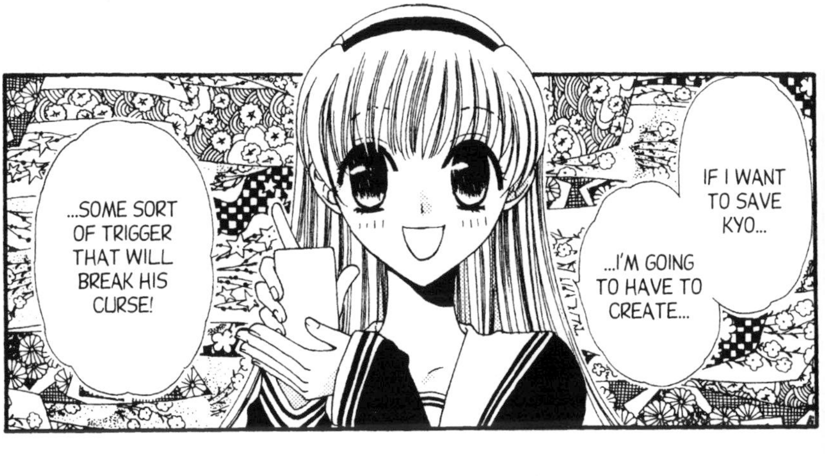
IF I WANT TO SAVE KYO...
...I'M GOING TO HAVE TO CREATE...
...SOME SORT OF TRIGGER THAT WILL BREAK HIS CURSE!

Tohru Honda

The ever-optimistic heroine of our story. An orphan, she now lives in Shigure's house, along with Yuki and Kyo, and is the only person outside of the family who knows the Sohma family's curse.

Yuki Sohma, the Rat

Soft-spoken. Self-esteem issues. At school, he's called "Prince Yuki."

Kyo Sohma, the Cat

The Cat who was left out of the Zodiac. Hates Yuki, leeks and miso. But mostly Yuki.

Kagura Sohma, the Boar

Bashful, yet headstrong. Determined to marry Kyo, even if it kills him.

Fruits Basket Characters

Mabudachi Trio

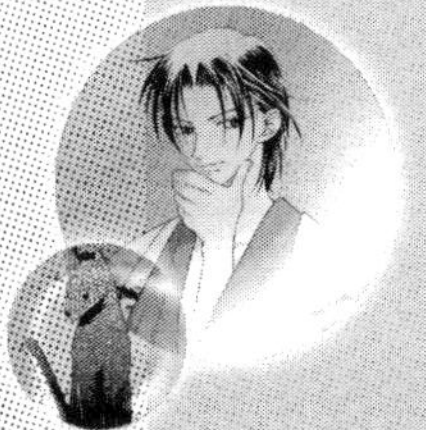

Shigure Sohma, the Dog

Enigmatic, mischievous and a little perverted. A popular novelist.

Hatori Sohma, the Dragon

Family doctor to the Sohmas. Only thing he can't cure is his broken heart.

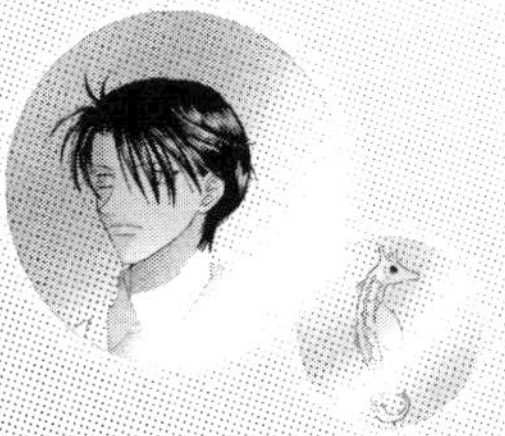

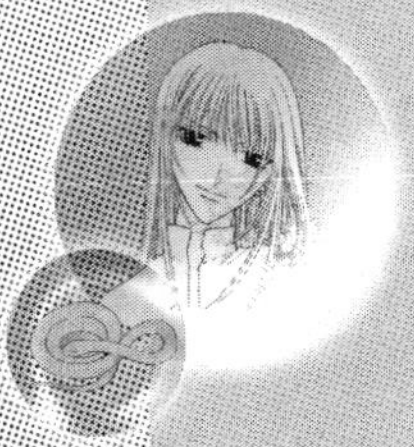

Ayame Sohma, the Snake

Yuki's older brother. A proud and playful drama queen…er, king. Runs a costume shop.

Saki Hanajima

"Hana-chan." Can sense people's "waves." Goth demeanor scares her classmates.

Arisa Uotani

"Uo-chan." A tough-talking "Yankee" who looks out for her friends.

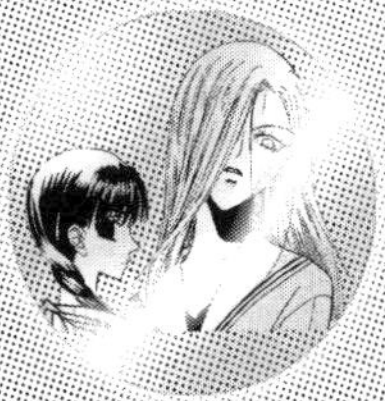

Tohru's Best Friends

Hiro Sohma, the Ram (or sheep)

This caustic tyke is skilled at throwing verbal barbs, but he has a soft spot for Kisa.

Momiji Sohma, the Rabbit

Half German. He's older than he looks. His mother rejected him because of the Sohma curse. His little sister, Momo, has been kept from him most of her life.

Hatsuharu Sohma, the Ox

The nicest of guys, except when he goes "Black." Then you'd better watch out. He was once in a relationship with Rin.

Kisa Sohma, the Tiger

Kisa became shy and self-conscious due to constant teasing by her classmates. Yuki, who has similar insecurities, feels particularly close to Kisa.

Fruits Basket Characters

Isuzu "Rin" Sohma, the Horse

She was once in a relationship with Hatsuharu (Haru)...and Tohru leaves her rather cold. Rin is full of pride, and she can't stand the amount of deference the other Sohma family members give Akito.

Ritsu Sohma, the Monkey

This shy, kimono-wearing member of the Sohma family is gorgeous. But this "she" is really a he!! Cross-dressing calms his nerves.

Kureno Sohma, the Rooster (or bird)

He is Akito's very favorite, and spends almost all of his time on the Sohma estate, tending to Akito's every desire. Kureno was born possessed by the spirit of the Bird, but his curse broke long ago...which means we've never seen him transformed. He pities Akito's loneliness, and can't bring himself to leave her.

"God"

Akito Sohma

The head of the Sohma clan. A dark figure of many secrets. Treated with fear and reverence. It has recently been revealed that Akito is actually a woman!

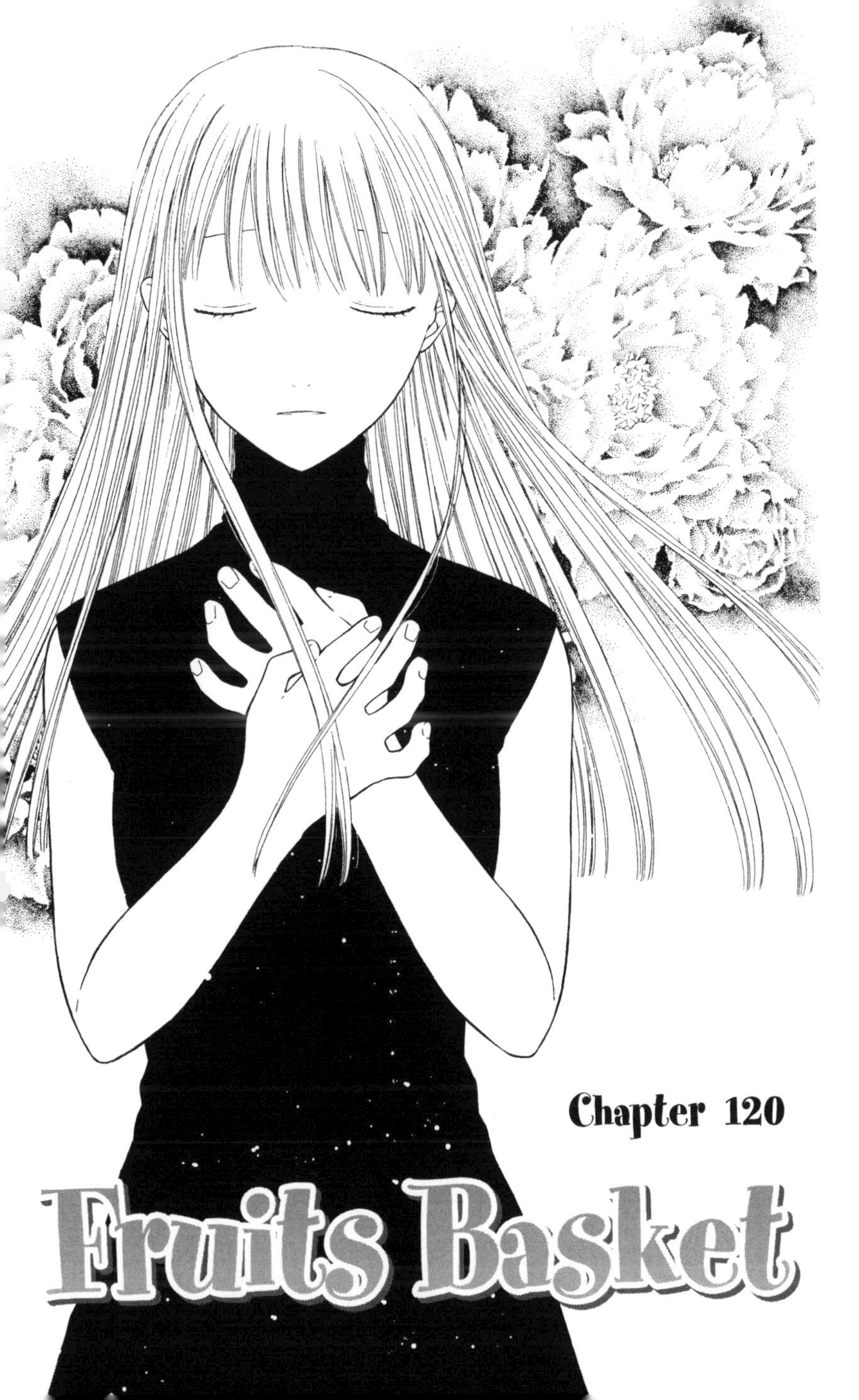
Chapter 120
Fruits Basket

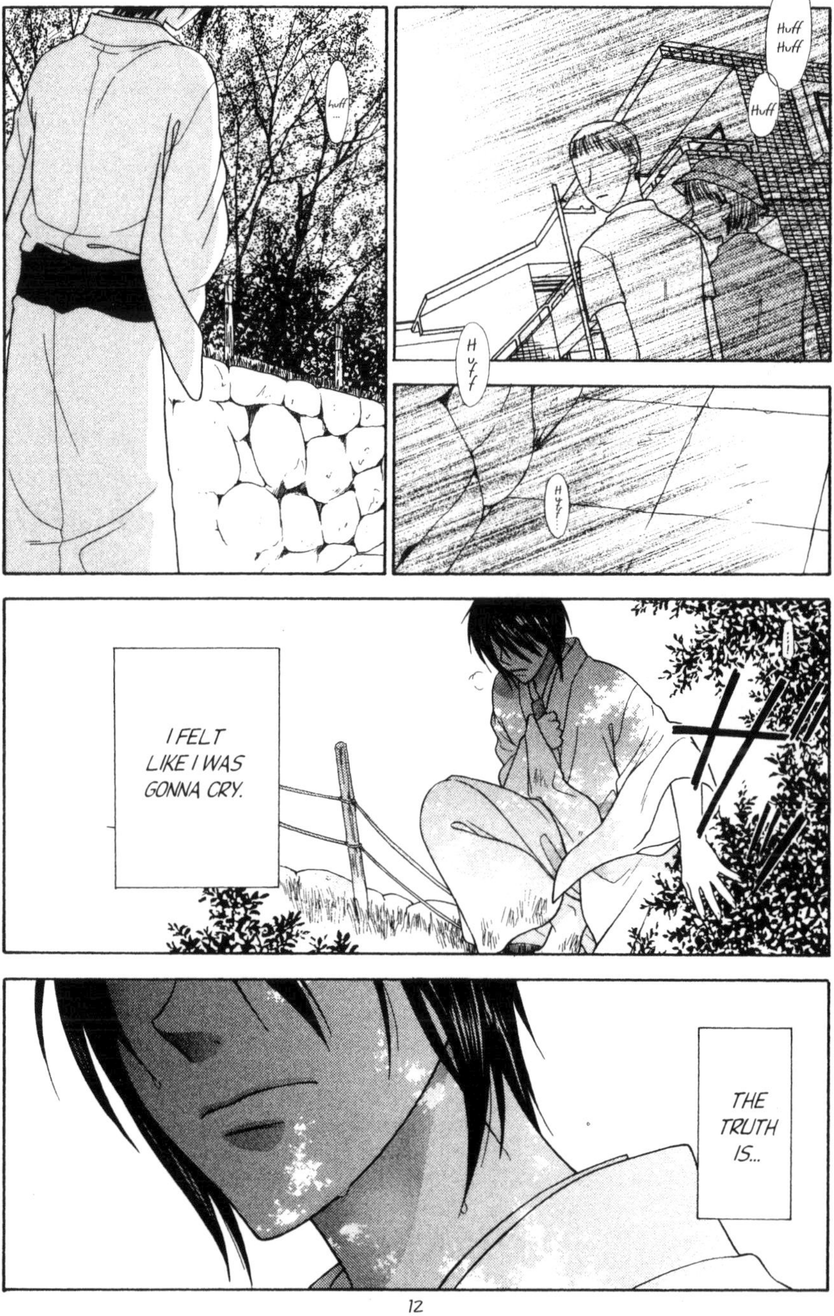
Huff Huff
Huff
Huff
Huff...
huff...
...!
I FELT LIKE I WAS GONNA CRY.
THE TRUTH IS...

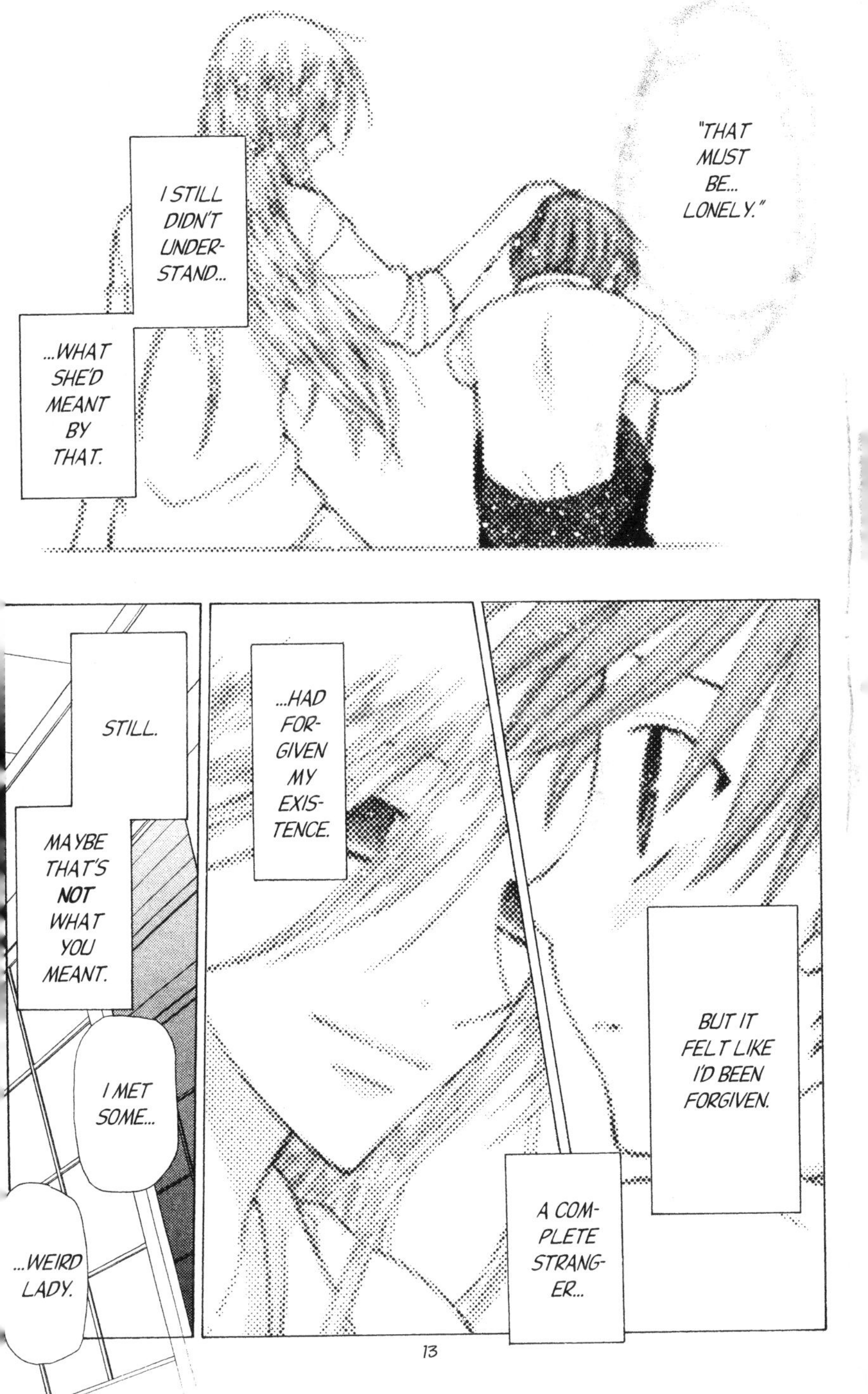
"THAT MUST BE... LONELY."
I STILL DIDN'T UNDER-STAND...
...WHAT SHE'D MEANT BY THAT.
BUT IT FELT LIKE I'D BEEN FORGIVEN.
A COM-PLETE STRANG-ER...
...HAD FOR-GIVEN MY EXIS-TENCE.
STILL.
MAYBE THAT'S **NOT** WHAT YOU MEANT.
I MET SOME...
...WEIRD LADY.

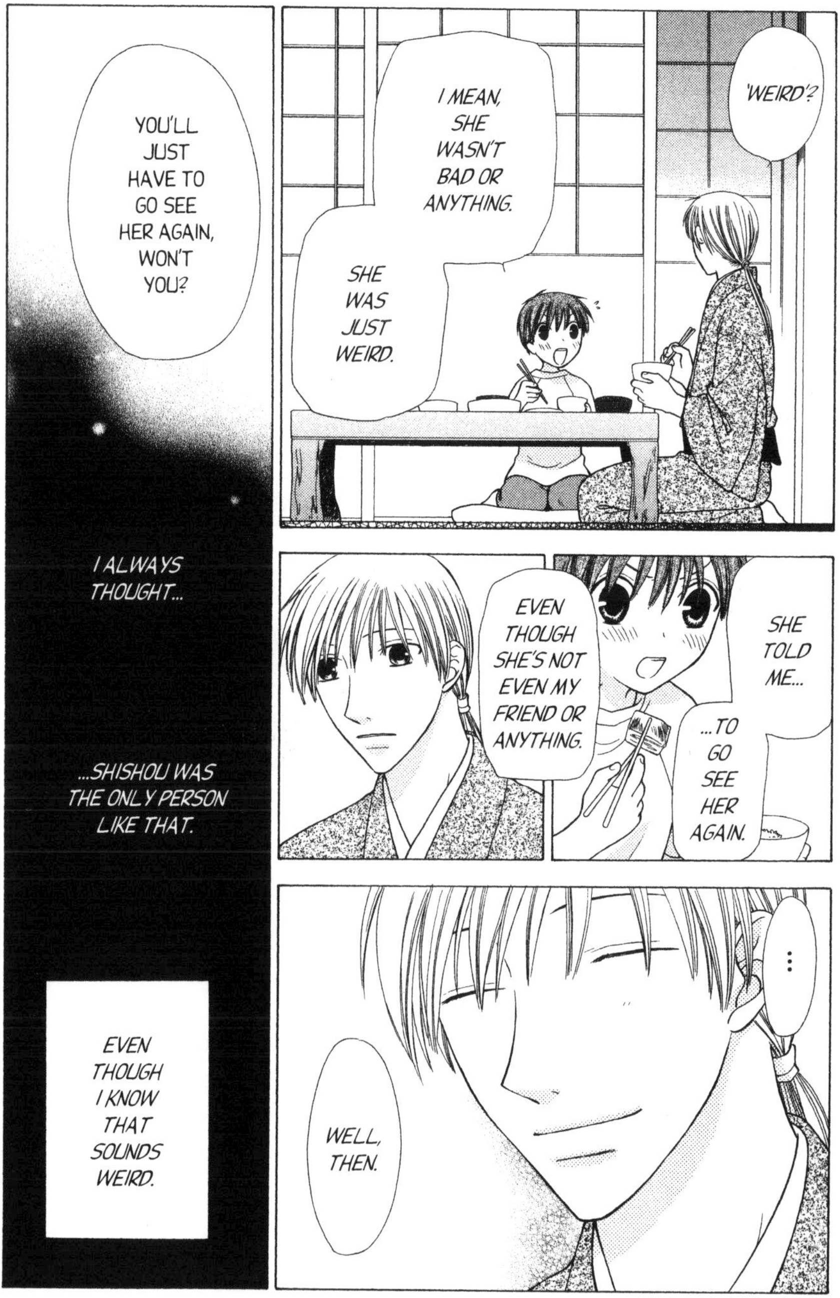
'WEIRD'?
I MEAN, SHE WASN'T BAD OR ANYTHING.
SHE WAS JUST WEIRD.
SHE TOLD ME...
...TO GO SEE HER AGAIN.
EVEN THOUGH SHE'S NOT EVEN MY FRIEND OR ANYTHING.
...
WELL, THEN.
YOU'LL JUST HAVE TO GO SEE HER AGAIN, WON'T YOU?
I ALWAYS THOUGHT...
...SHISHOU WAS THE ONLY PERSON LIKE THAT.
EVEN THOUGH I KNOW THAT SOUNDS WEIRD.

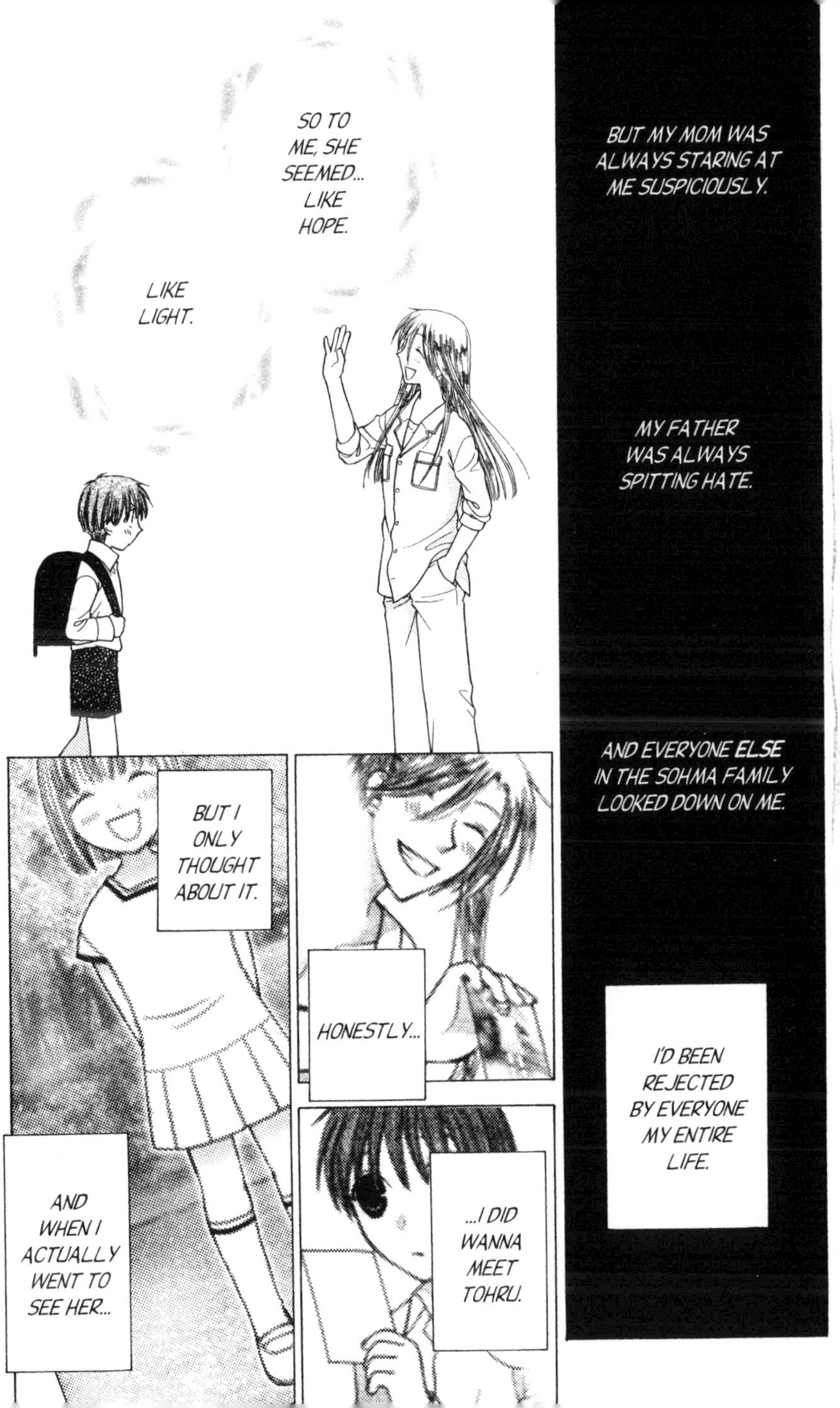
BUT MY MOM WAS ALWAYS STARING AT ME SUSPICIOUSLY.
MY FATHER WAS ALWAYS SPITTING HATE.
AND EVERYONE ELSE IN THE SOHMA FAMILY LOOKED DOWN ON ME.
I'D BEEN REJECTED BY EVERYONE MY ENTIRE LIFE.
SO TO ME, SHE SEEMED... LIKE HOPE.
LIKE LIGHT.
HONESTLY...
...I DID WANNA MEET TOHRU.
BUT I ONLY THOUGHT ABOUT IT.
AND WHEN I ACTUALLY WENT TO SEE HER...

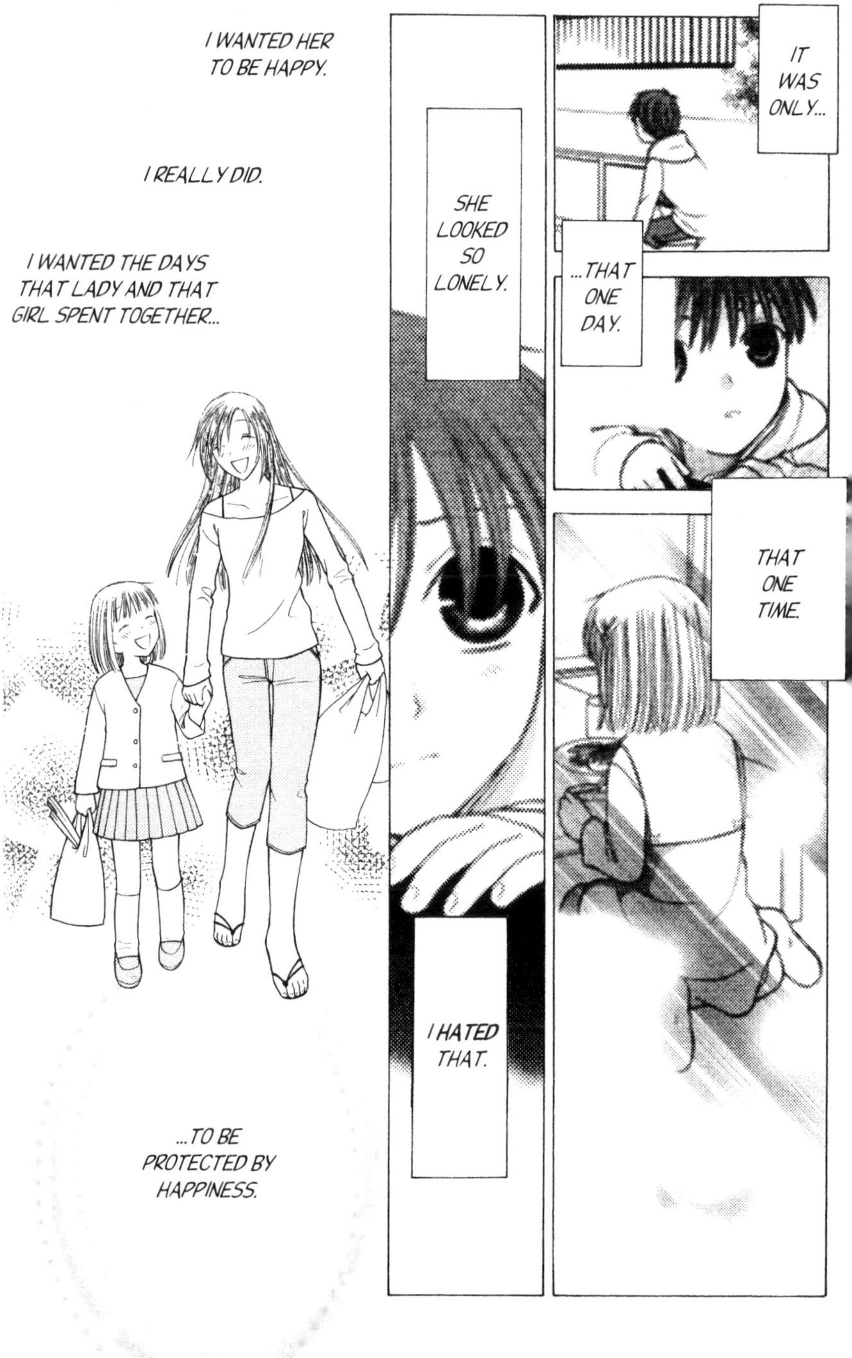
IT WAS ONLY...
...THAT ONE DAY.
THAT ONE TIME.
SHE LOOKED SO LONELY.
I HATED THAT.
I WANTED HER TO BE HAPPY.
I REALLY DID.
I WANTED THE DAYS THAT LADY AND THAT GIRL SPENT TOGETHER...
...TO BE PROTECTED BY HAPPINESS.

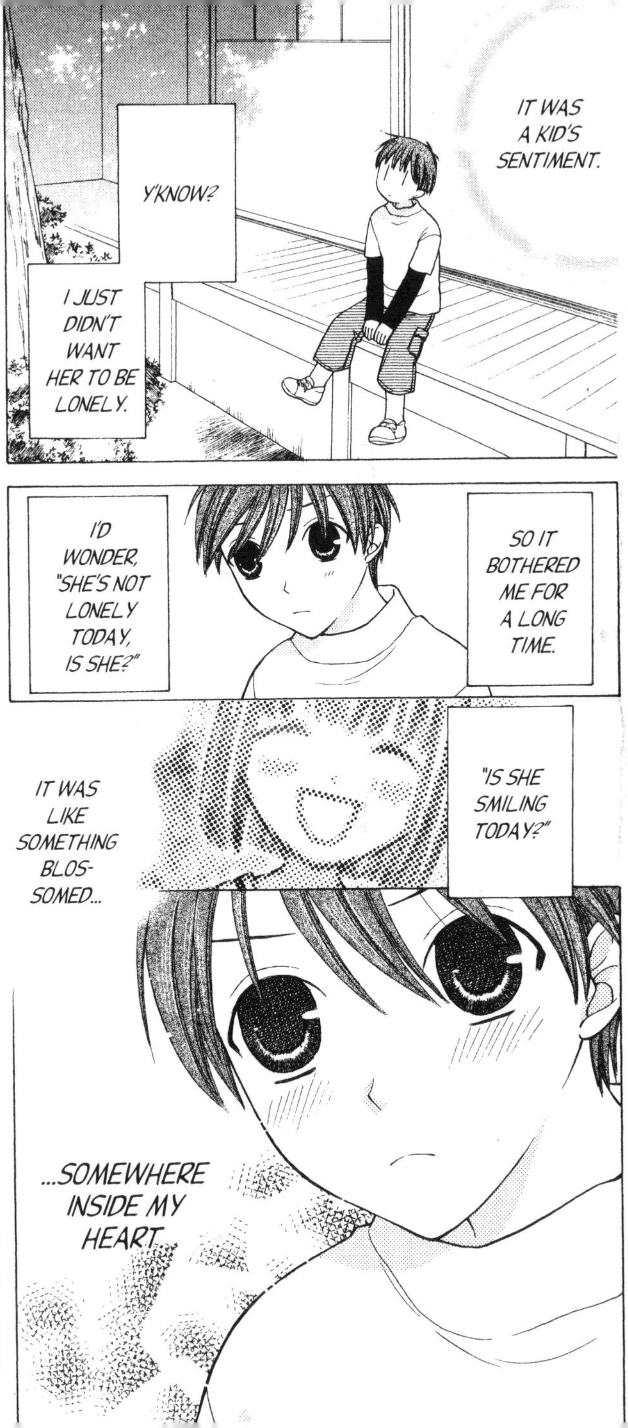
IT WAS A KID'S SENTIMENT.
Y'KNOW?
I JUST DIDN'T WANT HER TO BE LONELY.
SO IT BOTHERED ME FOR A LONG TIME.
I'D WONDER, "SHE'S NOT LONELY TODAY, IS SHE?"
"IS SHE SMILING TODAY?"
IT WAS LIKE SOMETHING BLOS-SOMED...
...SOMEWHERE INSIDE MY HEART.

Fruits Basket

Nice to meet you and hello. I'm Takaya, presenting Furuba Volume 21. The cover this time is Ren-san. Actually, Furuba ended up being one volume longer than I anticipated, and that meant there would have to be one more cover model than planned. "Oh, no!" I thought. "Who should it be?" I couldn't decide even up until Volume 20 came out, and I worried and worried, and then I ended up with Ren-san. So now you know. The truth is, there's a character other than Ren-san I wanted to put on a cover... (I'm sorry, Ren-san.) But thinking about it reasonably, it really should be Ren-san. Somehow, the "uniform cover project" (although it's not so great as to be called that) that I wished for since Volume 1 looks like it will be a success. (laugh) Now then, please enjoy Volume 21.

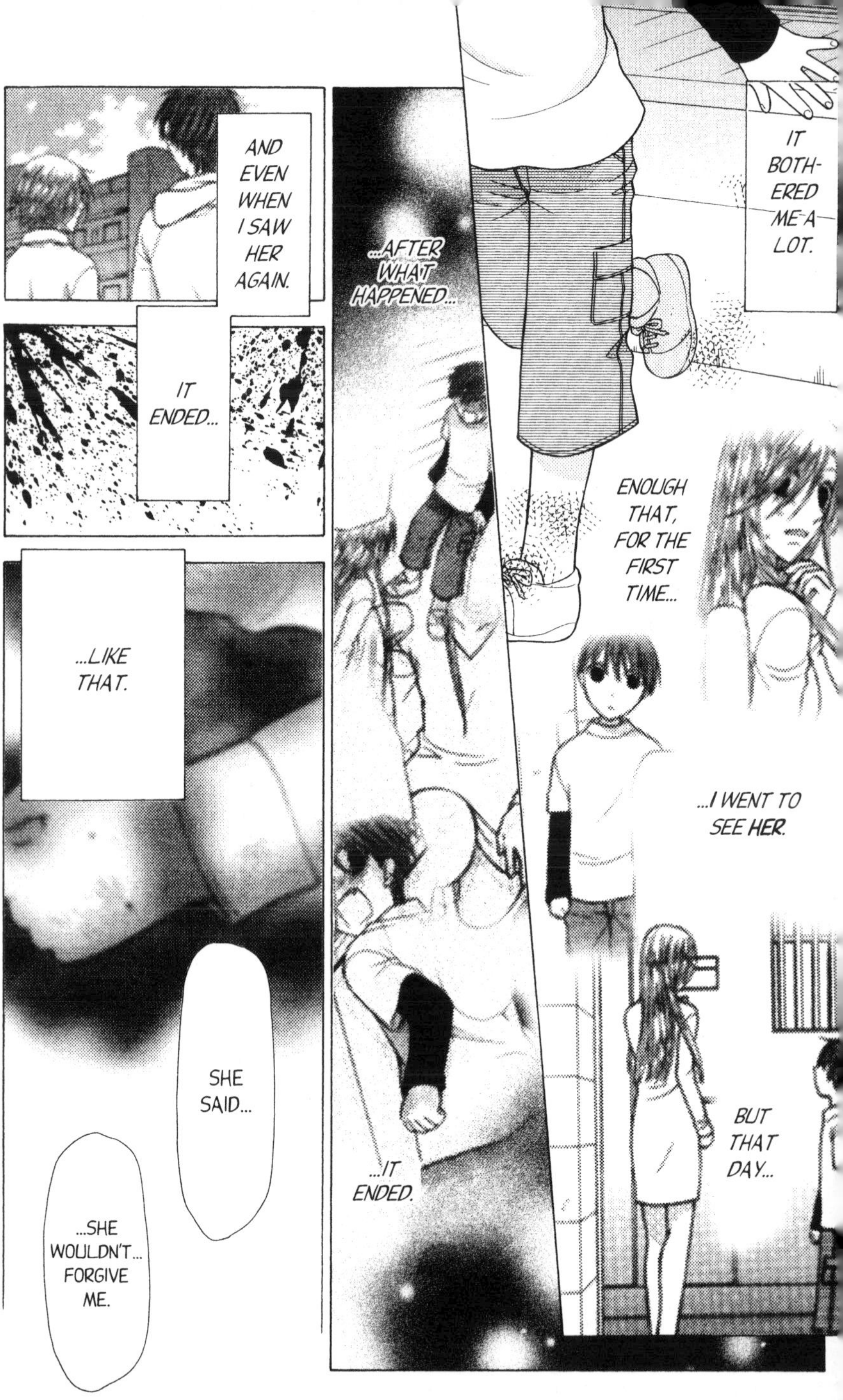
IT BOTHERED ME A LOT.
ENOUGH THAT, FOR THE FIRST TIME...
...I WENT TO SEE HER.
BUT THAT DAY...
...AFTER WHAT HAPPENED...
...IT ENDED.
AND EVEN WHEN I SAW HER AGAIN.
IT ENDED...
...LIKE THAT.
SHE SAID...
...SHE WOULDN'T... FORGIVE ME.

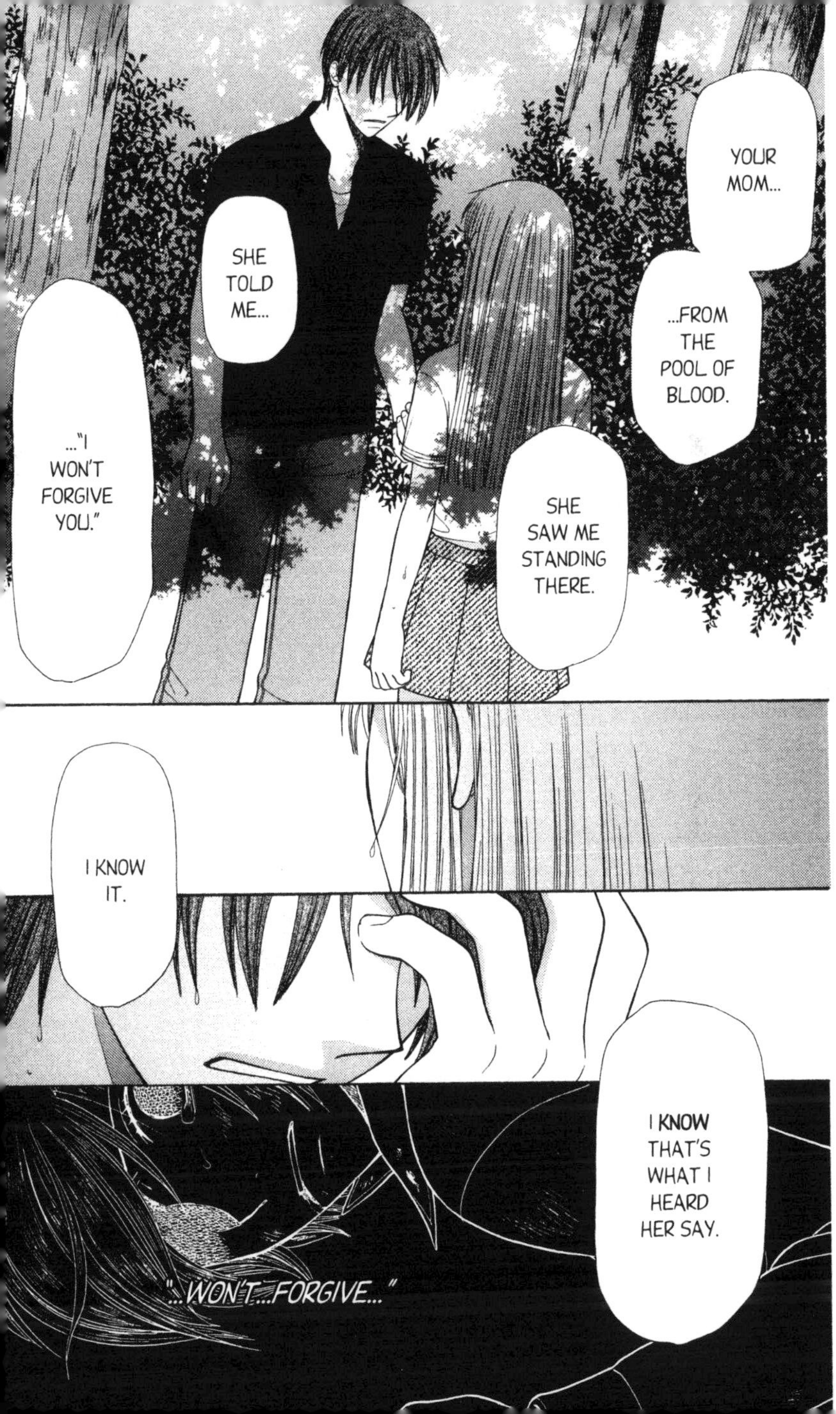
YOUR MOM...
...FROM THE POOL OF BLOOD.
SHE SAW ME STANDING THERE.
SHE TOLD ME...
..."I WON'T FORGIVE YOU."
I KNOW IT.
I KNOW THAT'S WHAT I HEARD HER SAY.
"...WON'T...FORGIVE..."

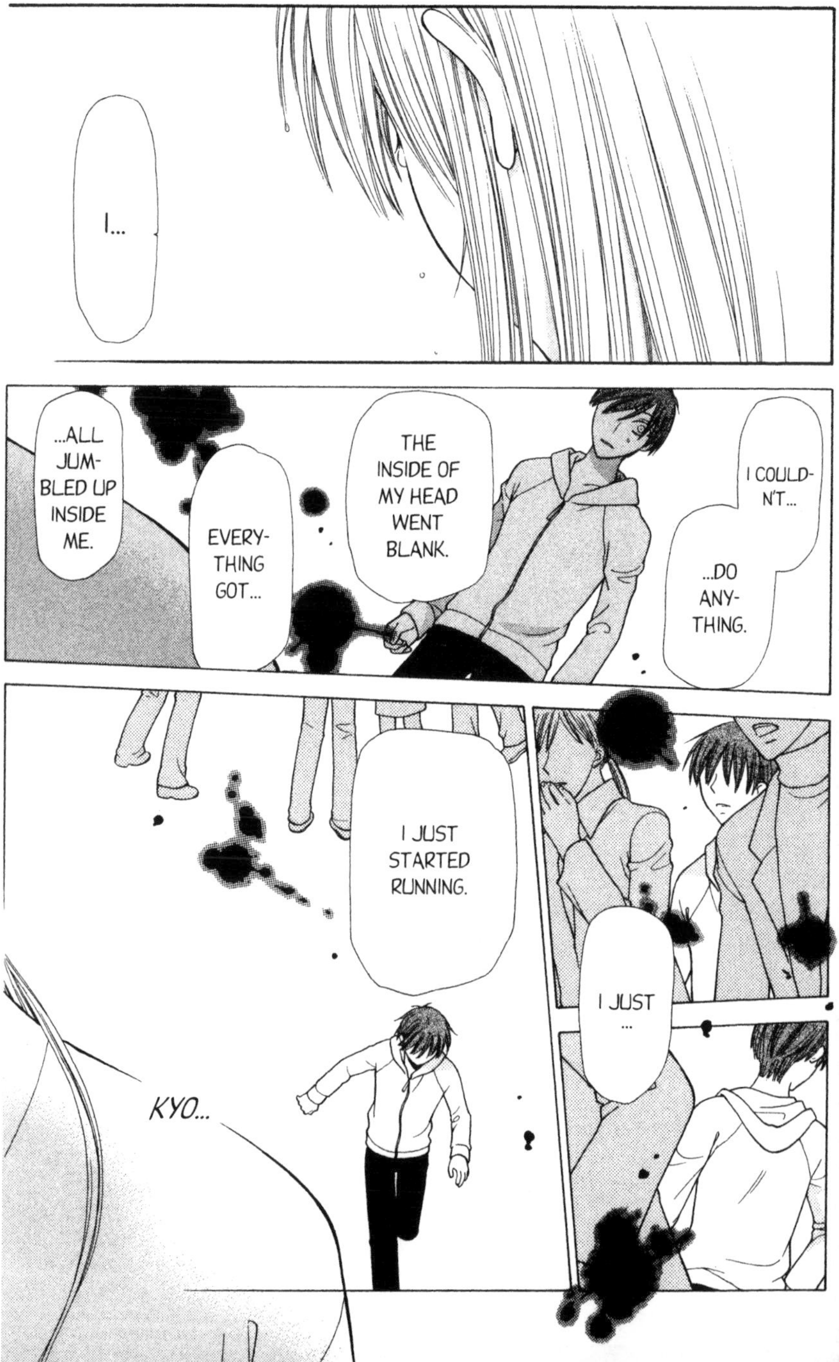
I...
I COULDN'T...
...DO ANYTHING.
THE INSIDE OF MY HEAD WENT BLANK.
EVERYTHING GOT...
...ALL JUMBLED UP INSIDE ME.
I JUST ...
I JUST STARTED RUNNING.
KYO...

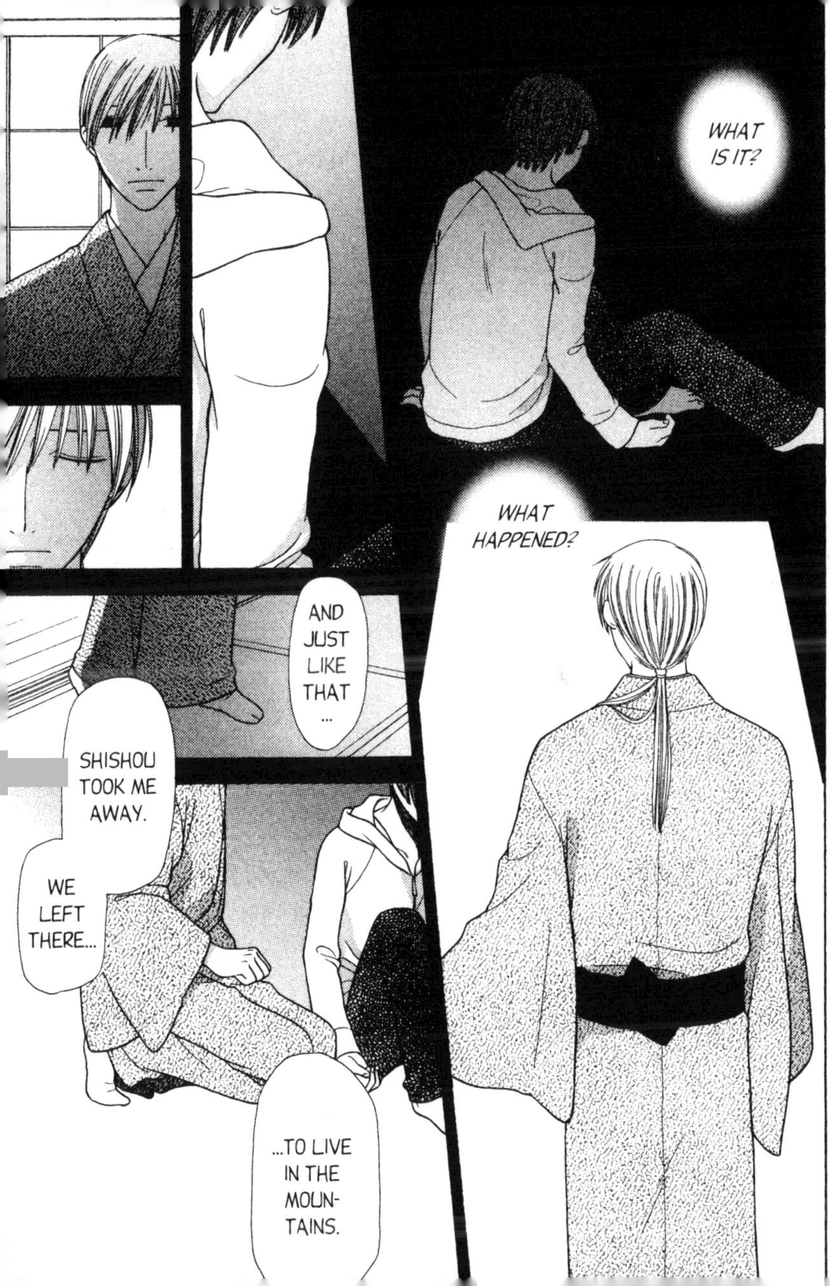
WHAT IS IT?
WHAT HAPPENED?
AND JUST LIKE THAT...
SHISHOU TOOK ME AWAY.
WE LEFT THERE...
...TO LIVE IN THE MOUNTAINS.

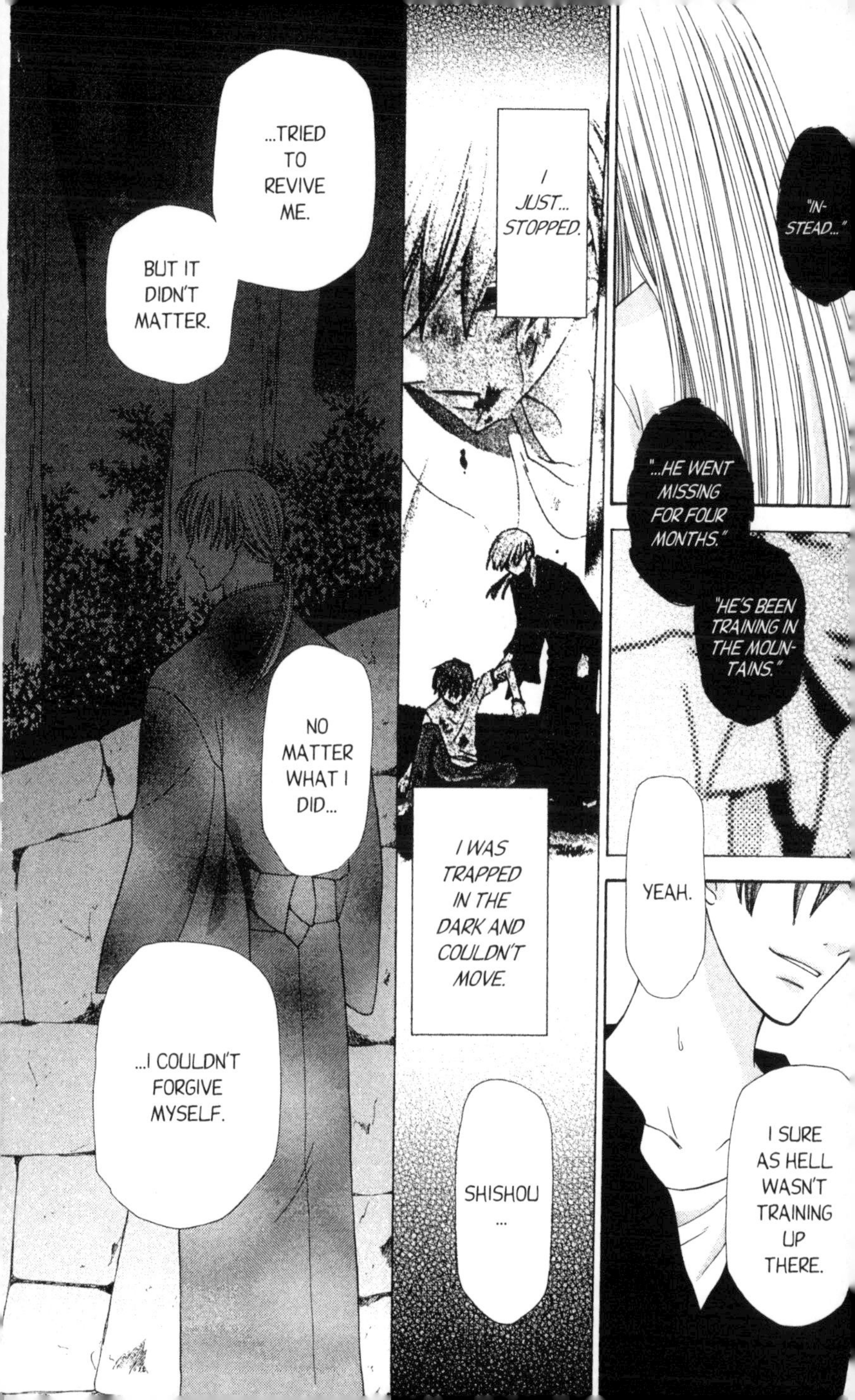
"IN-STEAD..."
"...HE WENT MISSING FOR FOUR MONTHS."
"HE'S BEEN TRAINING IN THE MOUN-TAINS."
YEAH.
I SURE AS HELL WASN'T TRAINING UP THERE.
I JUST... STOPPED.
I WAS TRAPPED IN THE DARK AND COULDN'T MOVE.
SHISHOU ...
...TRIED TO REVIVE ME.
BUT IT DIDN'T MATTER.
NO MATTER WHAT I DID...
...I COULDN'T FORGIVE MYSELF.

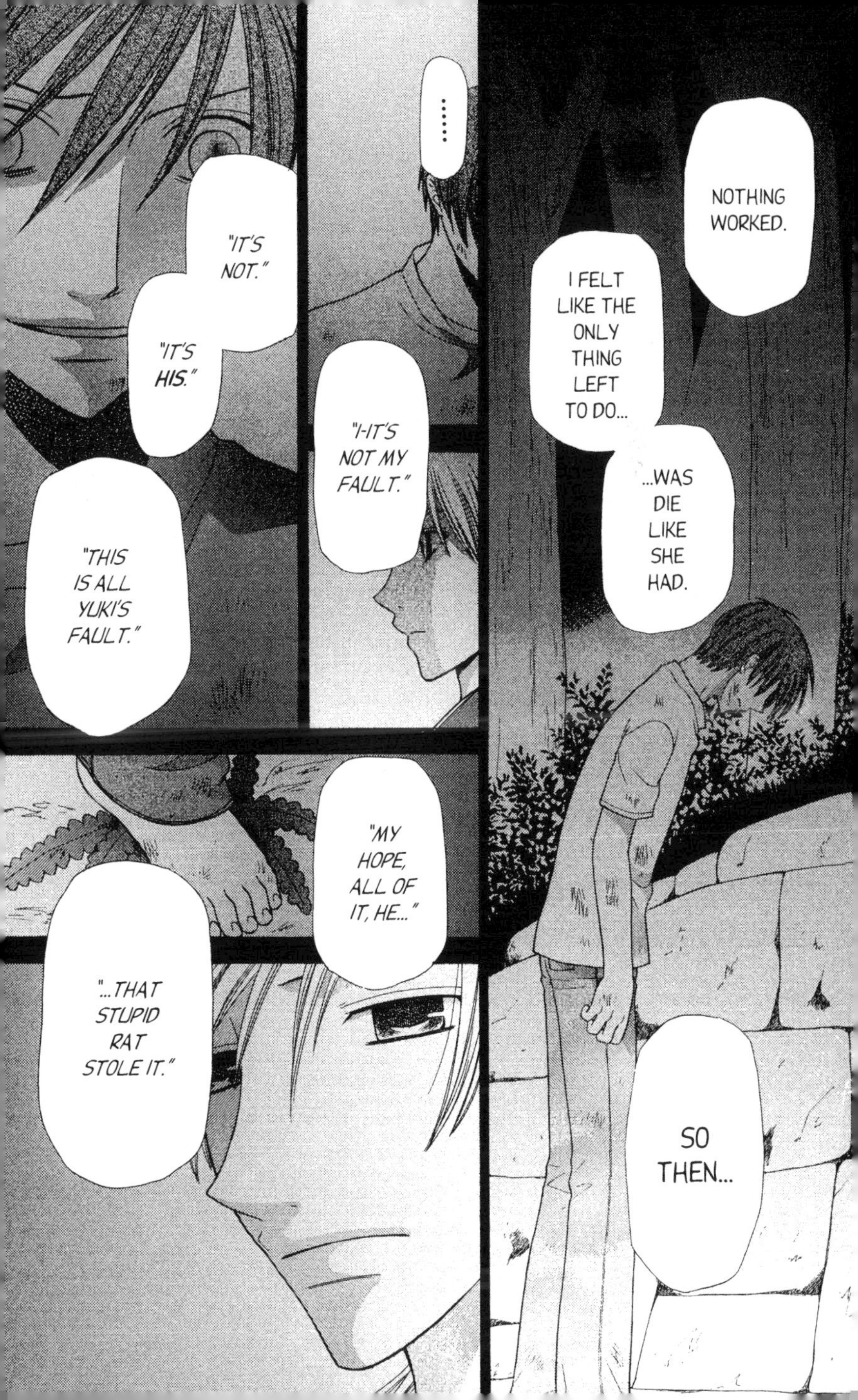
NOTHING WORKED.
I FELT LIKE THE ONLY THING LEFT TO DO...
...WAS DIE LIKE SHE HAD.
SO THEN...
......
"I-IT'S NOT MY FAULT."
"IT'S NOT."
"IT'S HIS."
"THIS IS ALL YUKI'S FAULT."
"MY HOPE, ALL OF IT, HE..."
"...THAT STUPID RAT STOLE IT."

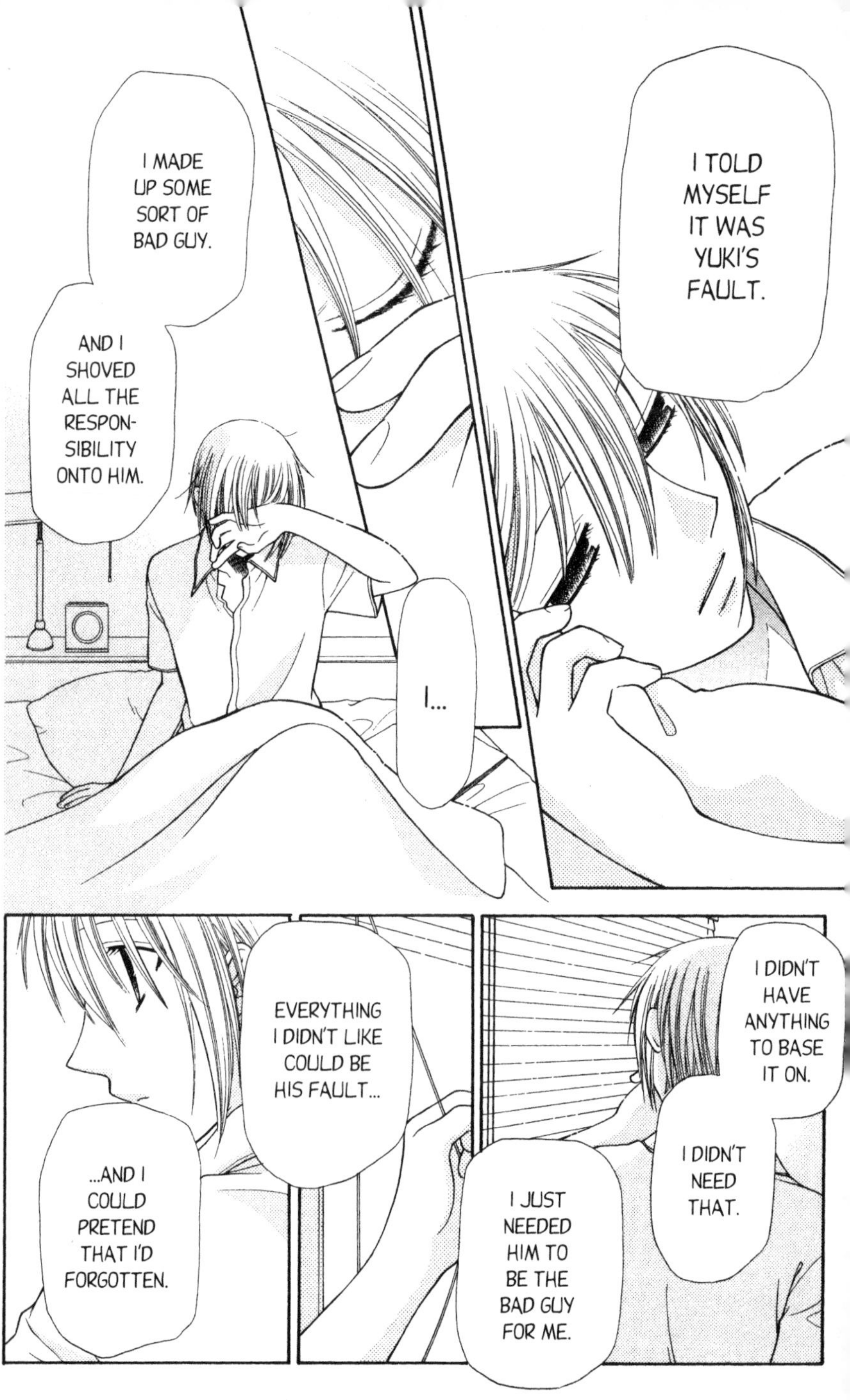
I TOLD MYSELF IT WAS YUKI'S FAULT.
I...
I MADE UP SOME SORT OF BAD GUY.
AND I SHOVED ALL THE RESPON-SIBILITY ONTO HIM.
I DIDN'T HAVE ANYTHING TO BASE IT ON.
I DIDN'T NEED THAT.
I JUST NEEDED HIM TO BE THE BAD GUY FOR ME.
EVERYTHING I DIDN'T LIKE COULD BE HIS FAULT...
...AND I COULD PRETEND THAT I'D FORGOTTEN.

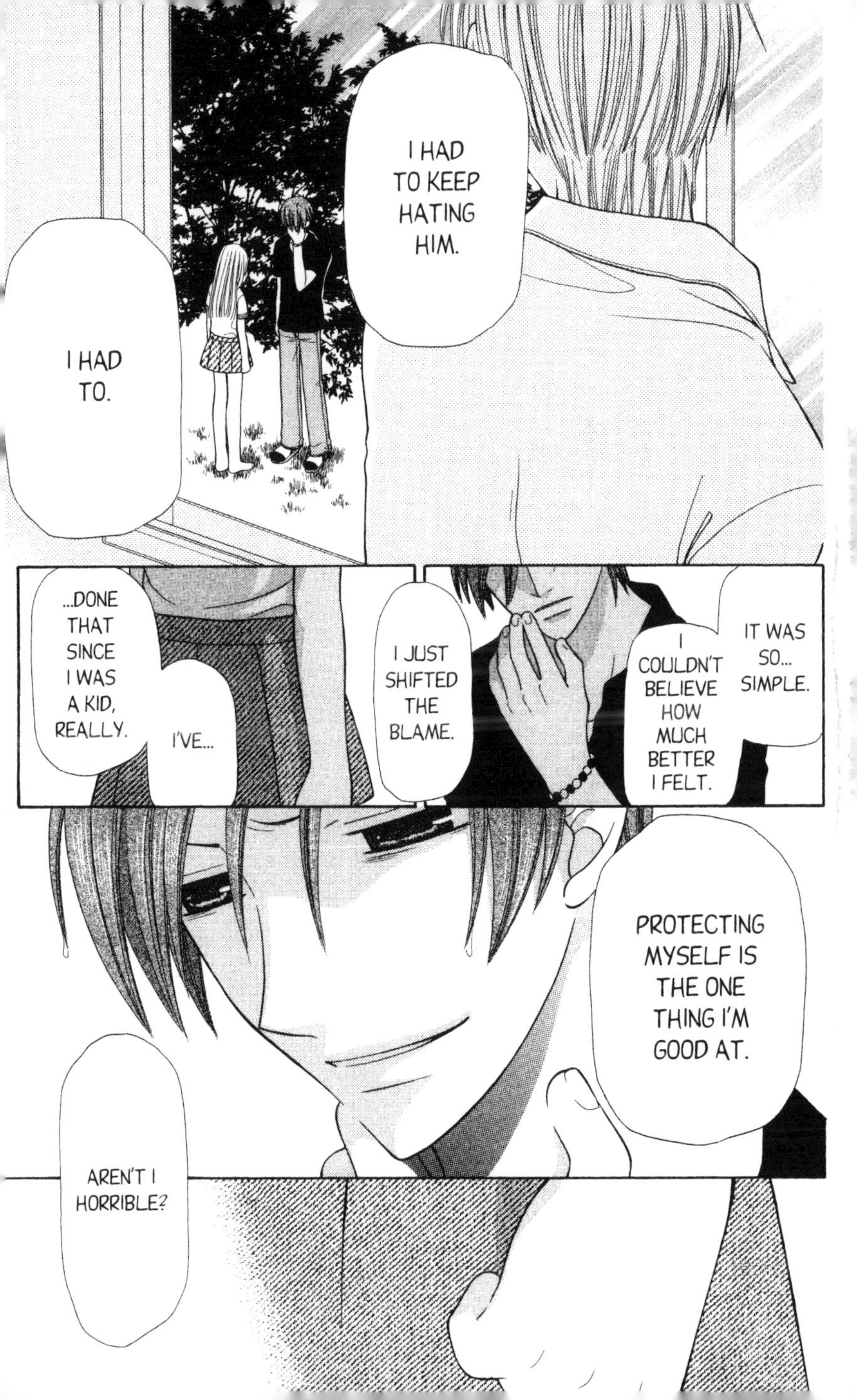
I HAD TO KEEP HATING HIM.
I HAD TO.
IT WAS SO... SIMPLE.
I COULDN'T BELIEVE HOW MUCH BETTER I FELT.
I JUST SHIFTED THE BLAME.
I'VE...
...DONE THAT SINCE I WAS A KID, REALLY.
PROTECTING MYSELF IS THE ONE THING I'M GOOD AT.
AREN'T I HORRIBLE?

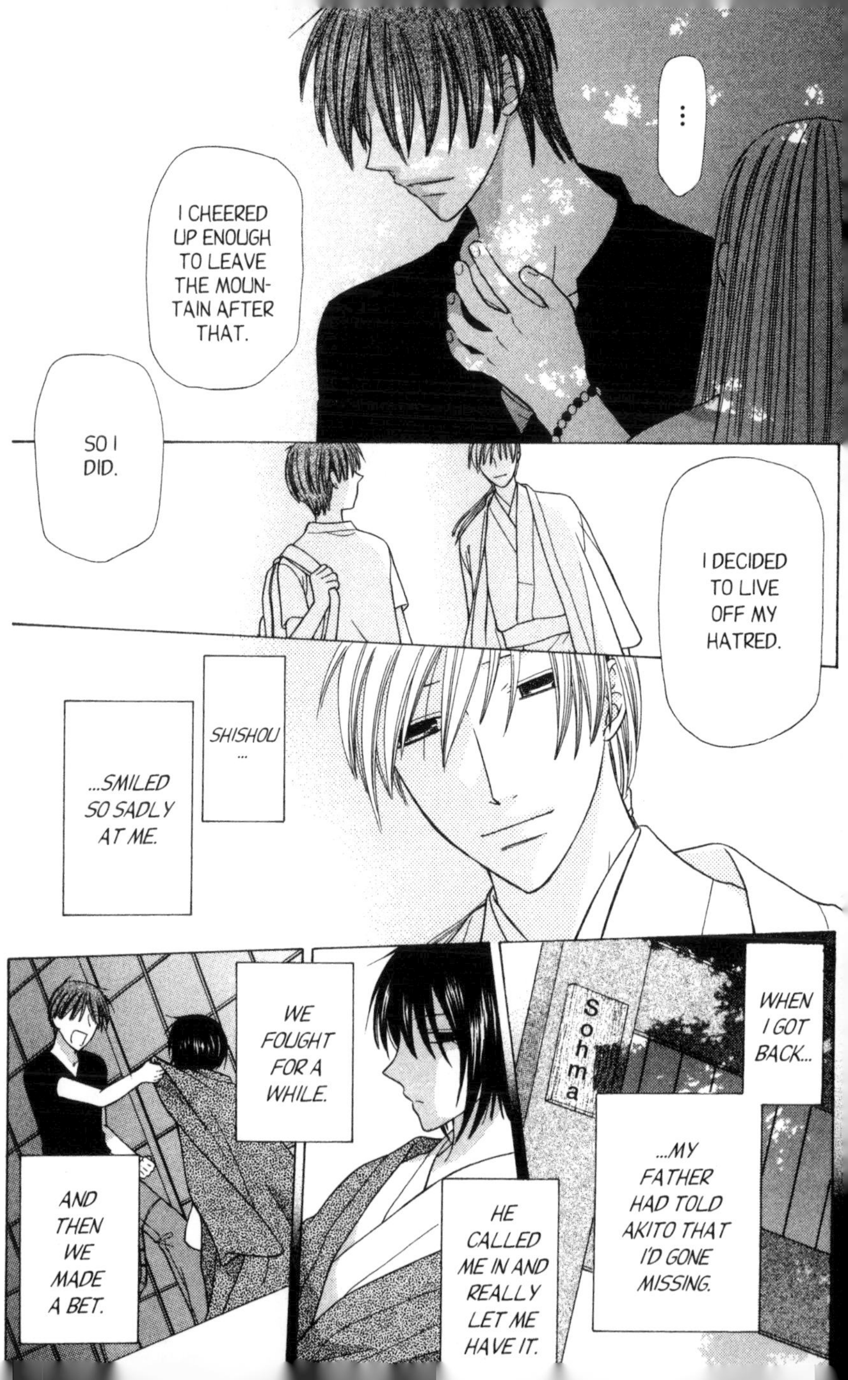
...
I CHEERED UP ENOUGH TO LEAVE THE MOUNTAIN AFTER THAT.
SO I DID.
I DECIDED TO LIVE OFF MY HATRED.
SHISHOU...
...SMILED SO SADLY AT ME.
WHEN I GOT BACK...
Sohma
...MY FATHER HAD TOLD AKITO THAT I'D GONE MISSING.
HE CALLED ME IN AND REALLY LET ME HAVE IT.
WE FOUGHT FOR A WHILE.
AND THEN WE MADE A BET.

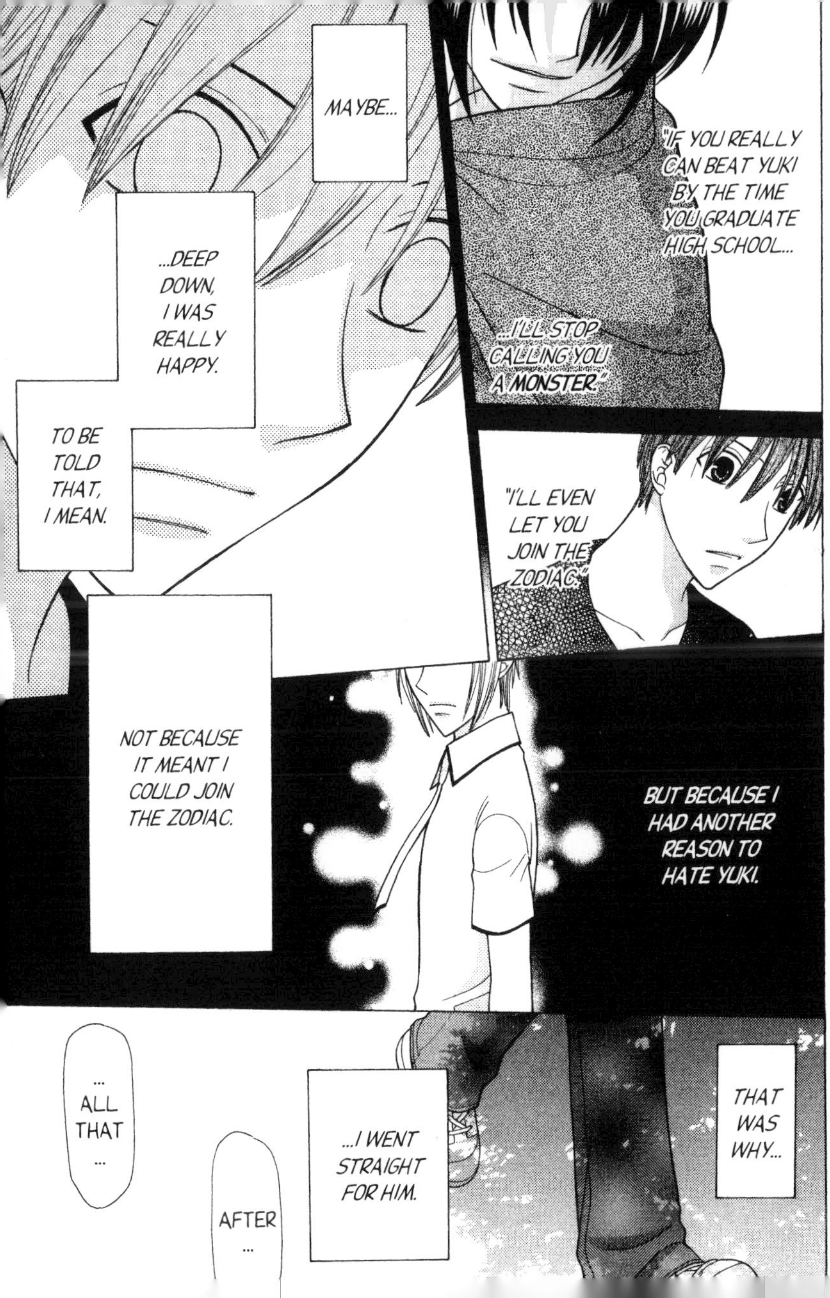
"IF YOU REALLY CAN BEAT YUKI BY THE TIME YOU GRADUATE HIGH SCHOOL...
...I'LL STOP CALLING YOU A MONSTER."
"I'LL EVEN LET YOU JOIN THE ZODIAC."
MAYBE...
...DEEP DOWN, I WAS REALLY HAPPY.
TO BE TOLD THAT, I MEAN.
NOT BECAUSE IT MEANT I COULD JOIN THE ZODIAC.
BUT BECAUSE I HAD ANOTHER REASON TO HATE YUKI.
THAT WAS WHY...
...I WENT STRAIGHT FOR HIM.
AFTER...
...ALL THAT...

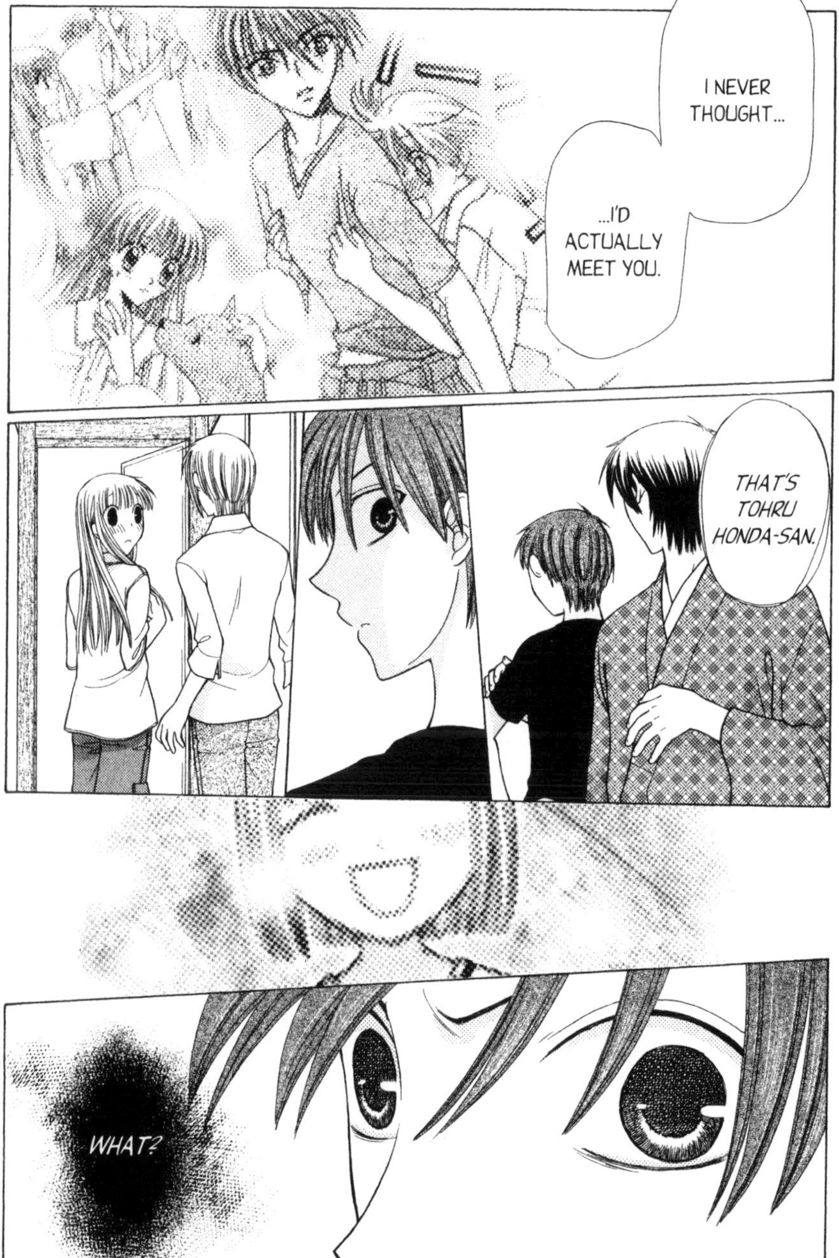
I NEVER THOUGHT...
...I'D ACTUALLY MEET YOU.
THAT'S TOHRU HONDA-SAN.
WHAT?

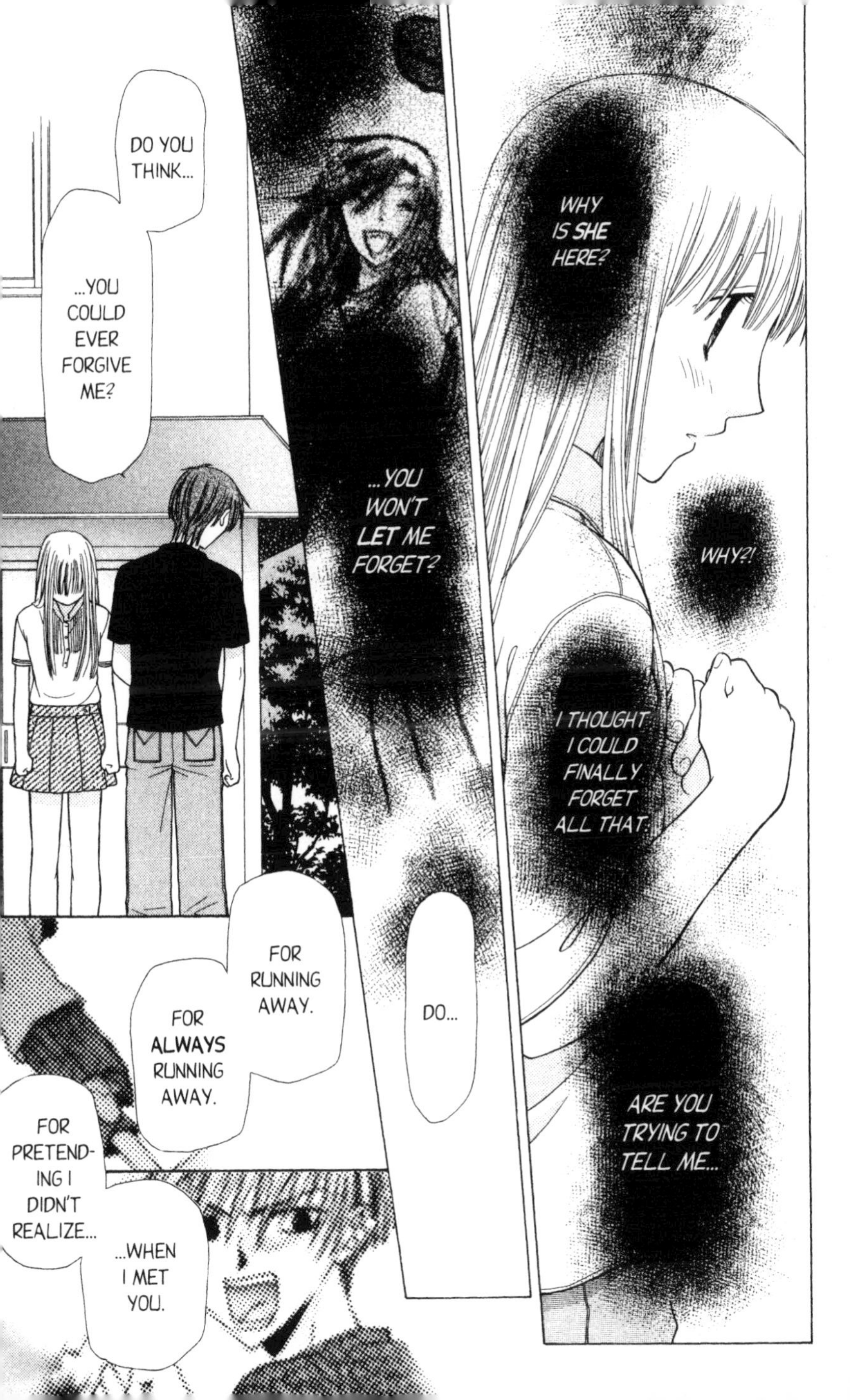
WHY IS SHE HERE?
WHY?!
I THOUGHT I COULD FINALLY FORGET ALL THAT.
ARE YOU TRYING TO TELL ME...
...YOU WON'T LET ME FORGET?
DO...
DO YOU THINK...
...YOU COULD EVER FORGIVE ME?
FOR RUNNING AWAY.
FOR **ALWAYS** RUNNING AWAY.
FOR PRETENDING I DIDN'T REALIZE...
...WHEN I MET YOU.

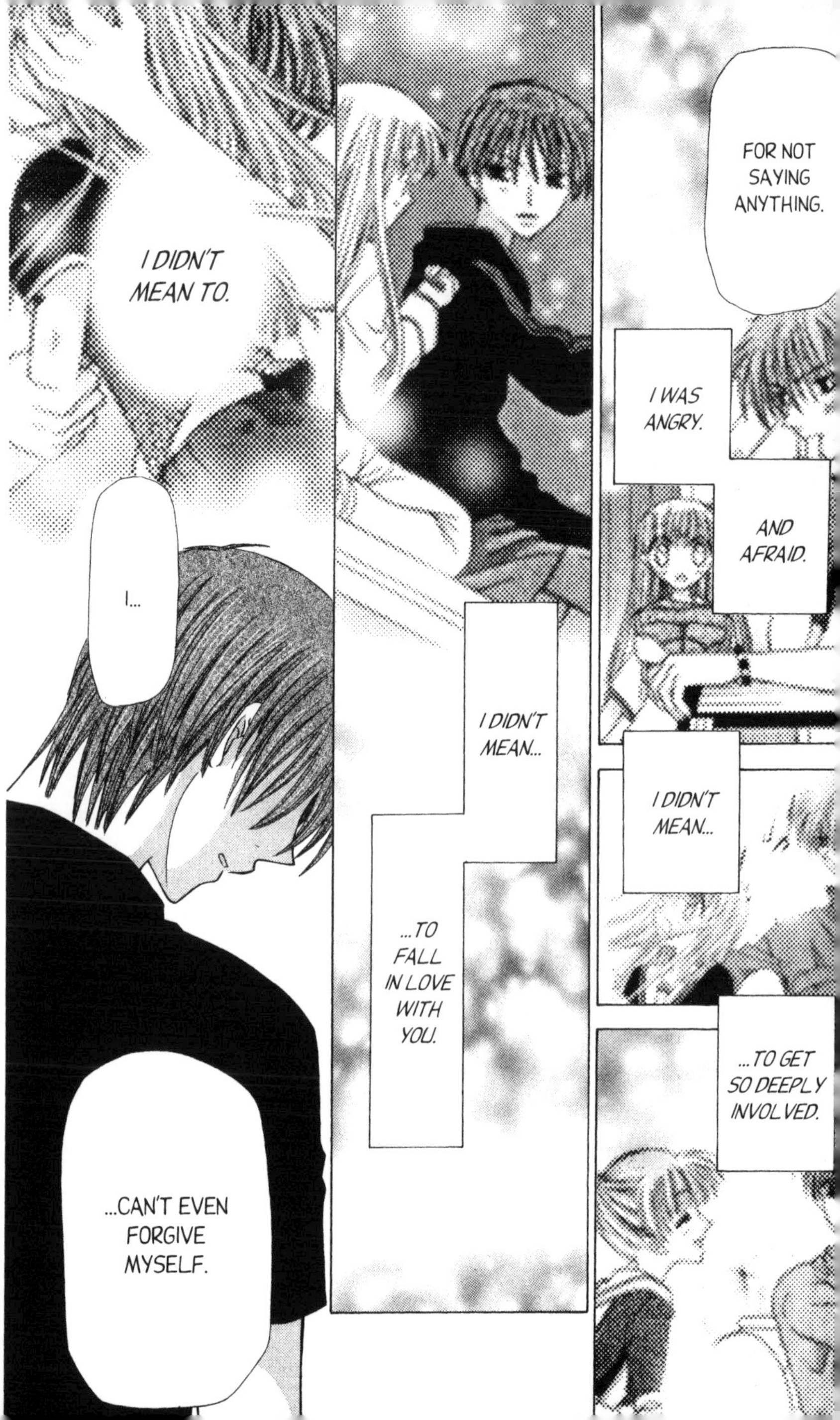
FOR NOT SAYING ANYTHING.
I WAS ANGRY.
AND AFRAID.
I DIDN'T MEAN...
...TO GET SO DEEPLY INVOLVED.
I DIDN'T MEAN...
...TO FALL IN LOVE WITH YOU.
I DIDN'T MEAN TO.
I...
...CAN'T EVEN FORGIVE MYSELF.

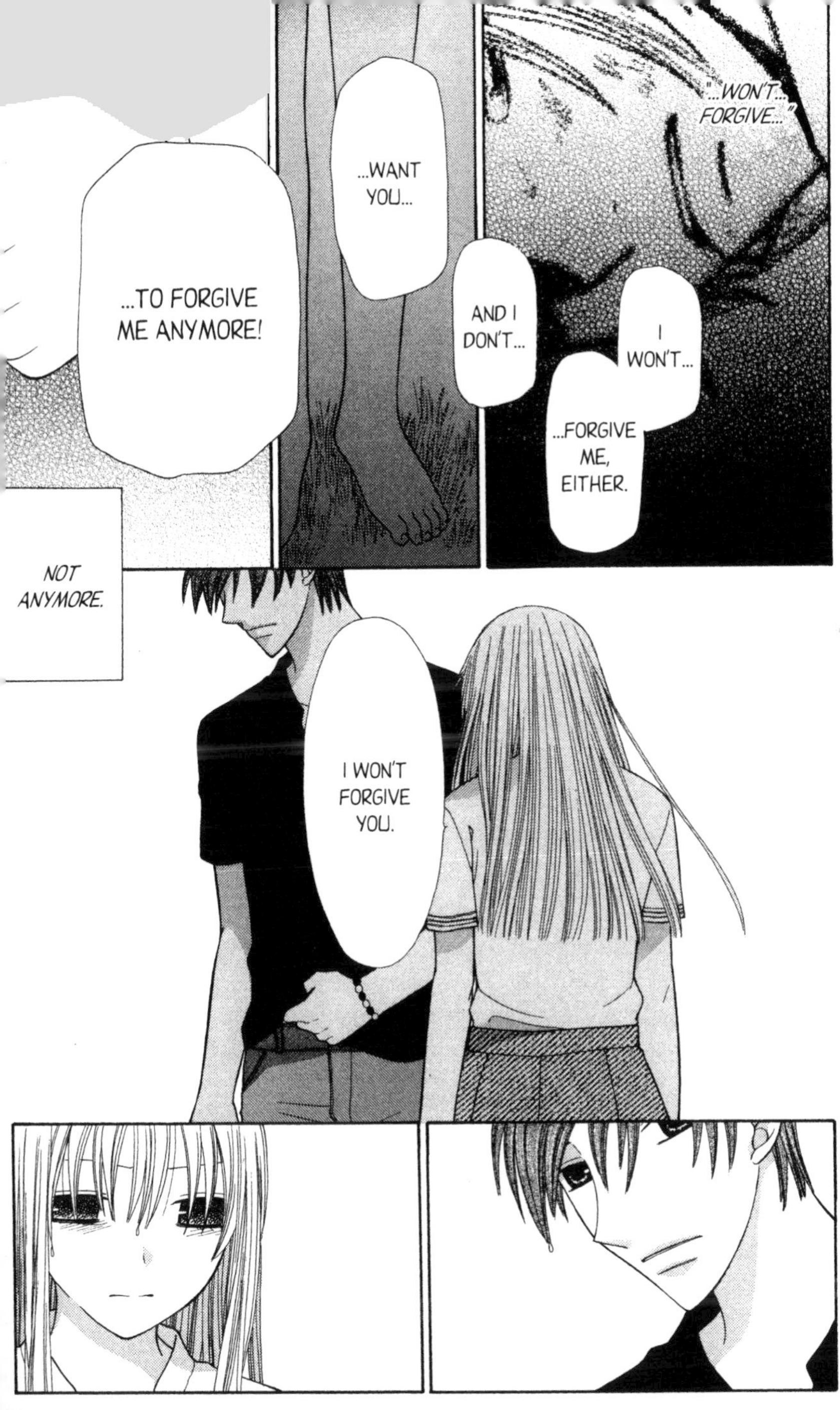
"...WON'T... FORGIVE..."
I WON'T...
...FORGIVE ME, EITHER.
AND I DON'T...
...WANT YOU...
...TO FORGIVE ME ANYMORE!
NOT ANYMORE.
I WON'T FORGIVE YOU.

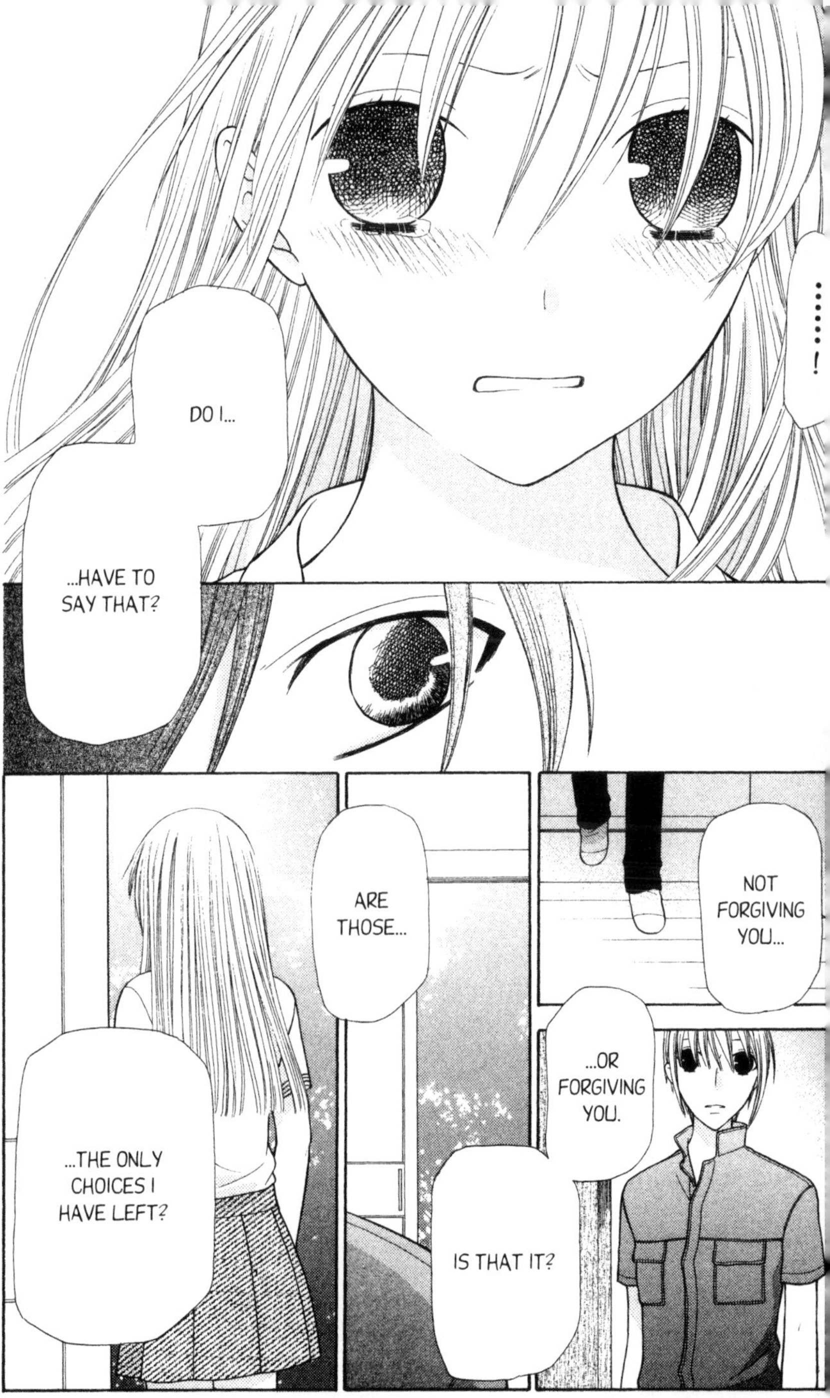
......!
DO I...
...HAVE TO SAY THAT?
NOT FORGIVING YOU...
...OR FORGIVING YOU.
ARE THOSE...
...THE ONLY CHOICES I HAVE LEFT?
IS THAT IT?

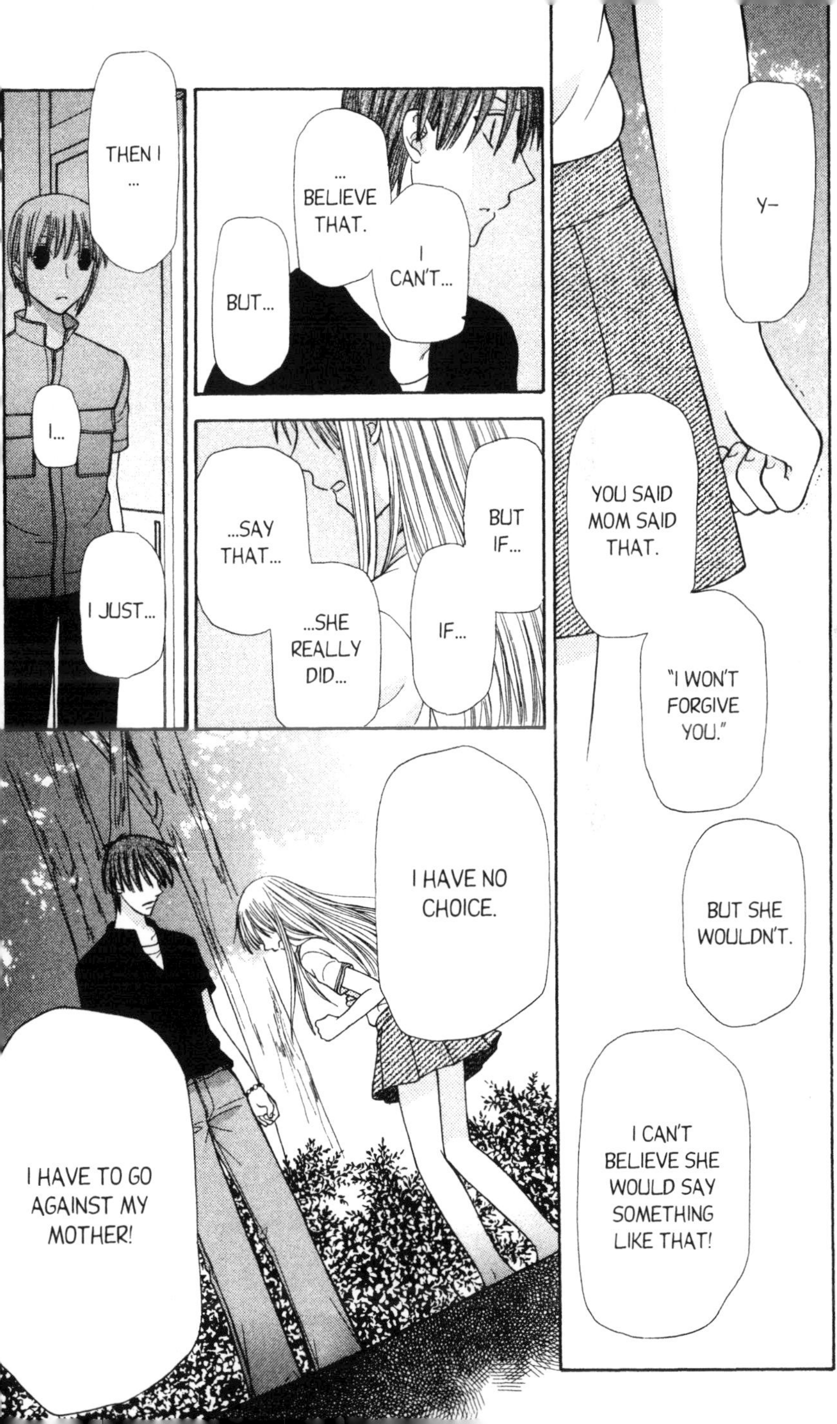
Y–
YOU SAID MOM SAID THAT.
"I WON'T FORGIVE YOU."
BUT SHE WOULDN'T.
I CAN'T BELIEVE SHE WOULD SAY SOMETHING LIKE THAT!
I CAN'T...
... BELIEVE THAT.
BUT...
BUT IF...
IF...
...SHE REALLY DID...
...SAY THAT...
THEN I ...
I...
I JUST...
I HAVE NO CHOICE.
I HAVE TO GO AGAINST MY MOTHER!

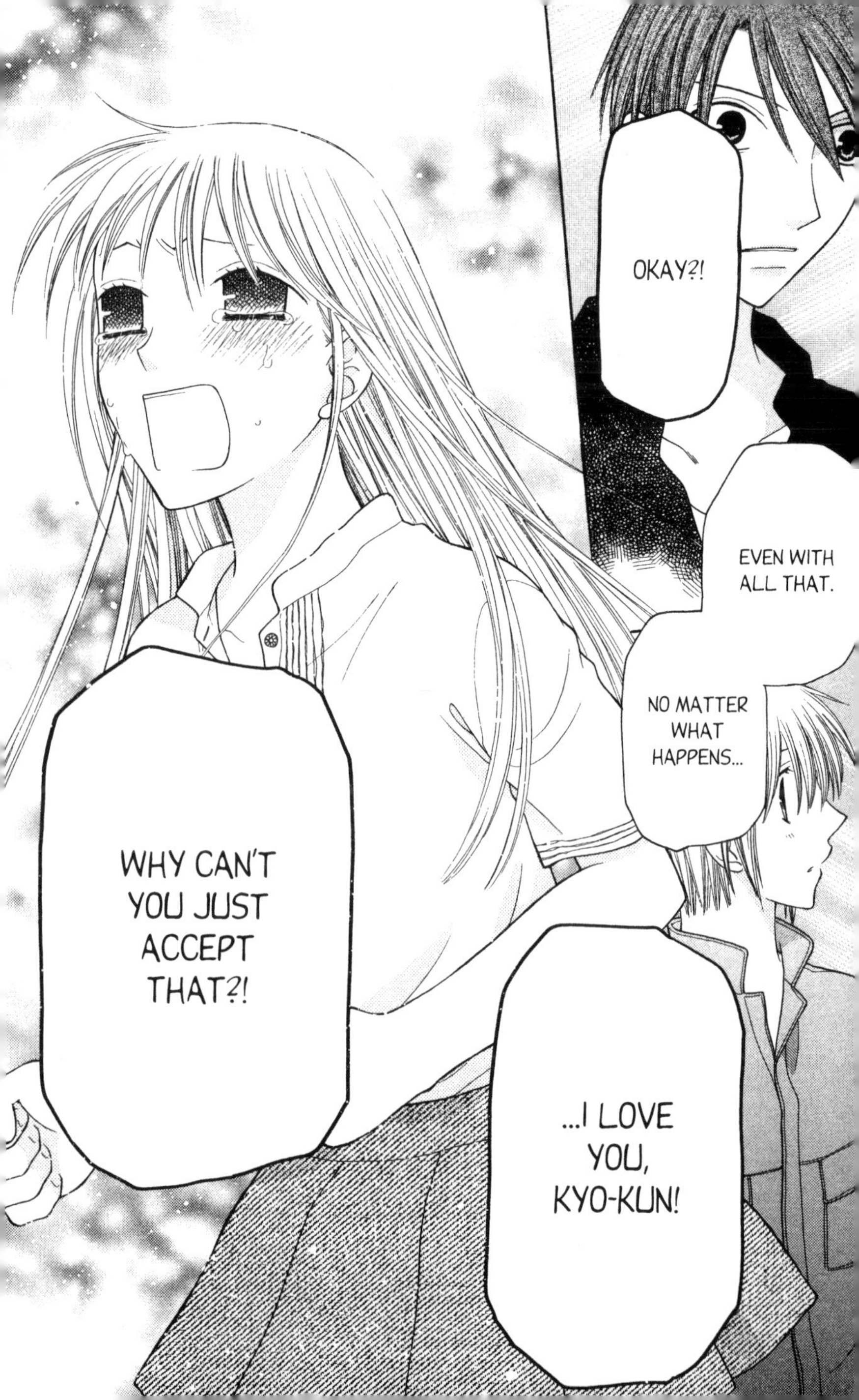
OKAY?!
EVEN WITH ALL THAT.
NO MATTER WHAT HAPPENS...
WHY CAN'T YOU JUST ACCEPT THAT?!
...I LOVE YOU, KYO-KUN!

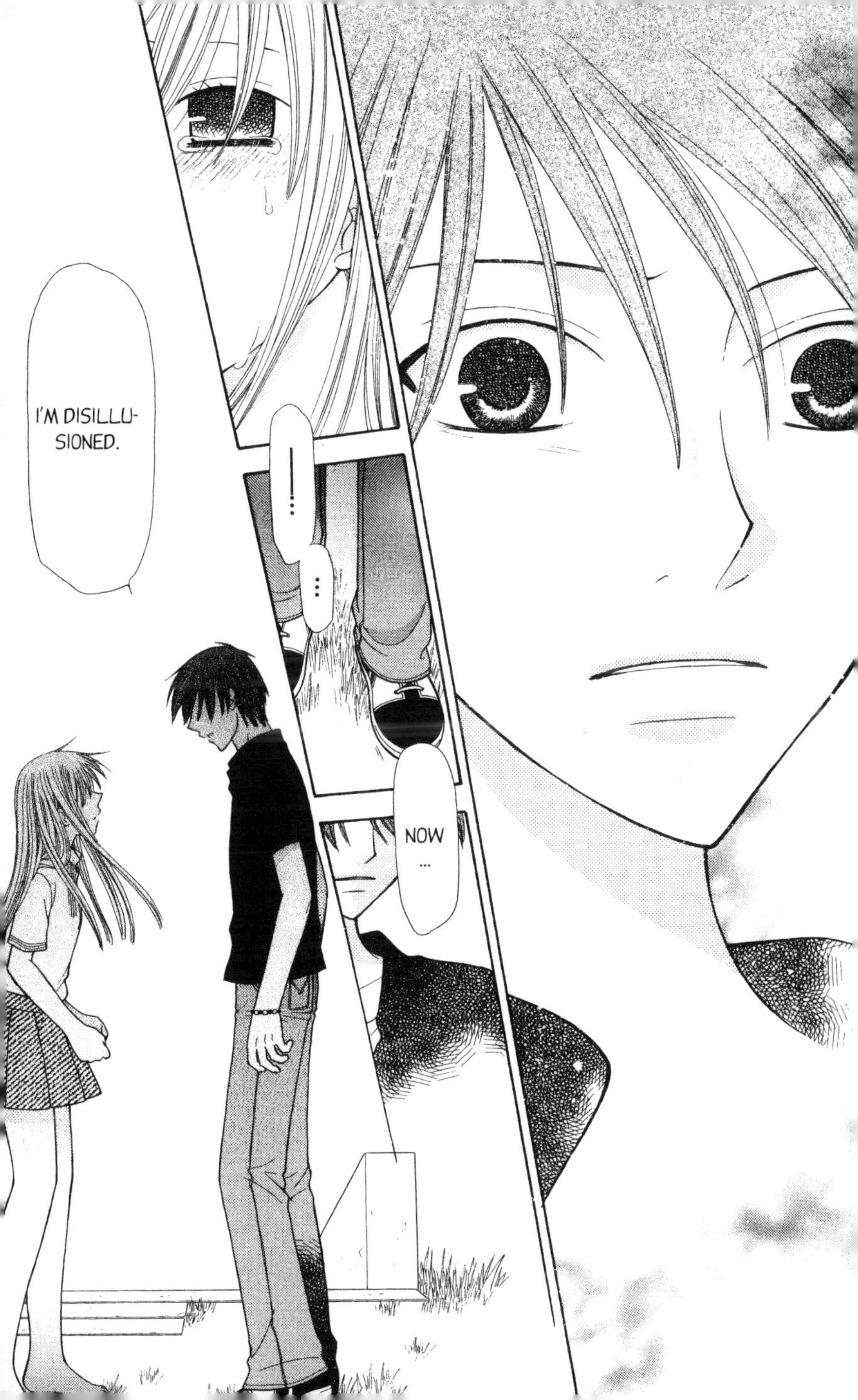
—...
...
NOW ...
I'M DISILLUSIONED.

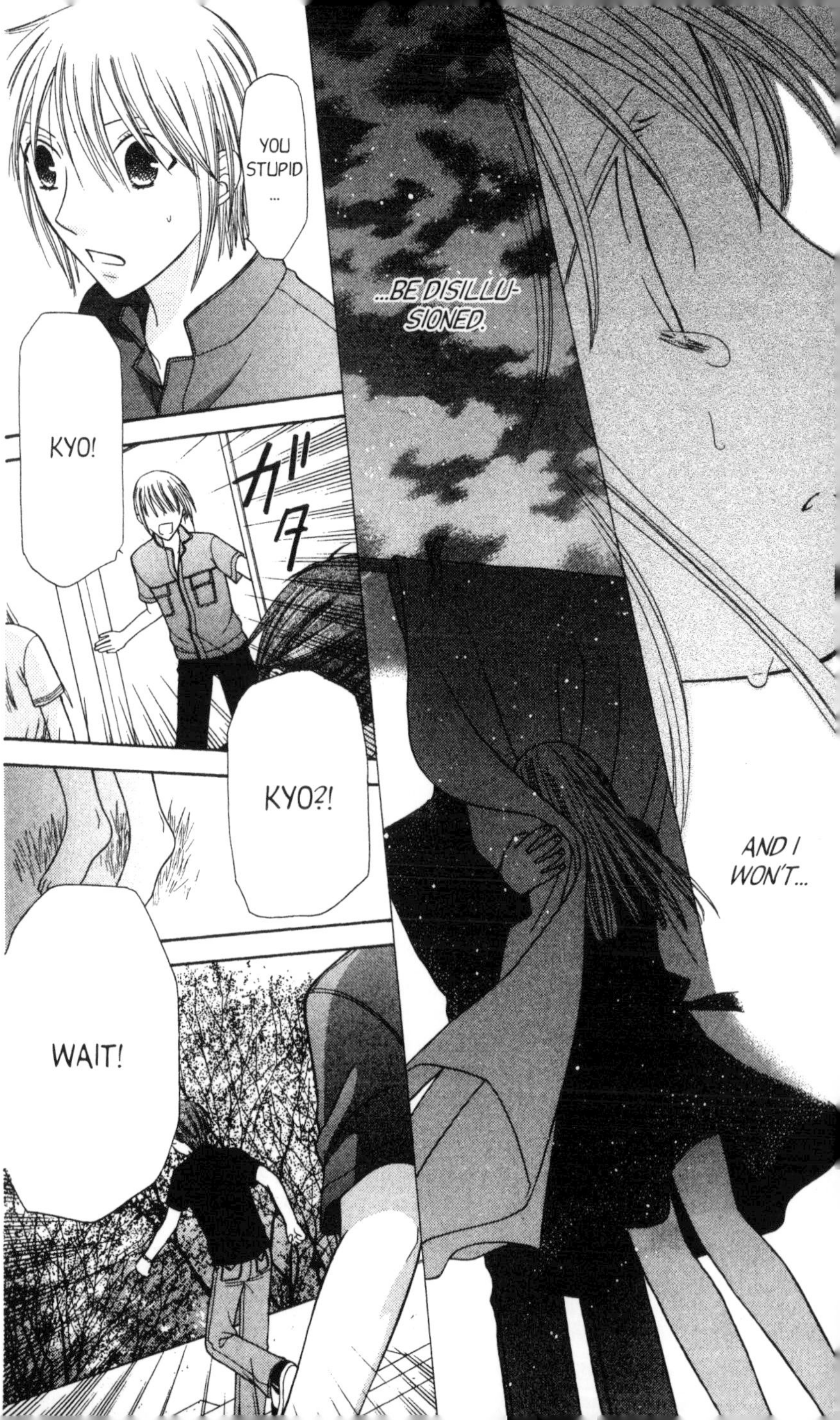
AND I WON'T...
...BE DISILLUSIONED.
YOU STUPID ...
KYO!
ガタ
KYO?!
WAIT!

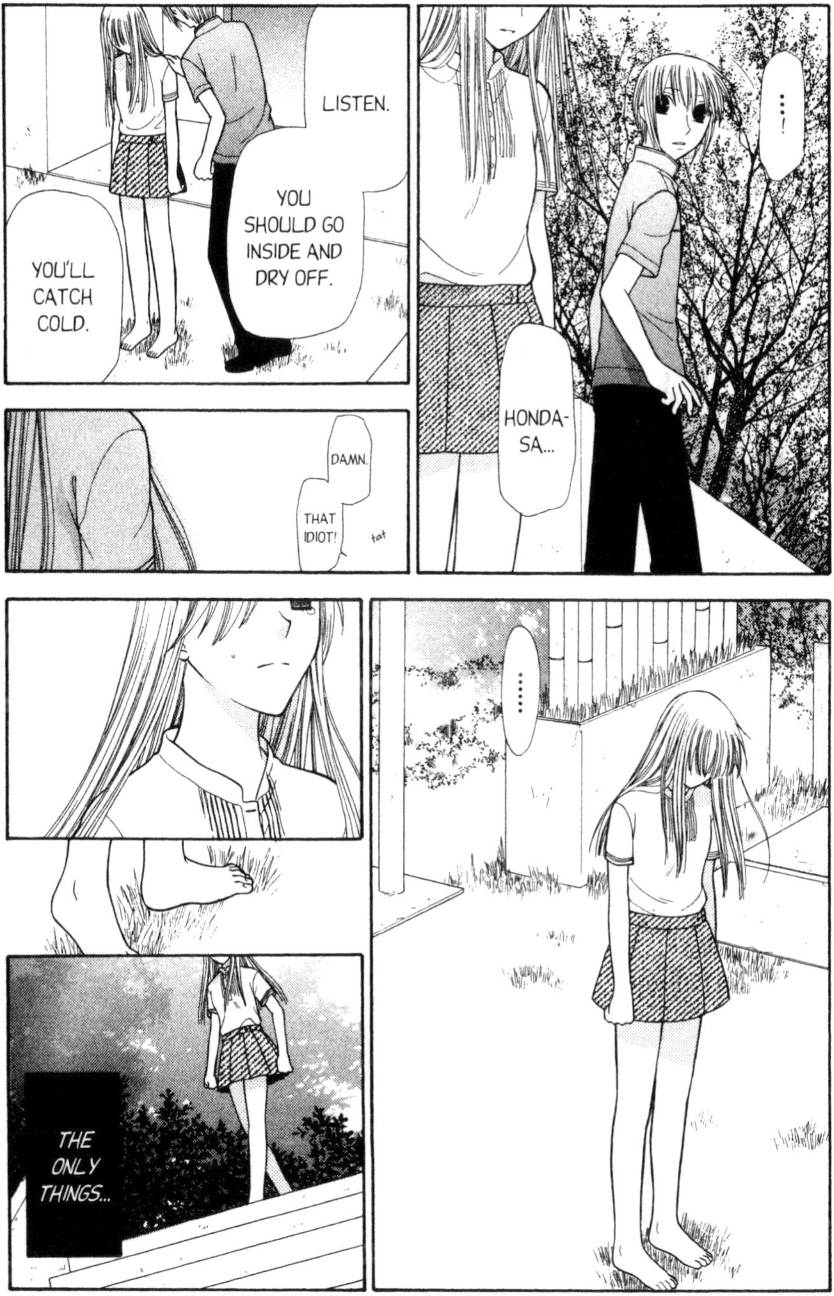
…!
HONDA-SA…
LISTEN.
YOU SHOULD GO INSIDE AND DRY OFF.
YOU'LL CATCH COLD.
DAMN.
THAT IDIOT!
tat
……
THE ONLY THINGS…

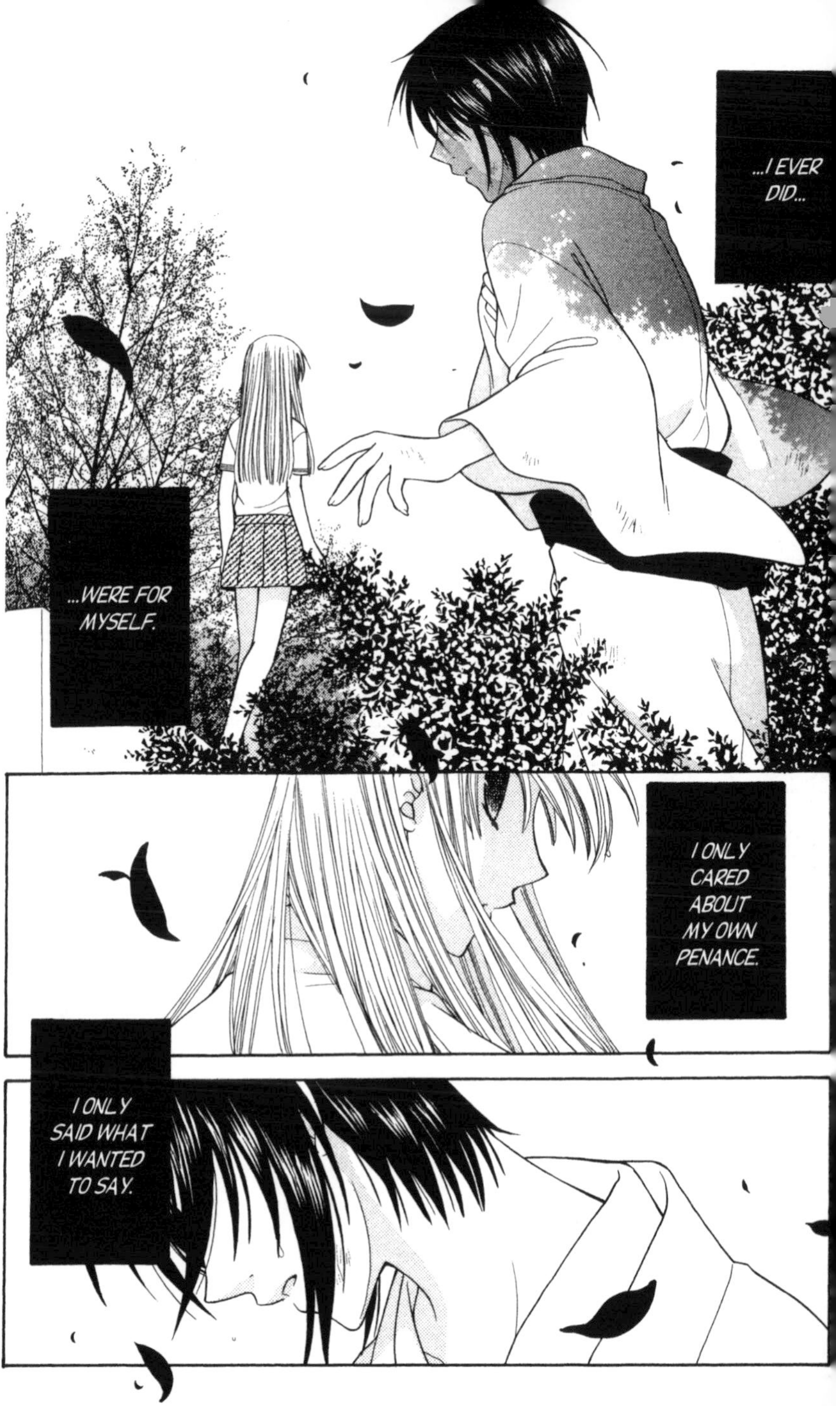
...I EVER DID...
...WERE FOR MYSELF.
I ONLY CARED ABOUT MY OWN PENANCE.
I ONLY SAID WHAT I WANTED TO SAY.

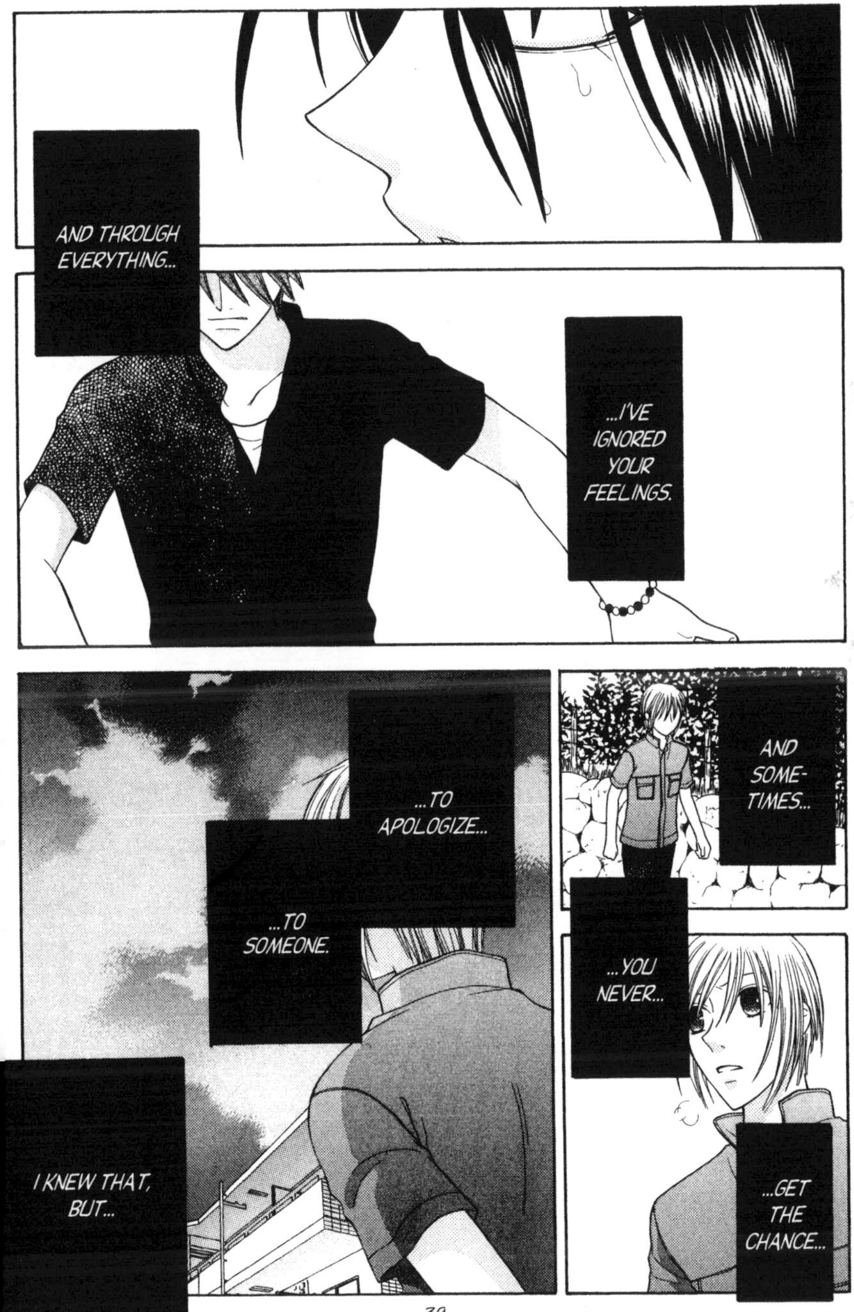
AND THROUGH EVERYTHING...
...I'VE IGNORED YOUR FEELINGS.
AND SOME-TIMES...
...YOU NEVER...
...GET THE CHANCE...
...TO APOLOGIZE...
...TO SOMEONE.
I KNEW THAT, BUT...

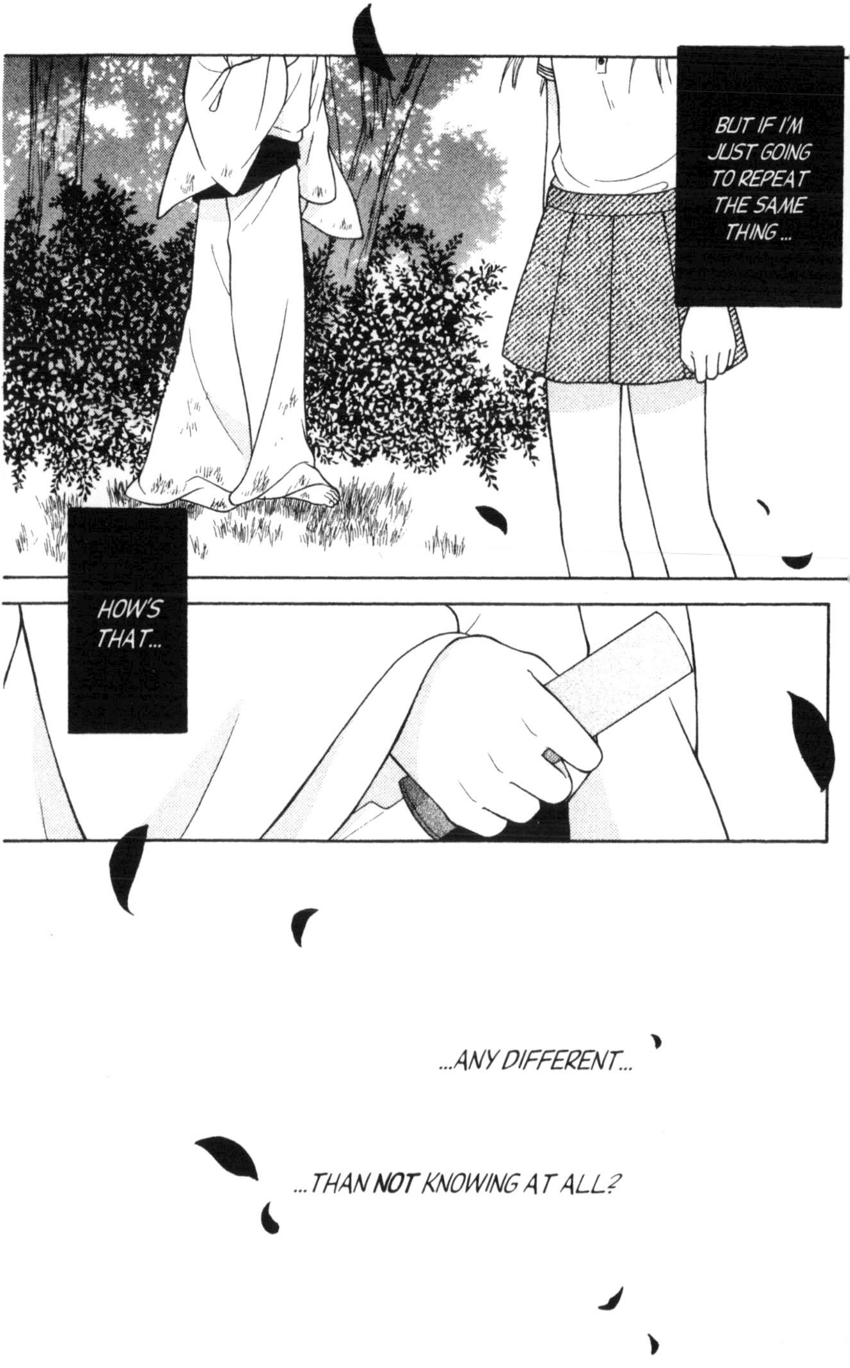
BUT IF I'M JUST GOING TO REPEAT THE SAME THING...
HOW'S THAT...
...ANY DIFFERENT...
...THAN **NOT** KNOWING AT ALL?

Filler Sketch

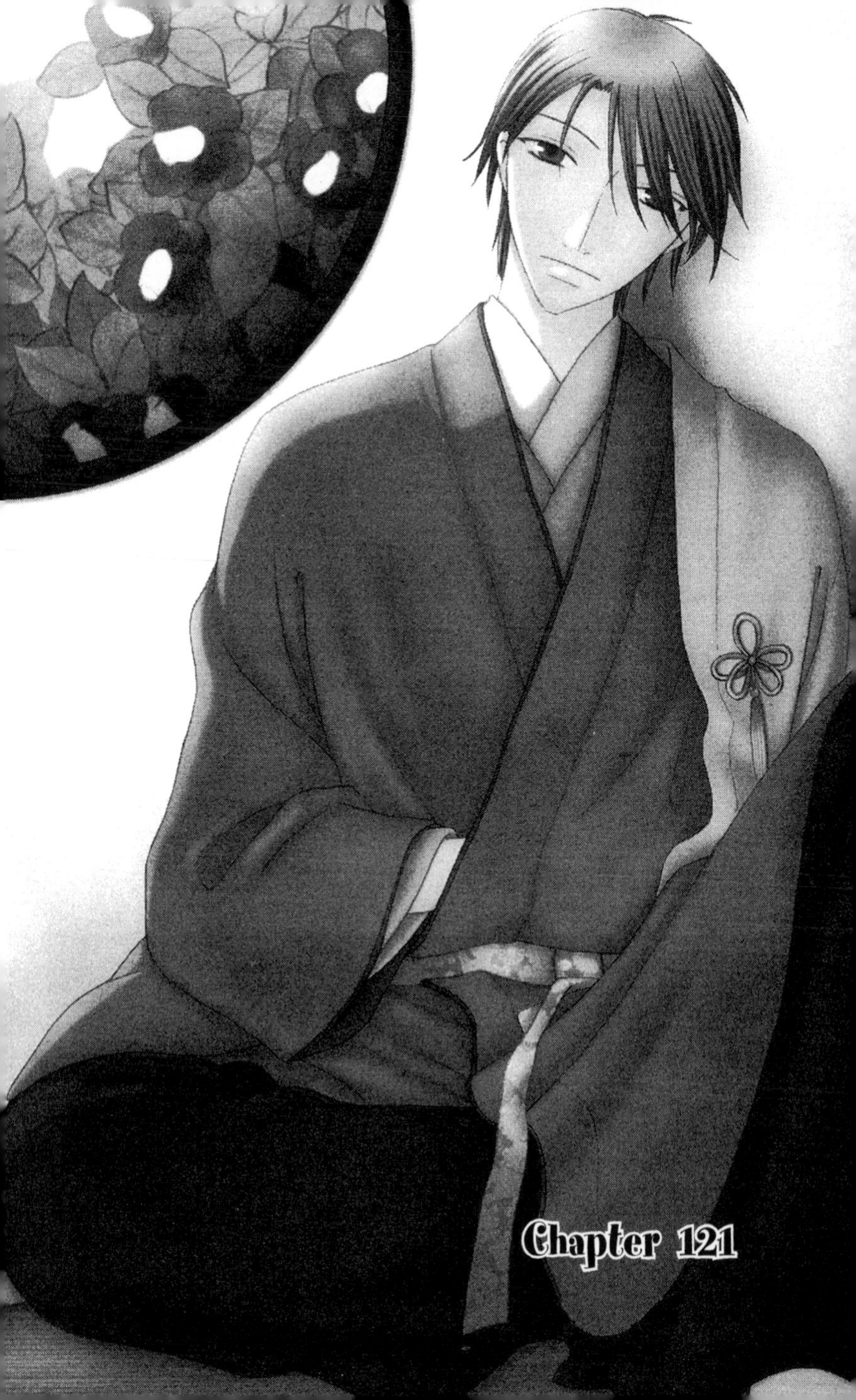
Chapter 121

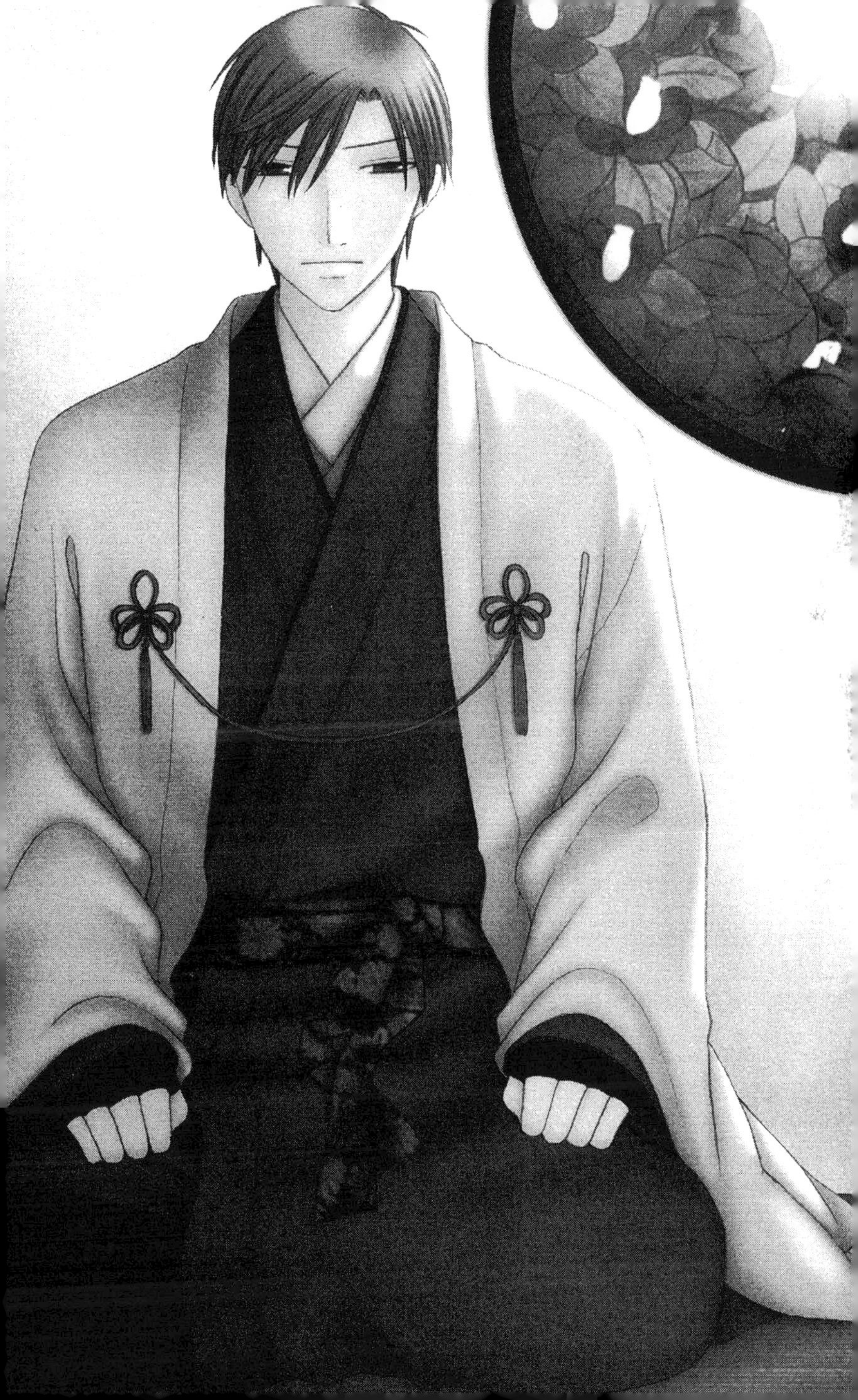

Filler Sketch

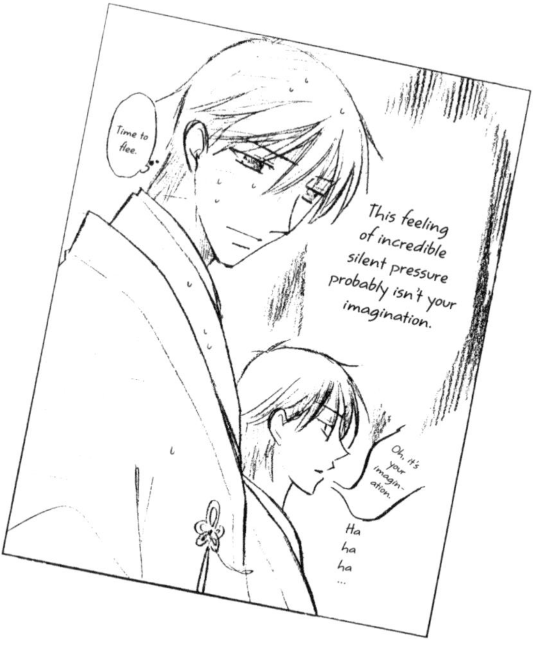
Time to flee.
This feeling of incredible silent pressure probably isn't your imagination.
Oh, it's your imagin-ation.
Ha ha ha...

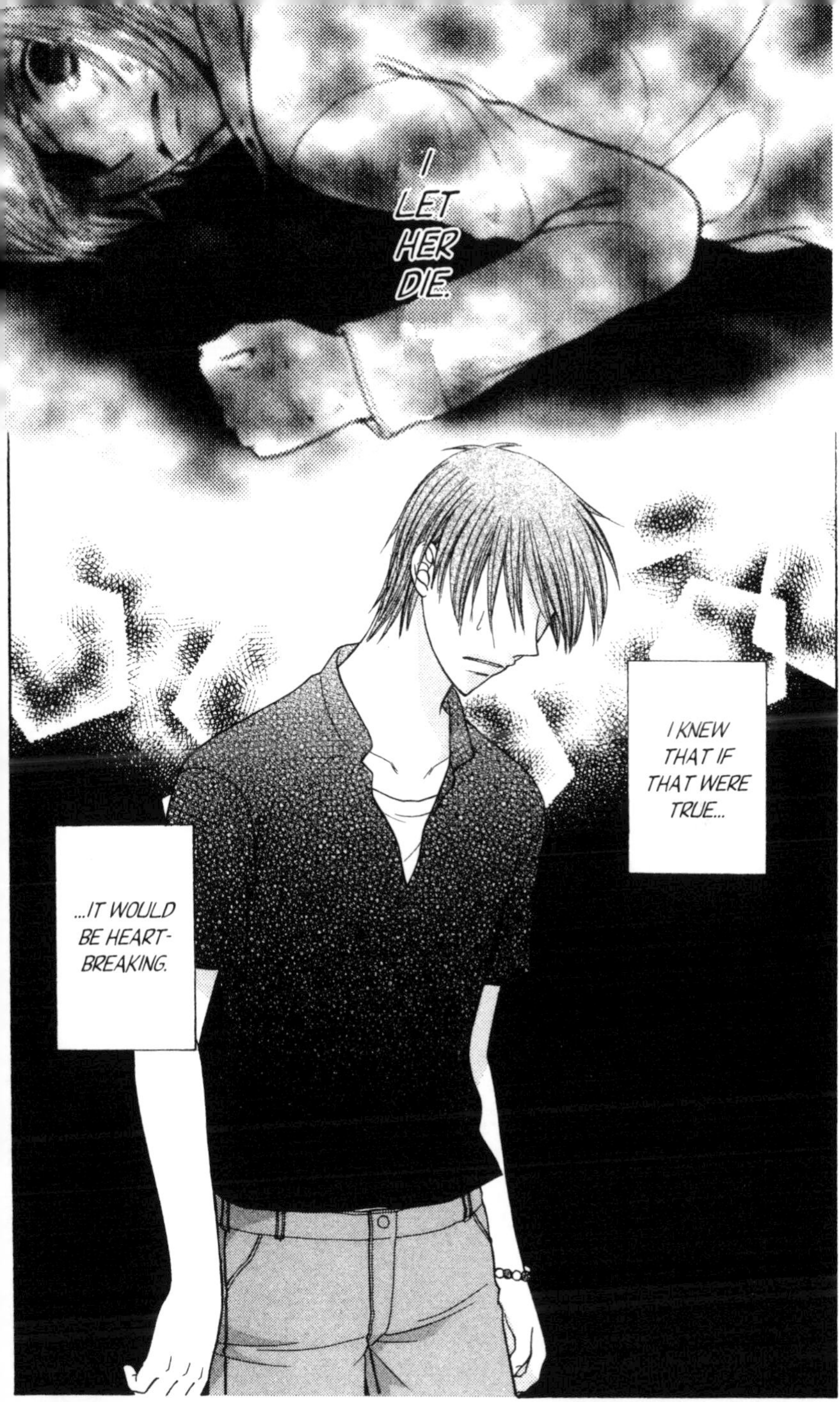
I LET HER DIE.
I KNEW THAT IF THAT WERE TRUE...
...IT WOULD BE HEART-BREAKING.

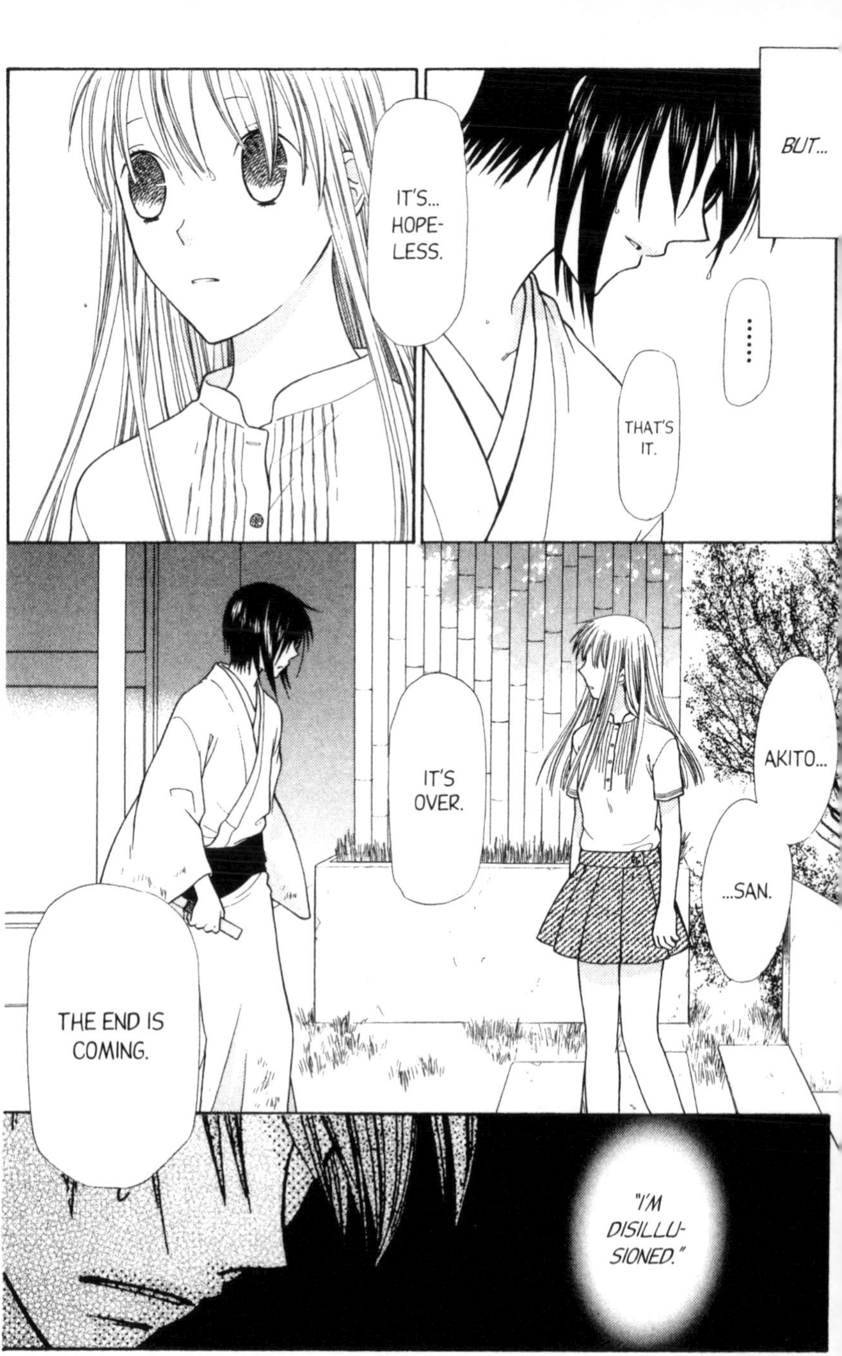
BUT...
......
THAT'S IT.
IT'S... HOPE-LESS.
AKITO...
...SAN.
IT'S OVER.
THE END IS COMING.
"I'M DISILLU-SIONED."

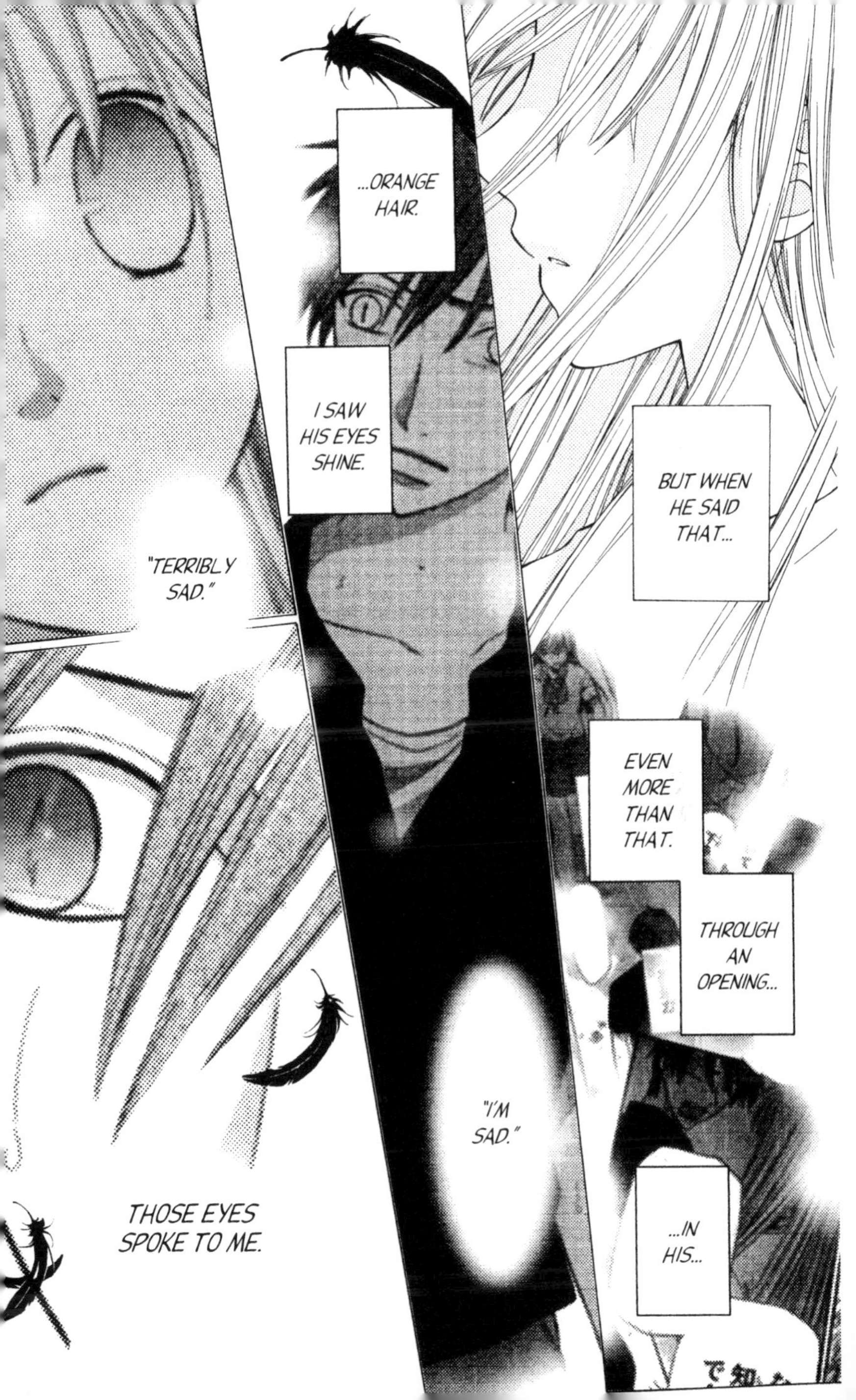
BUT WHEN HE SAID THAT...
EVEN MORE THAN THAT.
THROUGH AN OPENING...
...IN HIS...
...ORANGE HAIR.
I SAW HIS EYES SHINE.
"I'M SAD."
"TERRIBLY SAD."
THOSE EYES SPOKE TO ME.

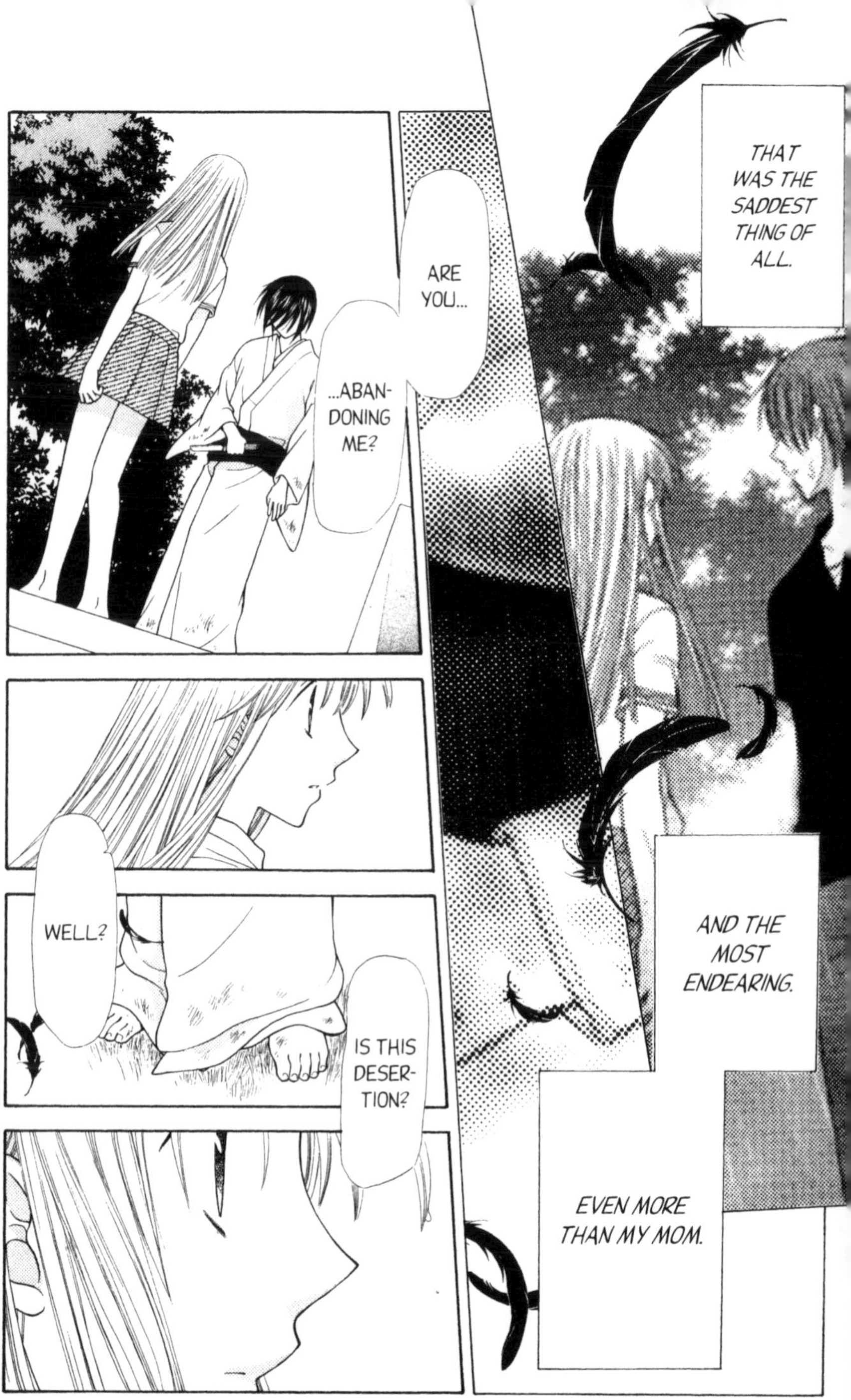

THAT WAS THE SADDEST THING OF ALL.
AND THE MOST ENDEARING.
EVEN MORE THAN MY MOM.
ARE YOU...
...ABAN-DONING ME?
WELL?
IS THIS DESER-TION?

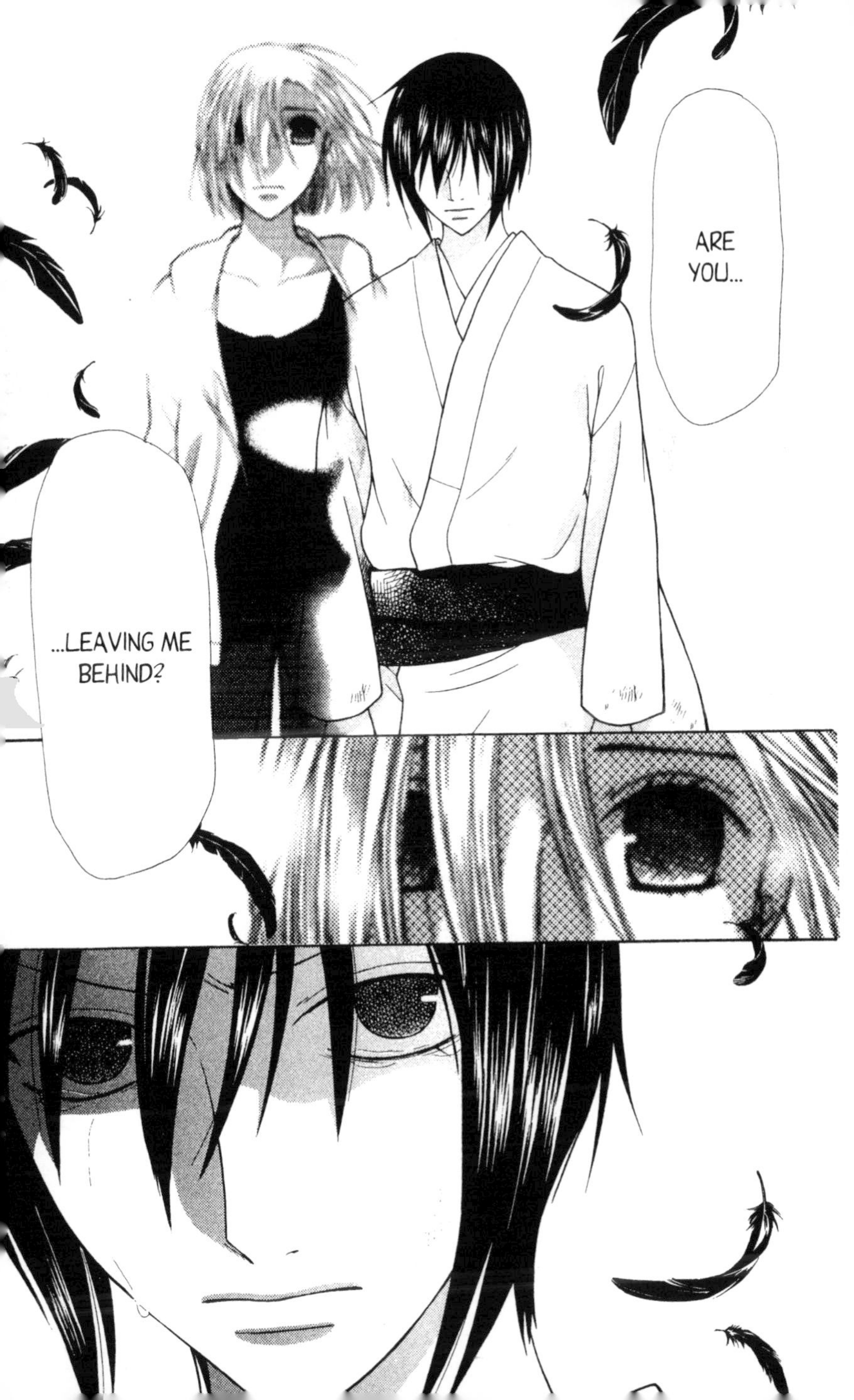
ARE YOU...
...LEAVING ME BEHIND?

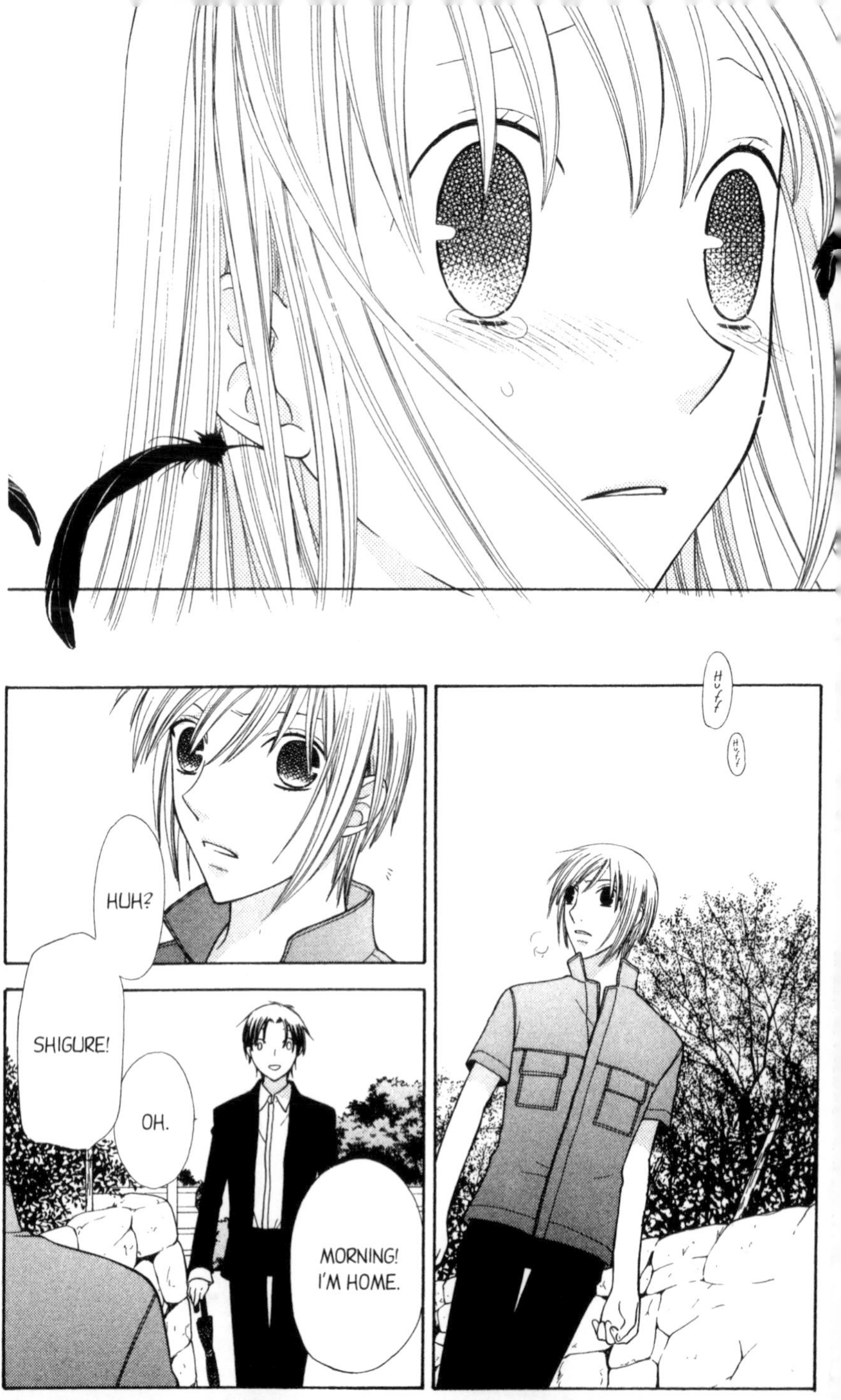
Huff
Huff
HUH?
SHIGURE!
OH.
MORNING! I'M HOME.

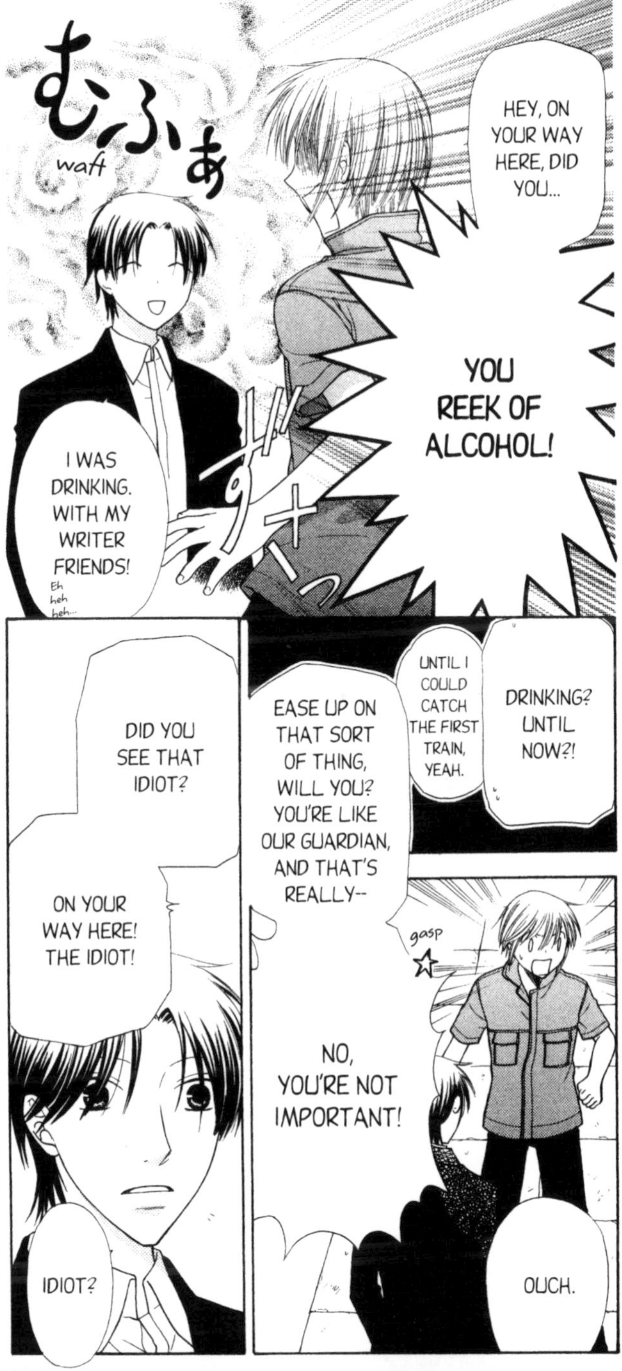
HEY, ON YOUR WAY HERE, DID YOU...
むふぁ
waft
YOU REEK OF ALCOHOL!
I WAS DRINKING. WITH MY WRITER FRIENDS!
Eh heh heh...
DRINKING? UNTIL NOW?!
UNTIL I COULD CATCH THE FIRST TRAIN, YEAH.
EASE UP ON THAT SORT OF THING, WILL YOU? YOU'RE LIKE OUR GUARDIAN, AND THAT'S REALLY--
gasp
NO, YOU'RE NOT IMPORTANT!
OUCH.
DID YOU SEE THAT IDIOT?
ON YOUR WAY HERE! THE IDIOT!
IDIOT?

Ren-san

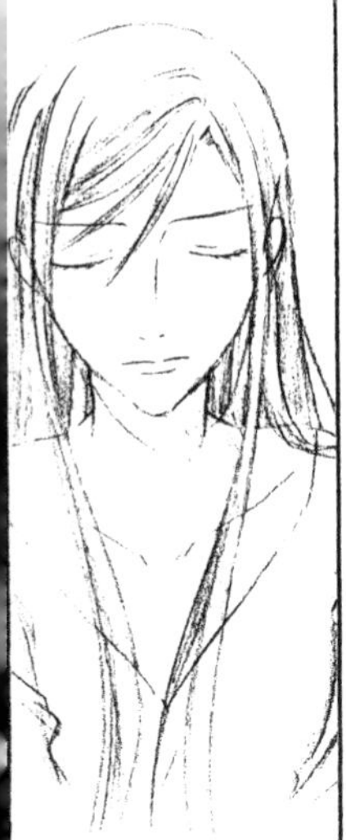

If I had to describe my strongest memory of Ren-san, it would be "my fingers hurt like crazy" (from inking).

- *The composition of her family before she came to the Sohma is unknown.*
- *Her age isn't clarified.*
- *I wanted to give the impression that her true identity is unknown.*
- *An impression like... she's not really human, she's a "spirit."*
- *Still, I also kinda wish I could have drawn her showing more of a backbone.*
- *But there's really no end to it, I held back.*
- *Akito takes after Ren-san. looks-wise.*

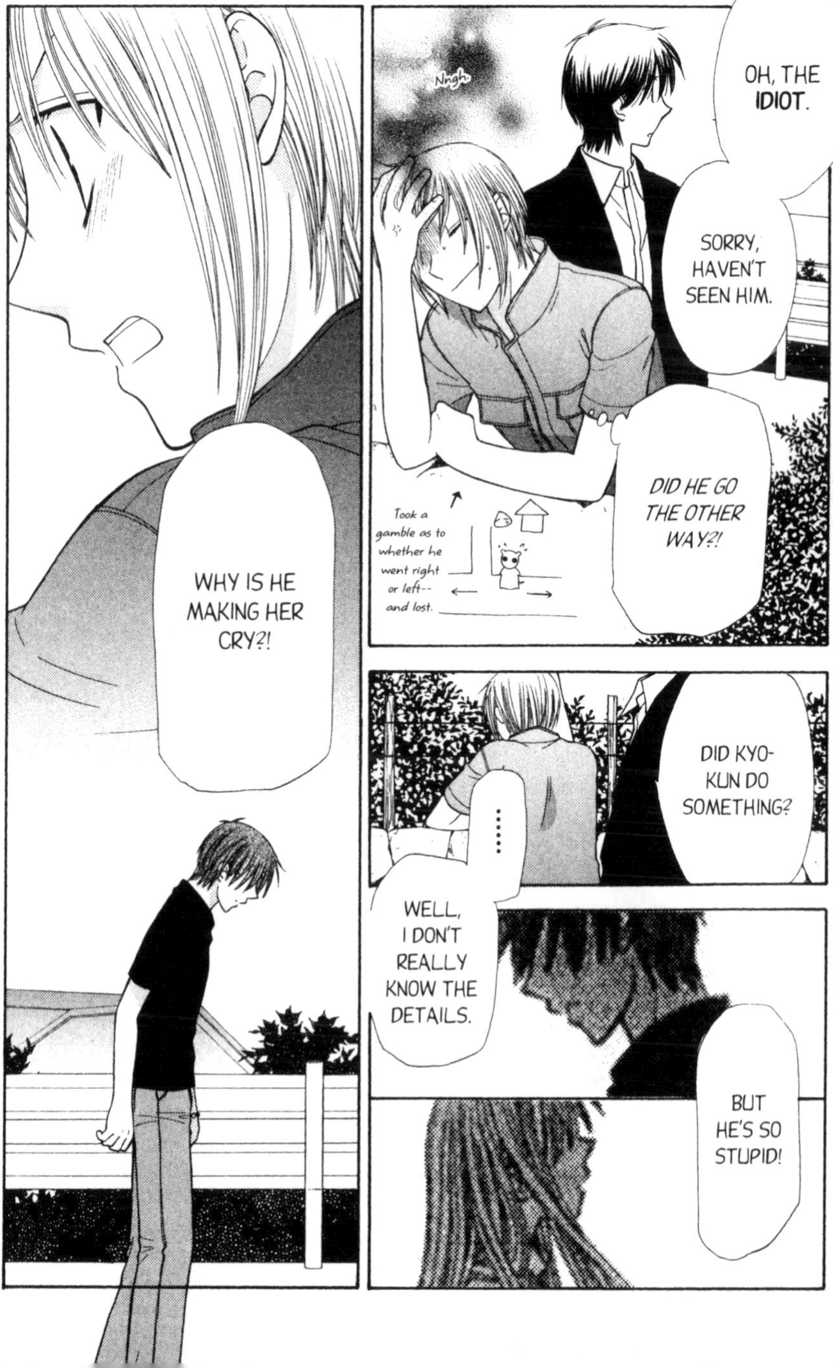
OH, THE **IDIOT**.
SORRY, HAVEN'T SEEN HIM.
Nngh.
DID HE GO THE OTHER WAY?!
Took a gamble as to whether he went right or left-- and lost.
DID KYO-KUN DO SOMETHING?
......
WELL, I DON'T REALLY KNOW THE DETAILS.
BUT HE'S SO STUPID!
WHY IS HE MAKING HER CRY?!

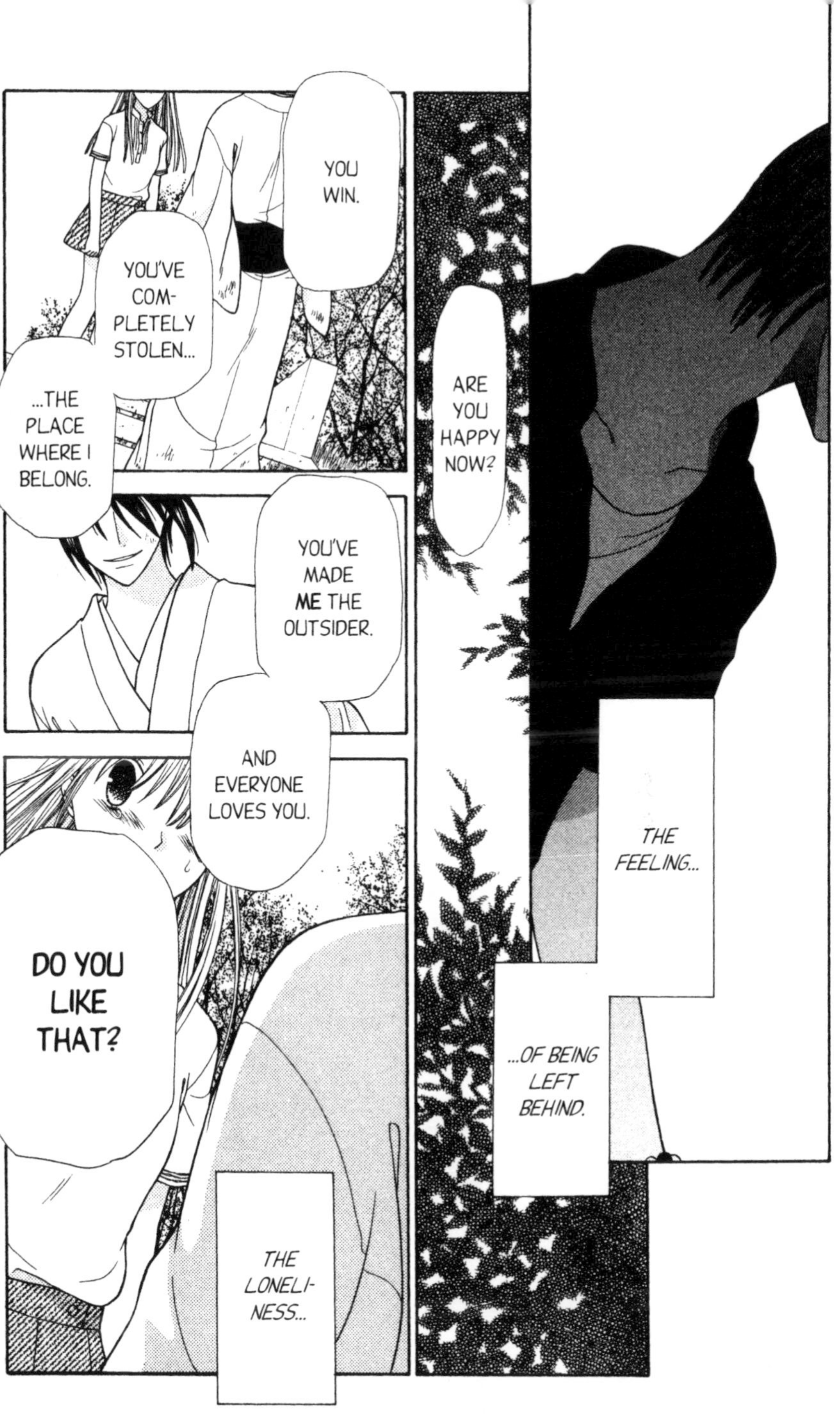
THE FEELING...
...OF BEING LEFT BEHIND.
ARE YOU HAPPY NOW?
YOU WIN.
YOU'VE COM-PLETELY STOLEN...
...THE PLACE WHERE I BELONG.
YOU'VE MADE **ME** THE OUTSIDER.
AND EVERYONE LOVES YOU.
DO YOU LIKE THAT?
THE LONELI-NESS...

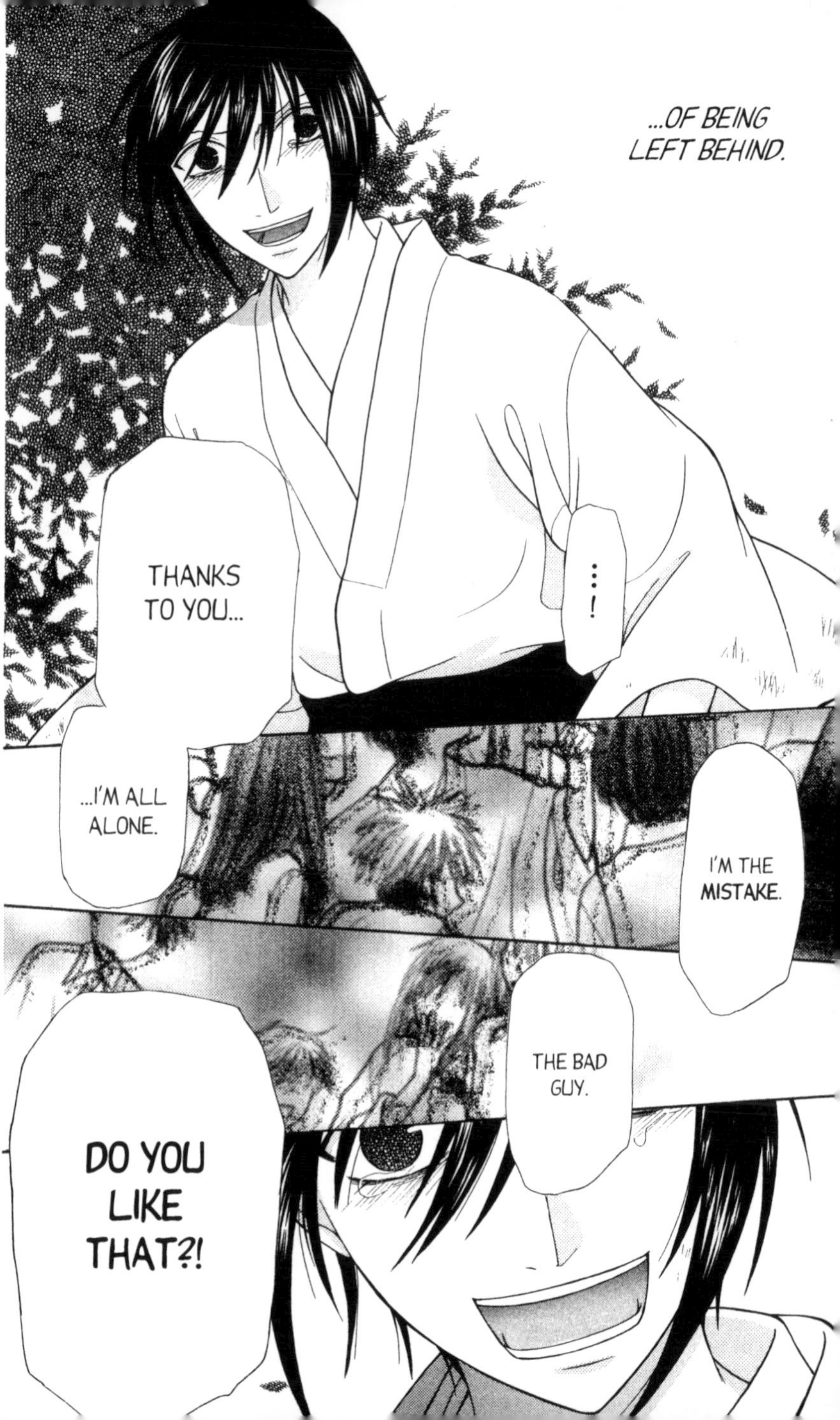

...OF BEING LEFT BEHIND.
...!
THANKS TO YOU...
...I'M ALL ALONE.
I'M THE MISTAKE.
THE BAD GUY.
DO YOU LIKE THAT?!

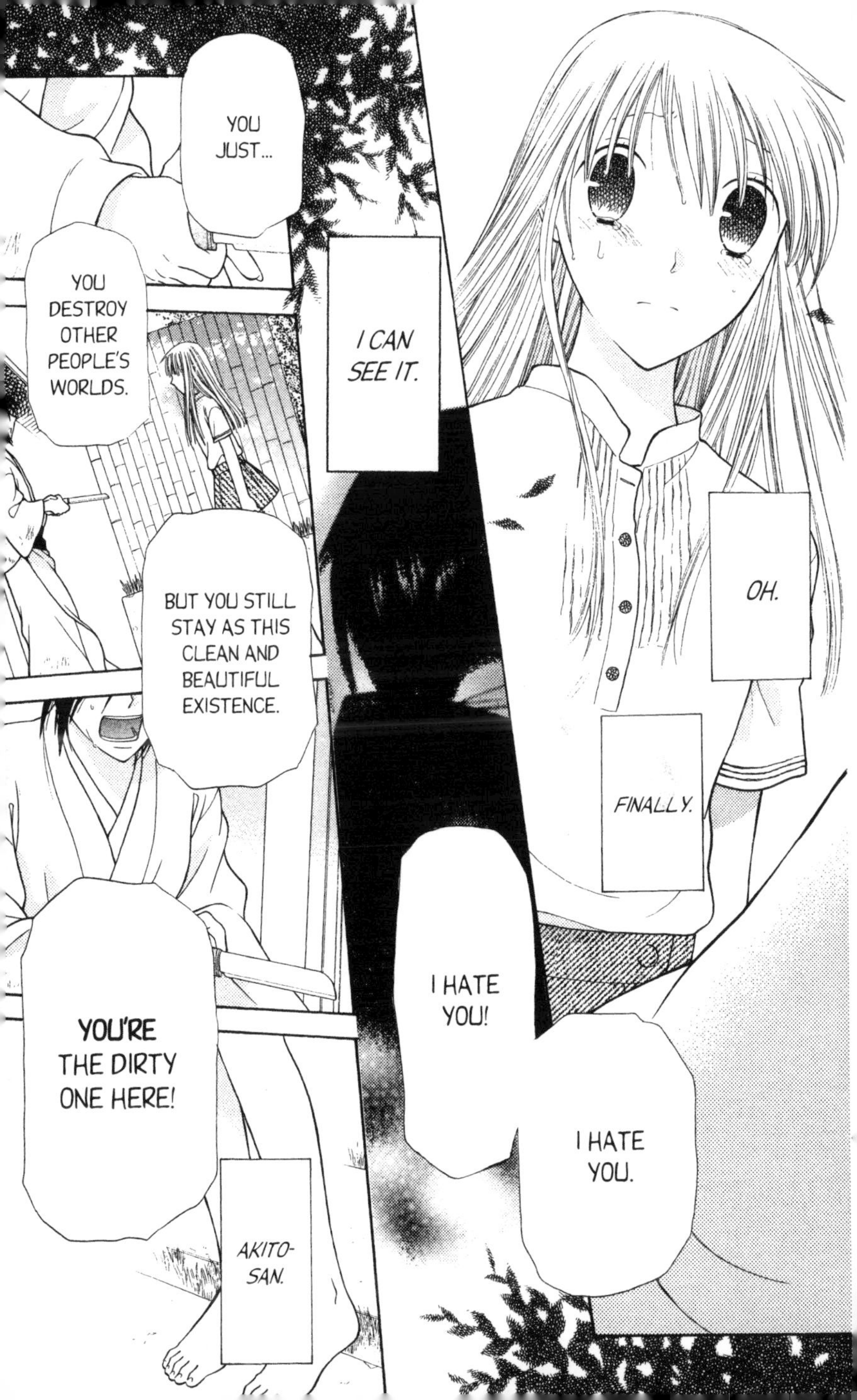

I CAN SEE IT.
OH.
FINALLY.
I HATE YOU!
I HATE YOU.
YOU JUST...
YOU DESTROY OTHER PEOPLE'S WORLDS.
BUT YOU STILL STAY AS THIS CLEAN AND BEAUTIFUL EXISTENCE.
YOU'RE THE DIRTY ONE HERE!
AKITO-SAN.

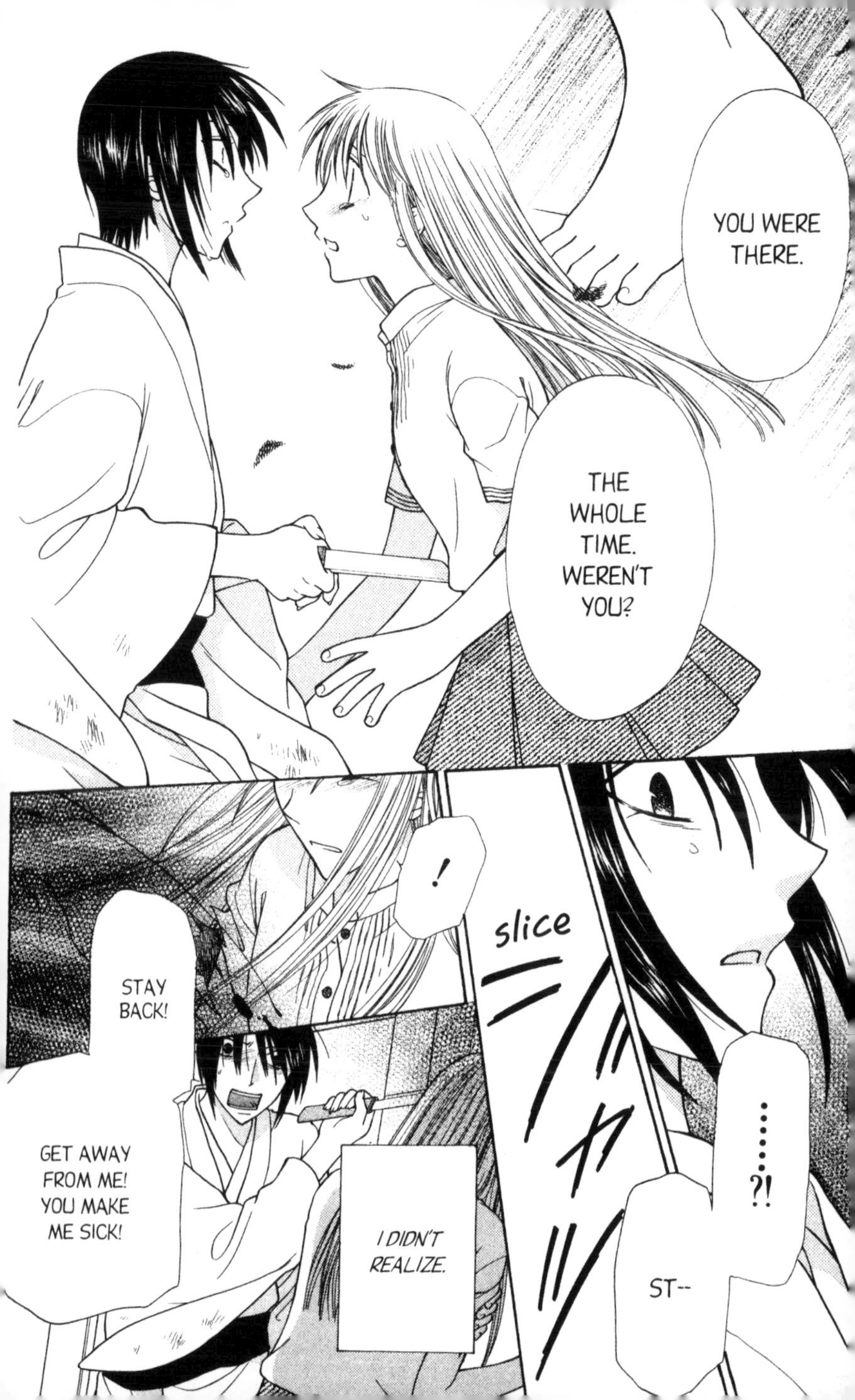
YOU WERE THERE.
THE WHOLE TIME. WEREN'T YOU?
......?!
ST--
slice
!
STAY BACK!
GET AWAY FROM ME! YOU MAKE ME SICK!
I DIDN'T REALIZE.

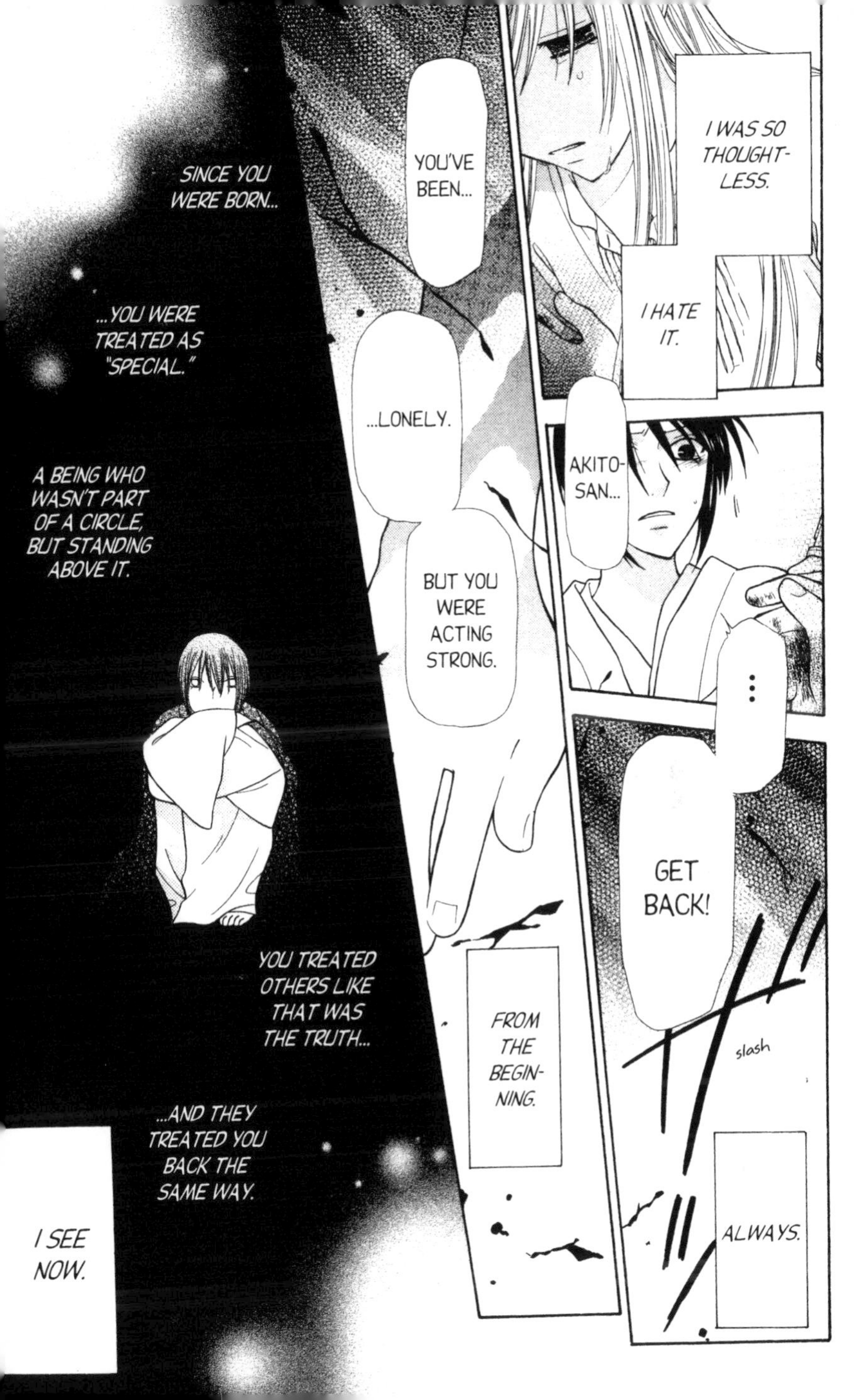
I WAS SO THOUGHT-LESS.
I HATE IT.
AKITO-SAN...
...
GET BACK!
slash
ALWAYS.
YOU'VE BEEN...
...LONELY.
BUT YOU WERE ACTING STRONG.
FROM THE BEGIN-NING.
SINCE YOU WERE BORN...
...YOU WERE TREATED AS "SPECIAL."
A BEING WHO WASN'T PART OF A CIRCLE, BUT STANDING ABOVE IT.
YOU TREATED OTHERS LIKE THAT WAS THE TRUTH...
...AND THEY TREATED YOU BACK THE SAME WAY.
I SEE NOW.

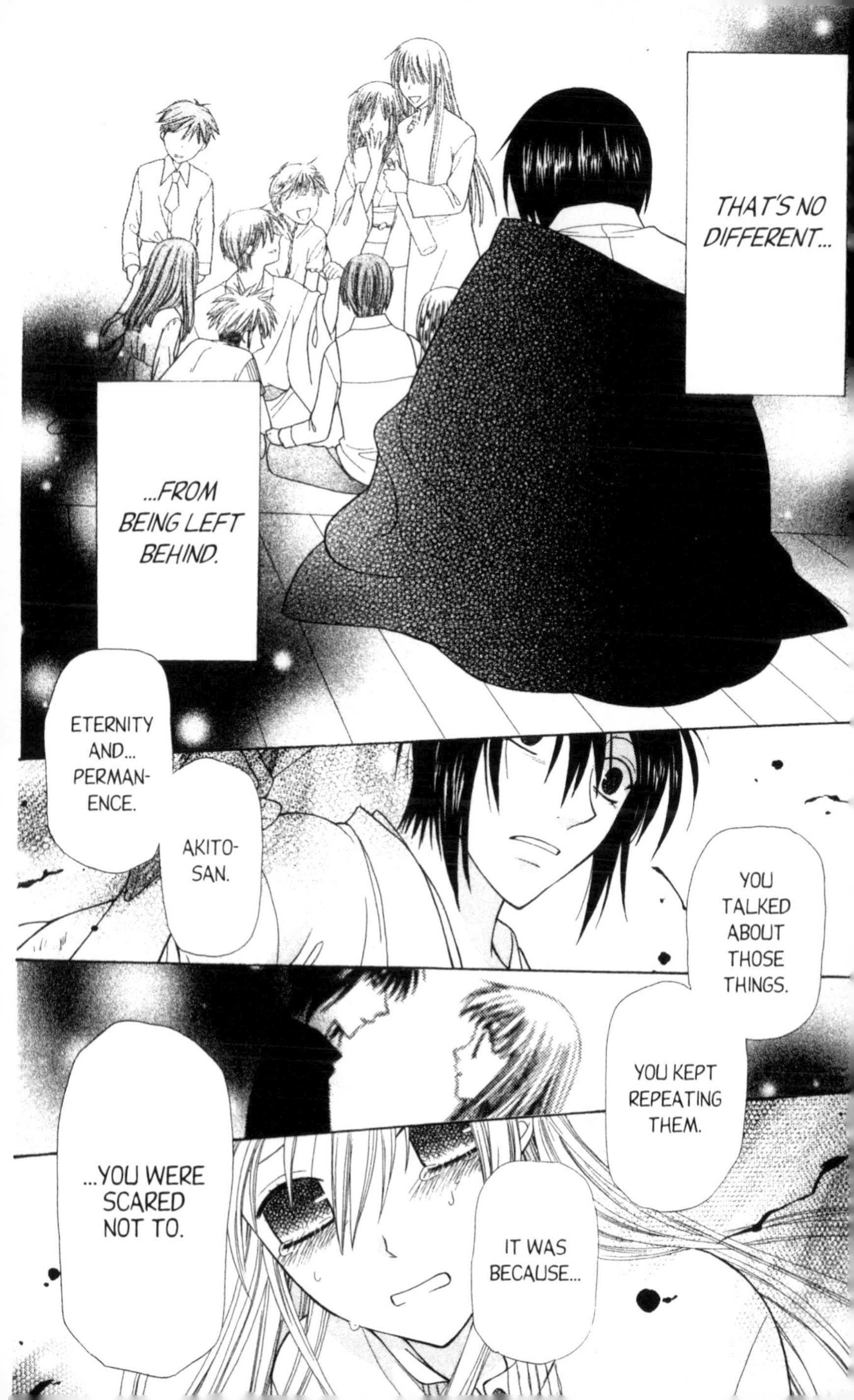
THAT'S NO DIFFERENT...
...FROM BEING LEFT BEHIND.
ETERNITY AND... PERMANENCE.
AKITO-SAN.
YOU TALKED ABOUT THOSE THINGS.
YOU KEPT REPEATING THEM.
IT WAS BECAUSE...
...YOU WERE SCARED NOT TO.

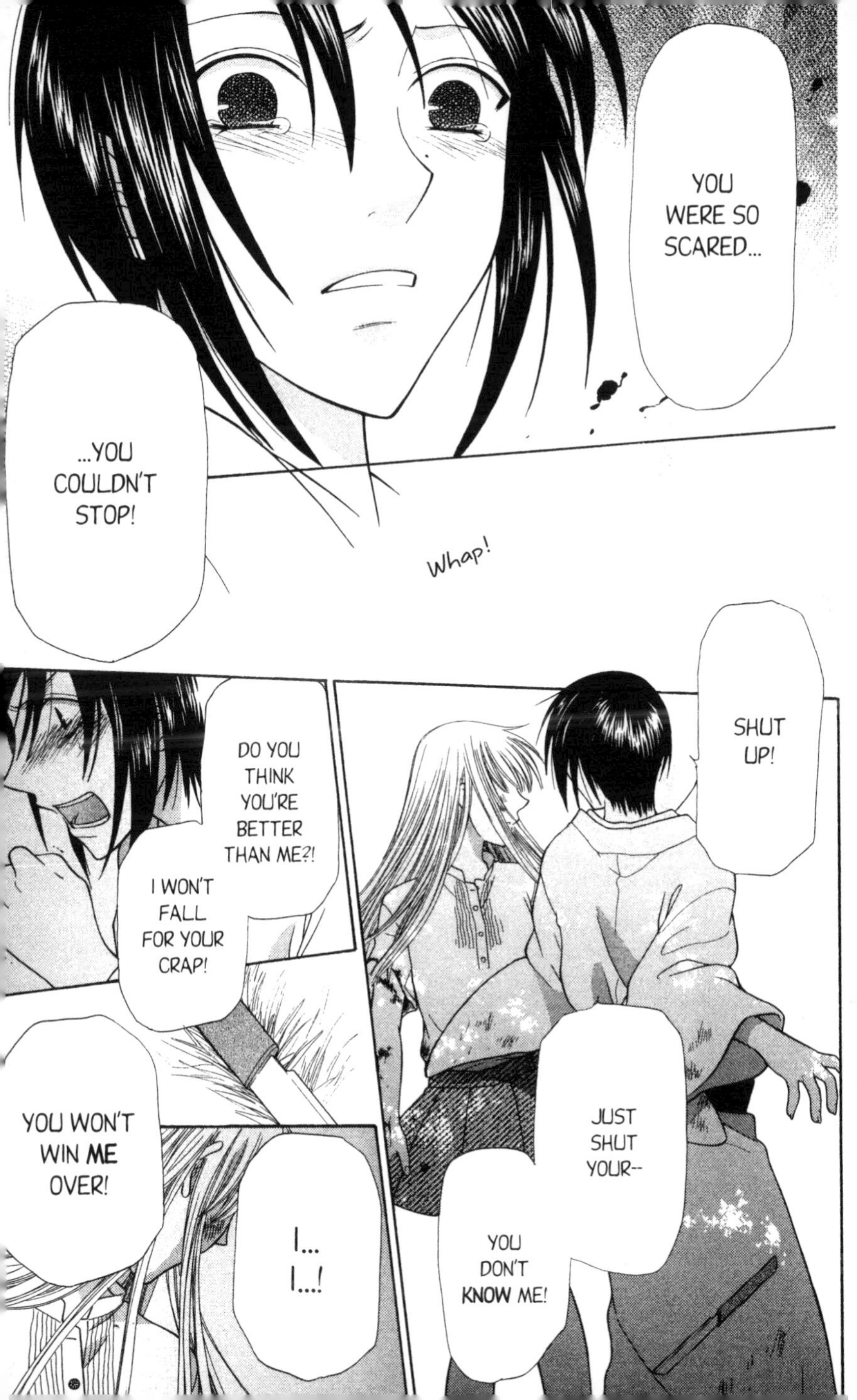
YOU WERE SO SCARED...
...YOU COULDN'T STOP!
Whap!
SHUT UP!
DO YOU THINK YOU'RE BETTER THAN ME?!
I WON'T FALL FOR YOUR CRAP!
JUST SHUT YOUR--
YOU WON'T WIN **ME** OVER!
YOU DON'T **KNOW** ME!
I... I...!

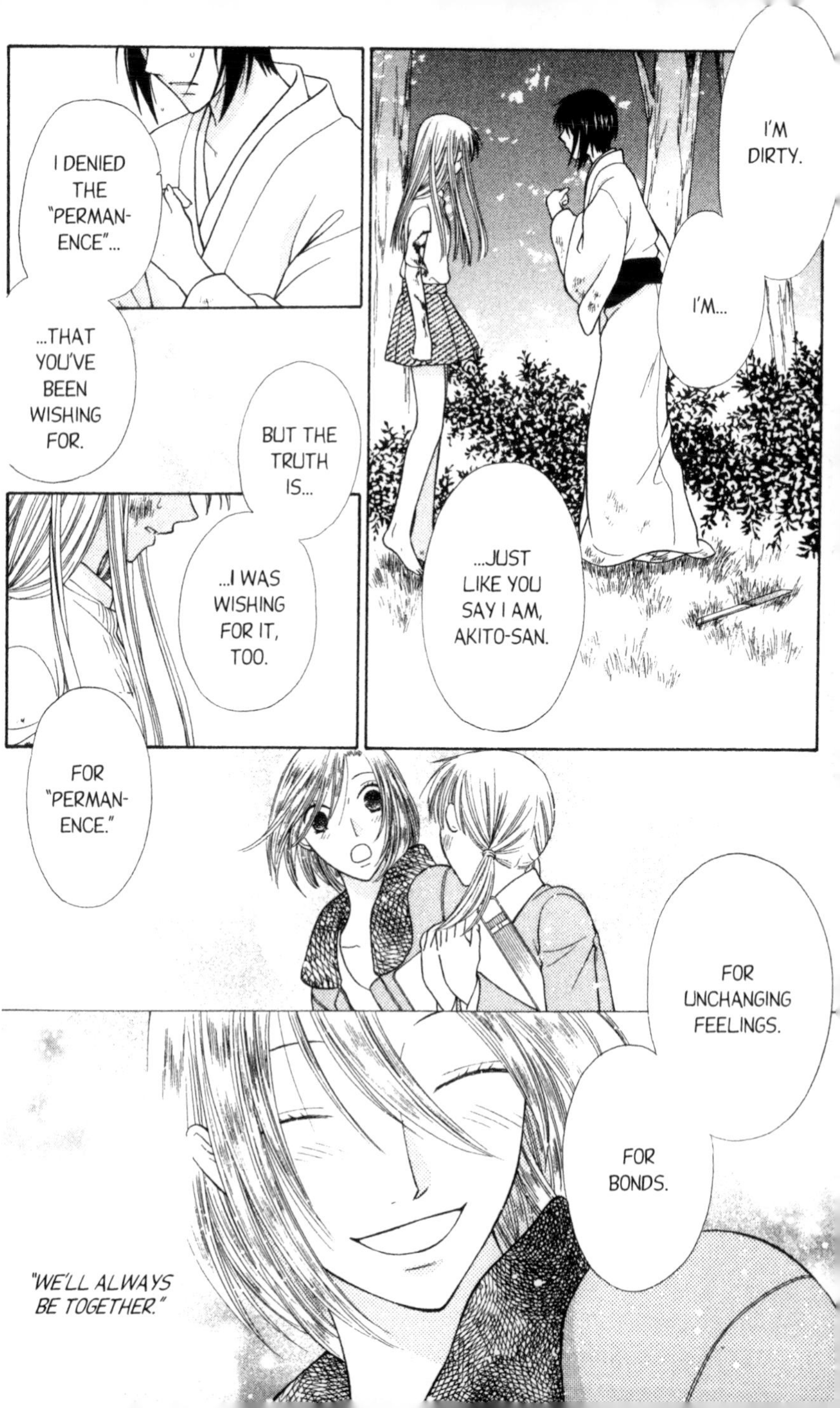
I'M DIRTY.
I'M...
...JUST LIKE YOU SAY I AM, AKITO-SAN.
I DENIED THE "PERMAN-ENCE"...
...THAT YOU'VE BEEN WISHING FOR.
BUT THE TRUTH IS...
...I WAS WISHING FOR IT, TOO.
FOR "PERMAN-ENCE."
FOR UNCHANGING FEELINGS.
FOR BONDS.
"WE'LL ALWAYS BE TOGETHER."

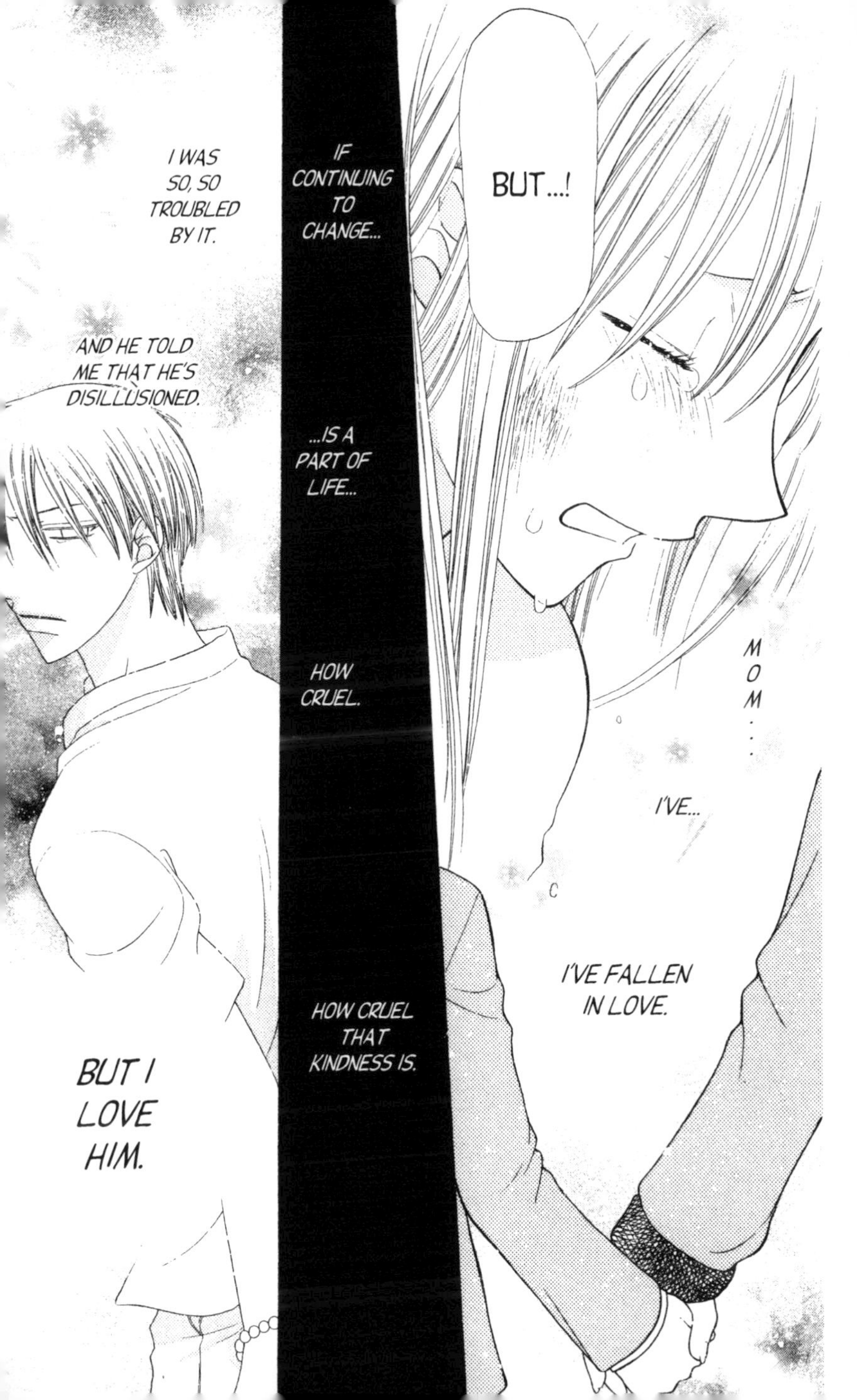
BUT...!
MOM...
I'VE...
I'VE FALLEN IN LOVE.
IF CONTINUING TO CHANGE...
...IS A PART OF LIFE...
HOW CRUEL.
HOW CRUEL THAT KINDNESS IS.
I WAS SO, SO TROUBLED BY IT.
AND HE TOLD ME THAT HE'S DISILLUSIONED.
BUT I LOVE HIM.

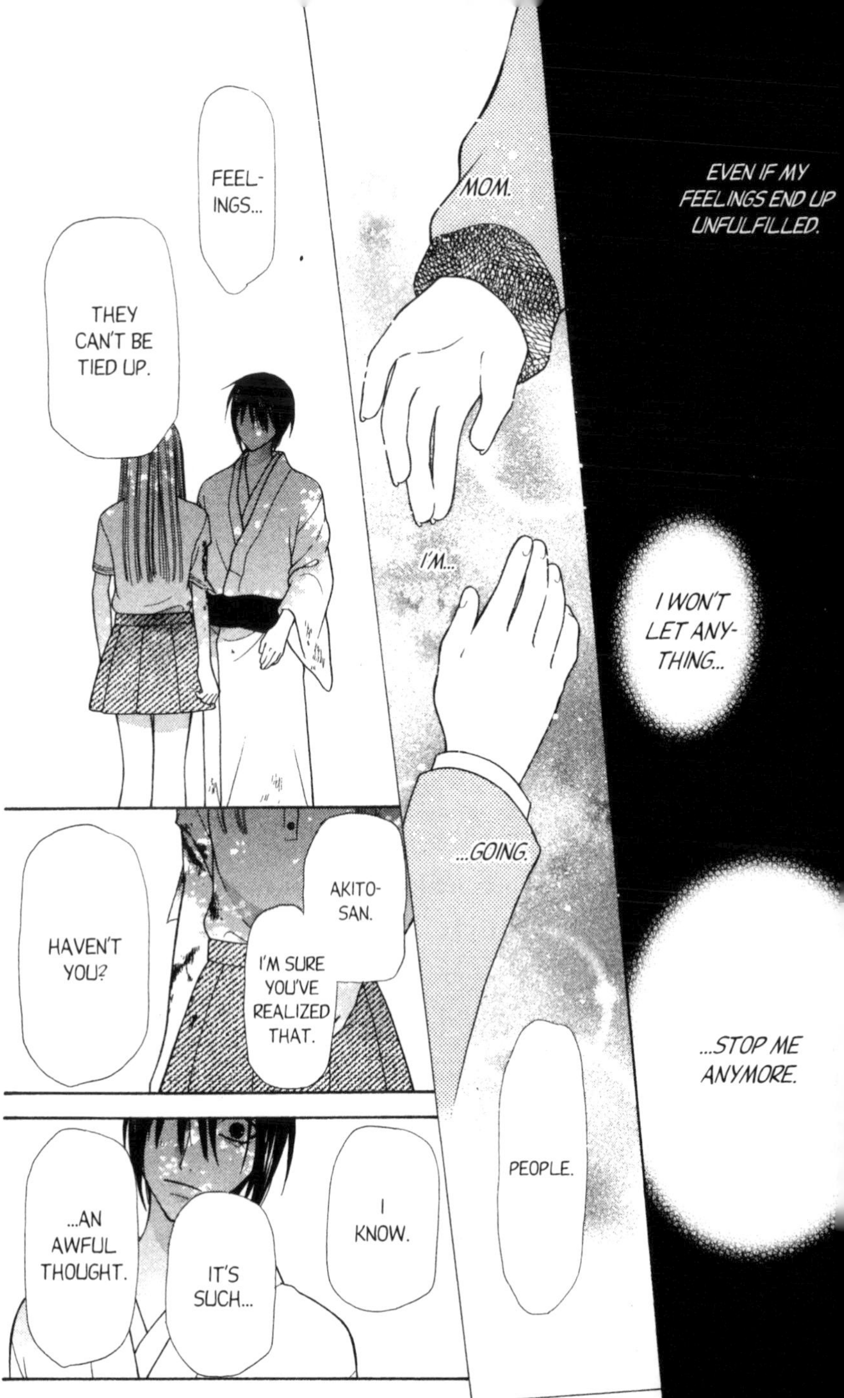
EVEN IF MY FEELINGS END UP UNFULFILLED.
I WON'T LET ANY-THING...
...STOP ME ANYMORE.
MOM.
I'M...
...GOING.
PEOPLE.
FEEL-INGS...
THEY CAN'T BE TIED UP.
AKITO-SAN.
I'M SURE YOU'VE REALIZED THAT.
HAVEN'T YOU?
I KNOW.
IT'S SUCH...
...AN AWFUL THOUGHT.

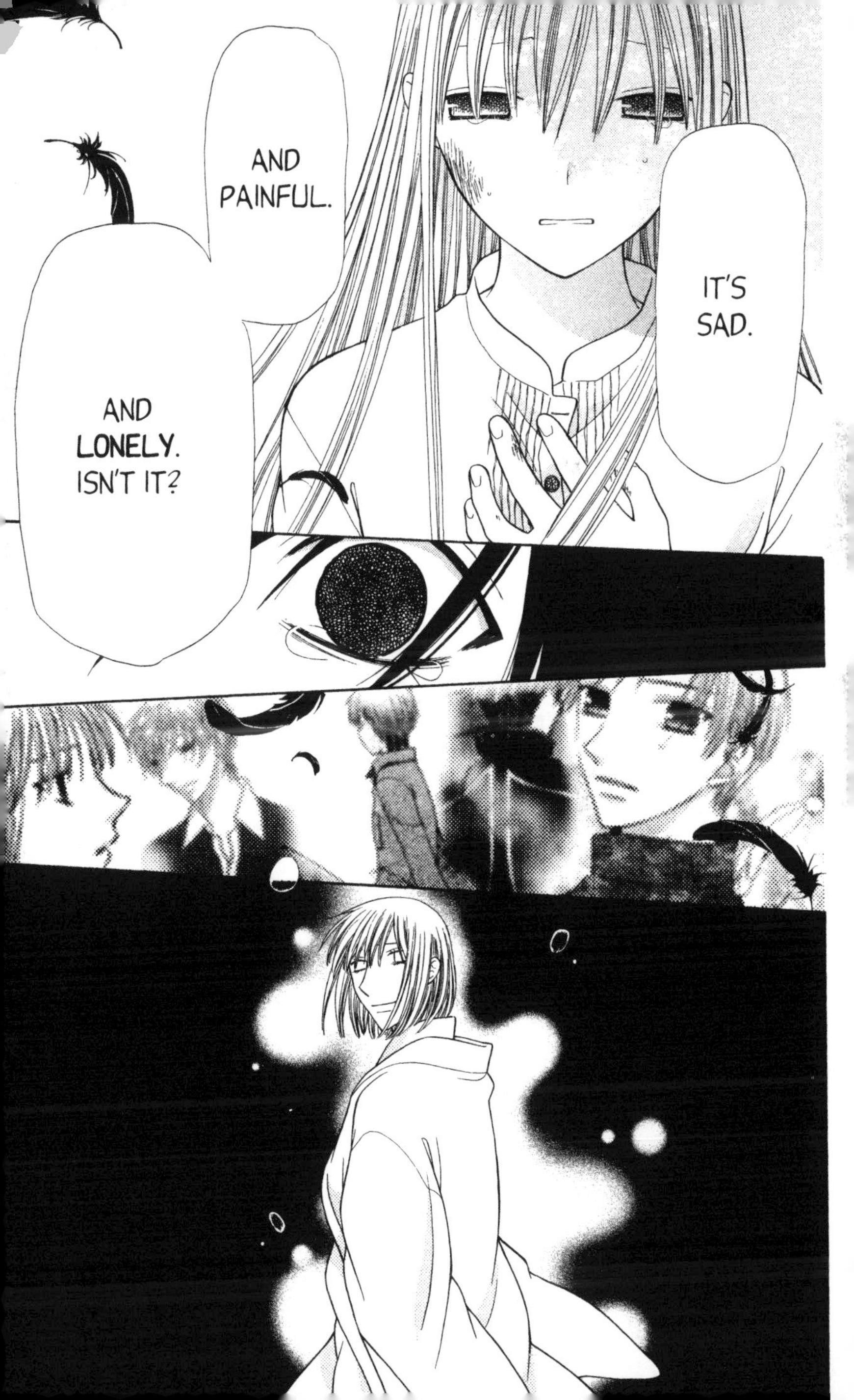
IT'S SAD.
AND PAINFUL.
AND LONELY. ISN'T IT?

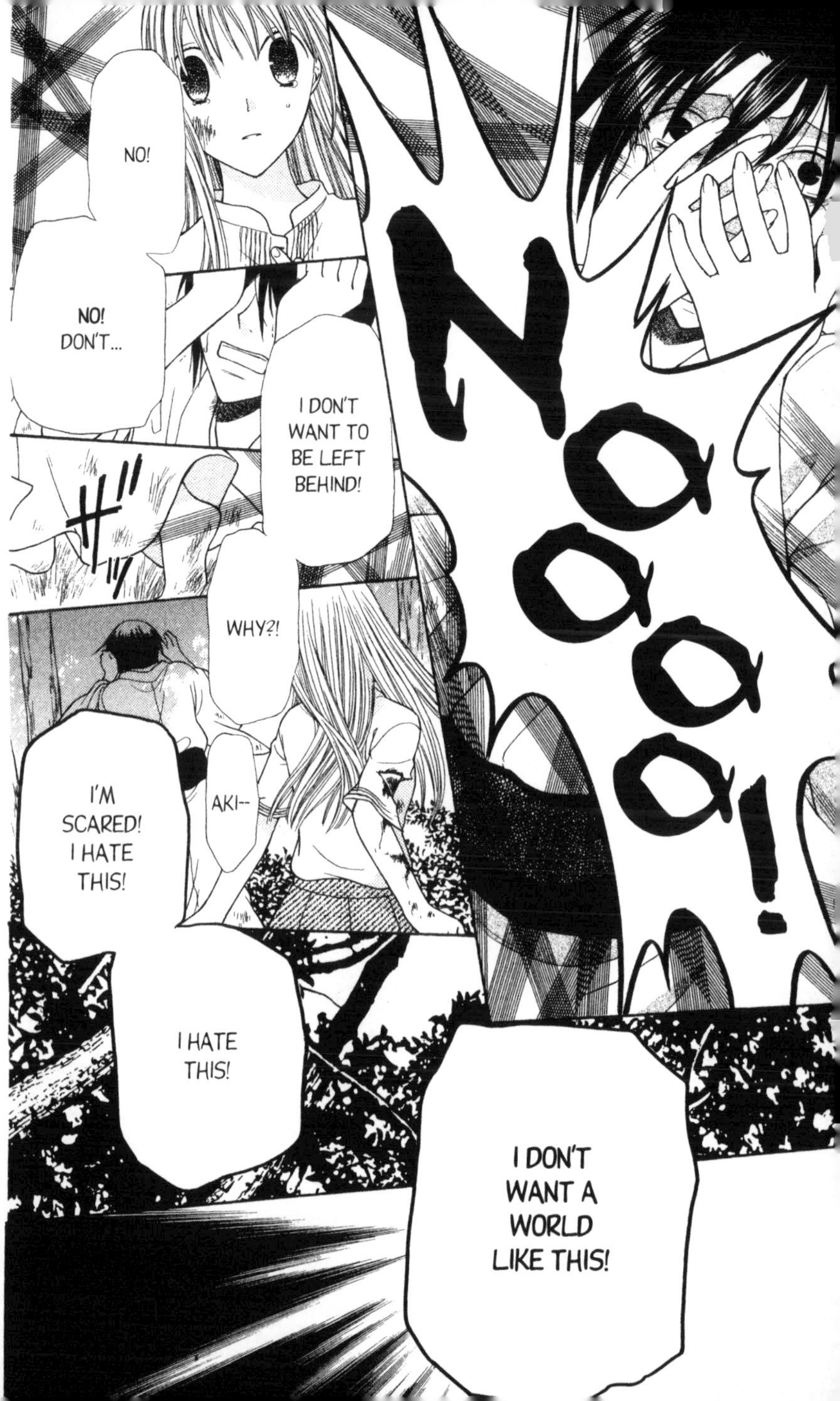
NOOOOO!
NO!
NO! DON'T...
I DON'T WANT TO BE LEFT BEHIND!
WHY?!
AKI--
I'M SCARED! I HATE THIS!
I HATE THIS!
I DON'T WANT A WORLD LIKE THIS!

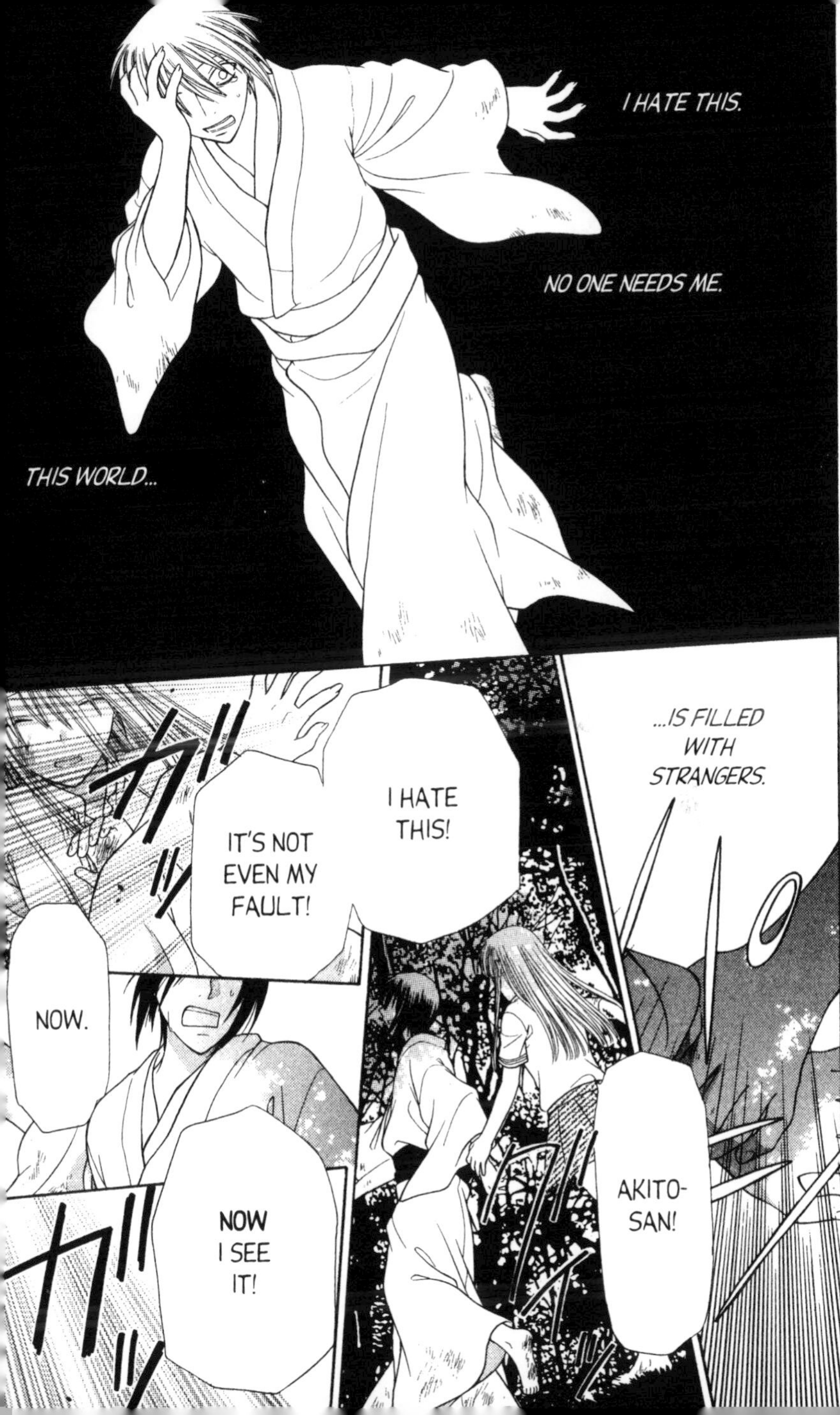
I HATE THIS.
NO ONE NEEDS ME.
THIS WORLD...
...IS FILLED WITH STRANGERS.
AKITO-SAN!
I HATE THIS!
IT'S NOT EVEN MY FAULT!
NOW.
NOW I SEE IT!

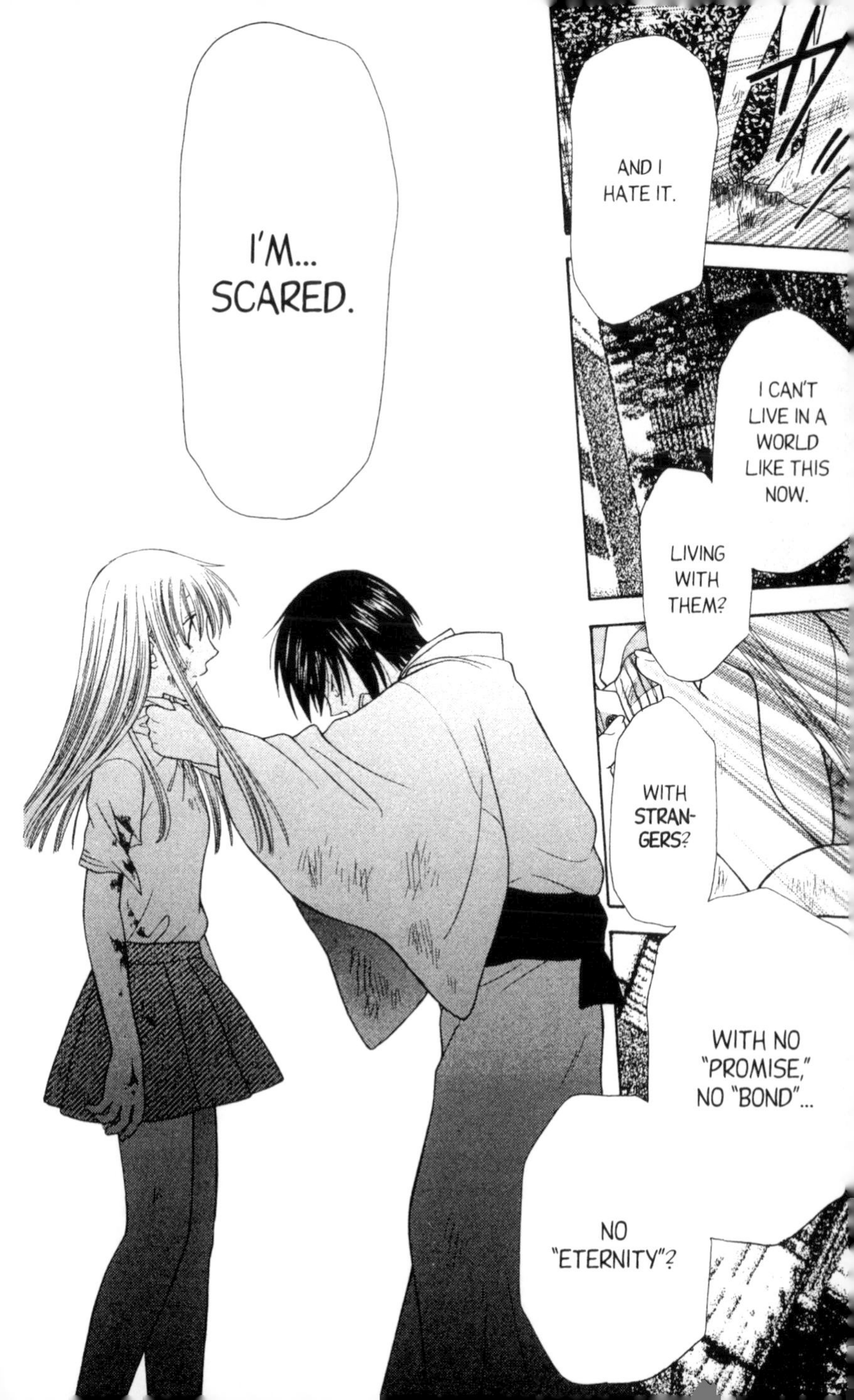
AND I HATE IT.
I CAN'T LIVE IN A WORLD LIKE THIS NOW.
LIVING WITH THEM?
WITH STRAN-GERS?
WITH NO "PROMISE," NO "BOND"...
NO "ETERNITY"?
I'M... SCARED.

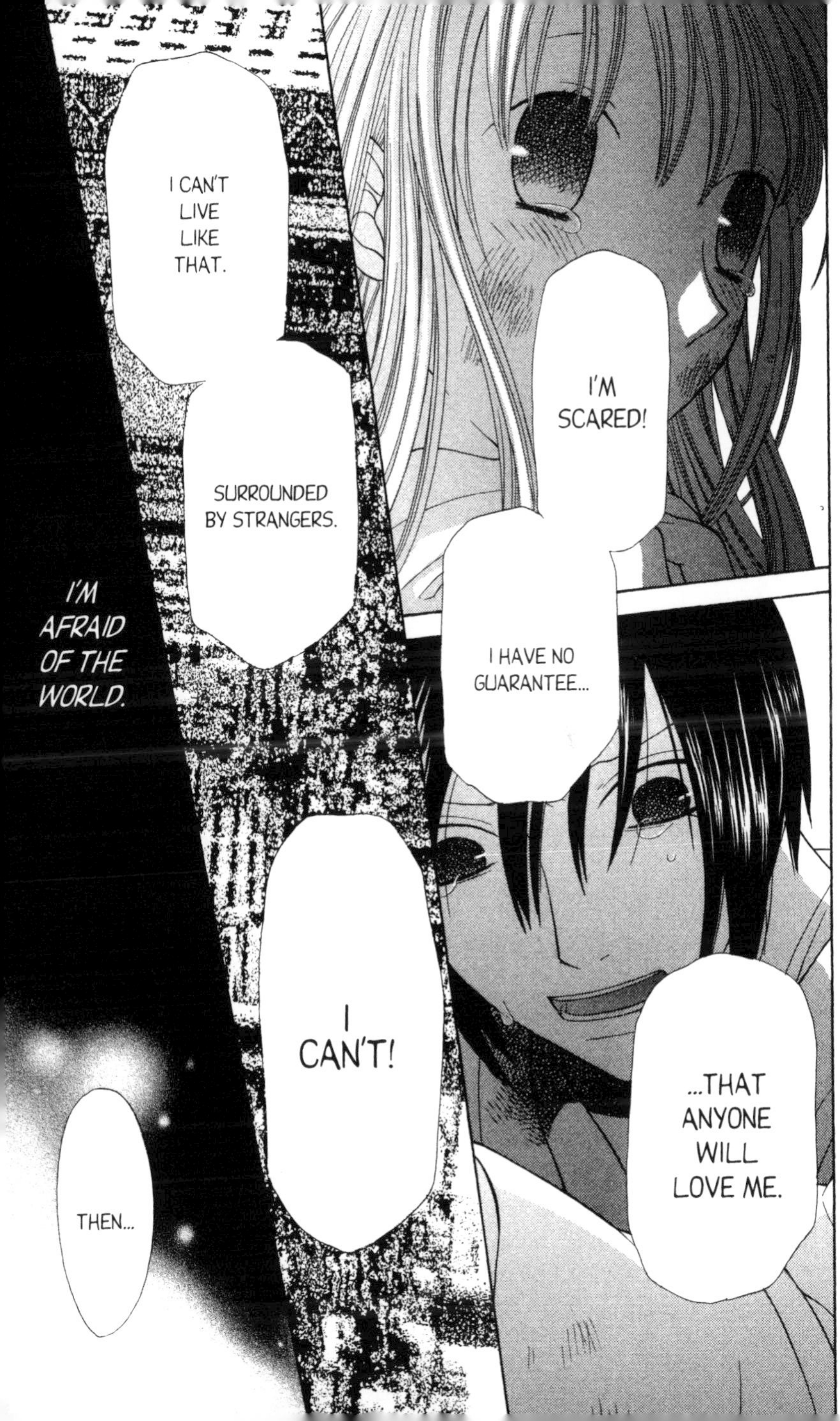
I'M SCARED!
I HAVE NO GUARANTEE...
...THAT ANYONE WILL LOVE ME.
I CAN'T LIVE LIKE THAT.
SURROUNDED BY STRANGERS.
I'M AFRAID OF THE WORLD.
I CAN'T!
THEN...

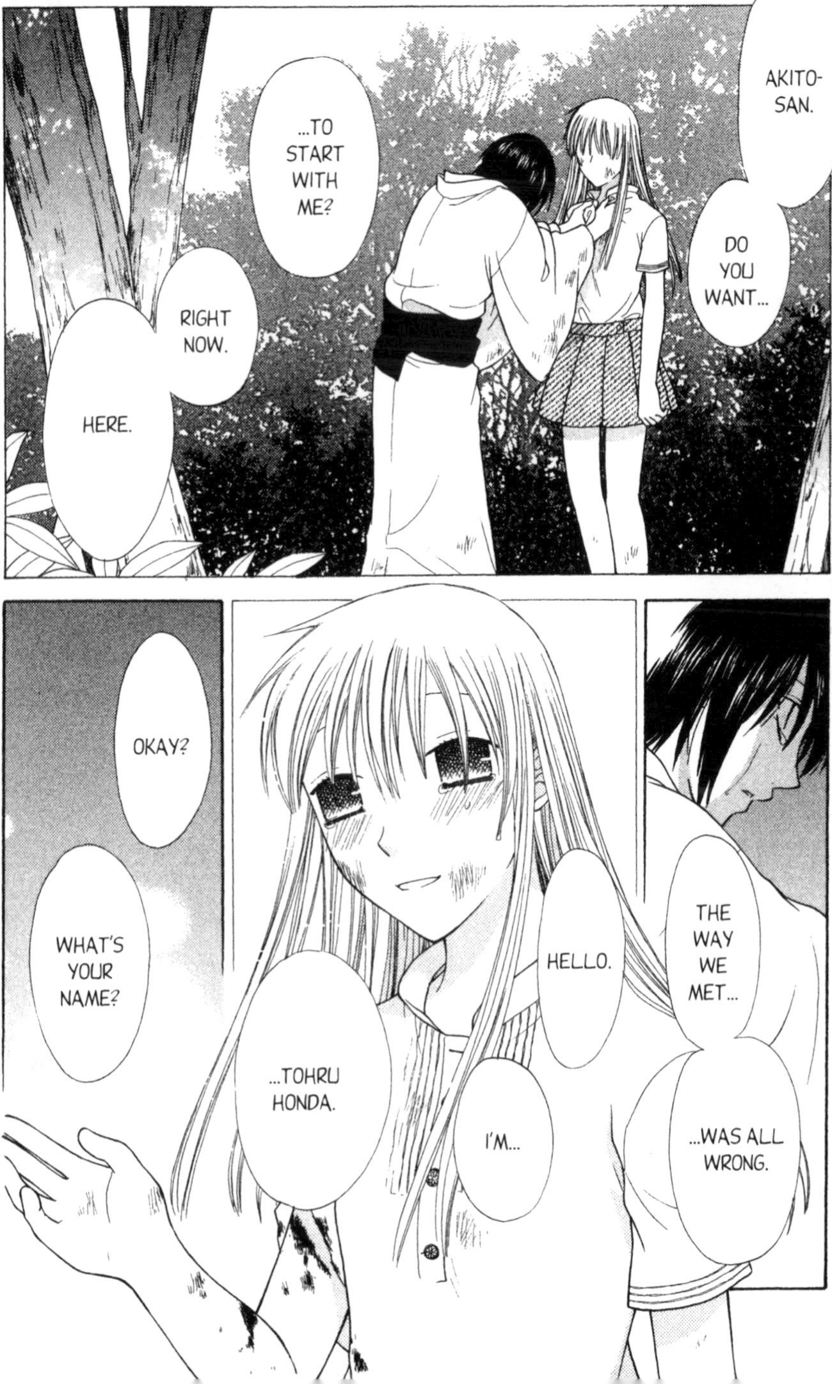
AKITO-SAN.
DO YOU WANT...
...TO START WITH ME?
RIGHT NOW.
HERE.
THE WAY WE MET...
...WAS ALL WRONG.
HELLO.
I'M...
...TOHRU HONDA.
OKAY?
WHAT'S YOUR NAME?

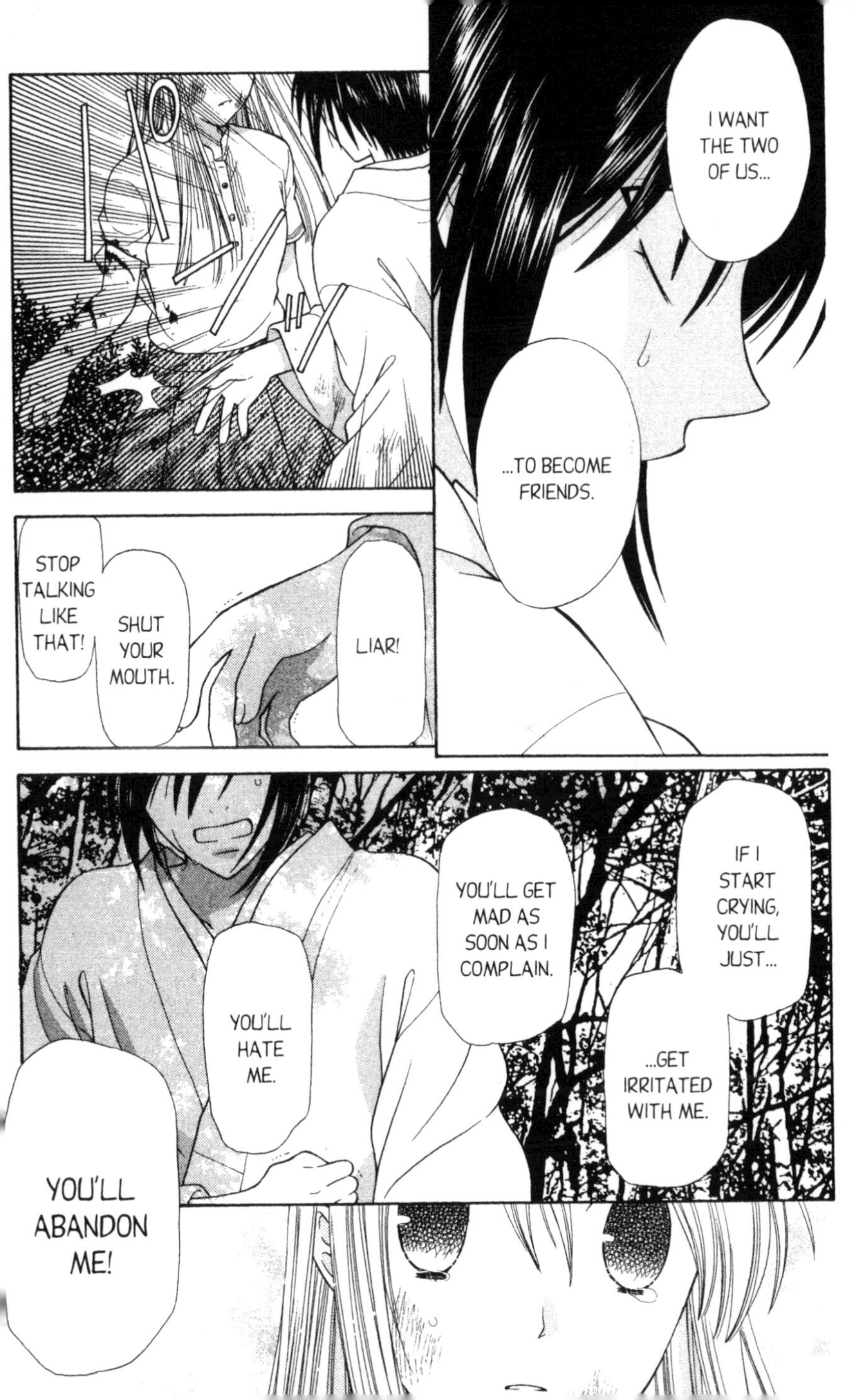
I WANT THE TWO OF US...
...TO BECOME FRIENDS.
LIAR!
SHUT YOUR MOUTH.
STOP TALKING LIKE THAT!
IF I START CRYING, YOU'LL JUST...
...GET IRRITATED WITH ME.
YOU'LL GET MAD AS SOON AS I COMPLAIN.
YOU'LL HATE ME.
YOU'LL ABANDON ME!

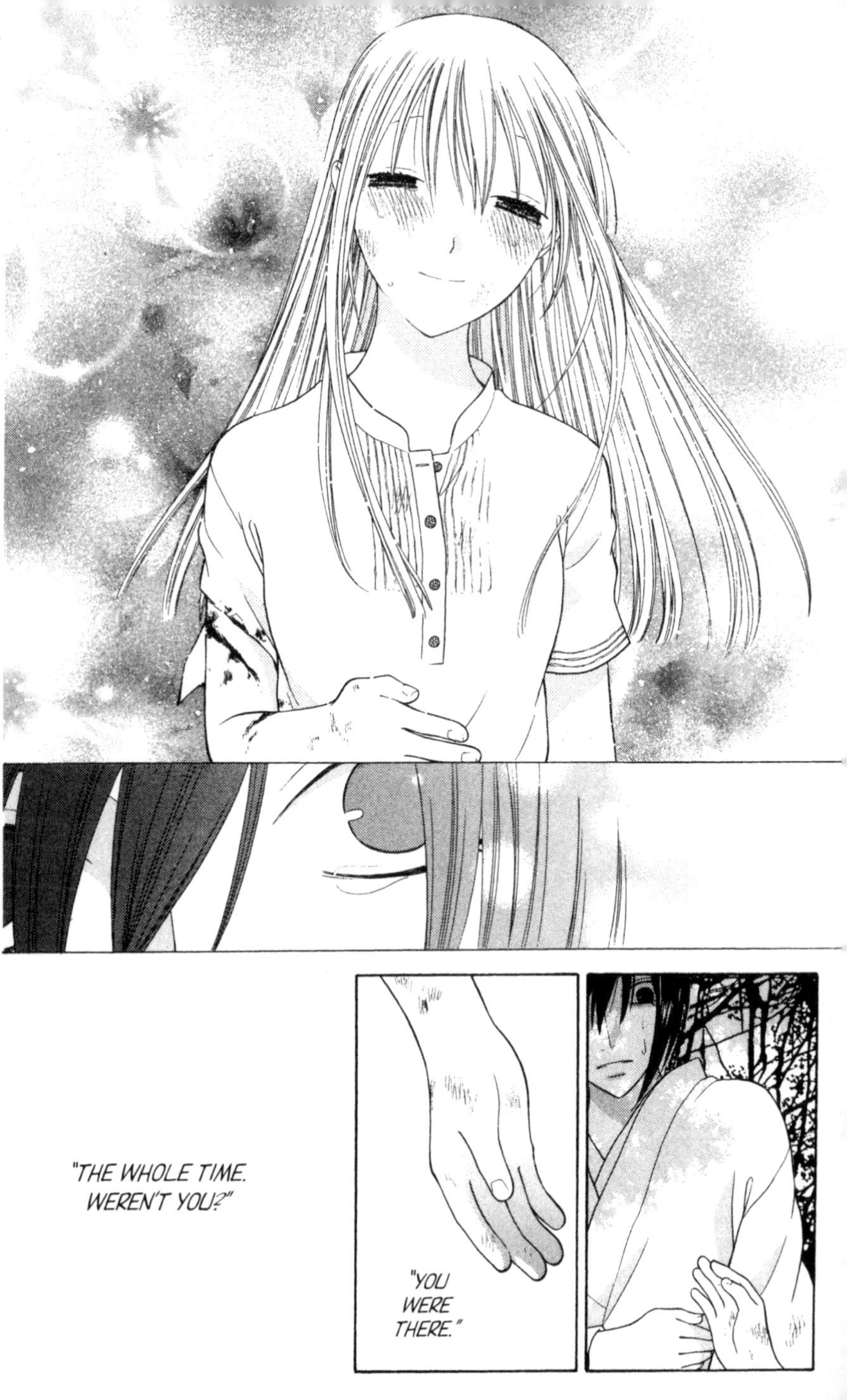
"YOU WERE THERE."
"THE WHOLE TIME. WEREN'T YOU?"

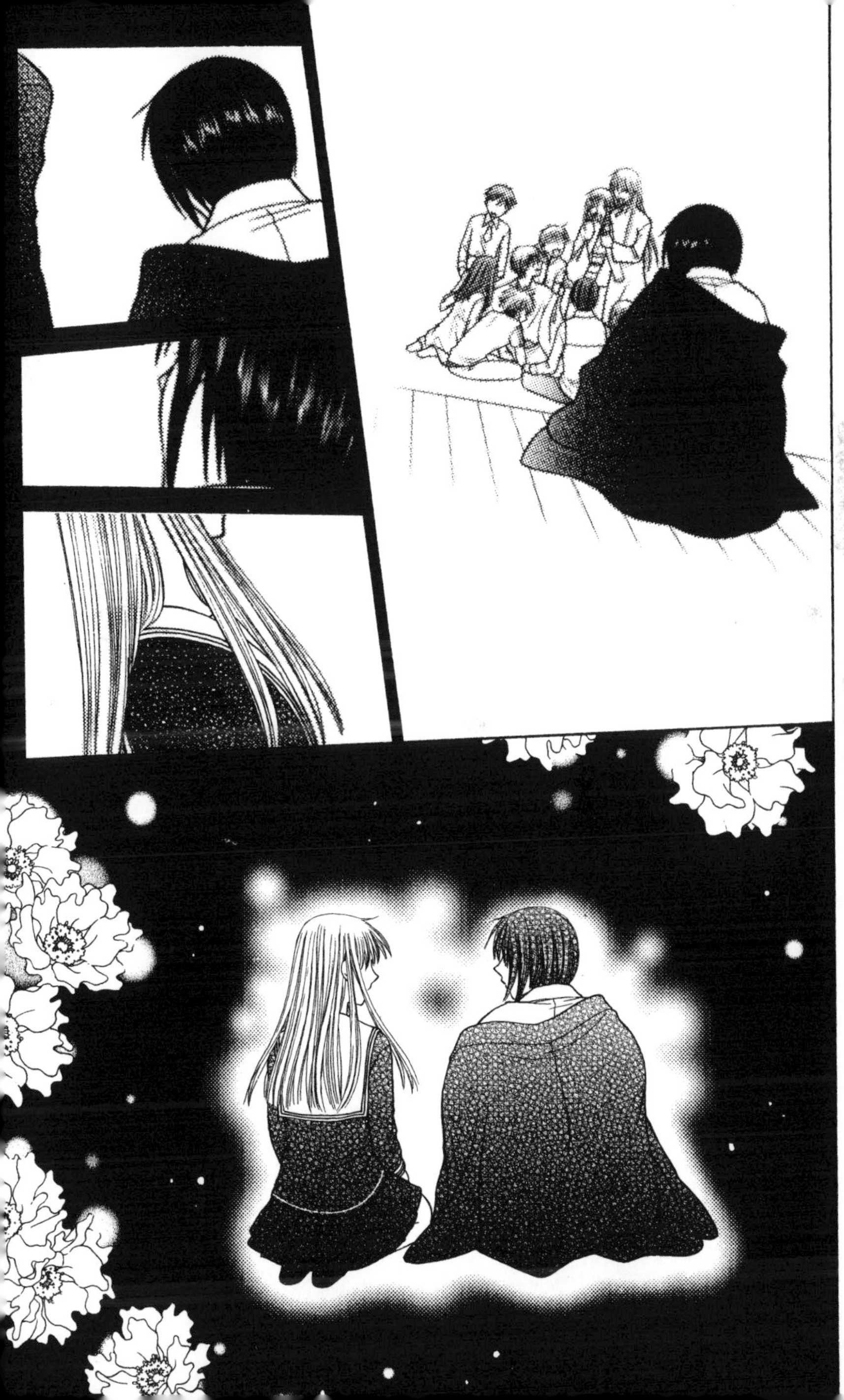

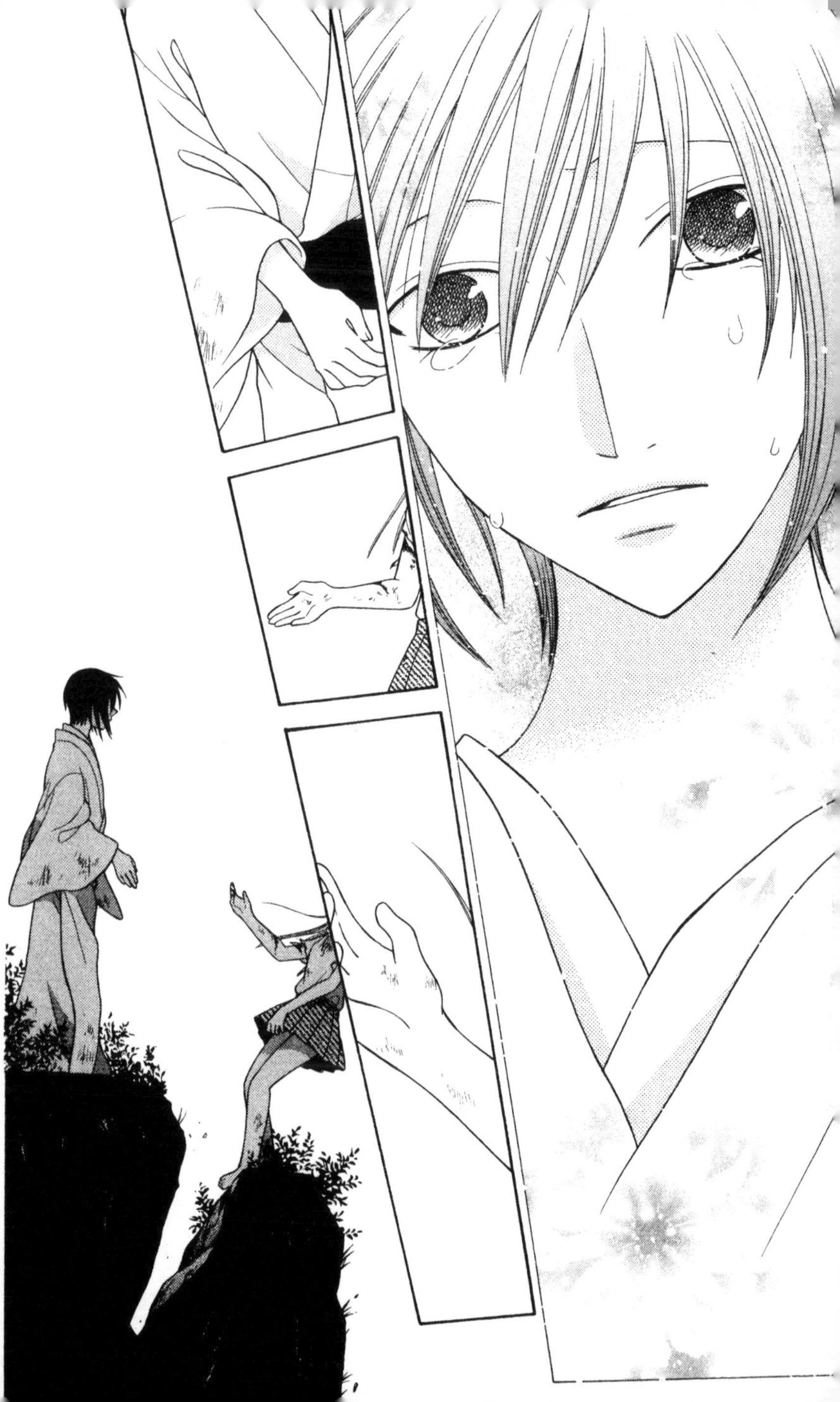

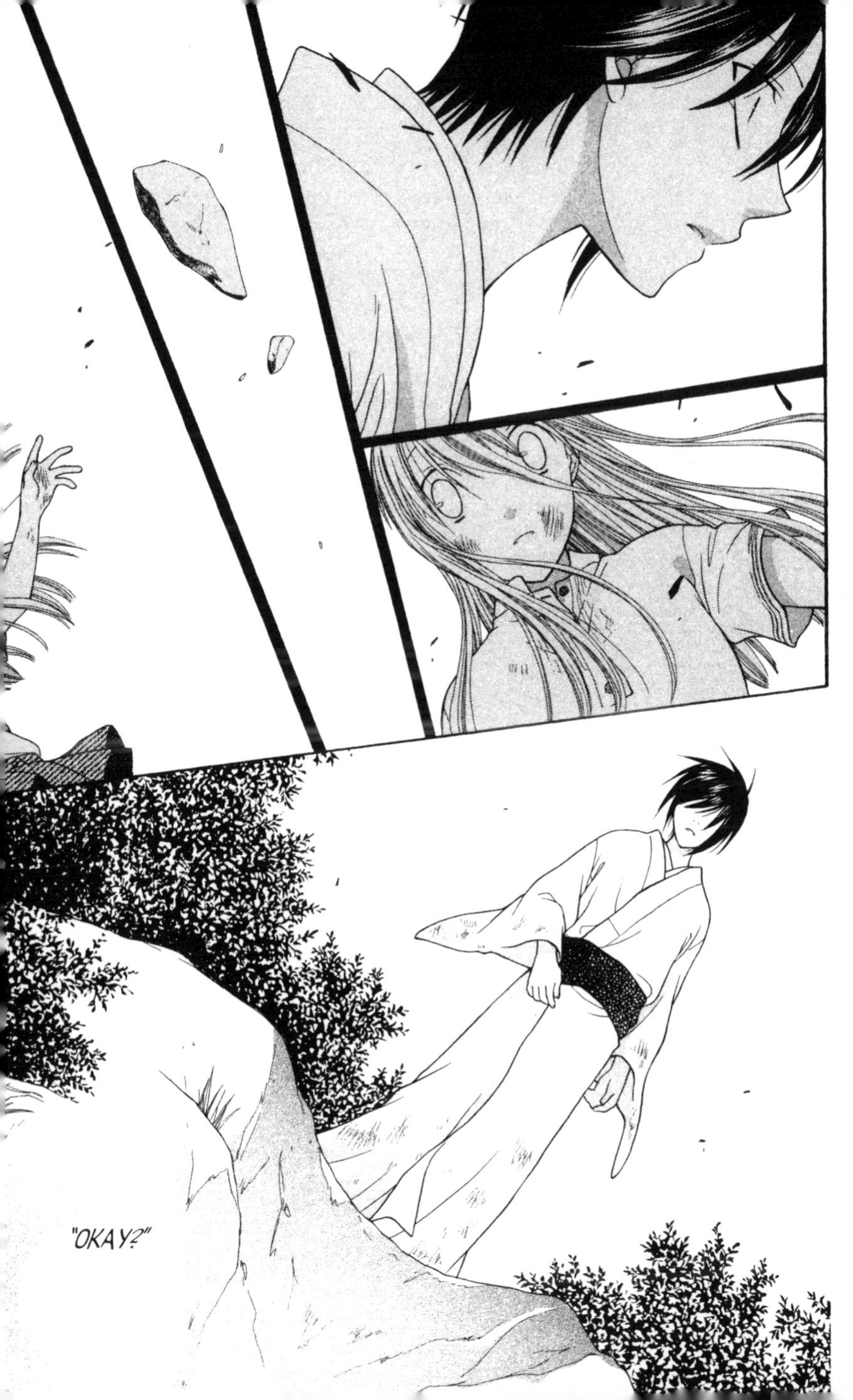
"OKAY?"

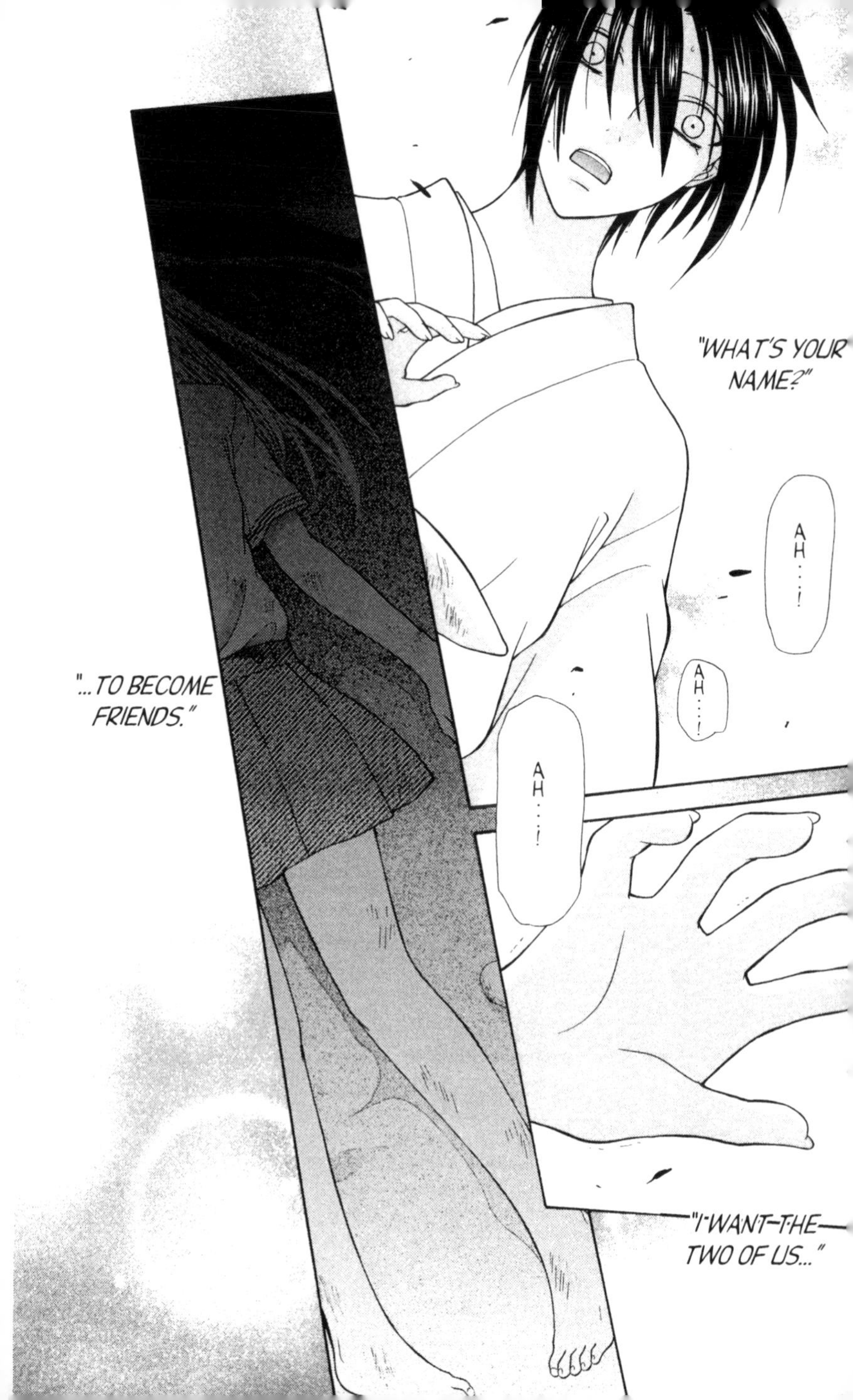
"WHAT'S YOUR NAME?"
AH...!
AH...!
AH...!
"I WANT THE TWO OF US..."
"...TO BECOME FRIENDS."

Chapter 122

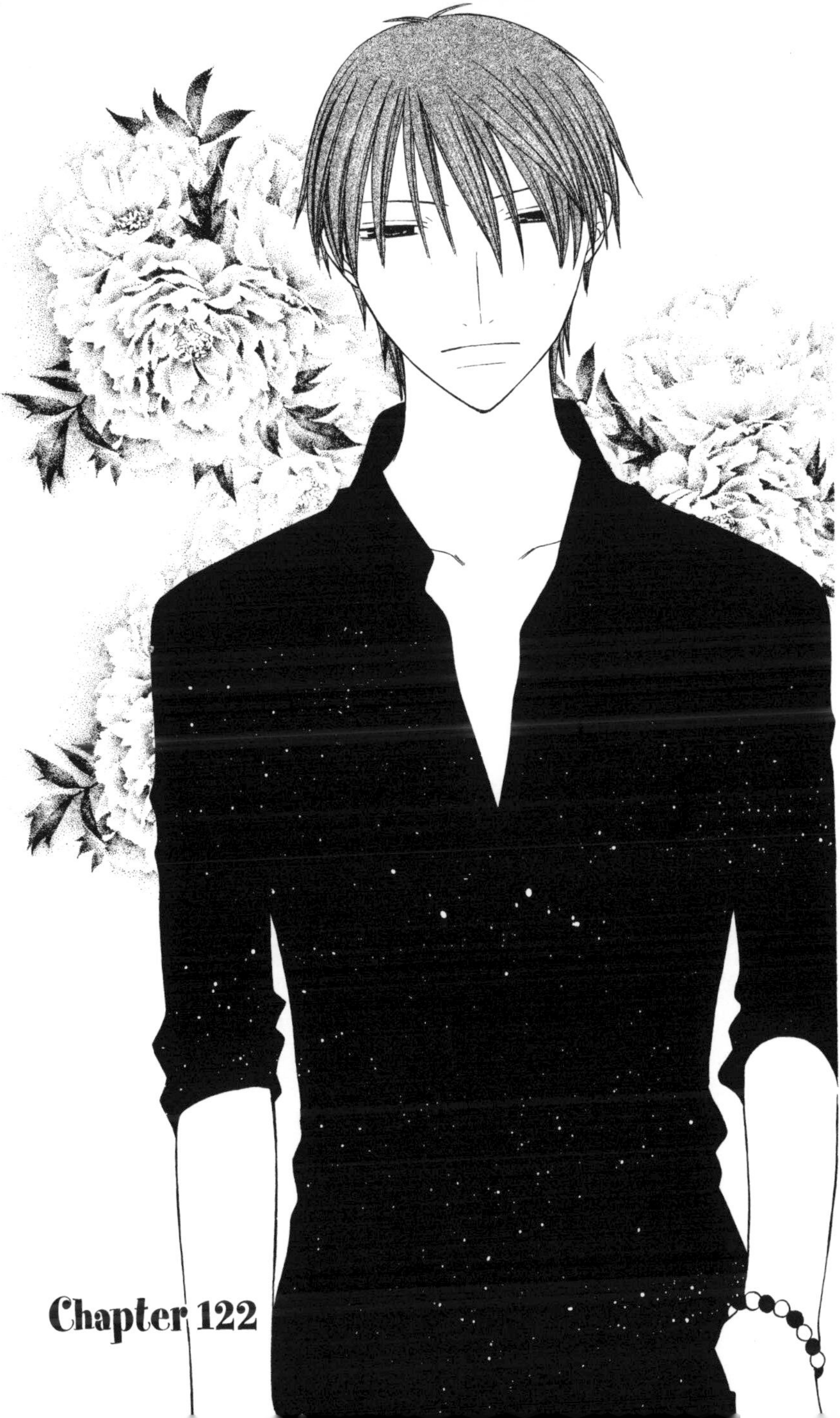

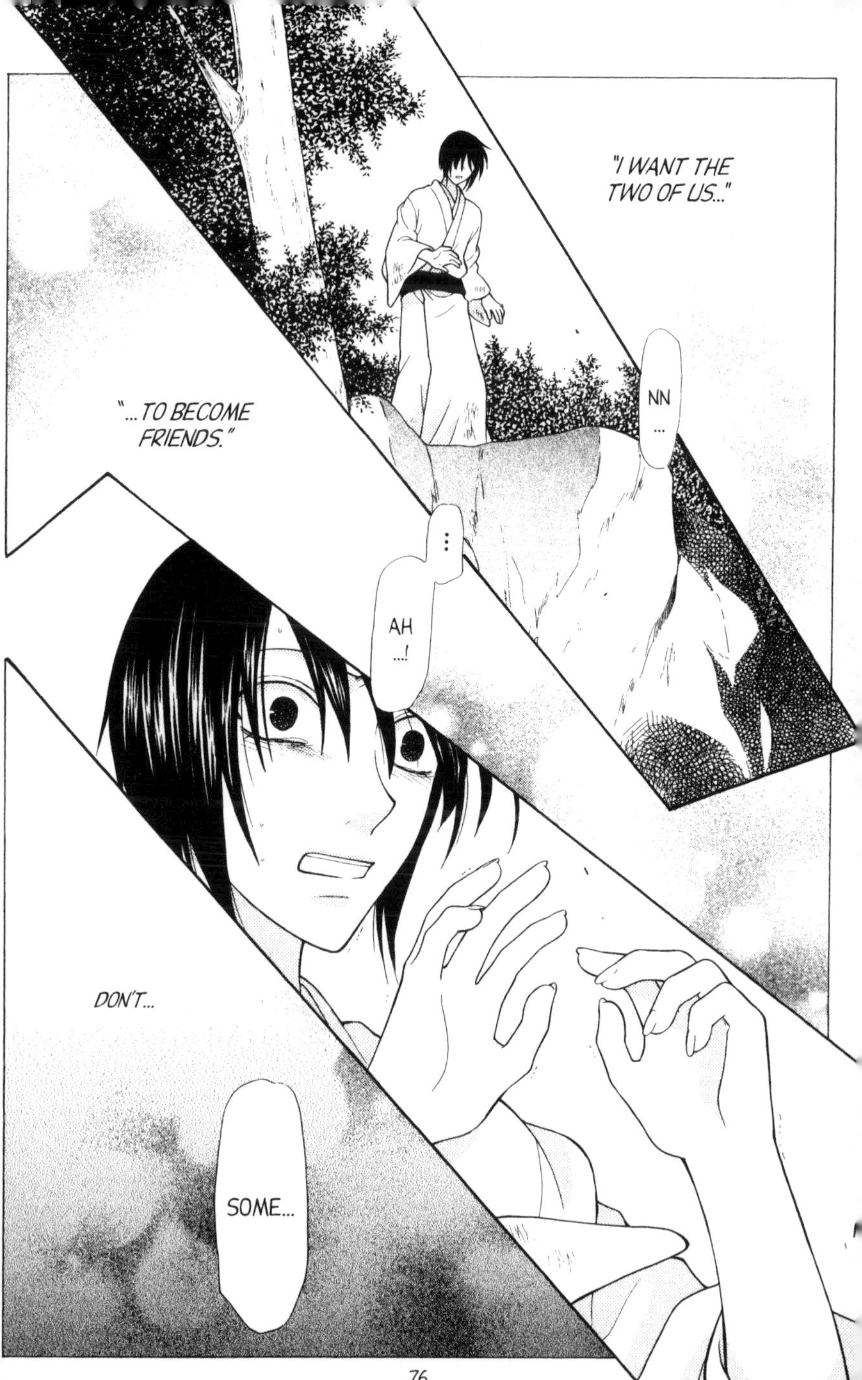
"I WANT THE TWO OF US..."
NN ...
"...TO BECOME FRIENDS."
...
AH ...!
DON'T...
SOME...

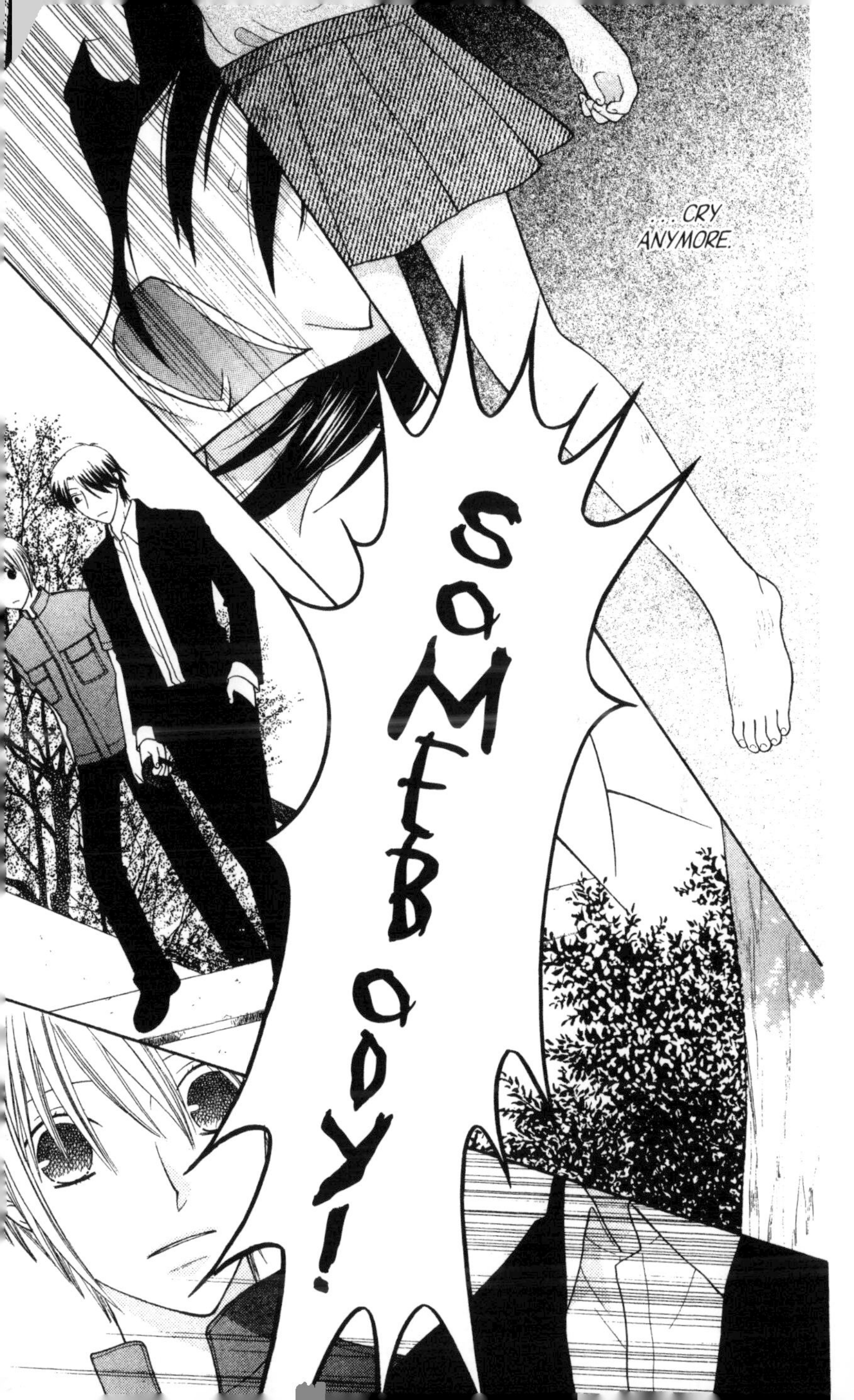
...CRY ANYMORE.
SOMEBODY!

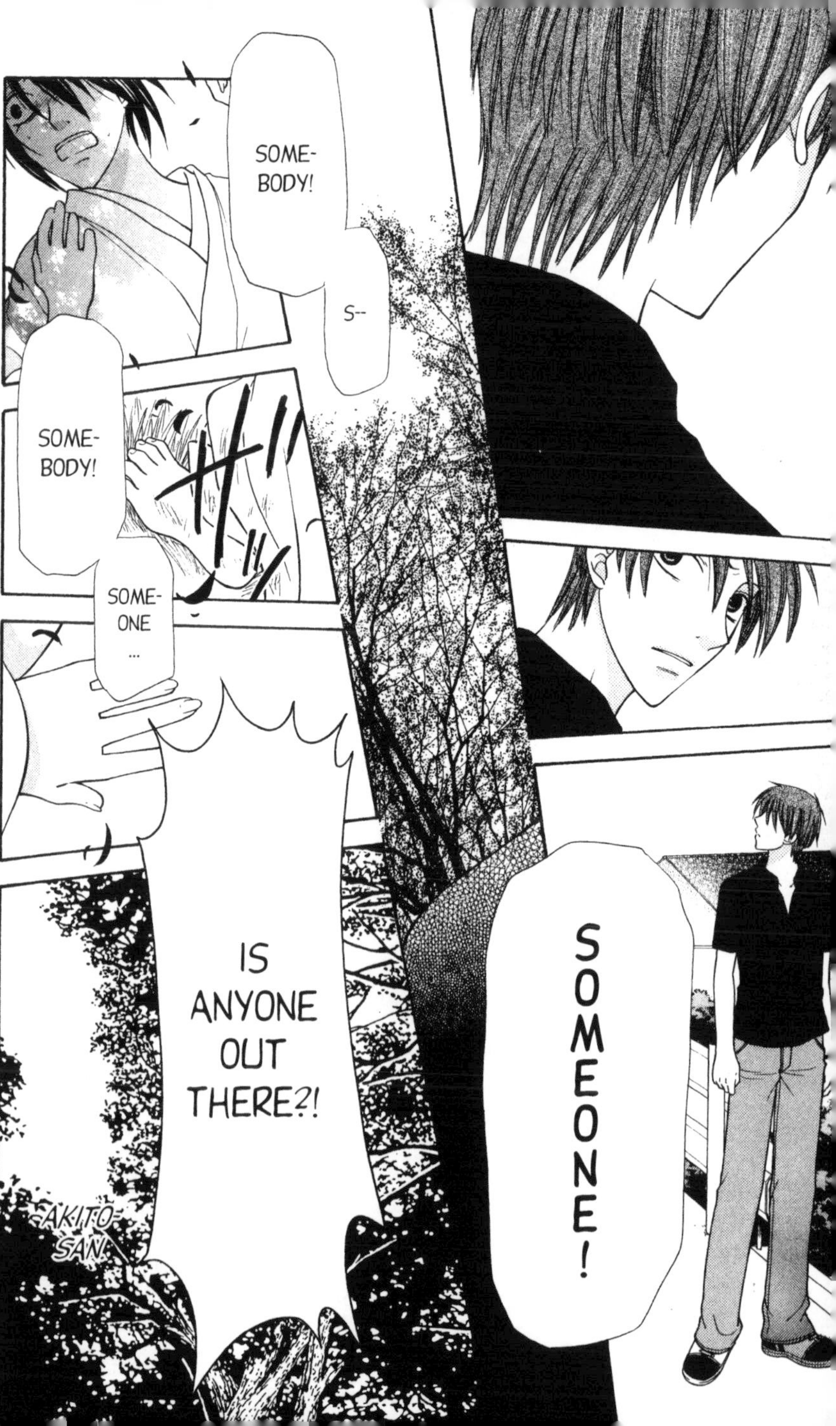
SOMEONE!
SOME-BODY!
S--
SOME-BODY!
SOME-ONE ...
IS ANYONE OUT THERE?!
AKITO-SAN

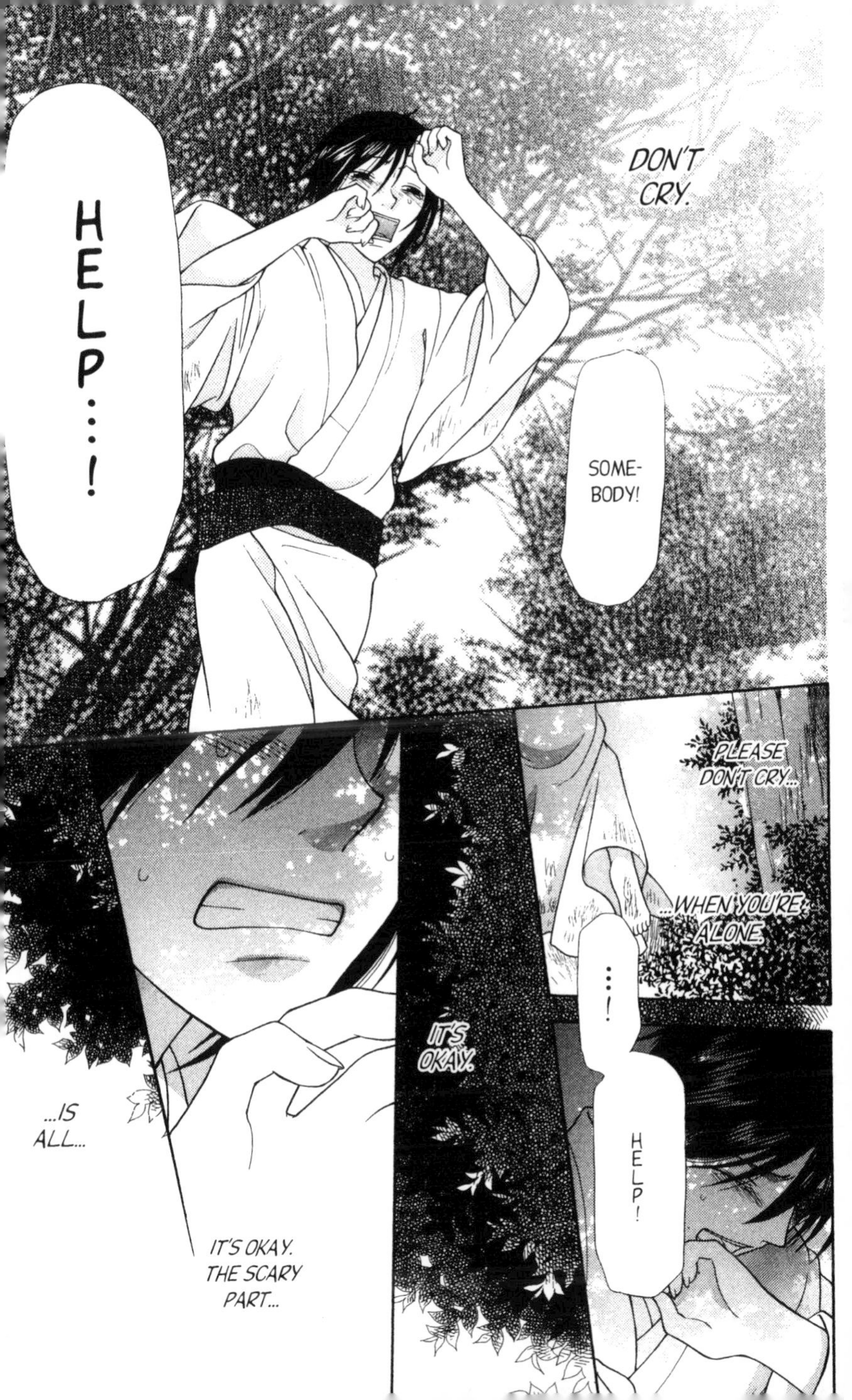
DON'T CRY.
SOME-BODY!
HELP...!
PLEASE DON'T CRY...
...WHEN YOU'RE ALONE.
...!
HELP!
IT'S OKAY.
IT'S OKAY. THE SCARY PART...
...IS ALL...

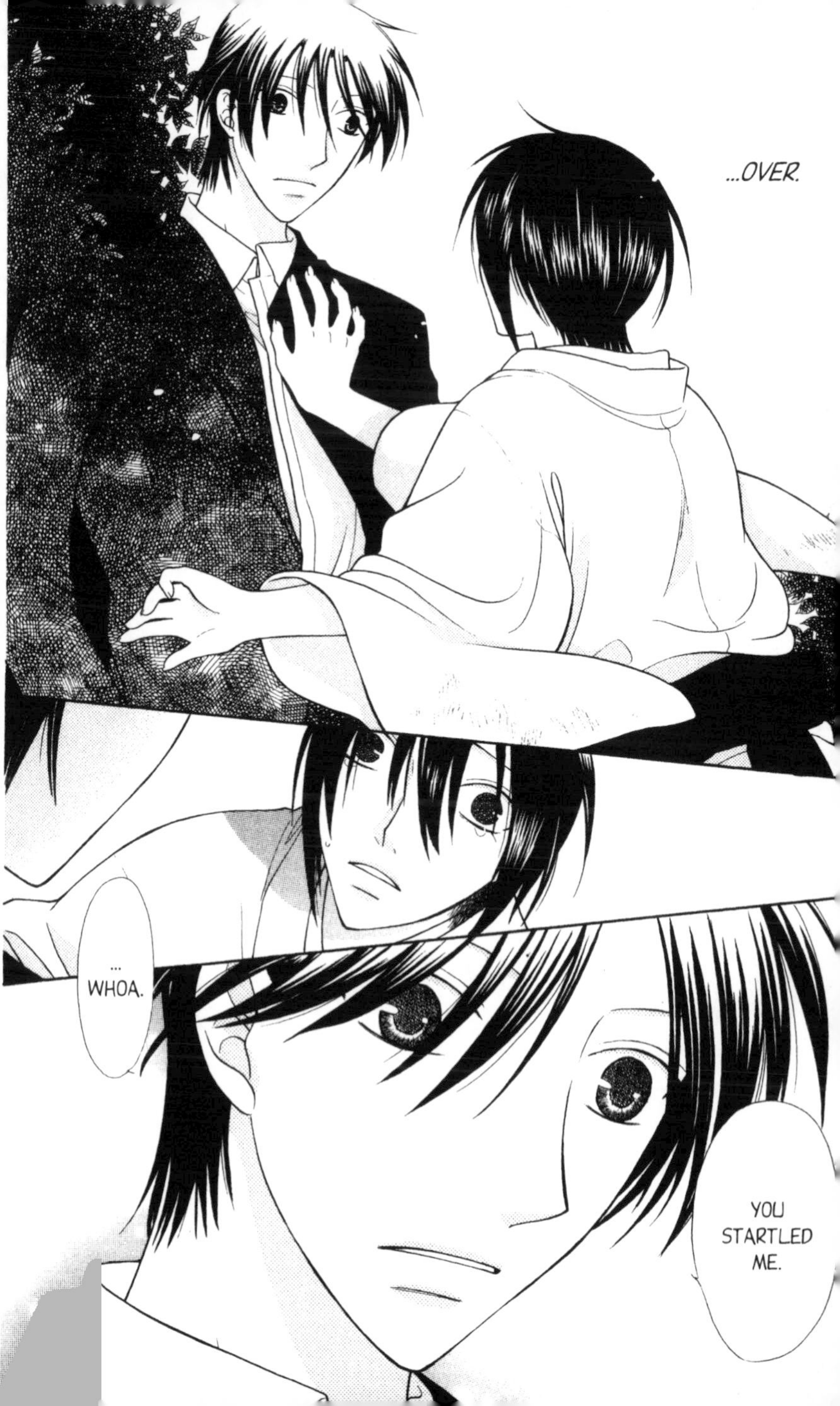
...OVER.
YOU STARTLED ME.
... WHOA.

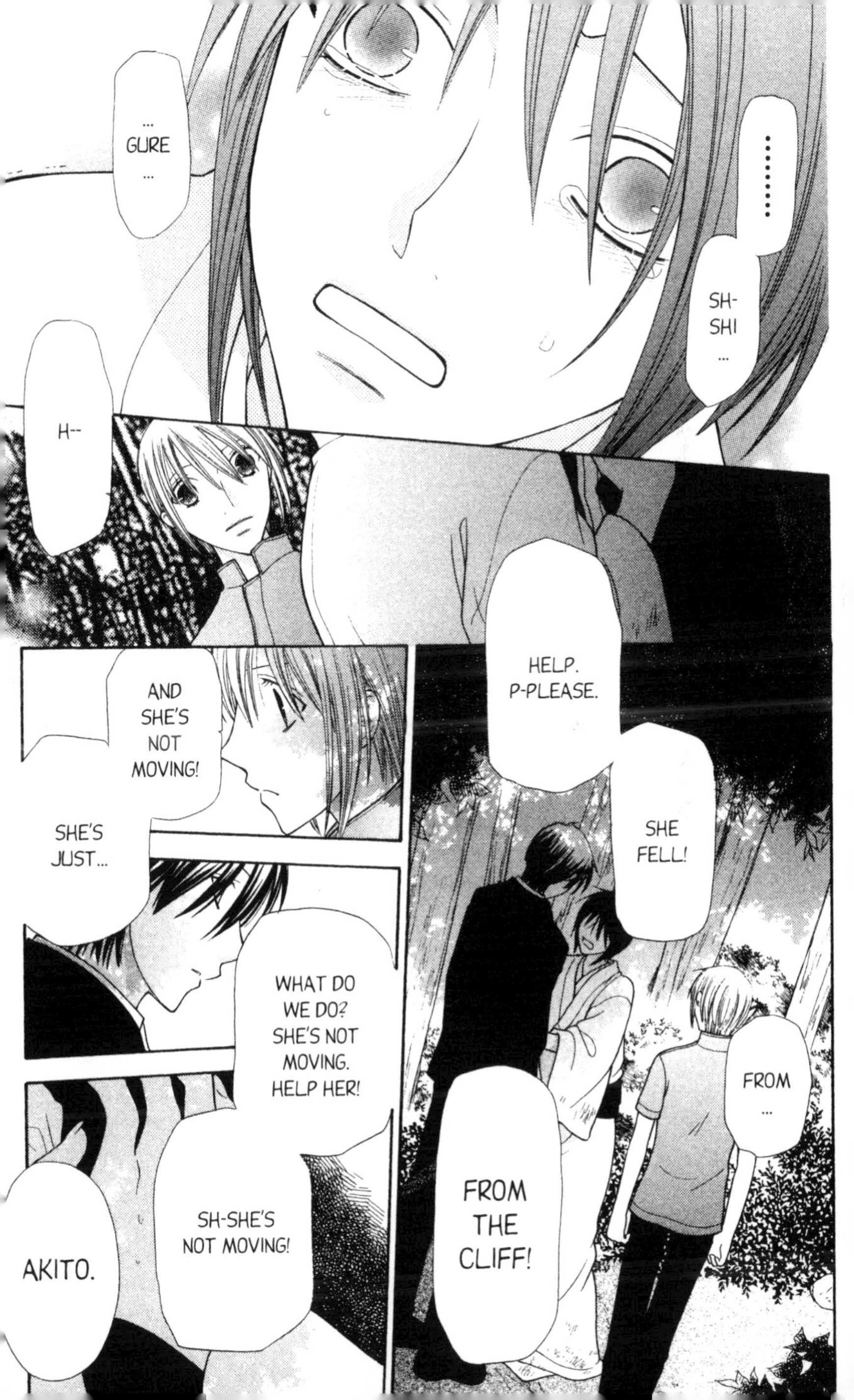
....
SH-SHI ...
... GURE ...
H--
HELP. P-PLEASE.
SHE FELL!
FROM ...
FROM THE CLIFF!
AND SHE'S NOT MOVING!
SHE'S JUST...
WHAT DO WE DO? SHE'S NOT MOVING. HELP HER!
SH-SHE'S NOT MOVING!
AKITO.

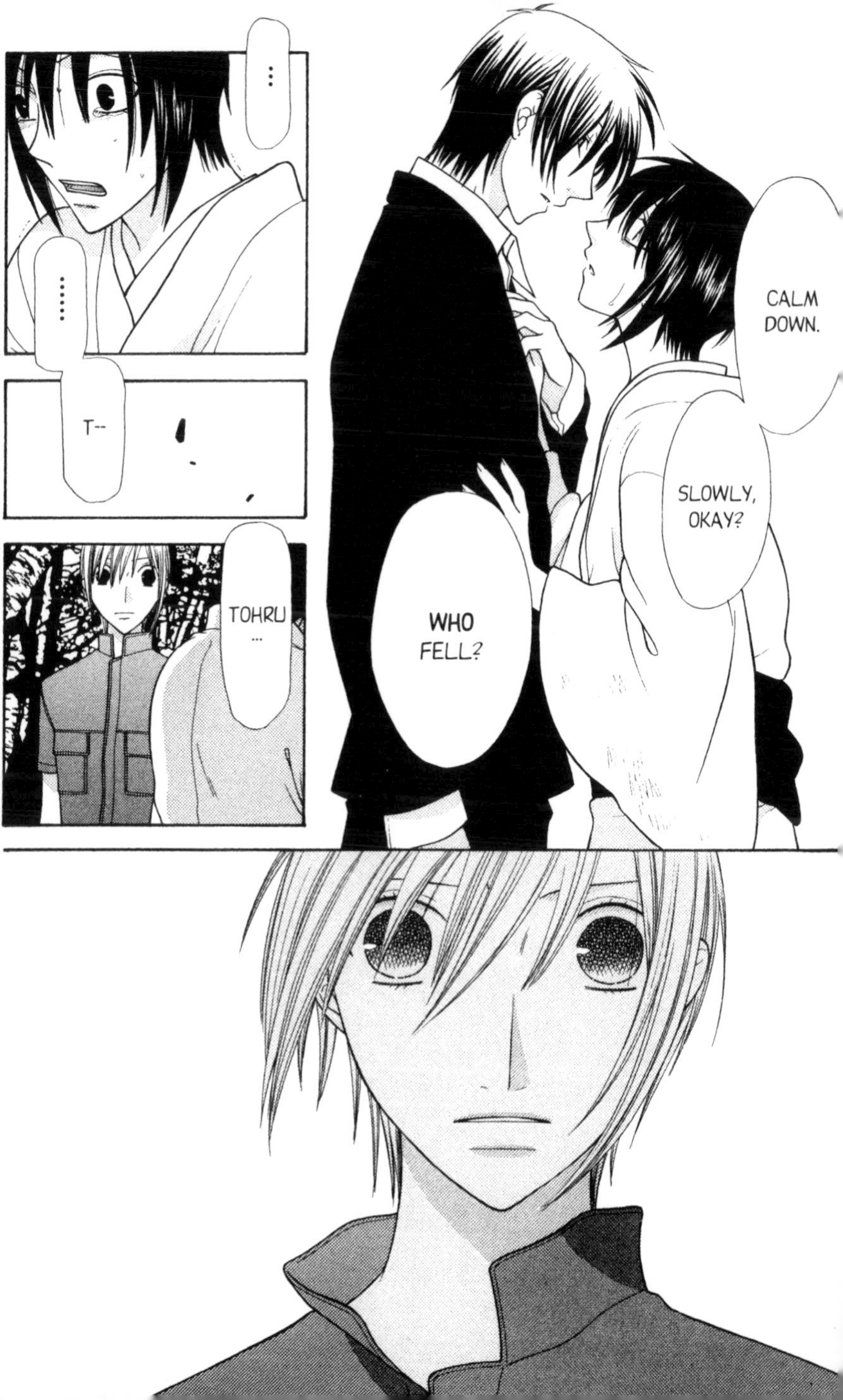
CALM DOWN.
SLOWLY, OKAY?
WHO FELL?
...
......
T--
TOHRU ...

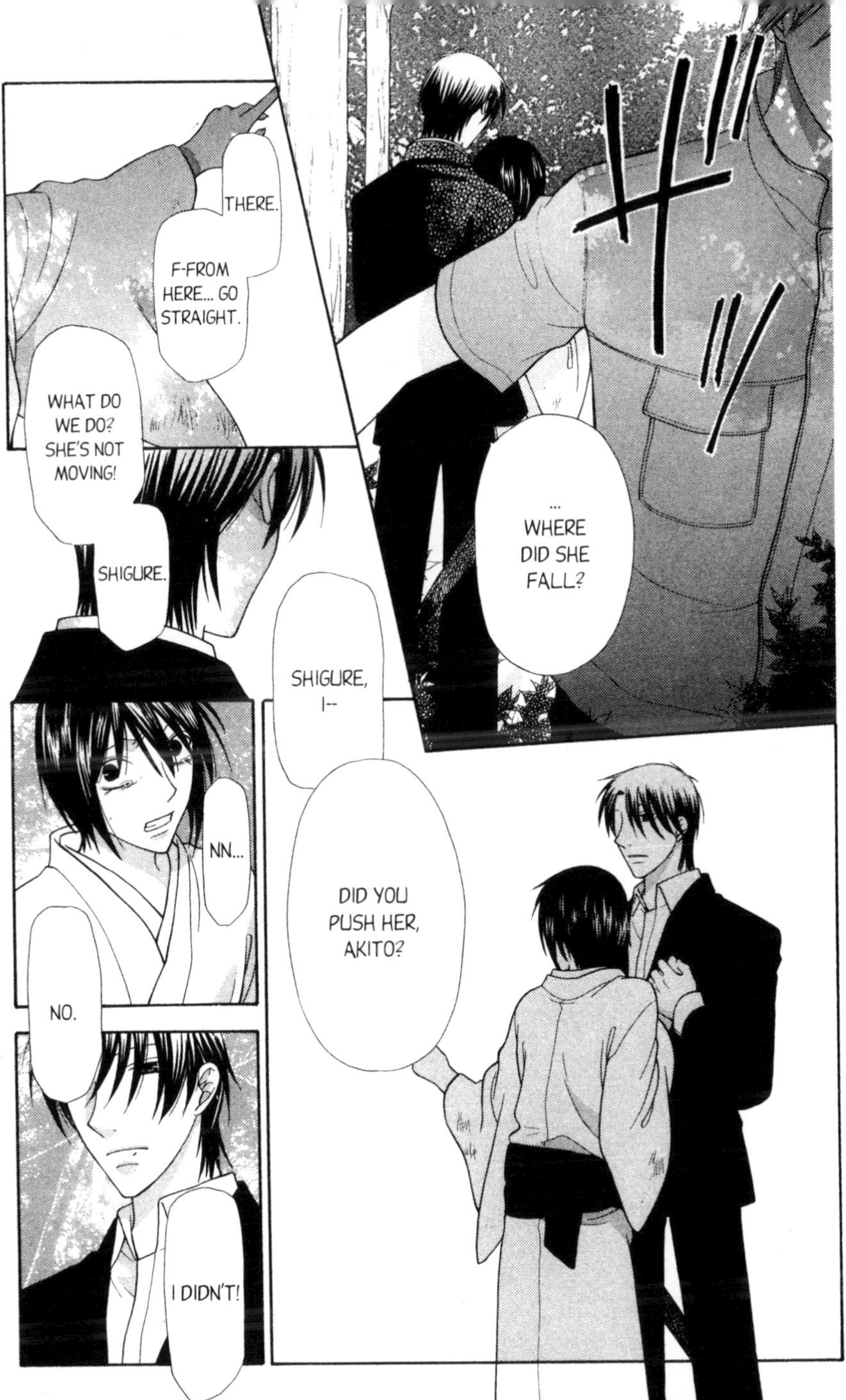

... WHERE DID SHE FALL?
THERE.
F-FROM HERE... GO STRAIGHT.
WHAT DO WE DO? SHE'S NOT MOVING!
SHIGURE.
SHIGURE, I--
DID YOU PUSH HER, AKITO?
NN...
NO.
I DIDN'T!

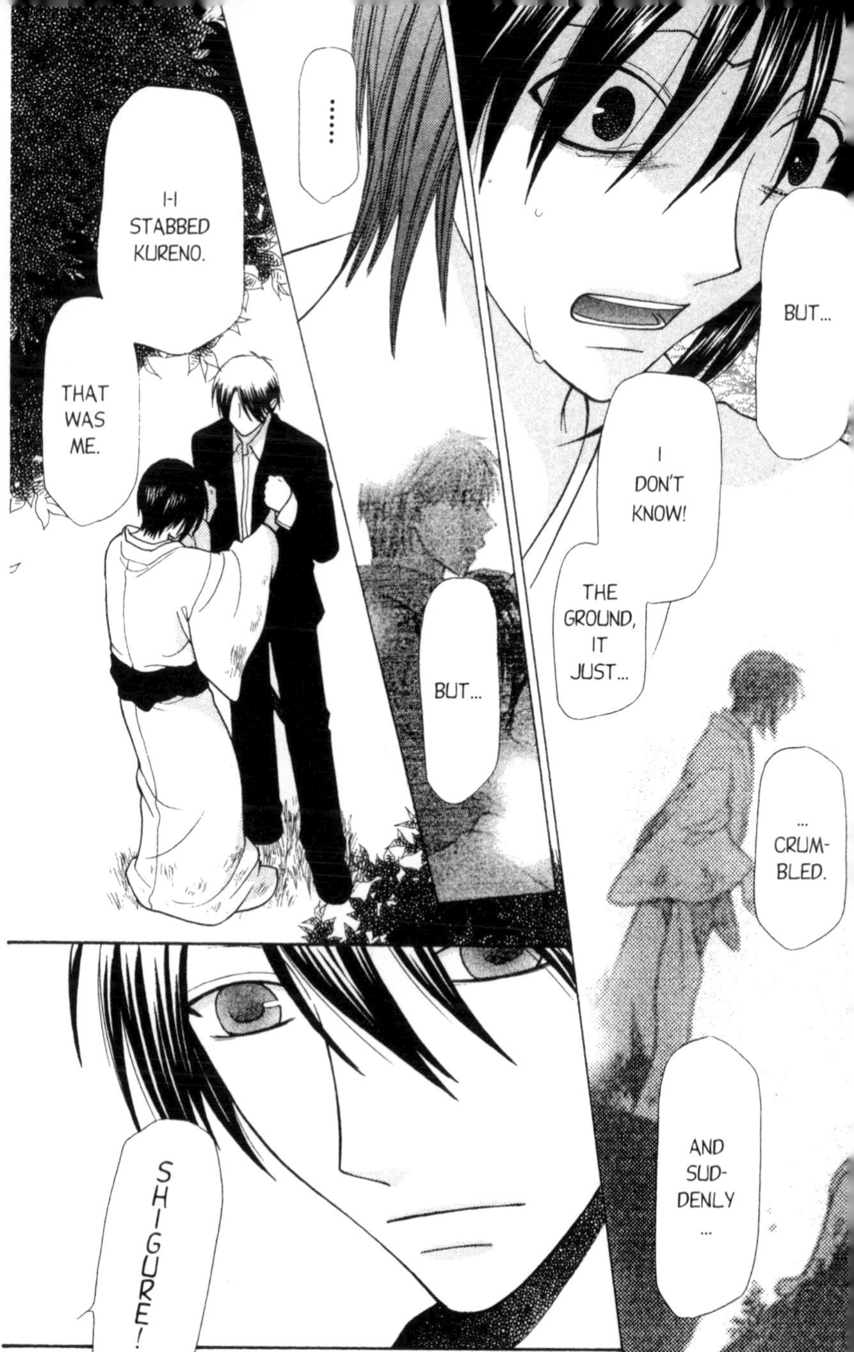
BUT...
I DON'T KNOW!
THE GROUND, IT JUST...
... CRUM-BLED.
AND SUD-DENLY ...
......
BUT...
I-I STABBED KURENO.
THAT WAS ME.
SHIGURE!

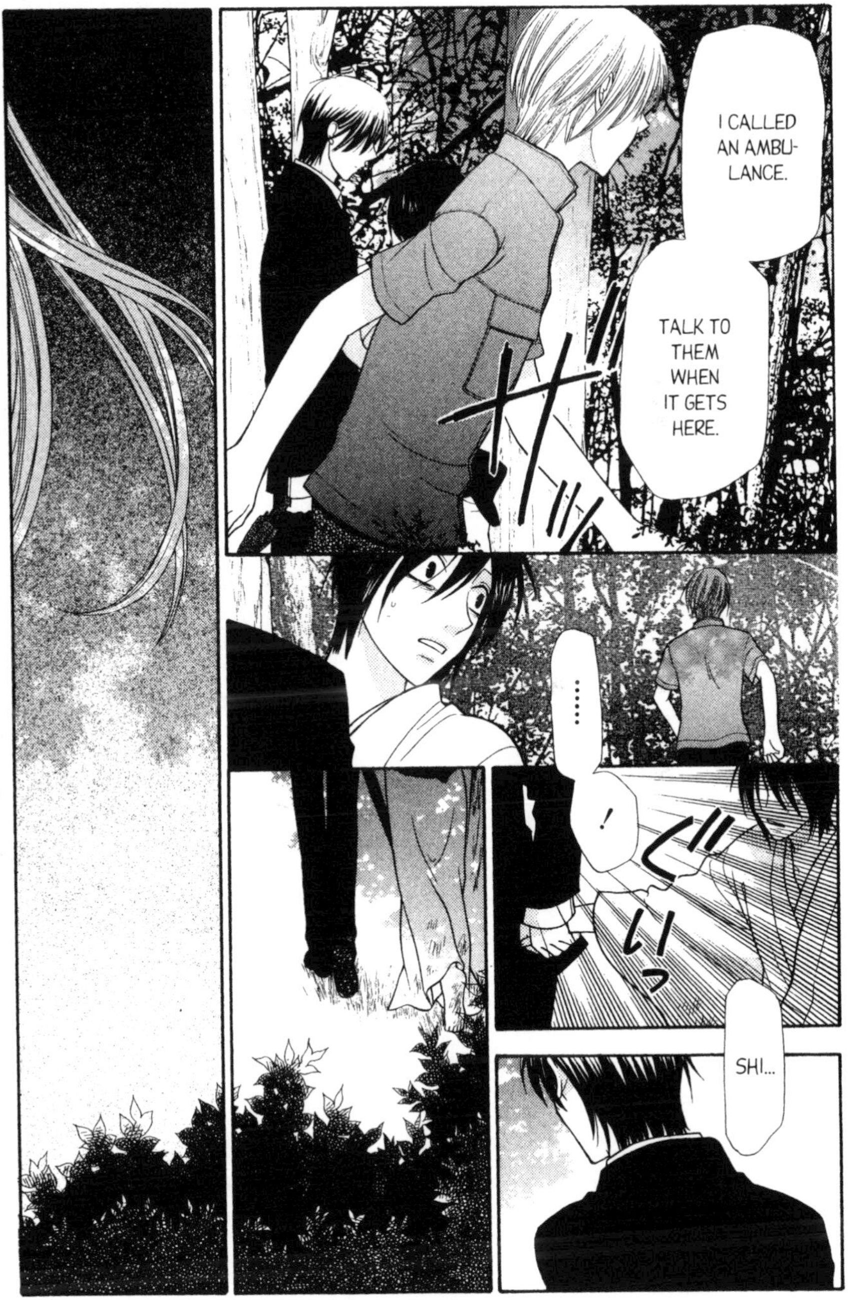
I CALLED AN AMBU-LANCE.
TALK TO THEM WHEN IT GETS HERE.
......
!
ぐいっ
SHI...

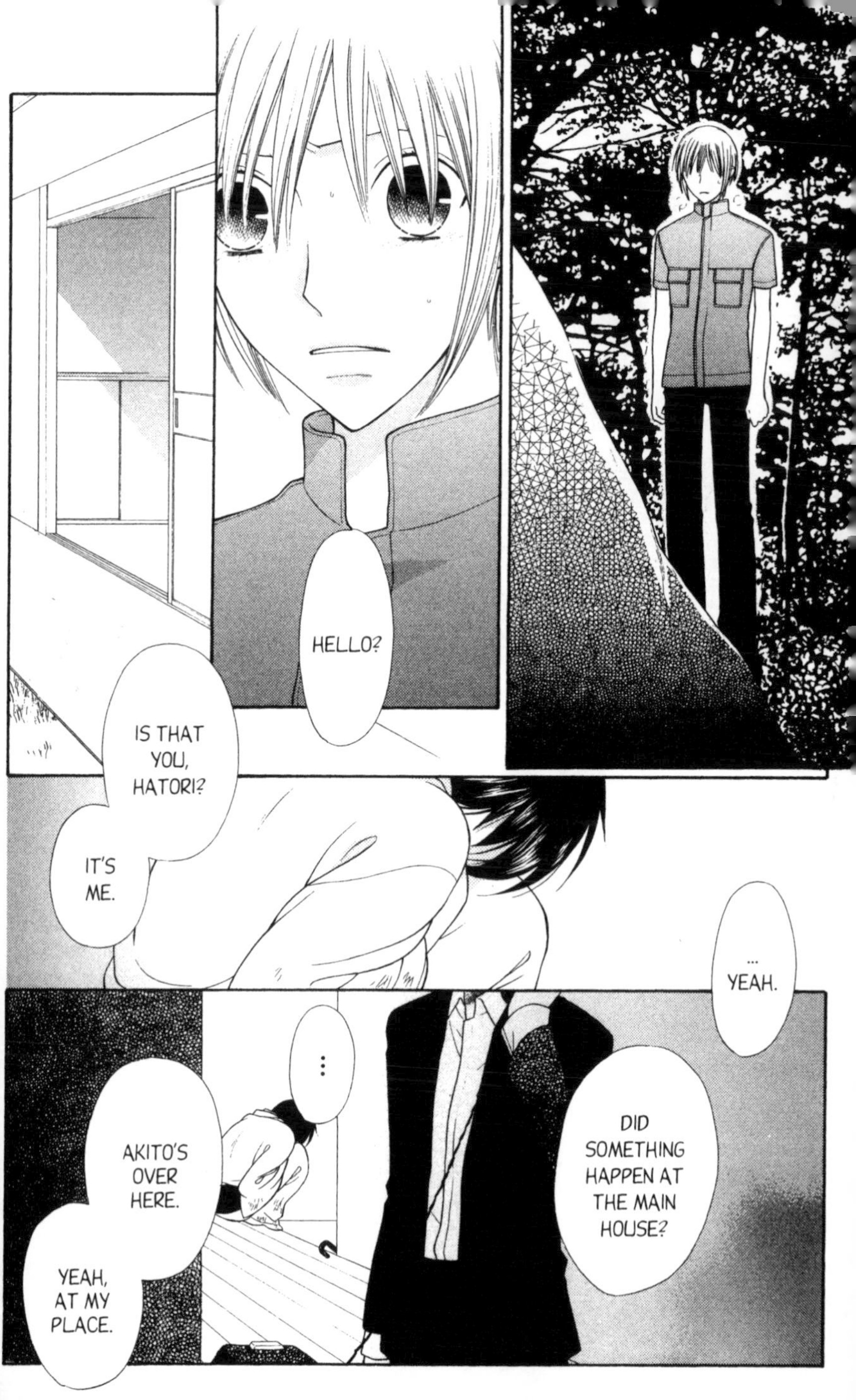
HELLO?
IS THAT YOU, HATORI?
IT'S ME.
...YEAH.
DID SOMETHING HAPPEN AT THE MAIN HOUSE?
...
AKITO'S OVER HERE.
YEAH, AT MY PLACE.

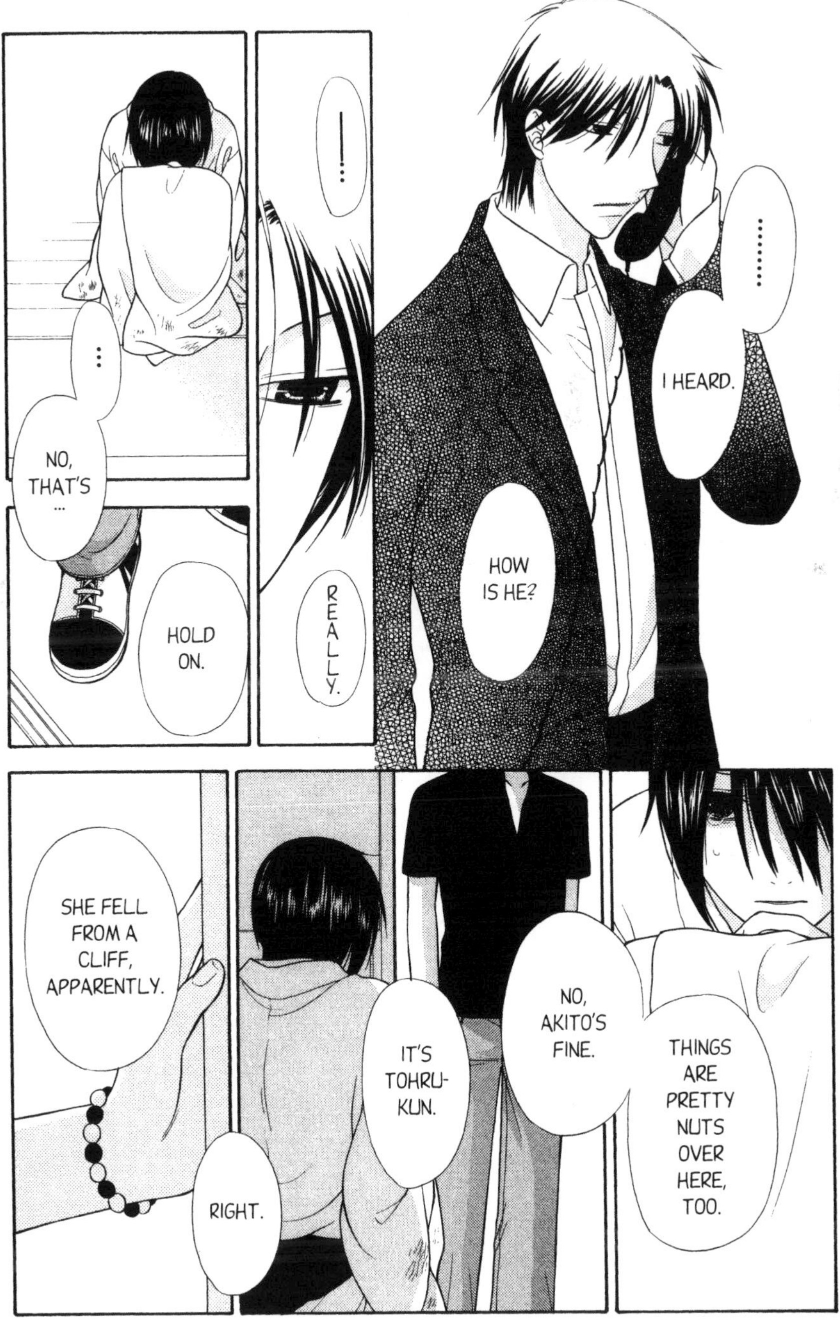
......
I HEARD.
HOW IS HE?
!...
REALLY.
...
NO, THAT'S ...
HOLD ON.
THINGS ARE PRETTY NUTS OVER HERE, TOO.
NO, AKITO'S FINE.
IT'S TOHRU-KUN.
RIGHT.
SHE FELL FROM A CLIFF, APPARENTLY.

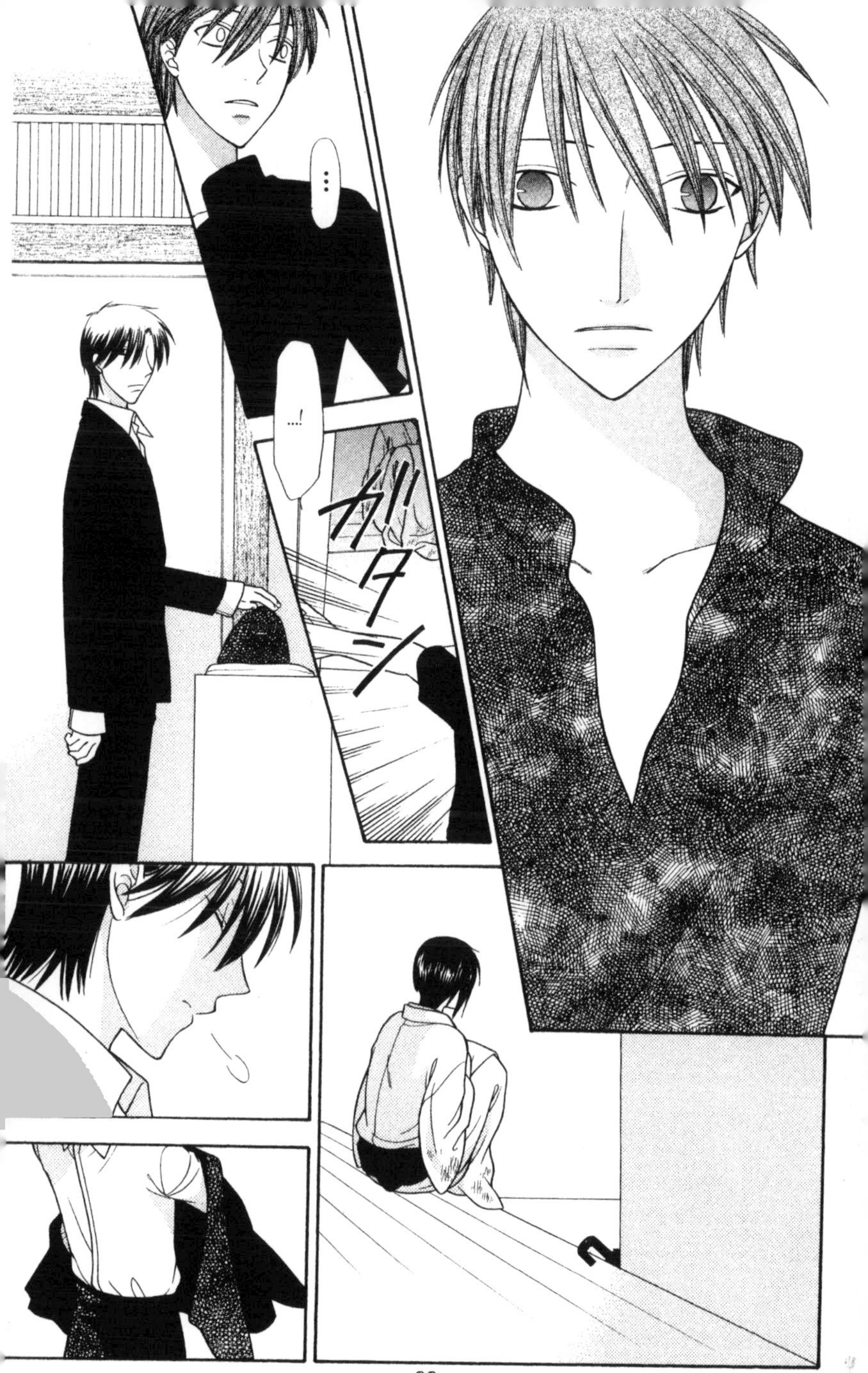
...
...!
ガターン

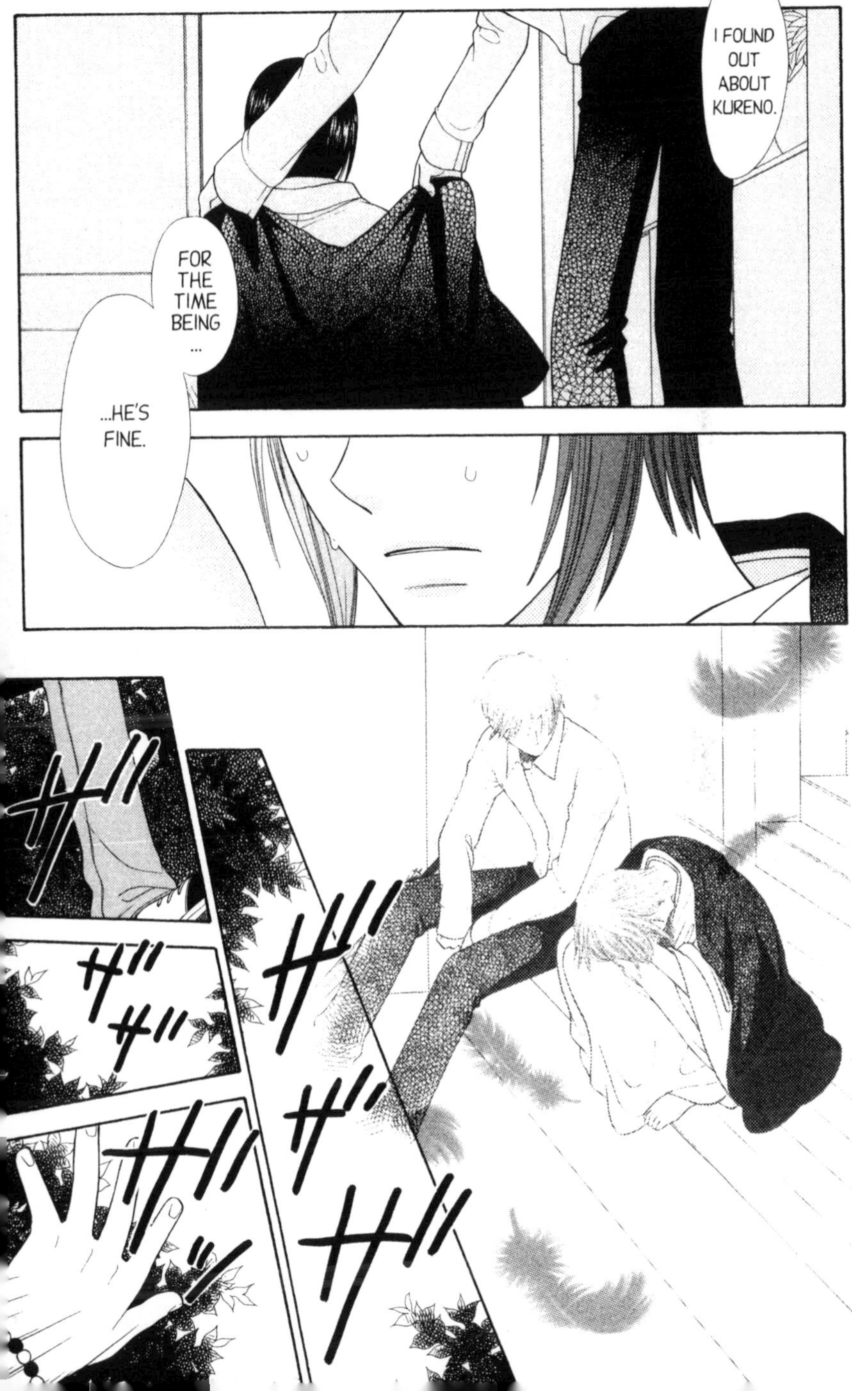
I FOUND OUT ABOUT KURENO.
FOR THE TIME BEING ...
...HE'S FINE.
ザッ
ザ
ザ
ザ
ザ
ザ
ザ
ザ

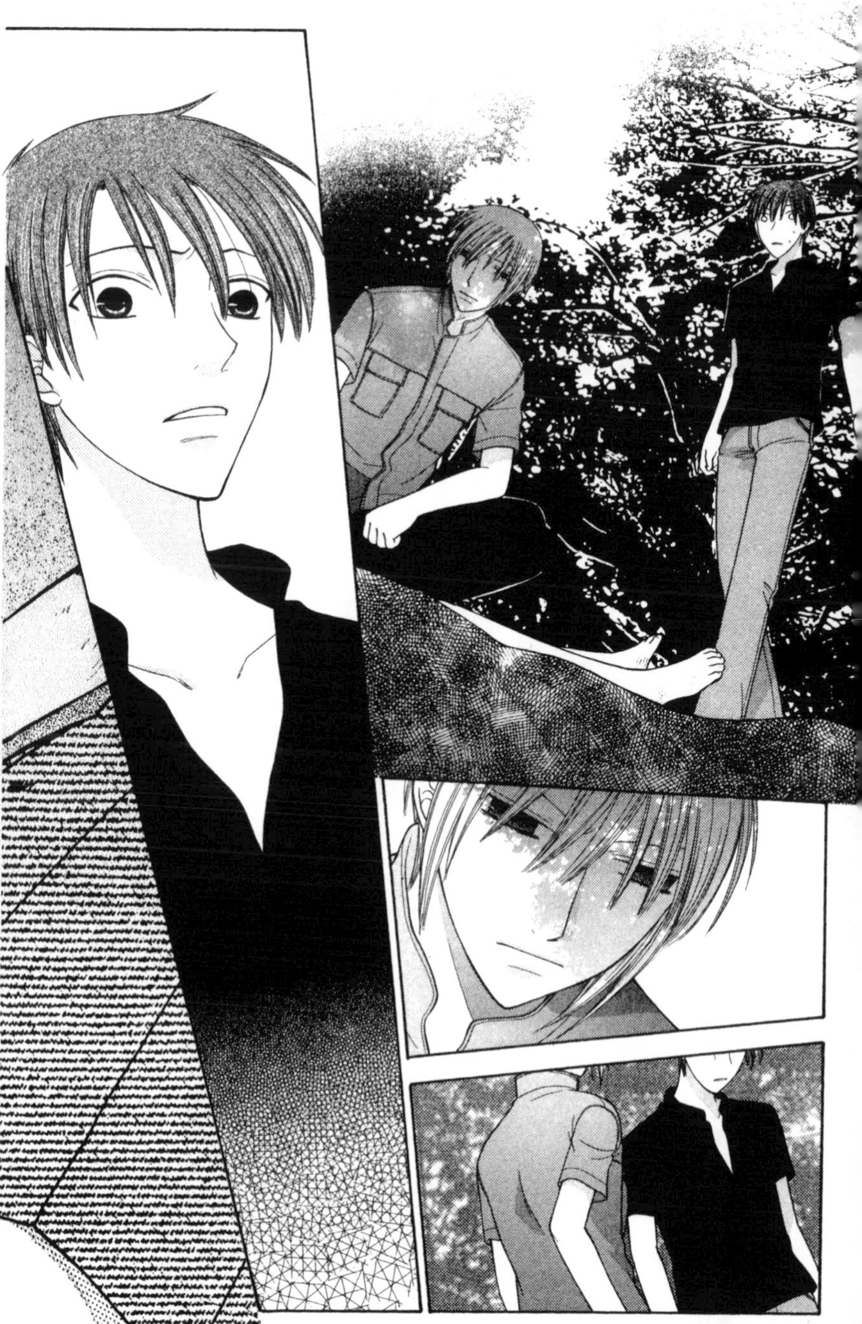

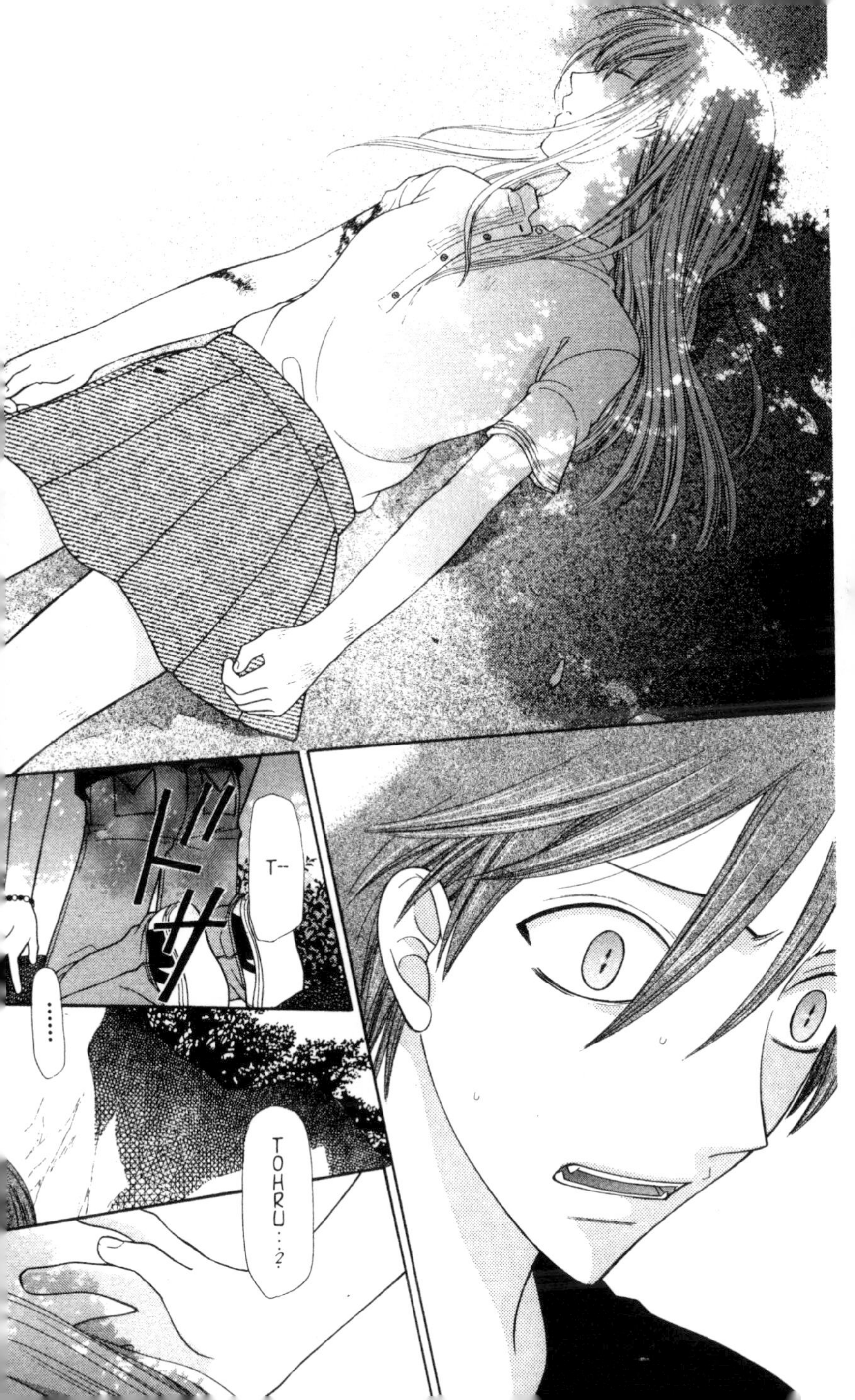
ドサ
T--
......
TOHRU...?

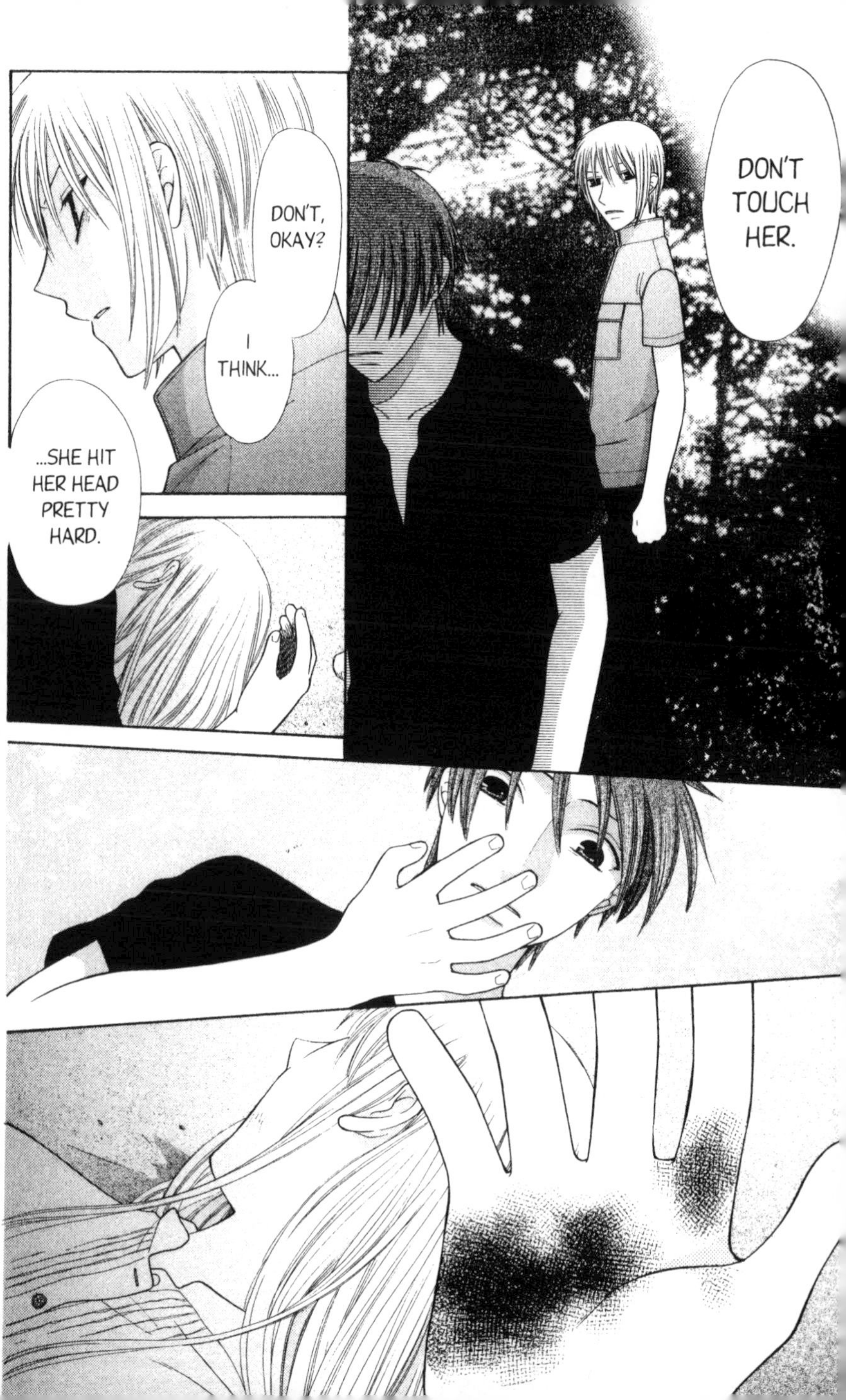
DON'T TOUCH HER.
DON'T, OKAY?
I THINK...
...SHE HIT HER HEAD PRETTY HARD.

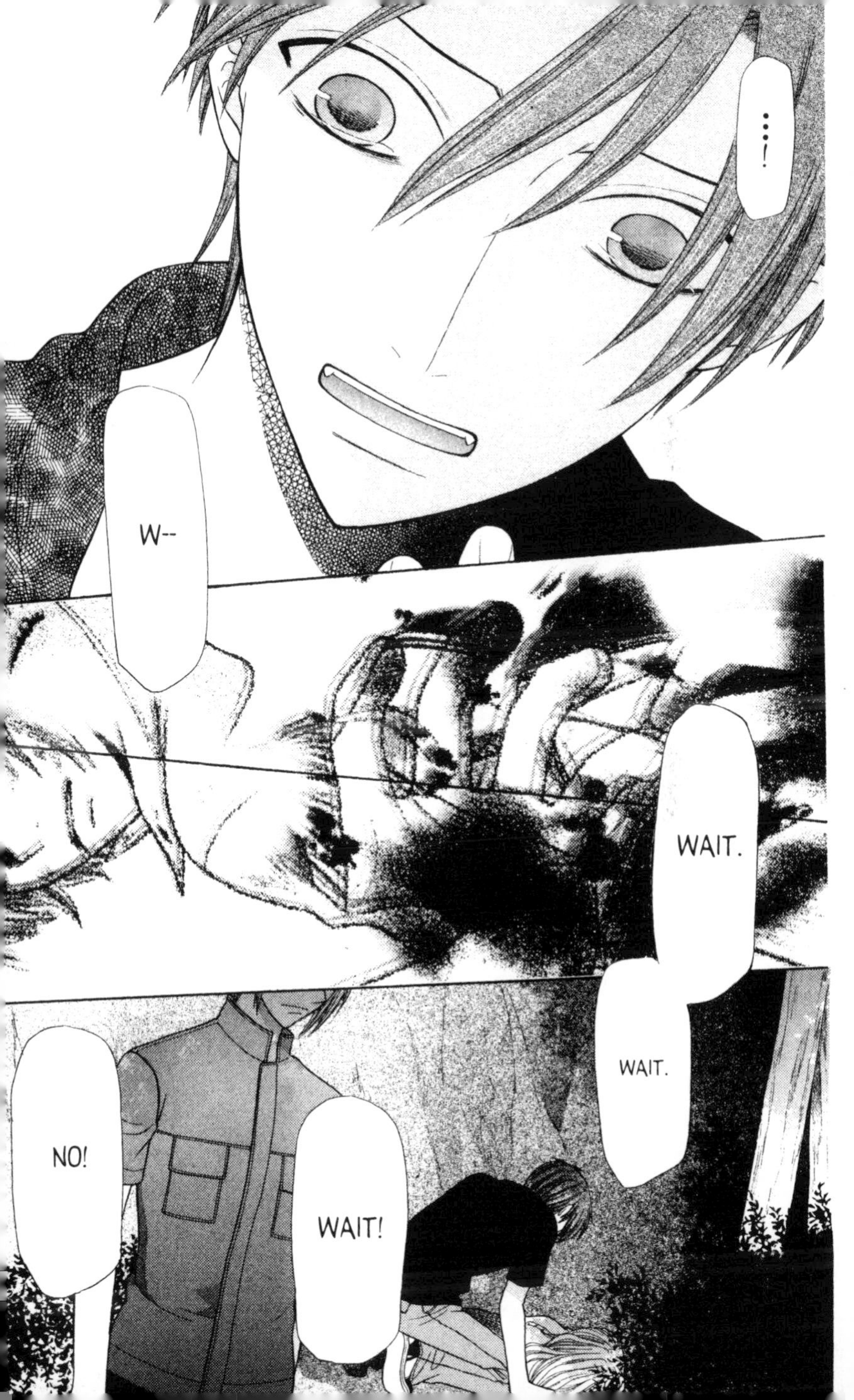

...!
W--
WAIT.
WAIT.
WAIT!
NO!

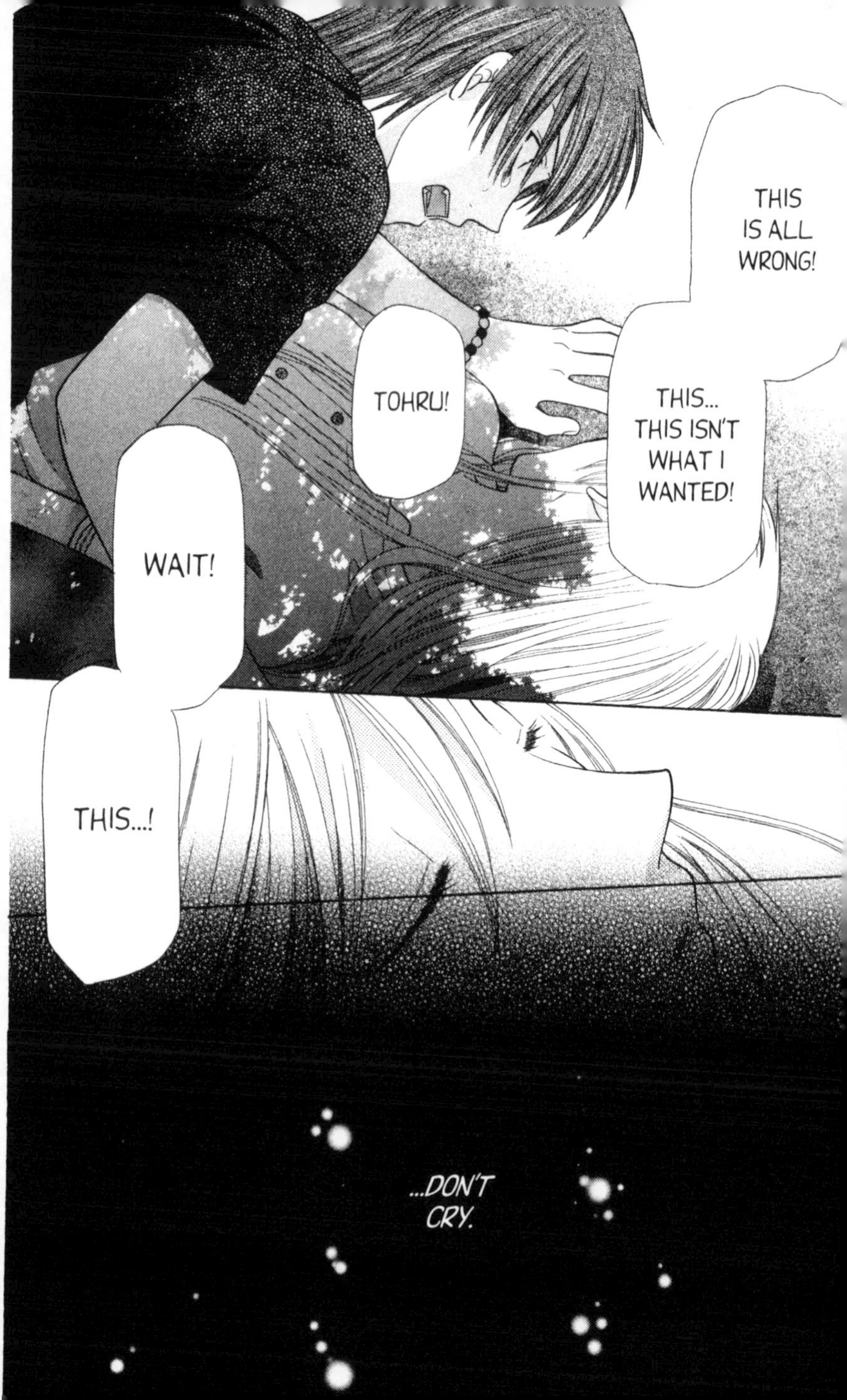
THIS IS ALL WRONG!
THIS... THIS ISN'T WHAT I WANTED!
TOHRU!
WAIT!
THIS...!
...DON'T CRY.

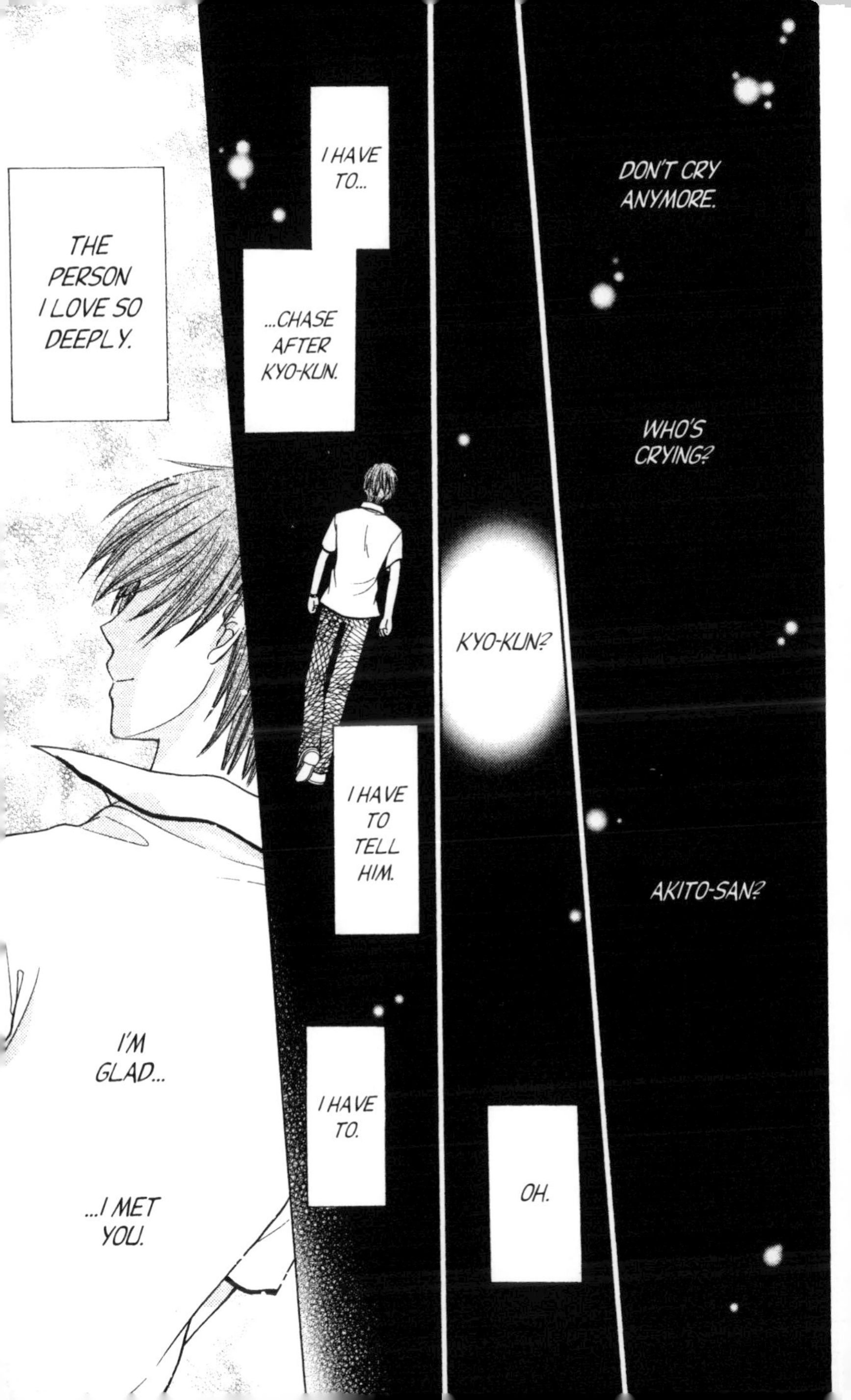
DON'T CRY ANYMORE.
WHO'S CRYING?
AKITO-SAN?
KYO-KUN?
OH.
I HAVE TO...
...CHASE AFTER KYO-KUN.
I HAVE TO TELL HIM.
I HAVE TO.
THE PERSON I LOVE SO DEEPLY.
I'M GLAD...
...I MET YOU.

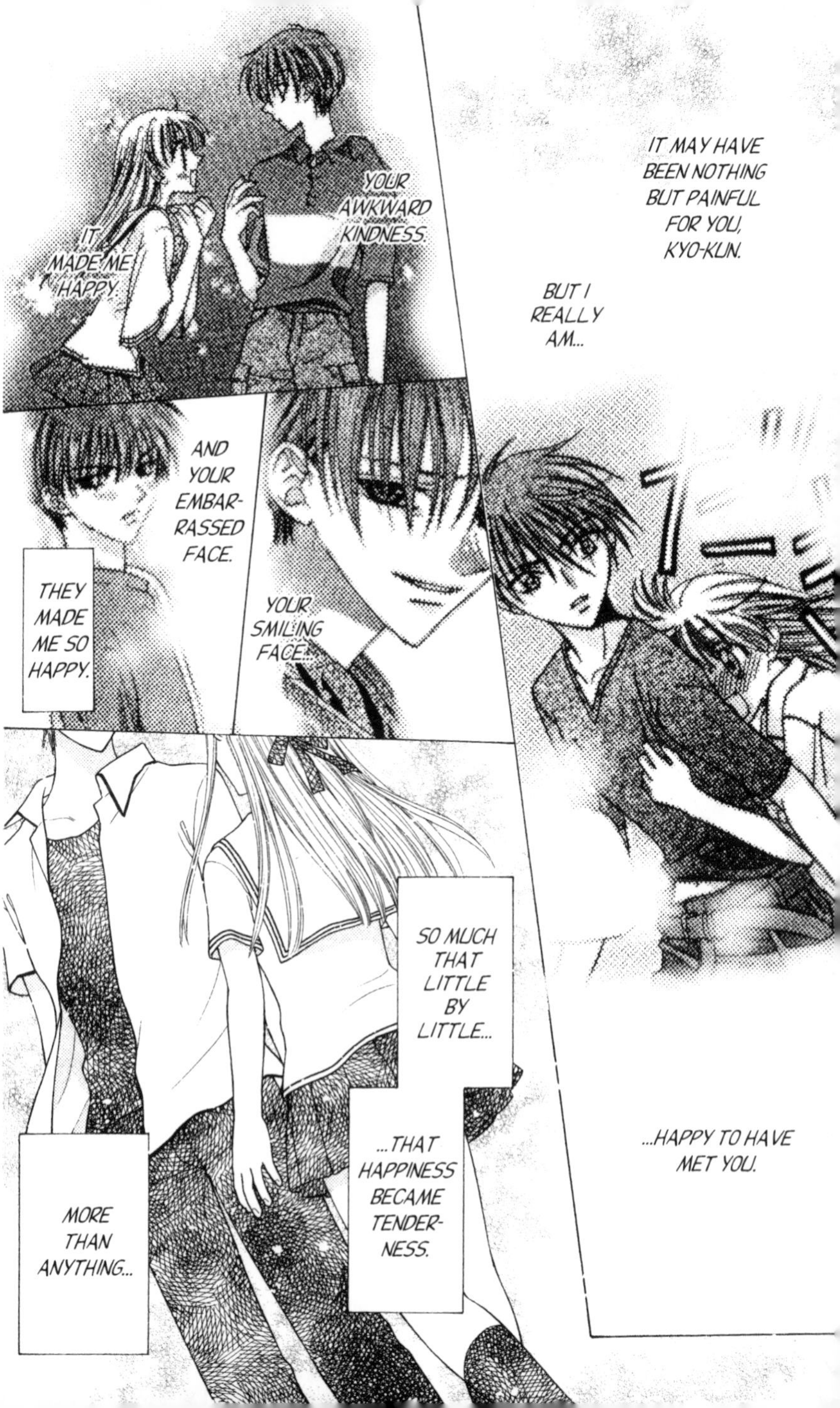
IT MAY HAVE BEEN NOTHING BUT PAINFUL FOR YOU, KYO-KUN.
BUT I REALLY AM...
...HAPPY TO HAVE MET YOU.
YOUR AWKWARD KINDNESS.
IT MADE ME HAPPY.
YOUR SMILING FACE...
AND YOUR EMBARRASSED FACE.
THEY MADE ME SO HAPPY.
SO MUCH THAT LITTLE BY LITTLE...
...THAT HAPPINESS BECAME TENDERNESS.
MORE THAN ANYTHING...

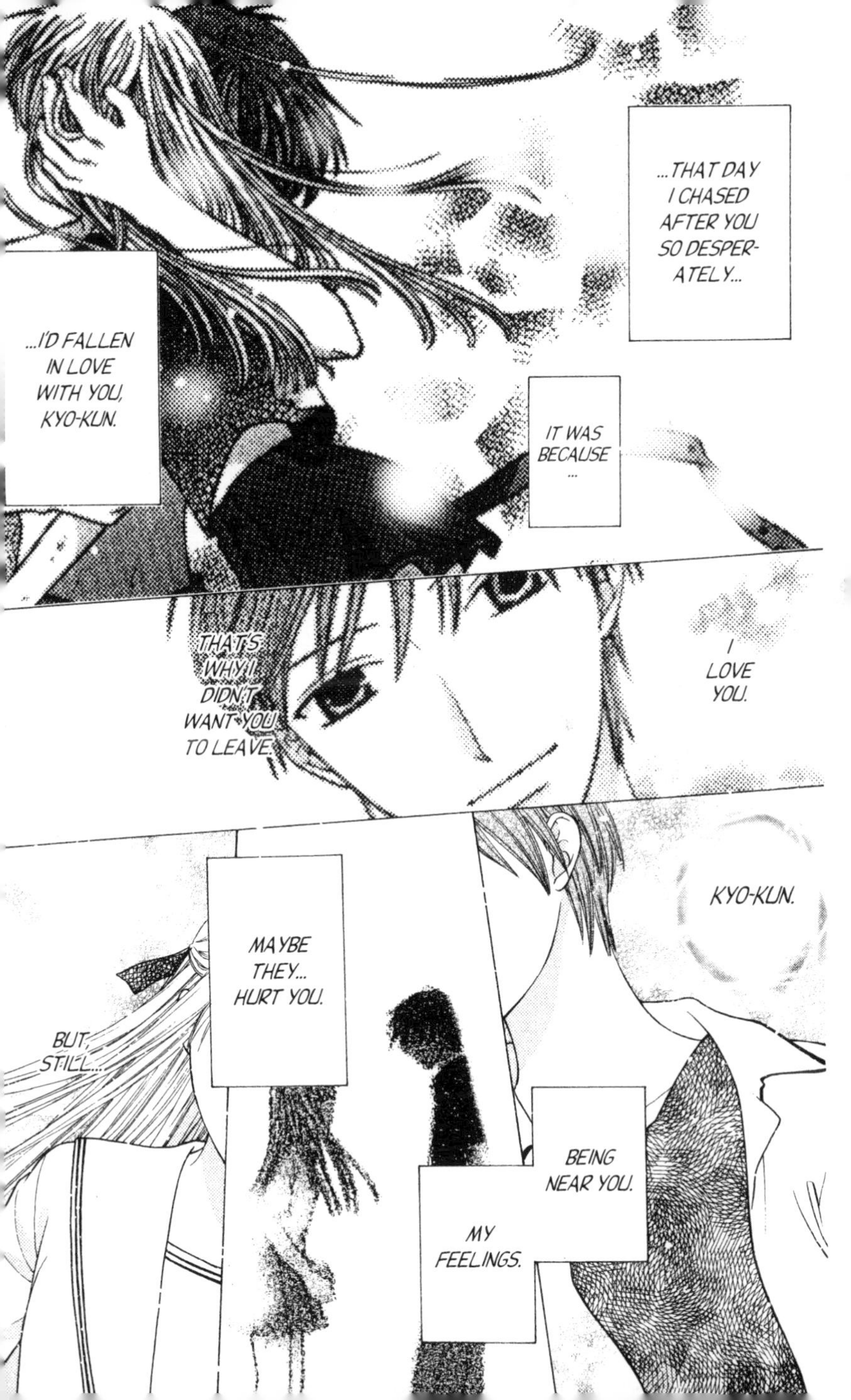

...THAT DAY I CHASED AFTER YOU SO DESPER-ATELY...
IT WAS BECAUSE ...
...I'D FALLEN IN LOVE WITH YOU, KYO-KUN.
I LOVE YOU.
THAT'S WHY I DIDN'T WANT YOU TO LEAVE.
KYO-KUN.
BEING NEAR YOU.
MY FEELINGS.
MAYBE THEY... HURT YOU.
BUT, STILL...

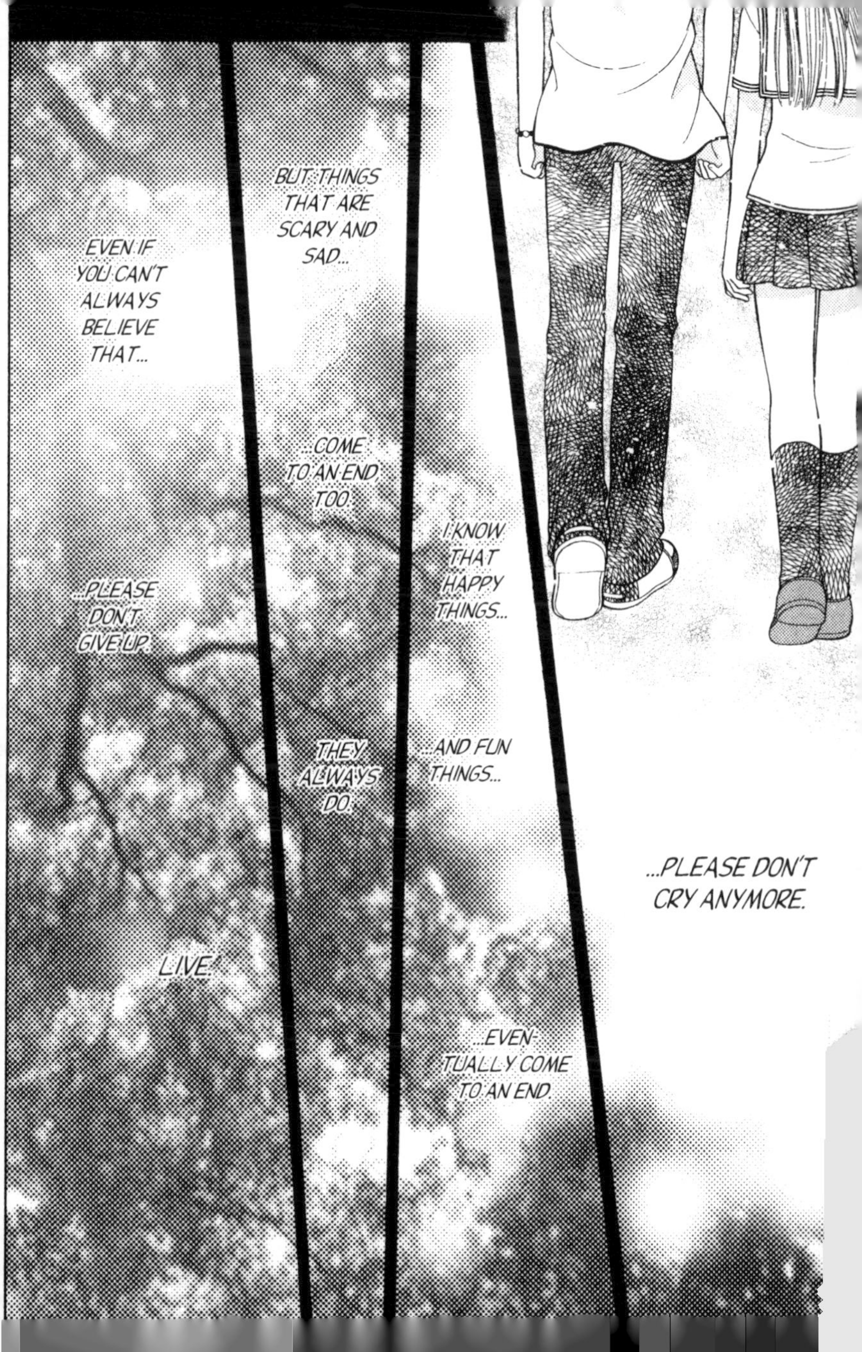
...PLEASE DON'T CRY ANYMORE.
I KNOW THAT HAPPY THINGS...
...AND FUN THINGS...
...EVEN-TUALLY COME TO AN END.
BUT THINGS THAT ARE SCARY AND SAD...
...COME TO AN END TOO.
THEY ALWAYS DO.
EVEN IF YOU CAN'T ALWAYS BELIEVE THAT...
...PLEASE DON'T GIVE UP.
LIVE.

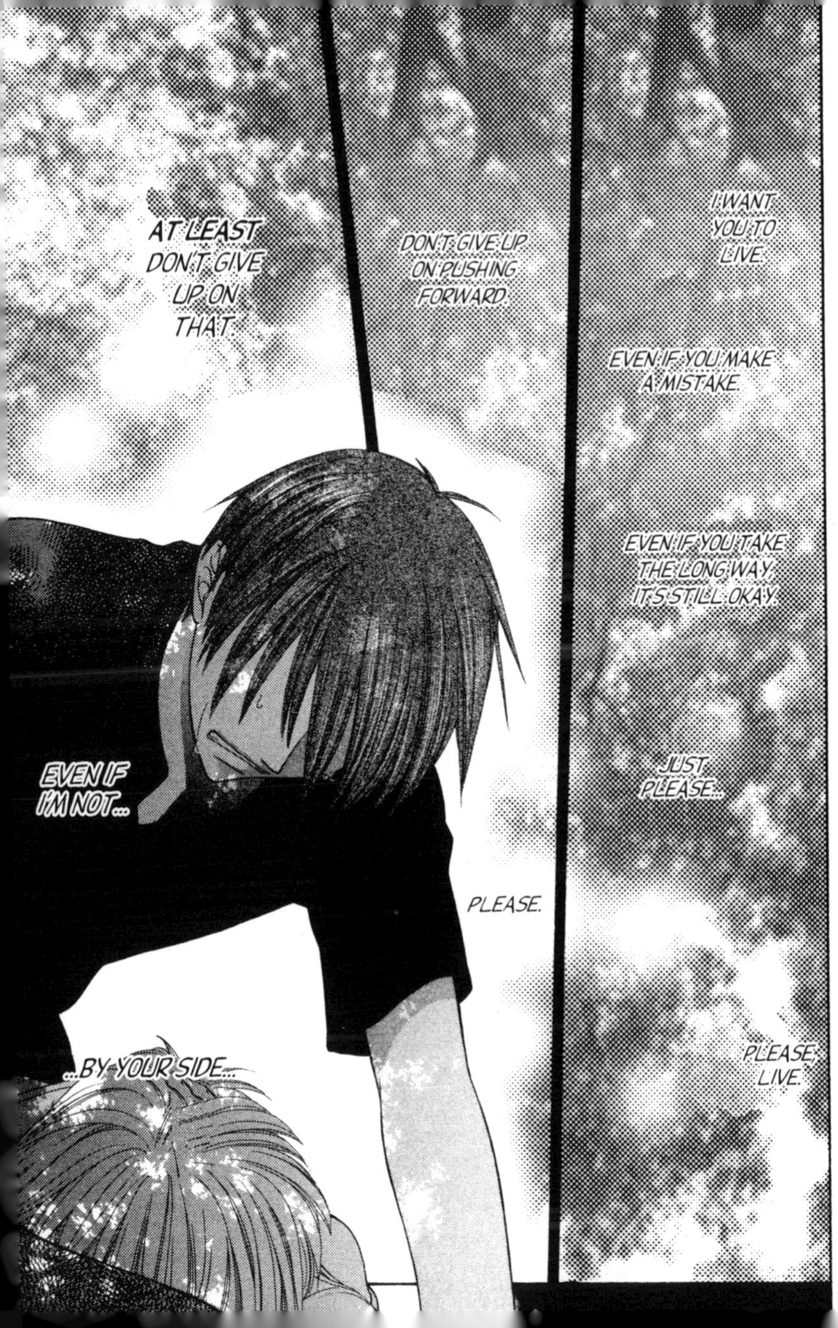
I WANT YOU TO LIVE.
EVEN IF YOU MAKE A MISTAKE.
EVEN IF YOU TAKE THE LONG WAY, IT'S STILL OKAY.
JUST PLEASE...
PLEASE, LIVE.
DON'T GIVE UP ON PUSHING FORWARD.
PLEASE.
AT LEAST DON'T GIVE UP ON THAT.
EVEN IF I'M NOT...
...BY YOUR SIDE...

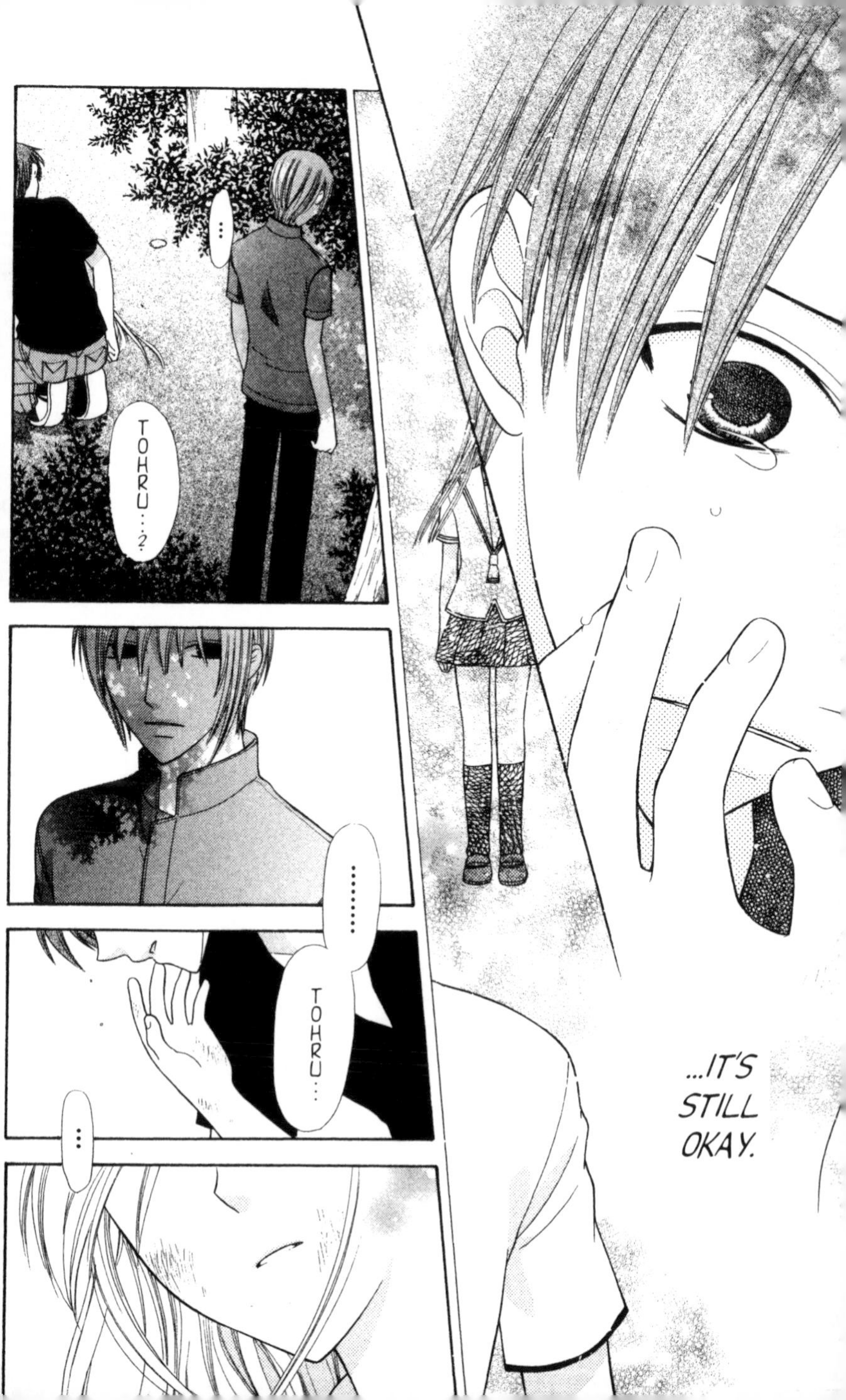
...IT'S STILL OKAY.
...
TOHRU...?
....
TOHRU...
...

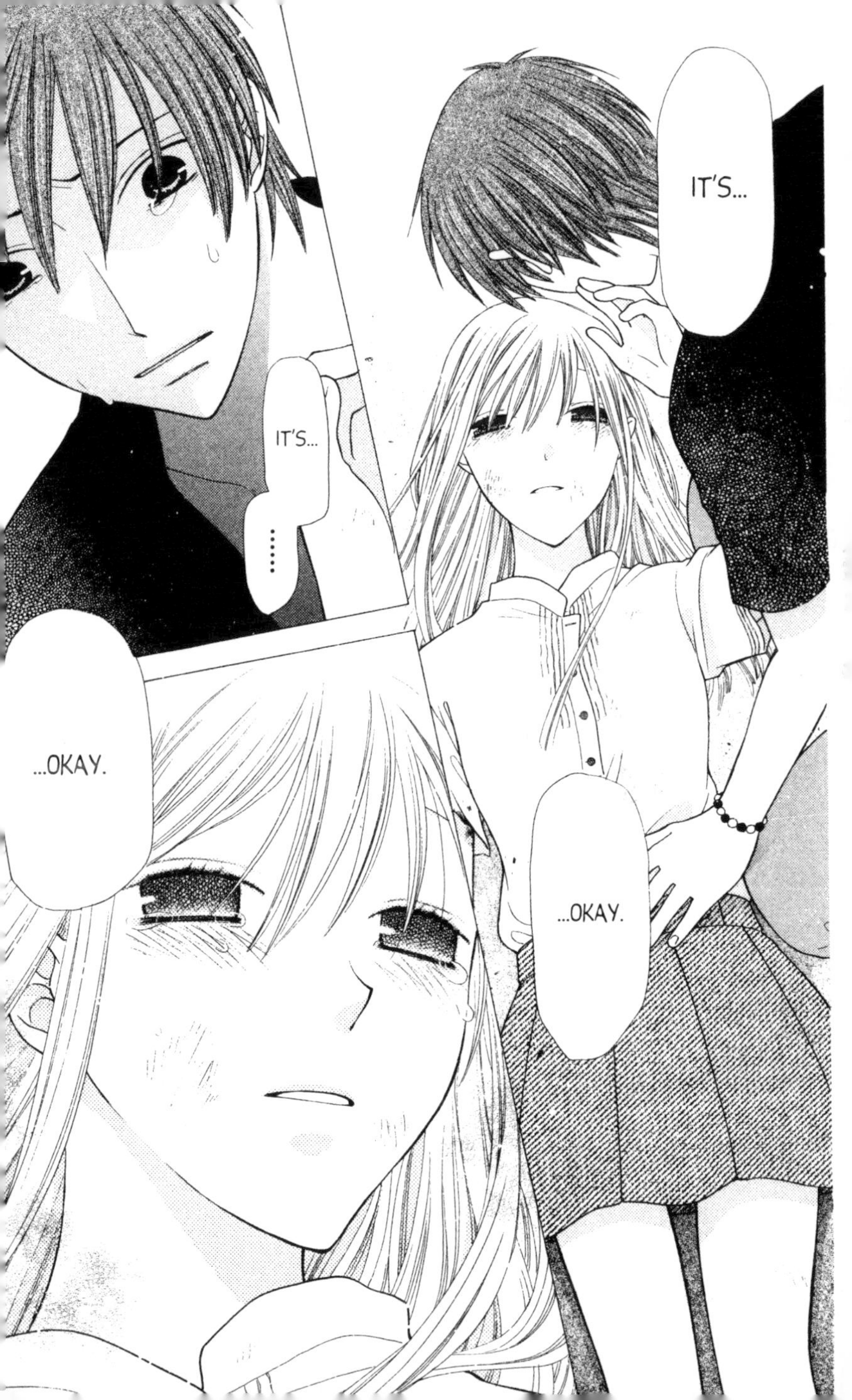
IT'S...
...OKAY.
IT'S...
......
...OKAY.

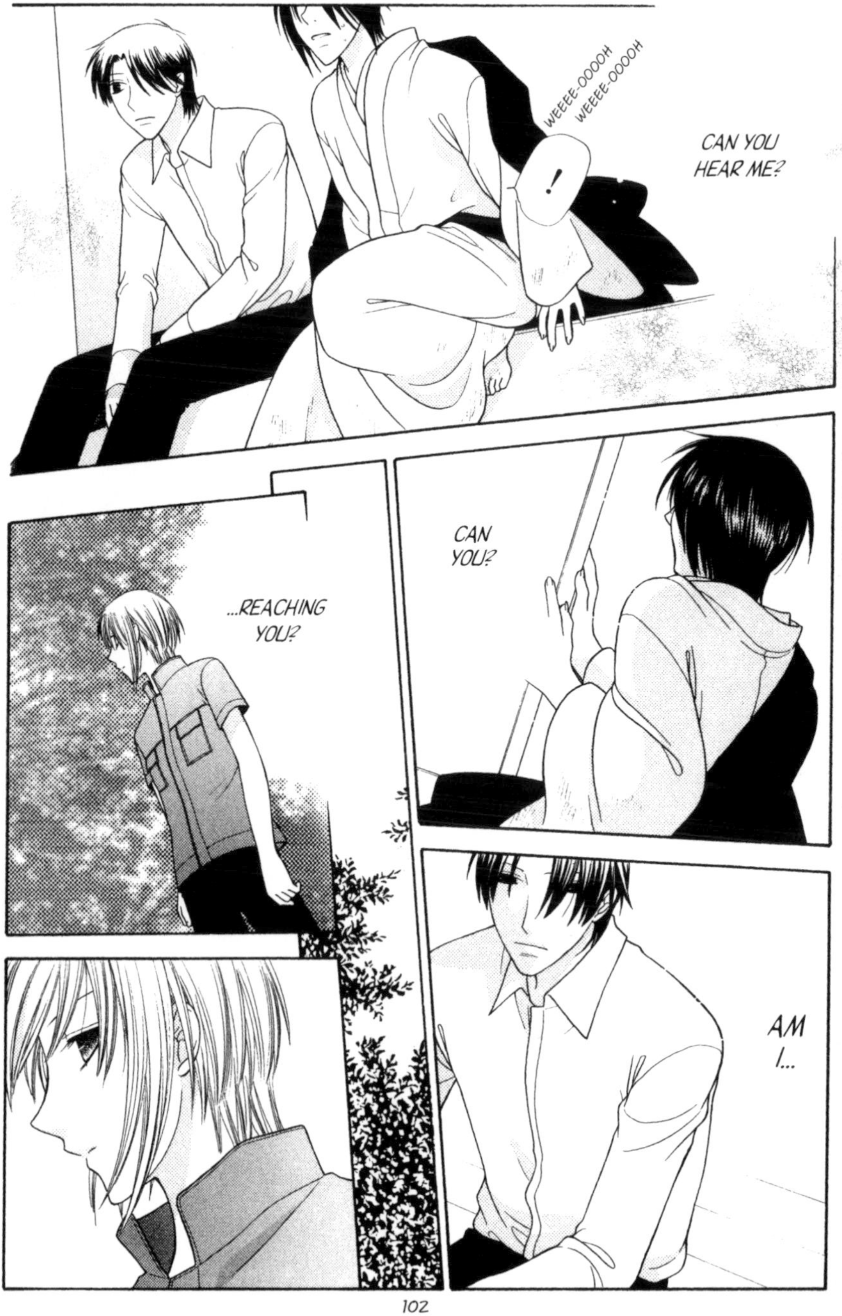
CAN YOU HEAR ME?
WEEEE-OOOOH WEEEE-OOOOH
!
CAN YOU?
AM I...
...REACHING YOU?

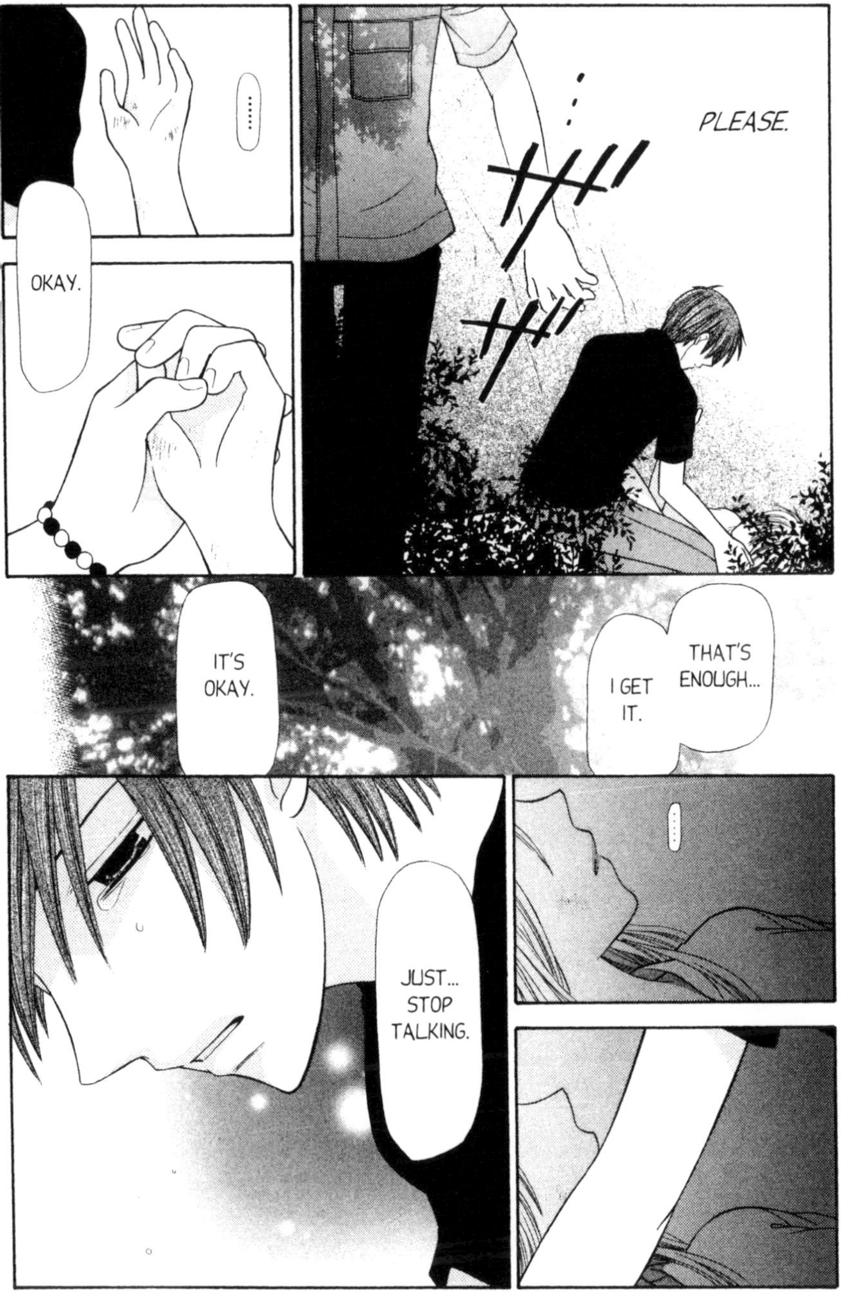

...
PLEASE.
......
OKAY.
THAT'S ENOUGH...
I GET IT.
IT'S OKAY.
......
JUST... STOP TALKING.

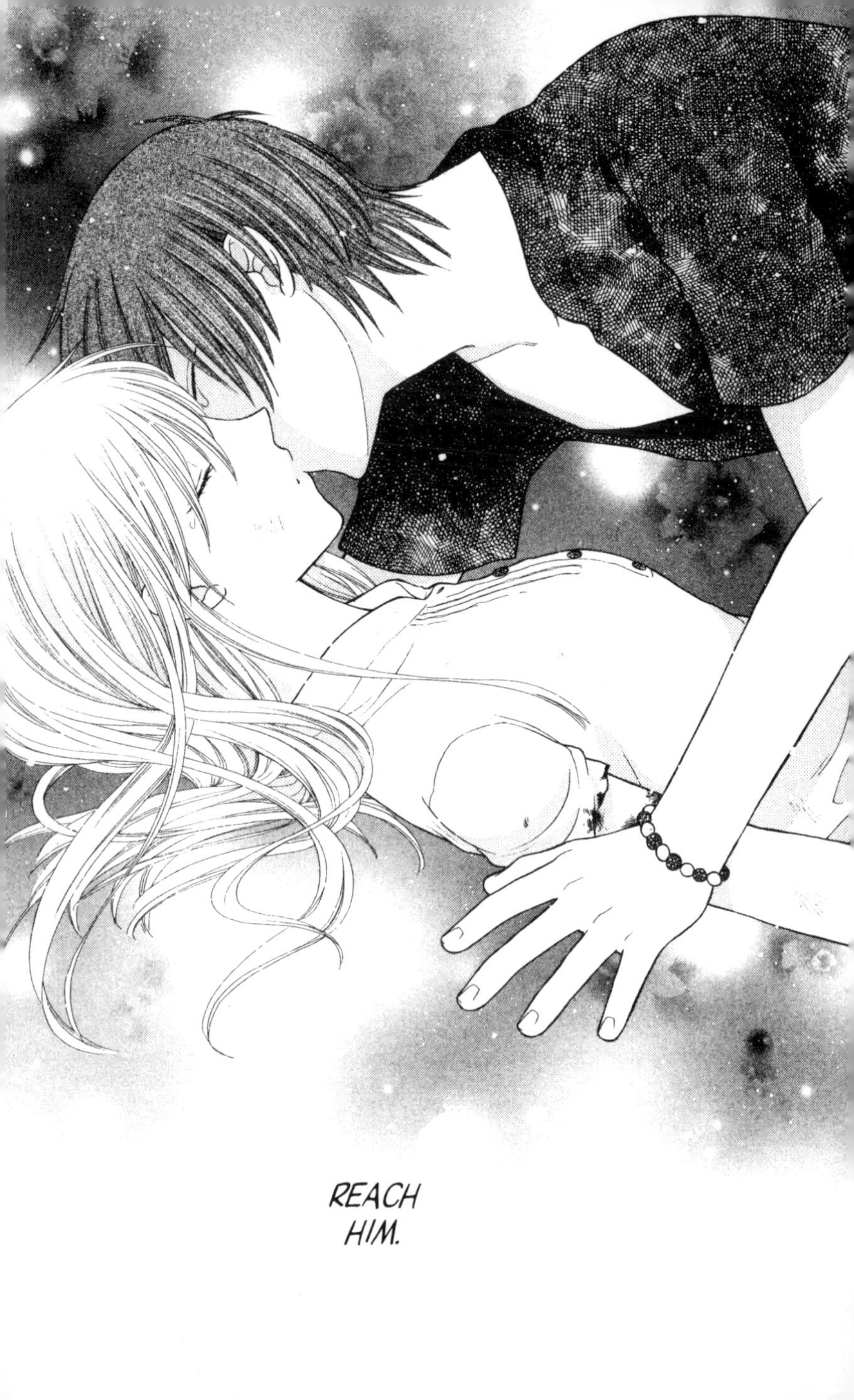
REACH
HIM.

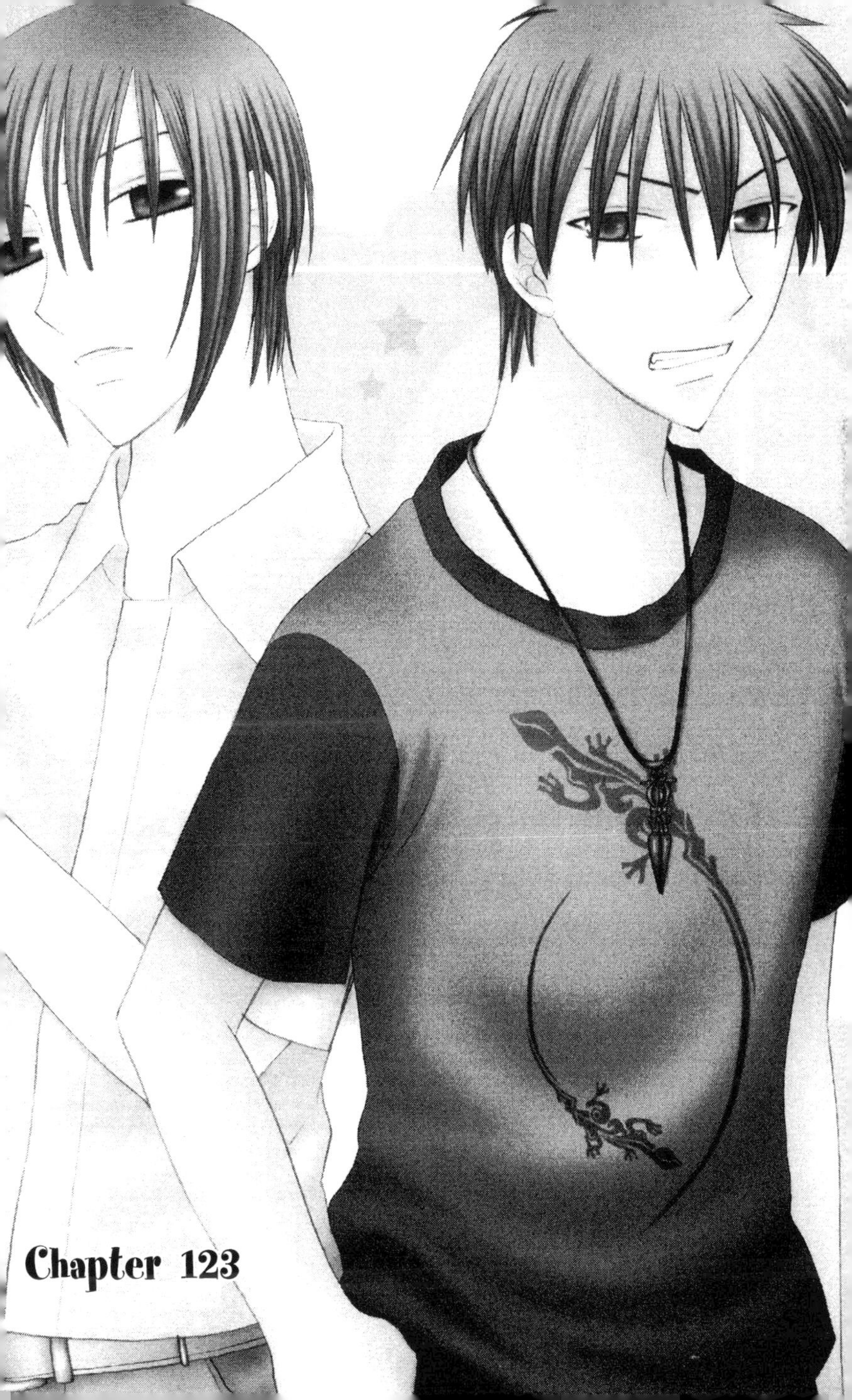

Chapter 123

Filler Sketch

Meet
Fight
Leader
Yuki.

Because I get
the feeling that
Yuki is actually
quicker to brawl.

Quicker than
Kyo, even.

His outfit's white, of course. The lining has Rat embroidery.

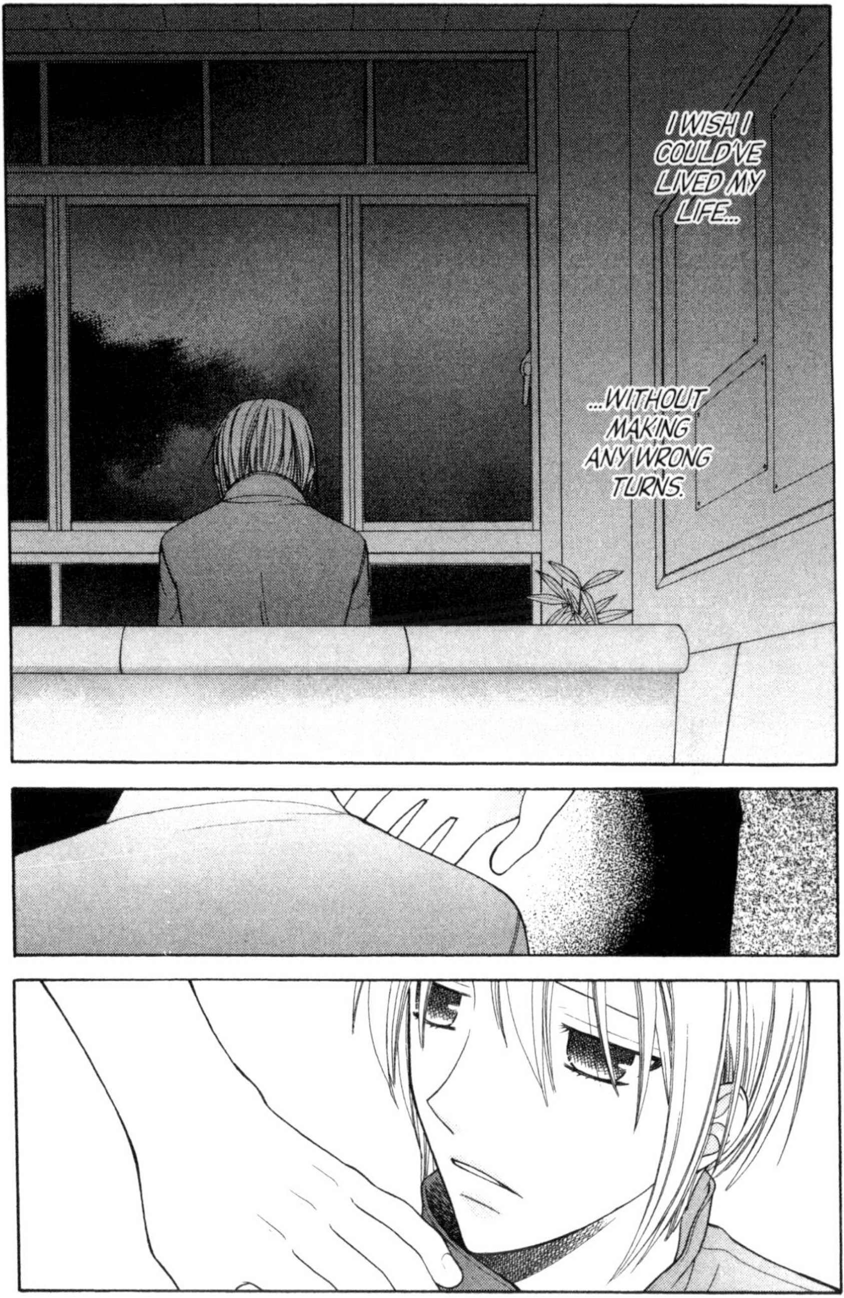
I WISH I COULD'VE LIVED MY LIFE...
...WITHOUT MAKING ANY WRONG TURNS.

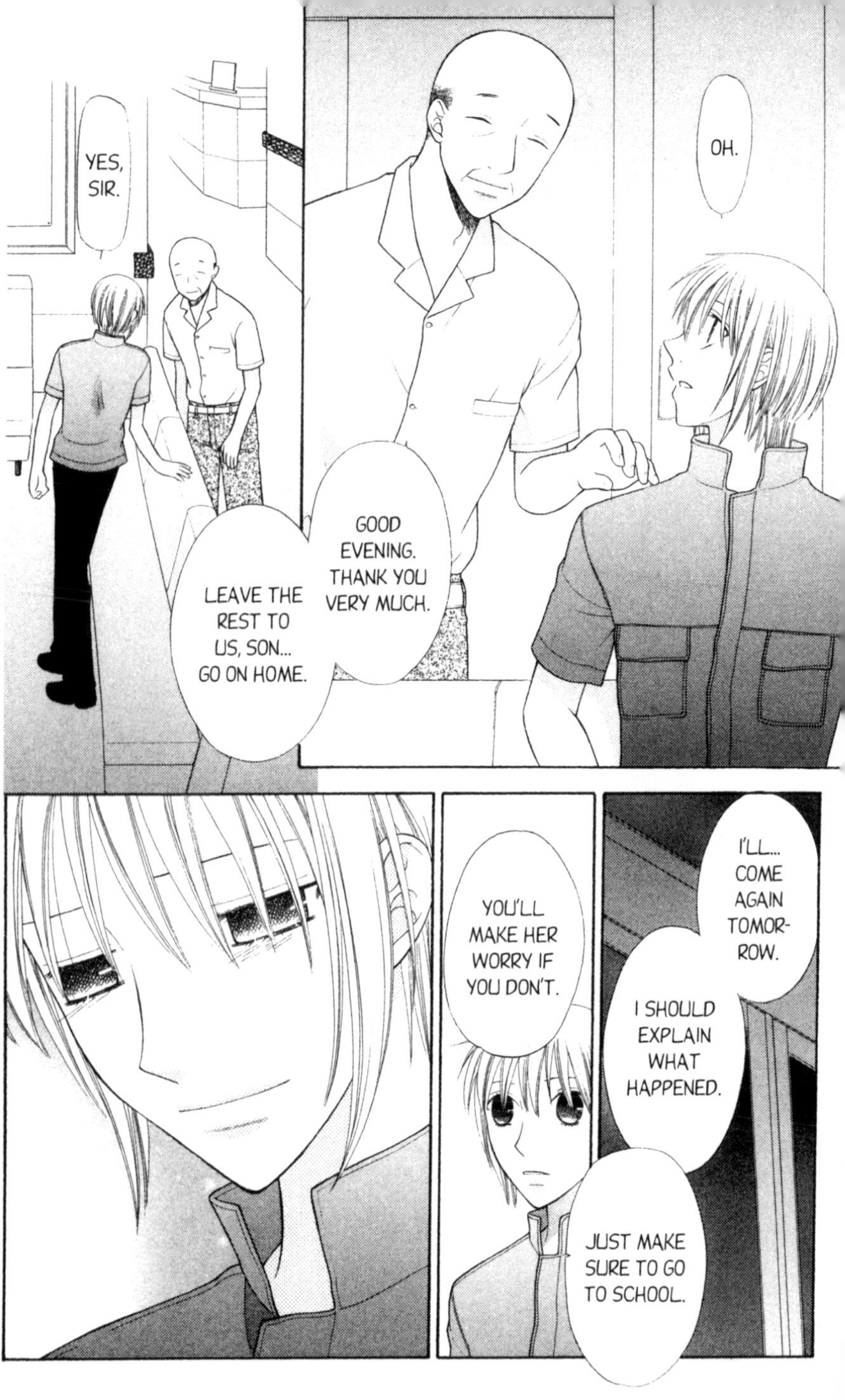
OH.
GOOD EVENING. THANK YOU VERY MUCH.
LEAVE THE REST TO US, SON... GO ON HOME.
YES, SIR.
I'LL... COME AGAIN TOMORROW.
I SHOULD EXPLAIN WHAT HAPPENED.
JUST MAKE SURE TO GO TO SCHOOL.
YOU'LL MAKE HER WORRY IF YOU DON'T.

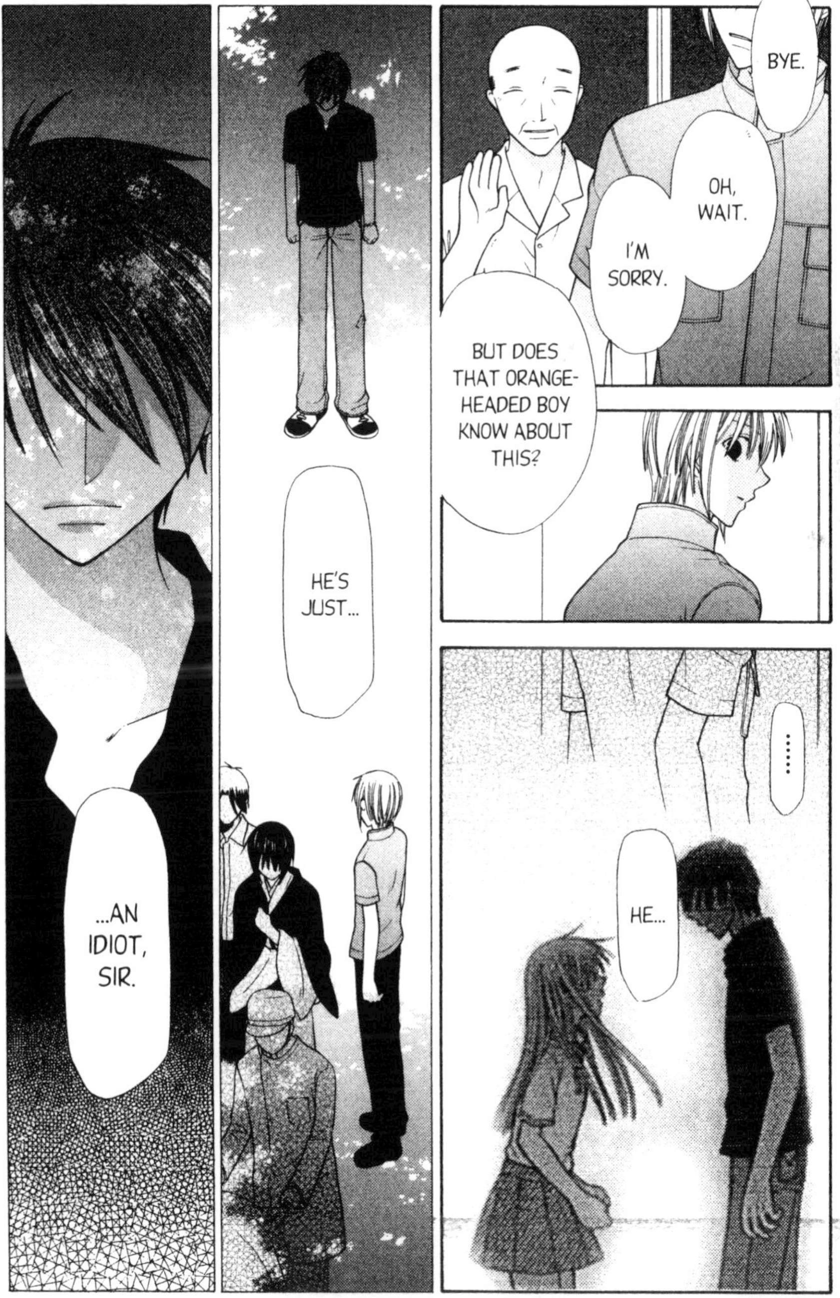

BYE.
OH, WAIT.
I'M SORRY.
BUT DOES THAT ORANGE-HEADED BOY KNOW ABOUT THIS?
......
HE...
HE'S JUST...
...AN IDIOT, SIR.

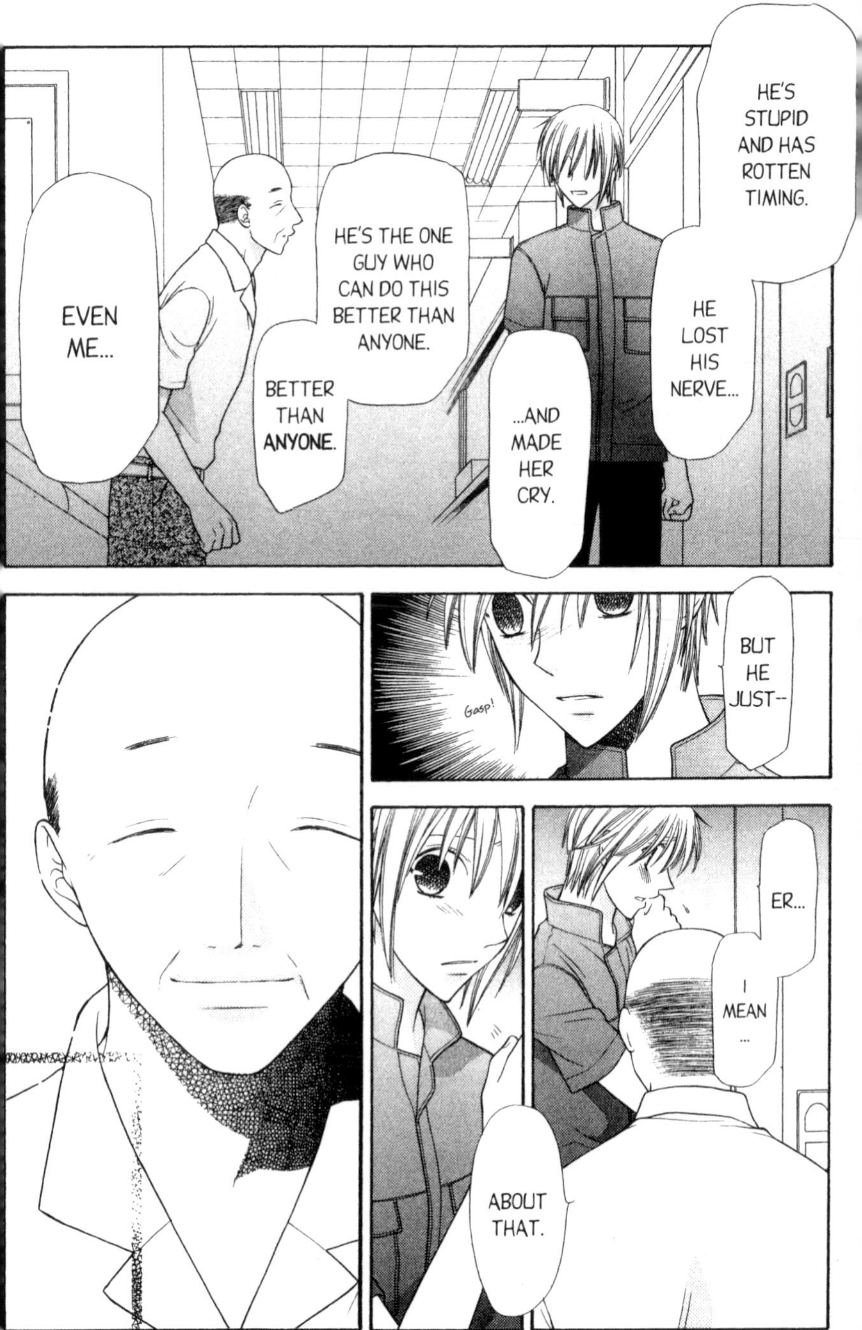
HE'S STUPID AND HAS ROTTEN TIMING.
HE LOST HIS NERVE...
...AND MADE HER CRY.
HE'S THE ONE GUY WHO CAN DO THIS BETTER THAN ANYONE.
BETTER THAN **ANYONE.**
EVEN ME...
BUT HE JUST--
Gasp!
ER...
I MEAN ...
ABOUT THAT.

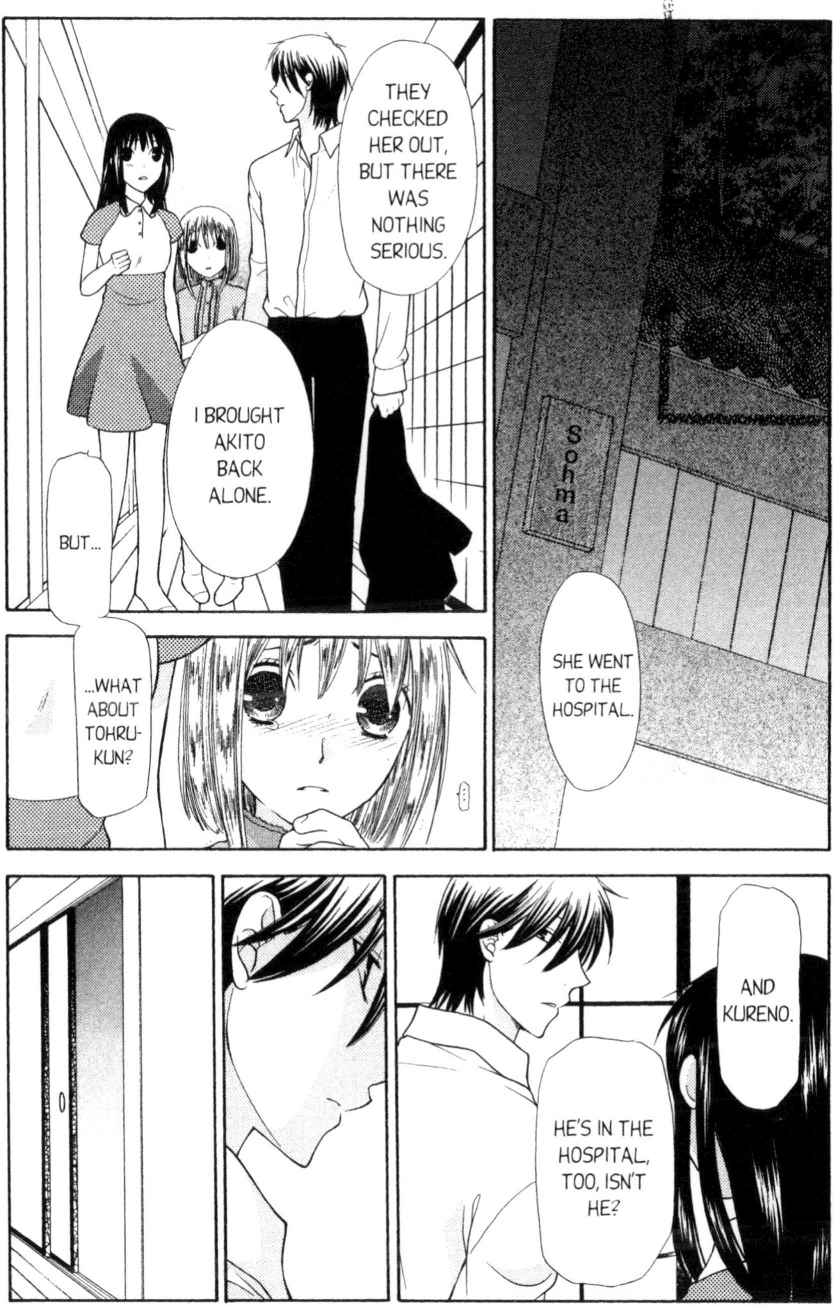
Sohma
SHE WENT TO THE HOSPITAL.
THEY CHECKED HER OUT, BUT THERE WAS NOTHING SERIOUS.
I BROUGHT AKITO BACK ALONE.
BUT...
...WHAT ABOUT TOHRU-KUN?
...
AND KURENO.
HE'S IN THE HOSPITAL, TOO, ISN'T HE?

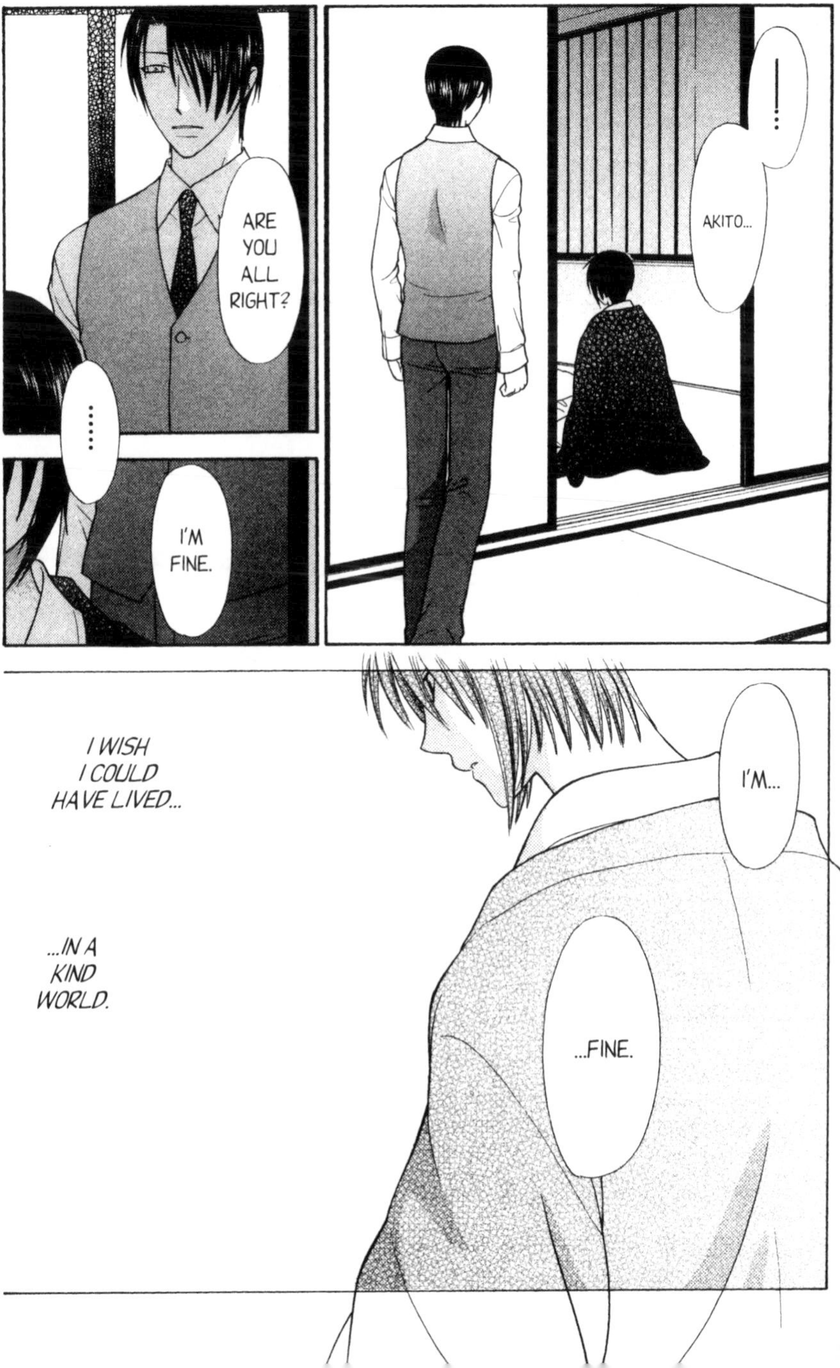
!
AKITO...
ARE YOU ALL RIGHT?
......
I'M FINE.
I'M...
...FINE.
I WISH I COULD HAVE LIVED...
...IN A KIND WORLD.

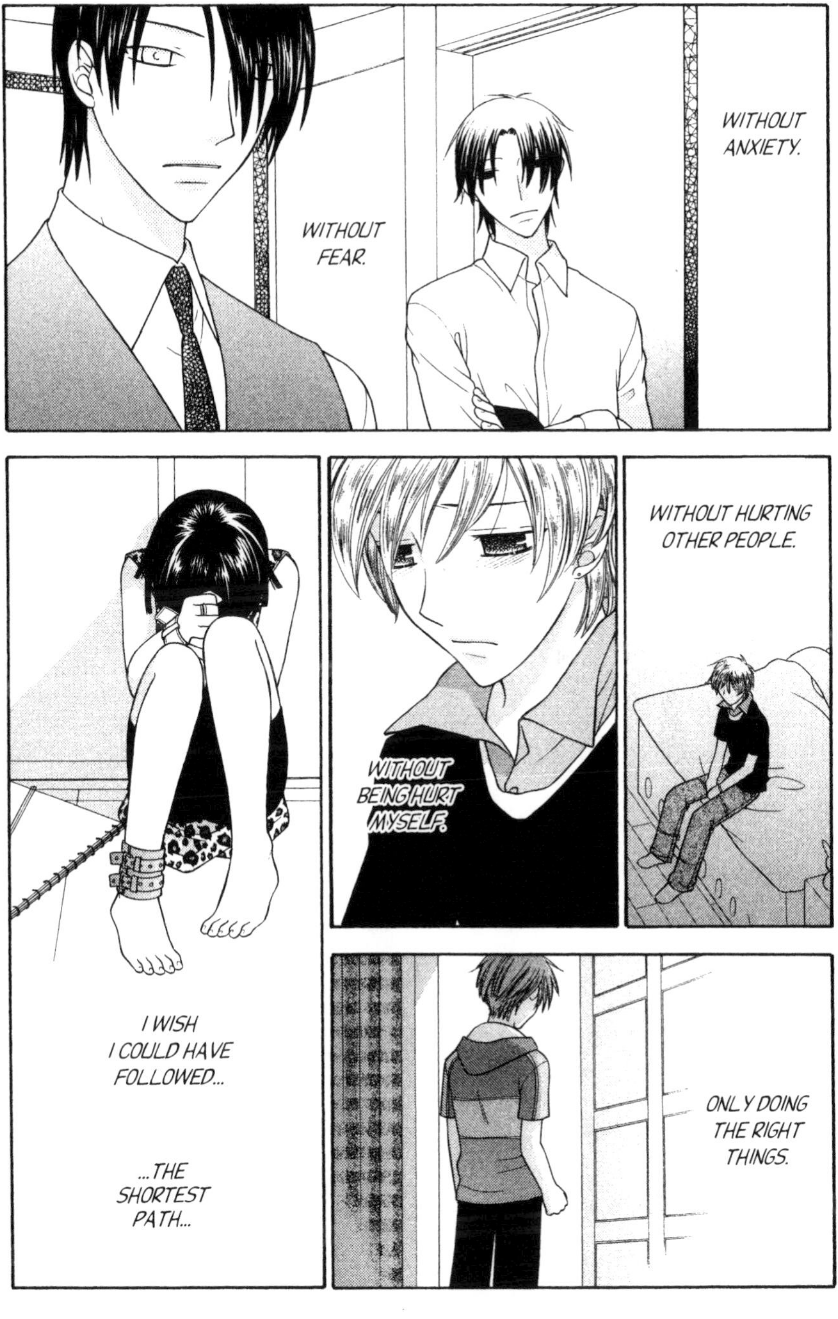
WITHOUT ANXIETY.
WITHOUT FEAR.
WITHOUT HURTING OTHER PEOPLE.
WITHOUT BEING HURT MYSELF.
ONLY DOING THE RIGHT THINGS.
I WISH I COULD HAVE FOLLOWED...
...THE SHORTEST PATH...

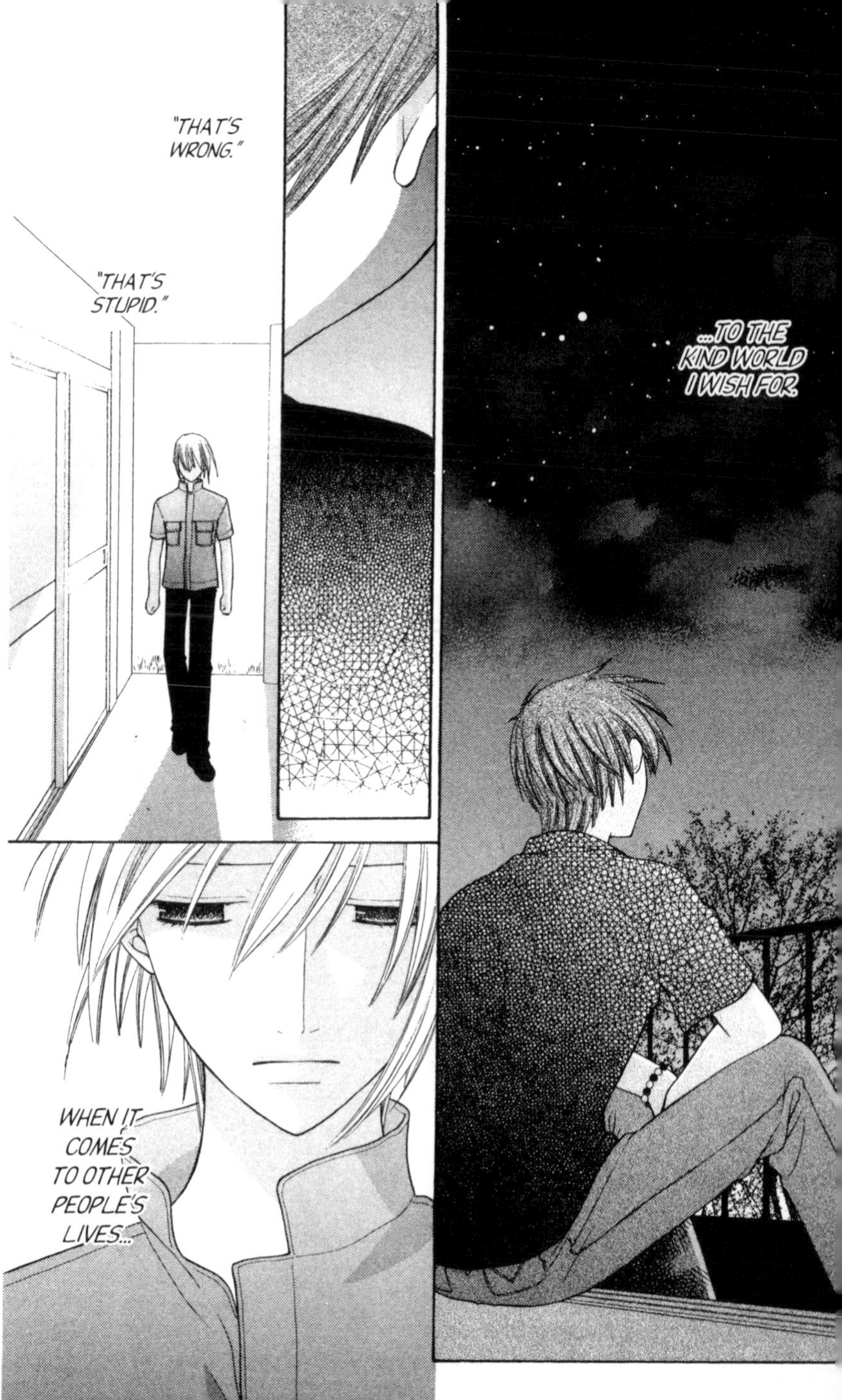
...TO THE KIND WORLD I WISH FOR.
"THAT'S WRONG."
"THAT'S STUPID."
WHEN IT COMES TO OTHER PEOPLE'S LIVES...

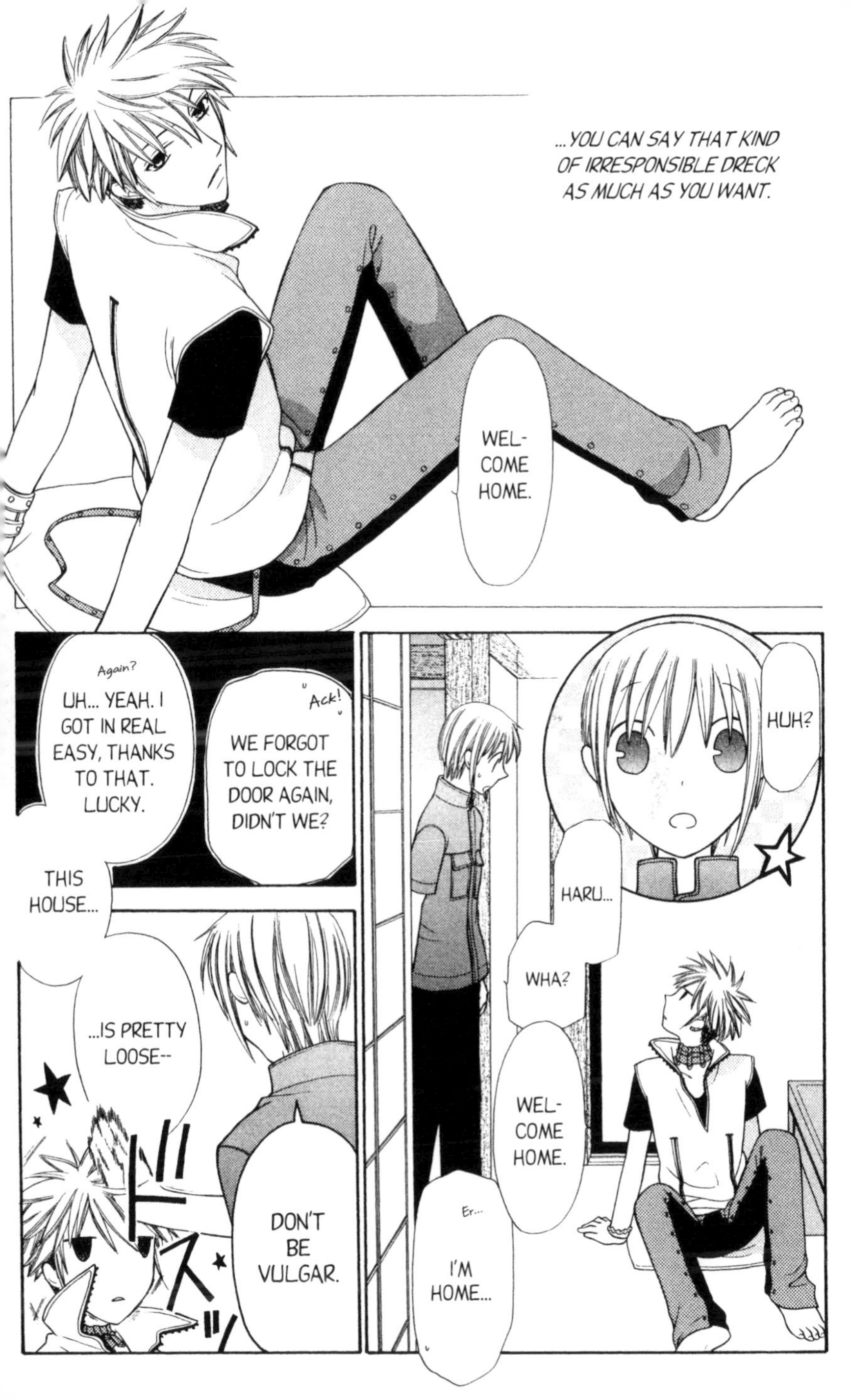
...YOU CAN SAY THAT KIND OF IRRESPONSIBLE DRECK AS MUCH AS YOU WANT.
WEL-COME HOME.
HUH?
HARU...
WHA?
WEL-COME HOME.
Er...
I'M HOME...
Ack!
WE FORGOT TO LOCK THE DOOR AGAIN, DIDN'T WE?
Again?
UH... YEAH. I GOT IN REAL EASY, THANKS TO THAT. LUCKY.
THIS HOUSE...
...IS PRETTY LOOSE--
DON'T BE VULGAR.

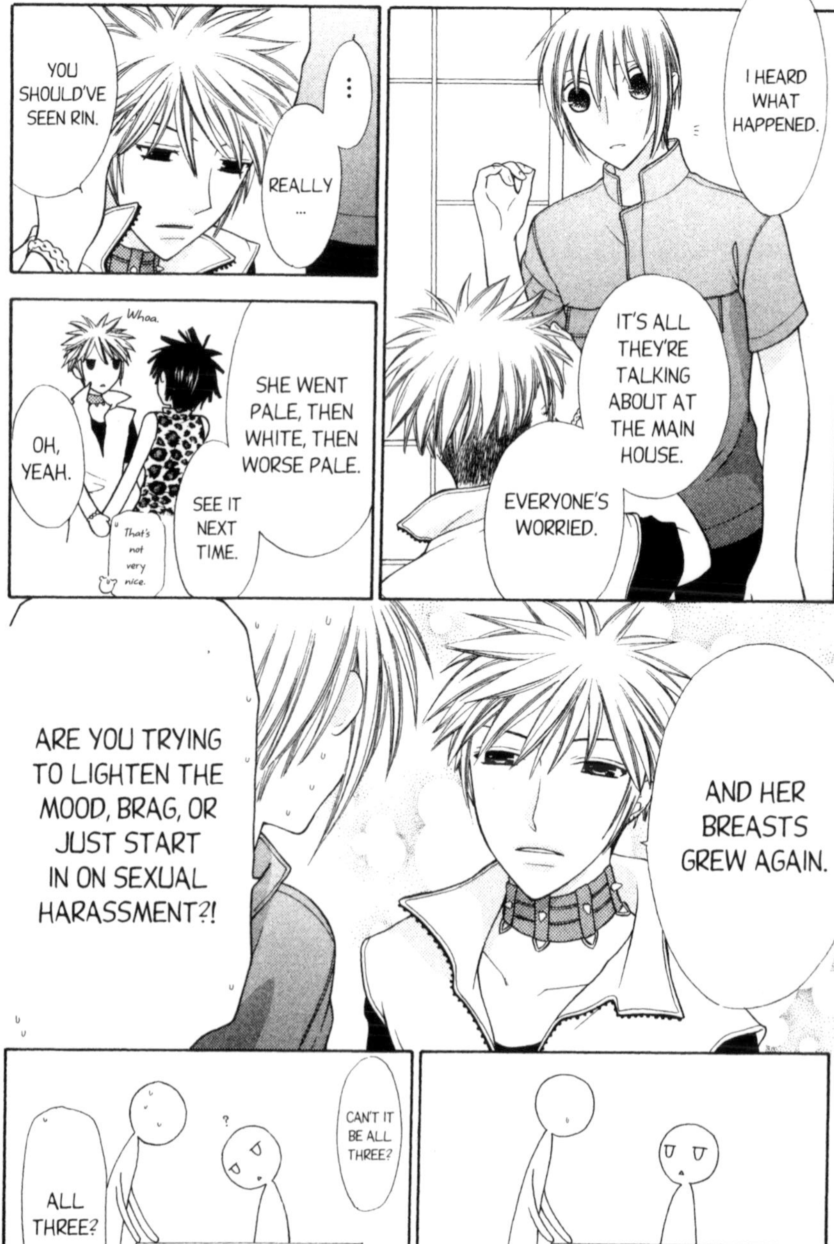
I HEARD WHAT HAPPENED.
IT'S ALL THEY'RE TALKING ABOUT AT THE MAIN HOUSE.
EVERYONE'S WORRIED.
...
YOU SHOULD'VE SEEN RIN.
REALLY ...
SHE WENT PALE, THEN WHITE, THEN WORSE PALE.
SEE IT NEXT TIME.
Whoa.
OH, YEAH.
That's not very nice.
AND HER BREASTS GREW AGAIN.
ARE YOU TRYING TO LIGHTEN THE MOOD, BRAG, OR JUST START IN ON SEXUAL HARASSMENT?!
CAN'T IT BE ALL THREE?
ALL THREE?

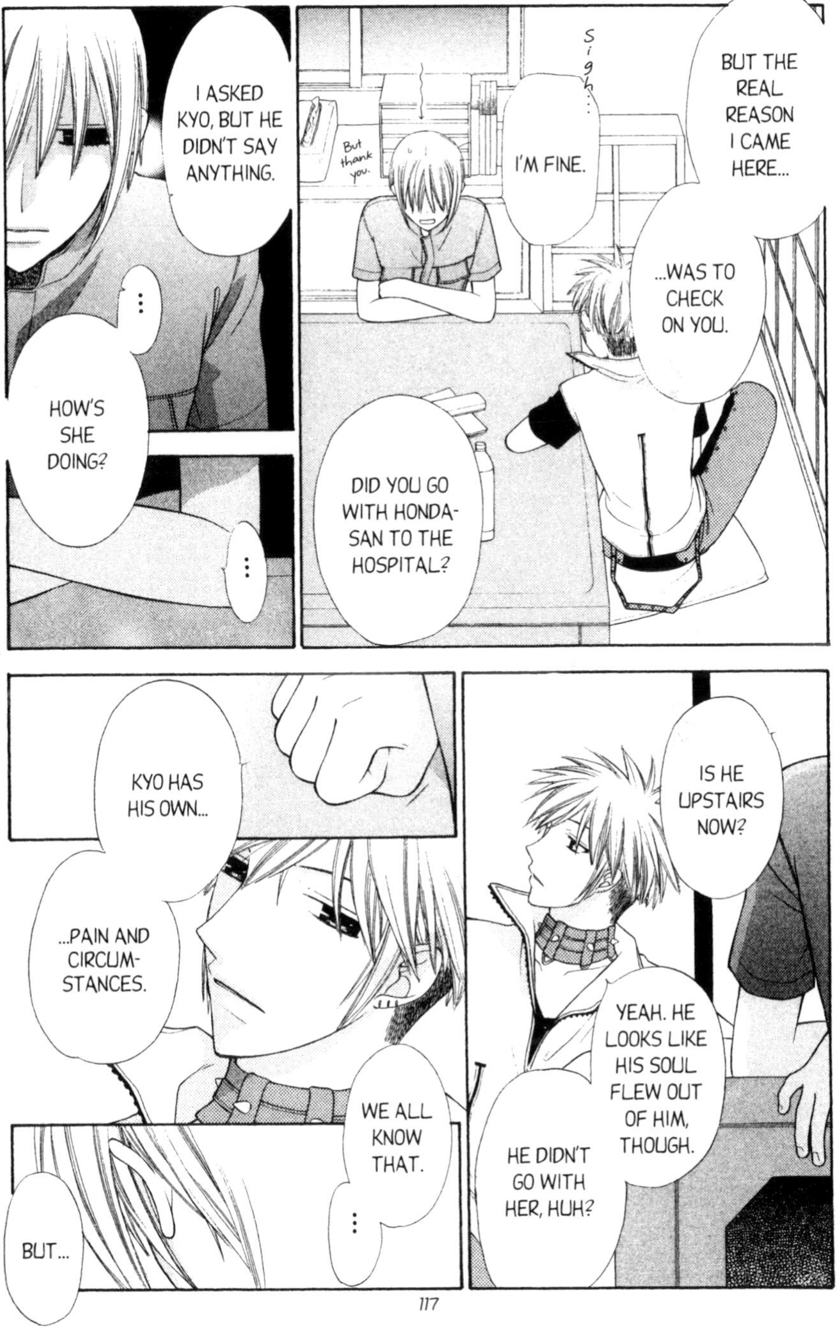

BUT THE REAL REASON I CAME HERE...
...WAS TO CHECK ON YOU.
Sigh...
I'M FINE.
But thank you.
DID YOU GO WITH HONDA-SAN TO THE HOSPITAL?
I ASKED KYO, BUT HE DIDN'T SAY ANYTHING.
...
HOW'S SHE DOING?
...
IS HE UPSTAIRS NOW?
YEAH. HE LOOKS LIKE HIS SOUL FLEW OUT OF HIM, THOUGH.
HE DIDN'T GO WITH HER, HUH?
KYO HAS HIS OWN...
...PAIN AND CIRCUM-STANCES.
WE ALL KNOW THAT.
...
BUT...

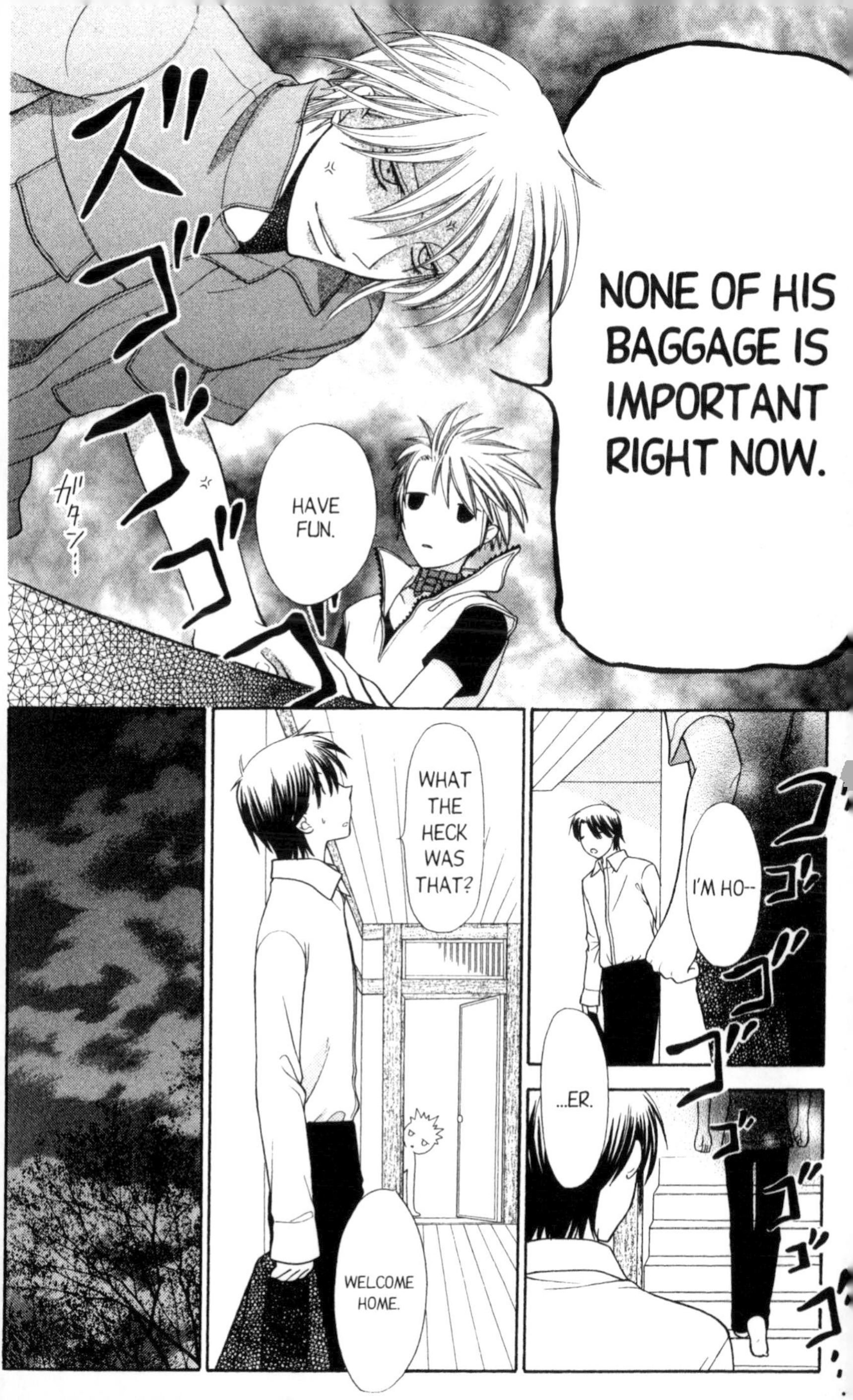

NONE OF HIS BAGGAGE IS IMPORTANT RIGHT NOW.
ズゴゴゴ
HAVE FUN.
ガタン…
I'M HO--
...ER.
WHAT THE HECK WAS THAT?
WELCOME HOME.

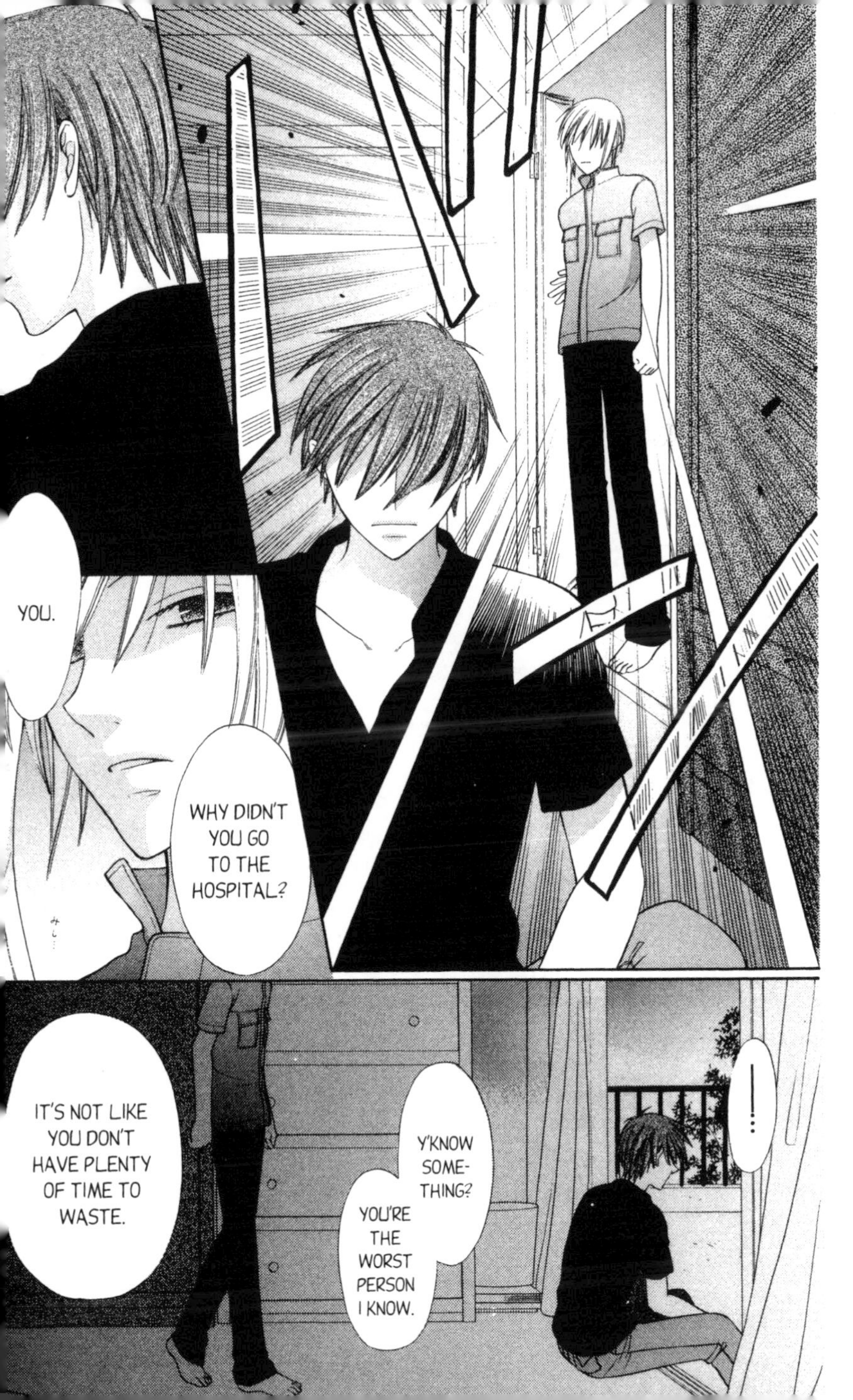
YOU.
WHY DIDN'T YOU GO TO THE HOSPITAL?
みし…
!…
Y'KNOW SOMETHING?
YOU'RE THE WORST PERSON I KNOW.
IT'S NOT LIKE YOU DON'T HAVE PLENTY OF TIME TO WASTE.

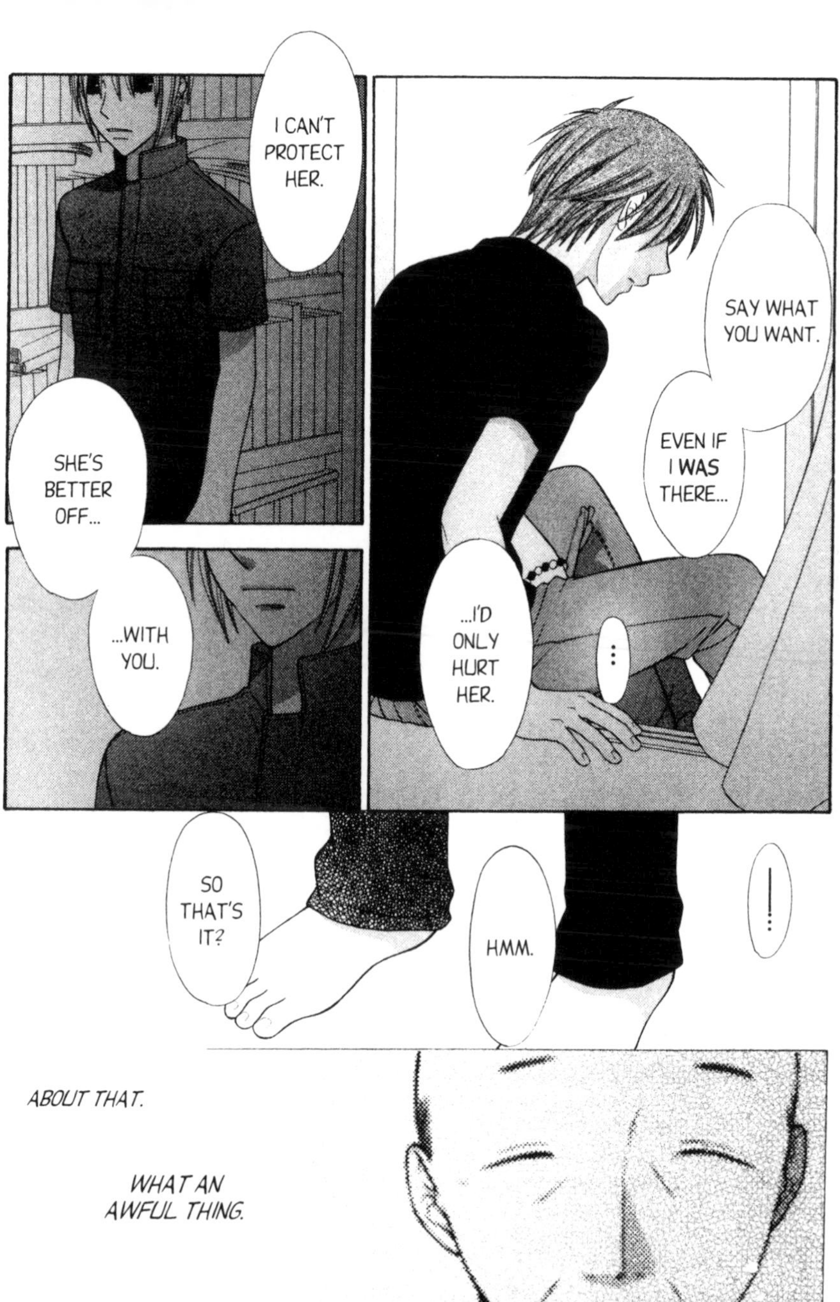

SAY WHAT YOU WANT.
EVEN IF I WAS THERE...
...I'D ONLY HURT HER.
...
I CAN'T PROTECT HER.
SHE'S BETTER OFF...
...WITH YOU.
!
HMM.
SO THAT'S IT?
ABOUT THAT.
WHAT AN AWFUL THING.

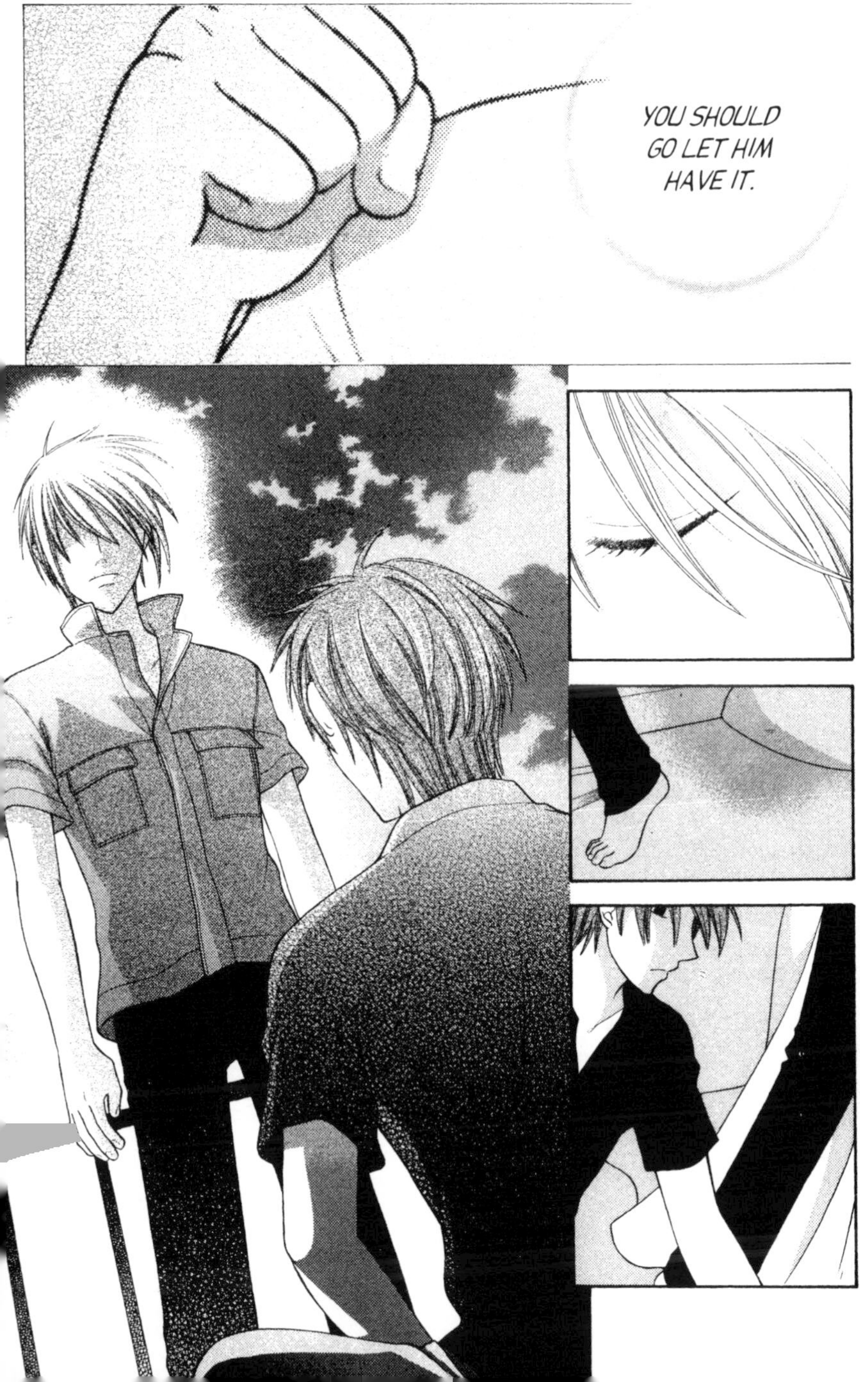
YOU SHOULD GO LET HIM HAVE IT.

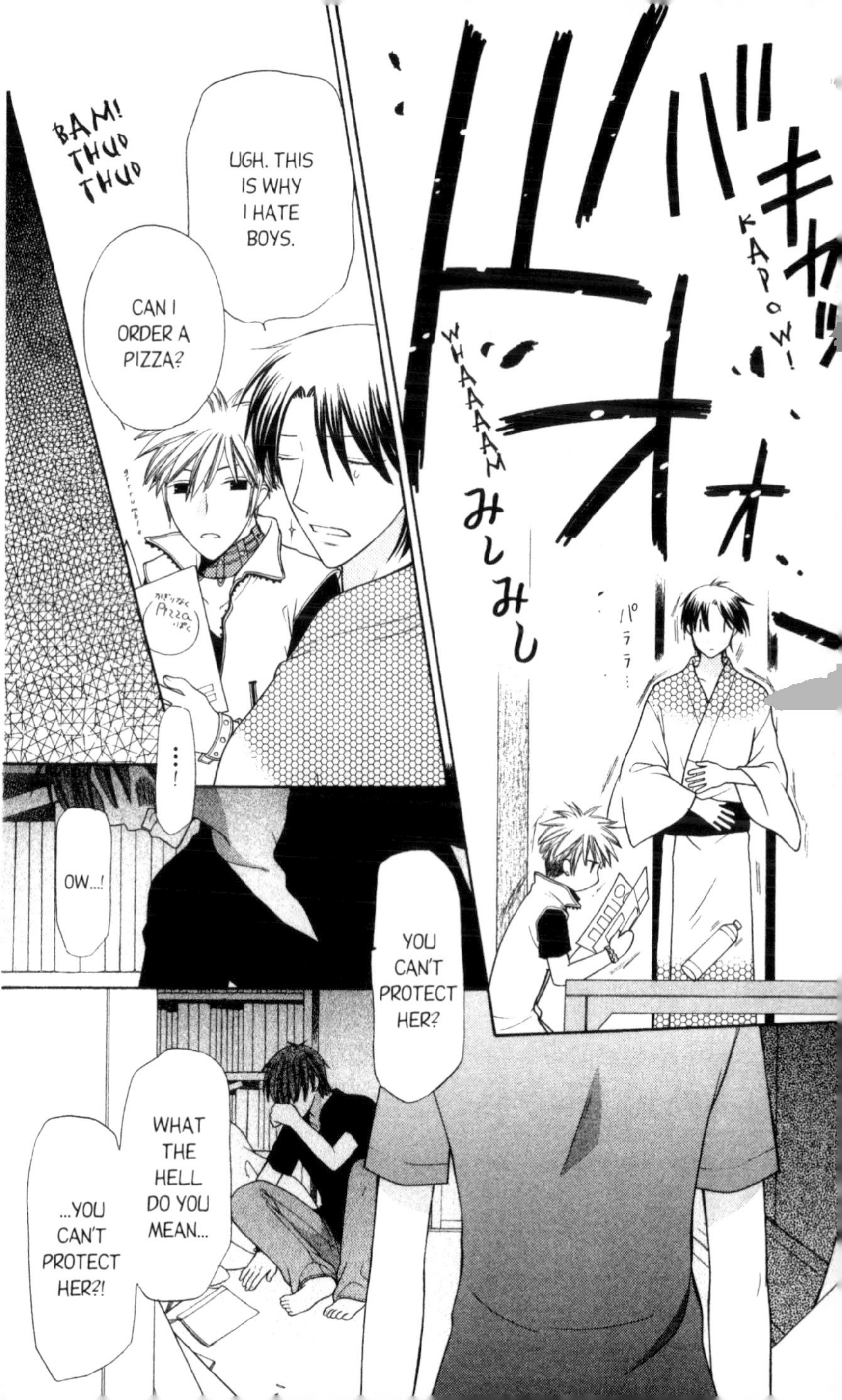
バキャッ
KAPOW!
ドオォ
WHAAAAAM
みしみし
パラ…
BAM! THUD THUD
UGH. THIS IS WHY I HATE BOYS.
CAN I ORDER A PIZZA?
Pizza
...!
OW...!
YOU CAN'T PROTECT HER?
WHAT THE HELL DO YOU MEAN...
...YOU CAN'T PROTECT HER?!

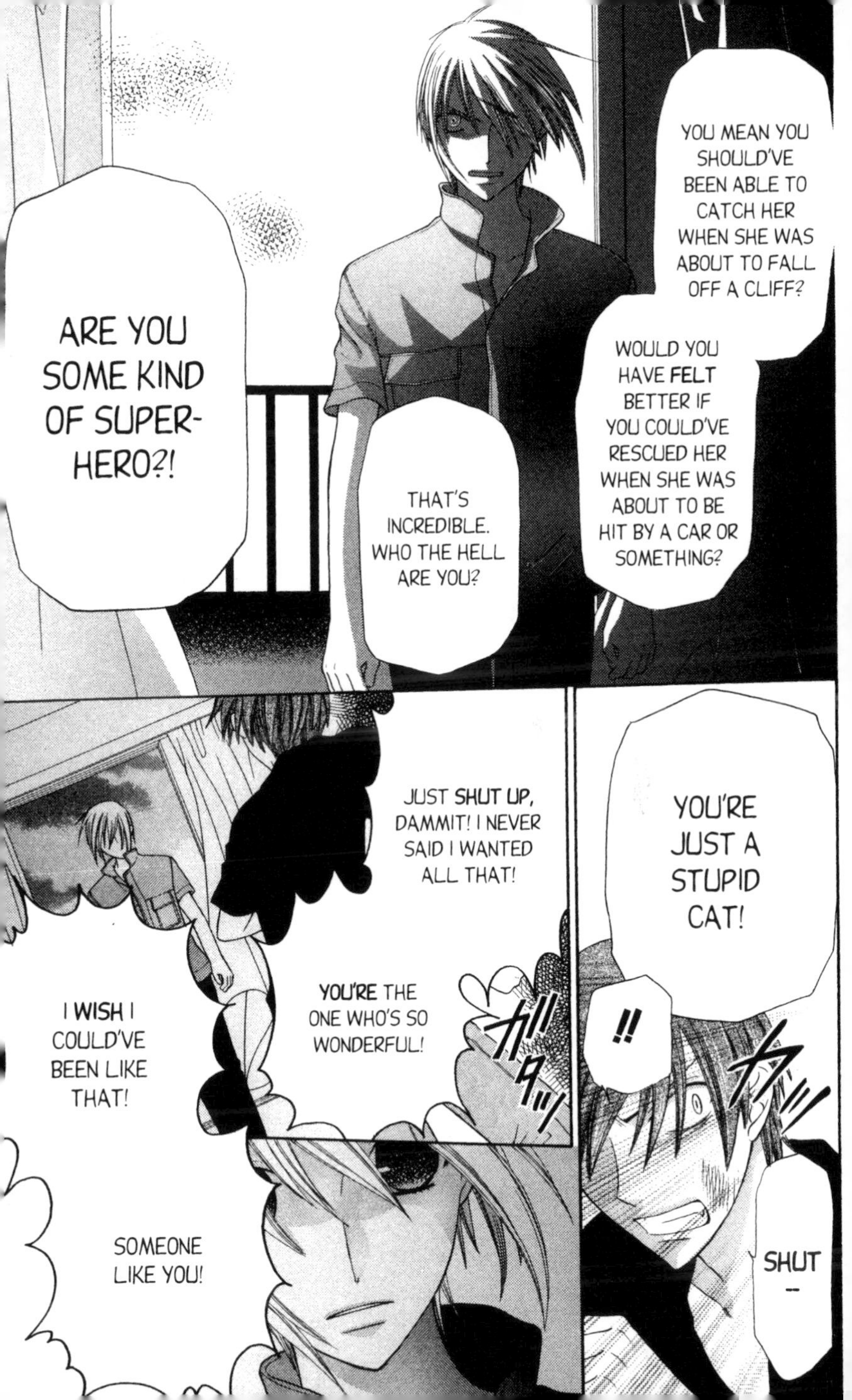
YOU MEAN YOU SHOULD'VE BEEN ABLE TO CATCH HER WHEN SHE WAS ABOUT TO FALL OFF A CLIFF?
WOULD YOU HAVE **FELT** BETTER IF YOU COULD'VE RESCUED HER WHEN SHE WAS ABOUT TO BE HIT BY A CAR OR SOMETHING?
THAT'S INCREDIBLE. WHO THE HELL ARE YOU?
ARE YOU SOME KIND OF SUPER-HERO?!
YOU'RE JUST A STUPID CAT!
!!
SHUT --
ガタッ
JUST **SHUT UP,** DAMMIT! I NEVER SAID I WANTED ALL THAT!
YOU'RE THE ONE WHO'S SO WONDERFUL!
I **WISH** I COULD'VE BEEN LIKE THAT!
SOMEONE LIKE YOU!

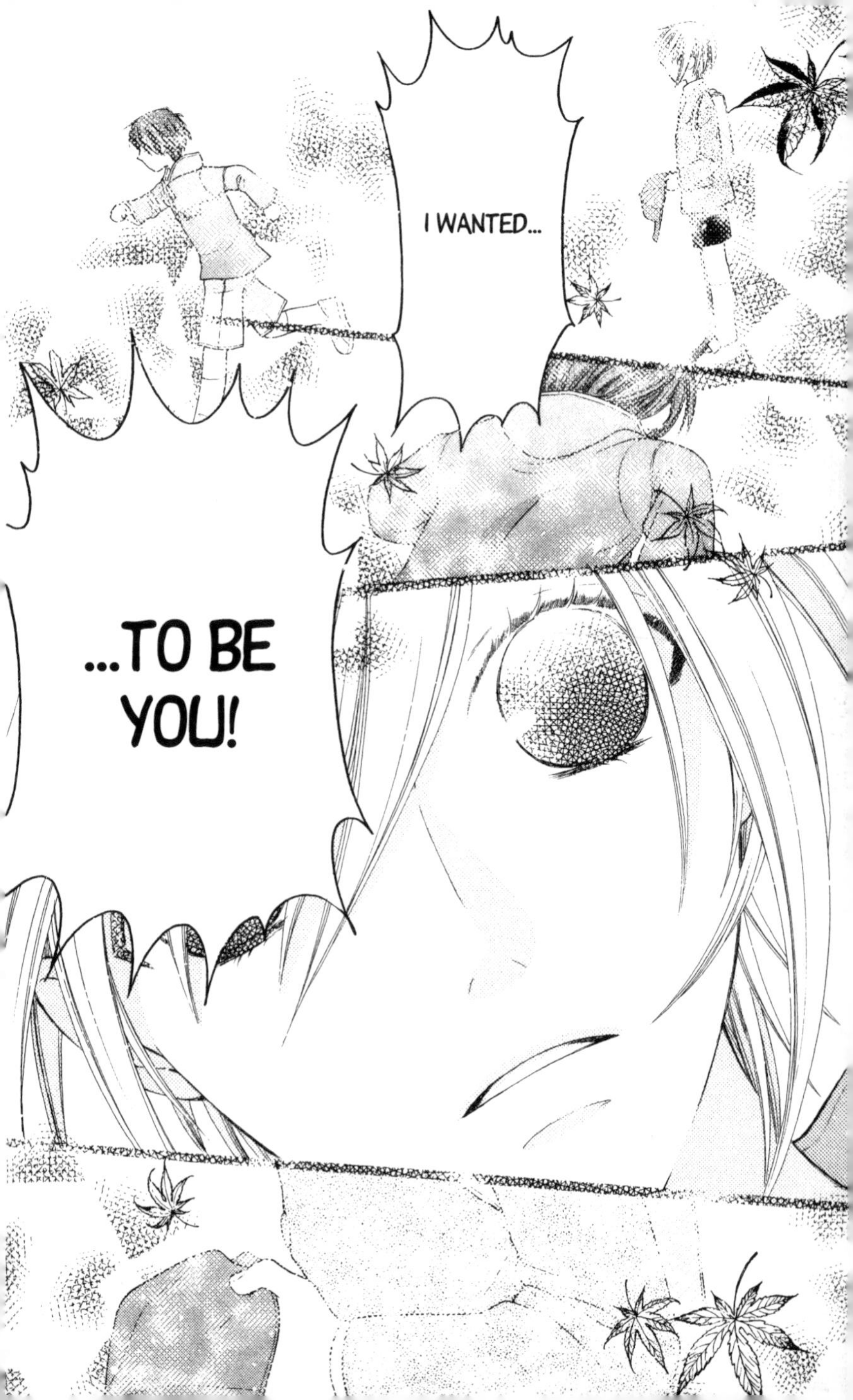
I WANTED...
...TO BE YOU!

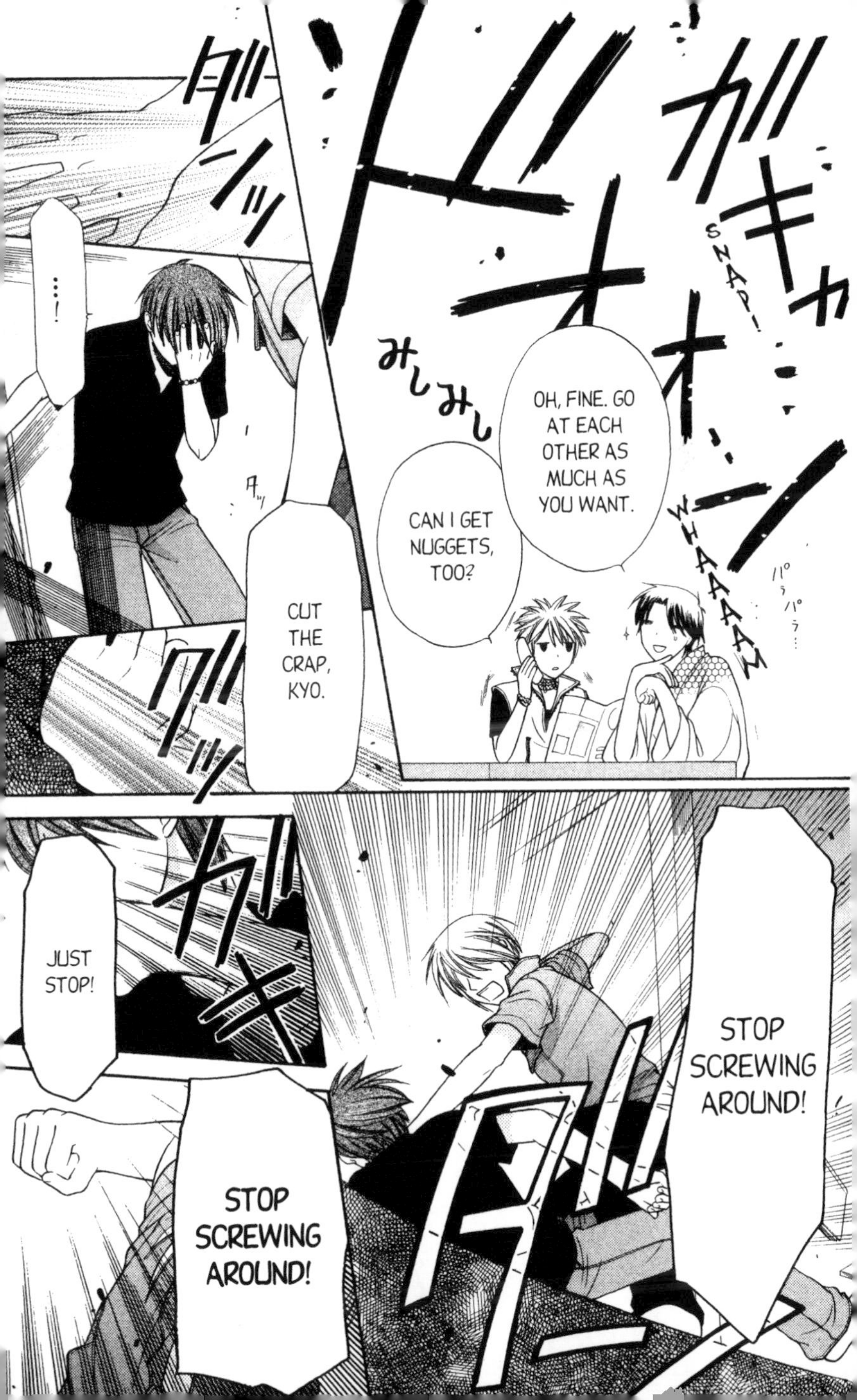
SNAP!
WHAAAAAM
みしみし
OH, FINE. GO AT EACH OTHER AS MUCH AS YOU WANT.
CAN I GET NUGGETS, TOO?
CUT THE CRAP, KYO.
...!
STOP SCREWING AROUND!
JUST STOP!
STOP SCREWING AROUND!

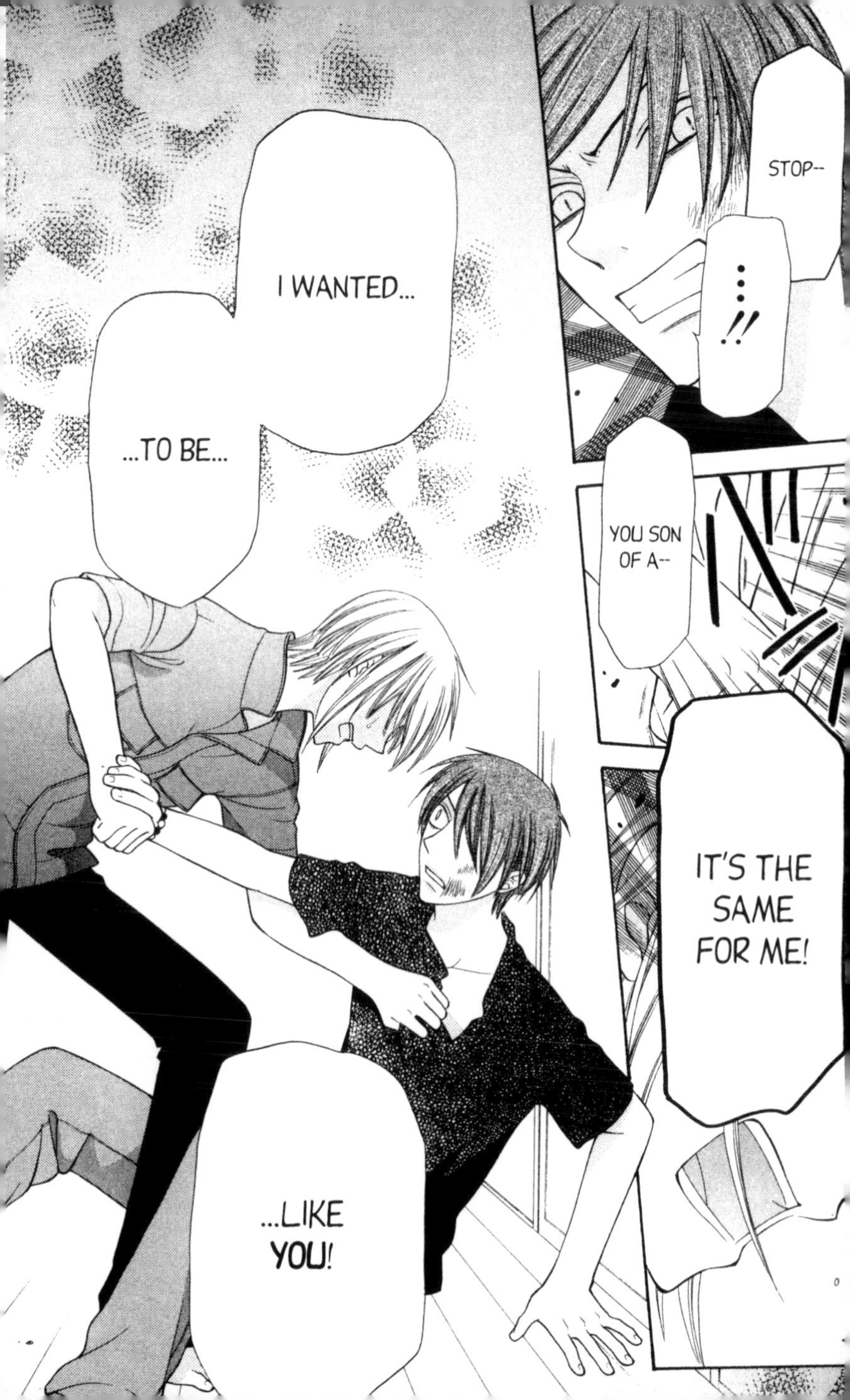
STOP--
......!!
YOU SON OF A--
IT'S THE SAME FOR ME!
I WANTED...
...TO BE...
...LIKE YOU!

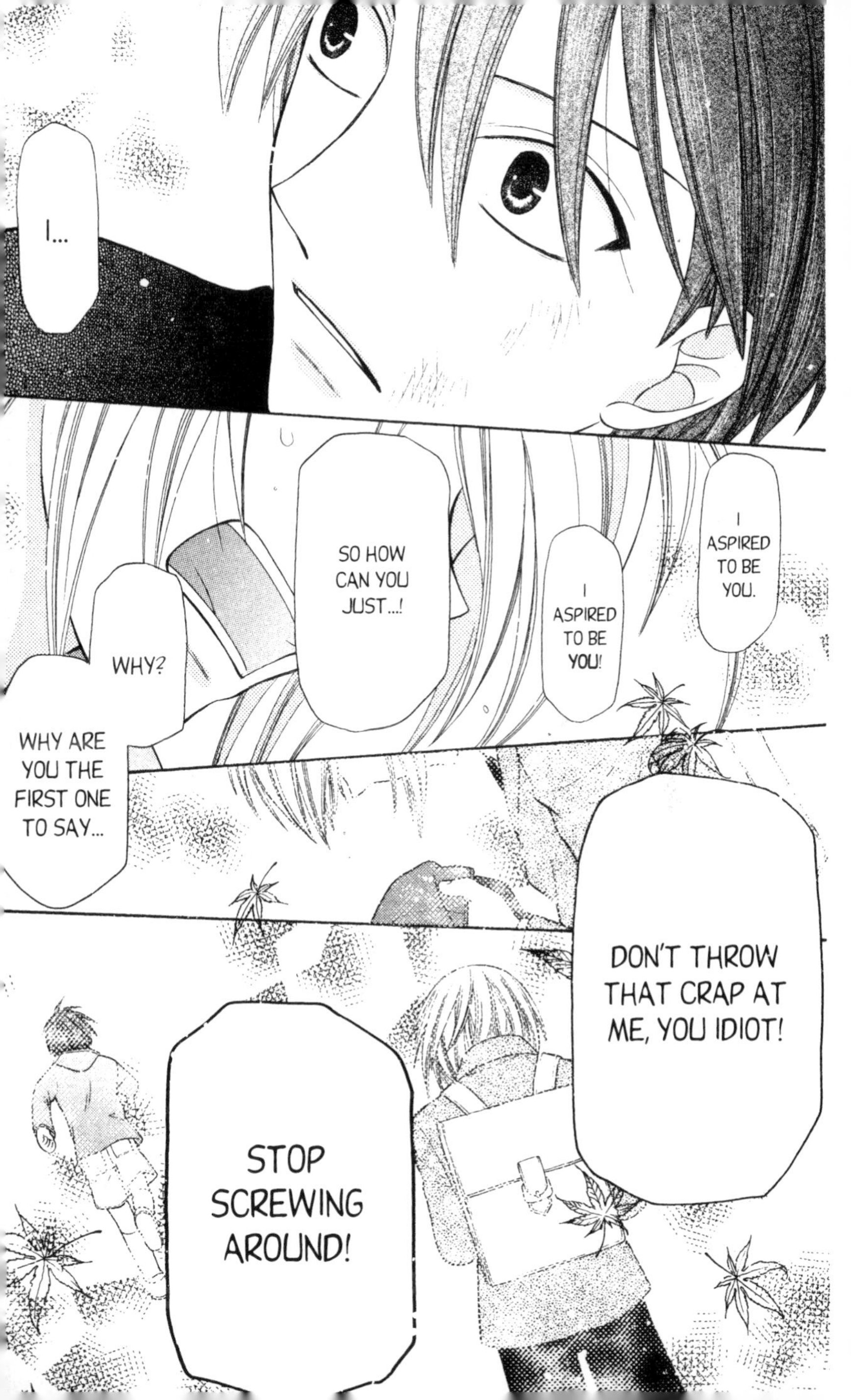
I...
I ASPIRED TO BE YOU.
I ASPIRED TO BE YOU!
SO HOW CAN YOU JUST...!
WHY?
WHY ARE YOU THE FIRST ONE TO SAY...
DON'T THROW THAT CRAP AT ME, YOU IDIOT!
STOP SCREWING AROUND!

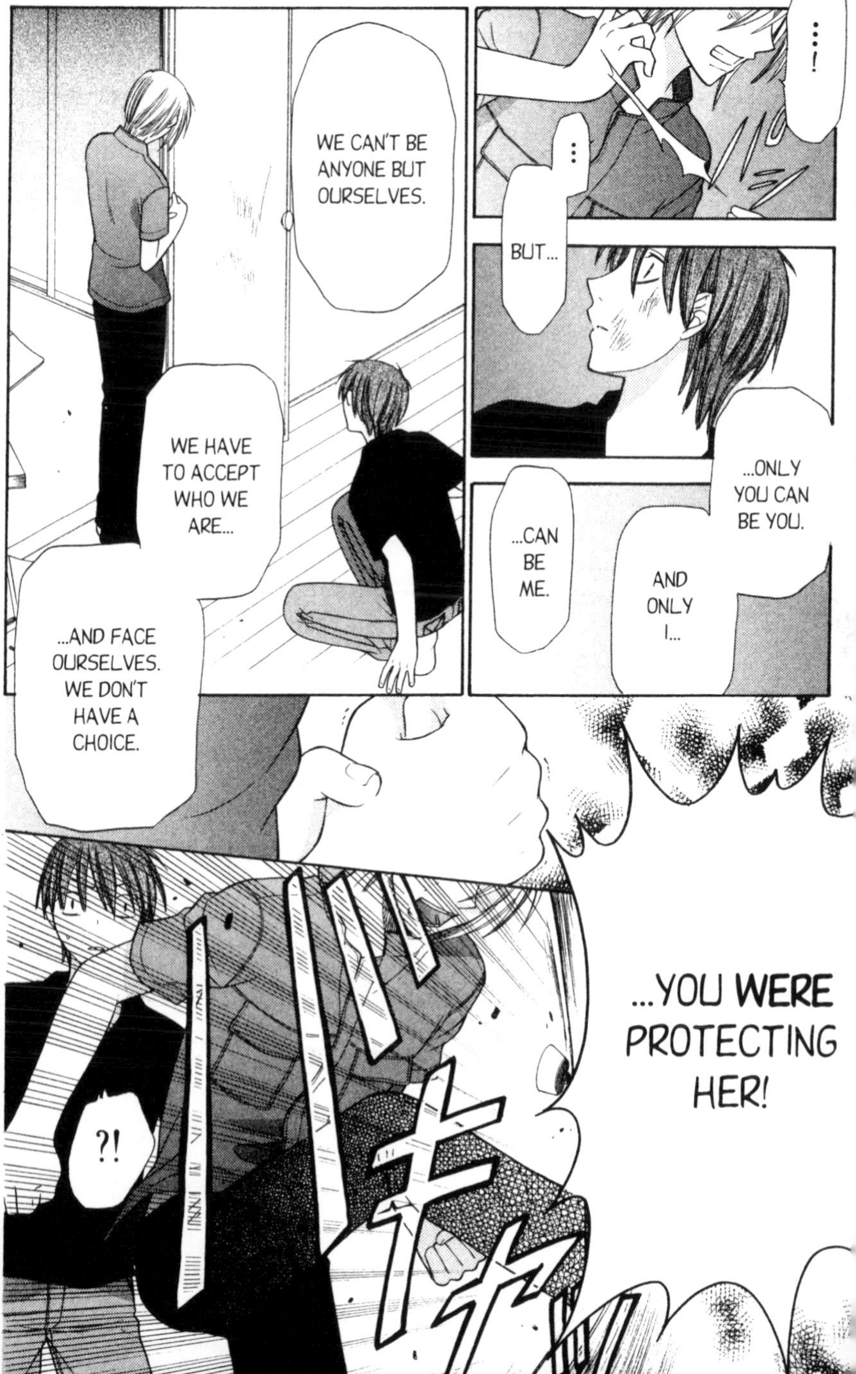
...!
...
BUT...
...ONLY YOU CAN BE YOU.
AND ONLY I...
...CAN BE ME.
WE CAN'T BE ANYONE BUT OURSELVES.
WE HAVE TO ACCEPT WHO WE ARE...
...AND FACE OURSELVES. WE DON'T HAVE A CHOICE.
...YOU **WERE** PROTECTING HER!
?!

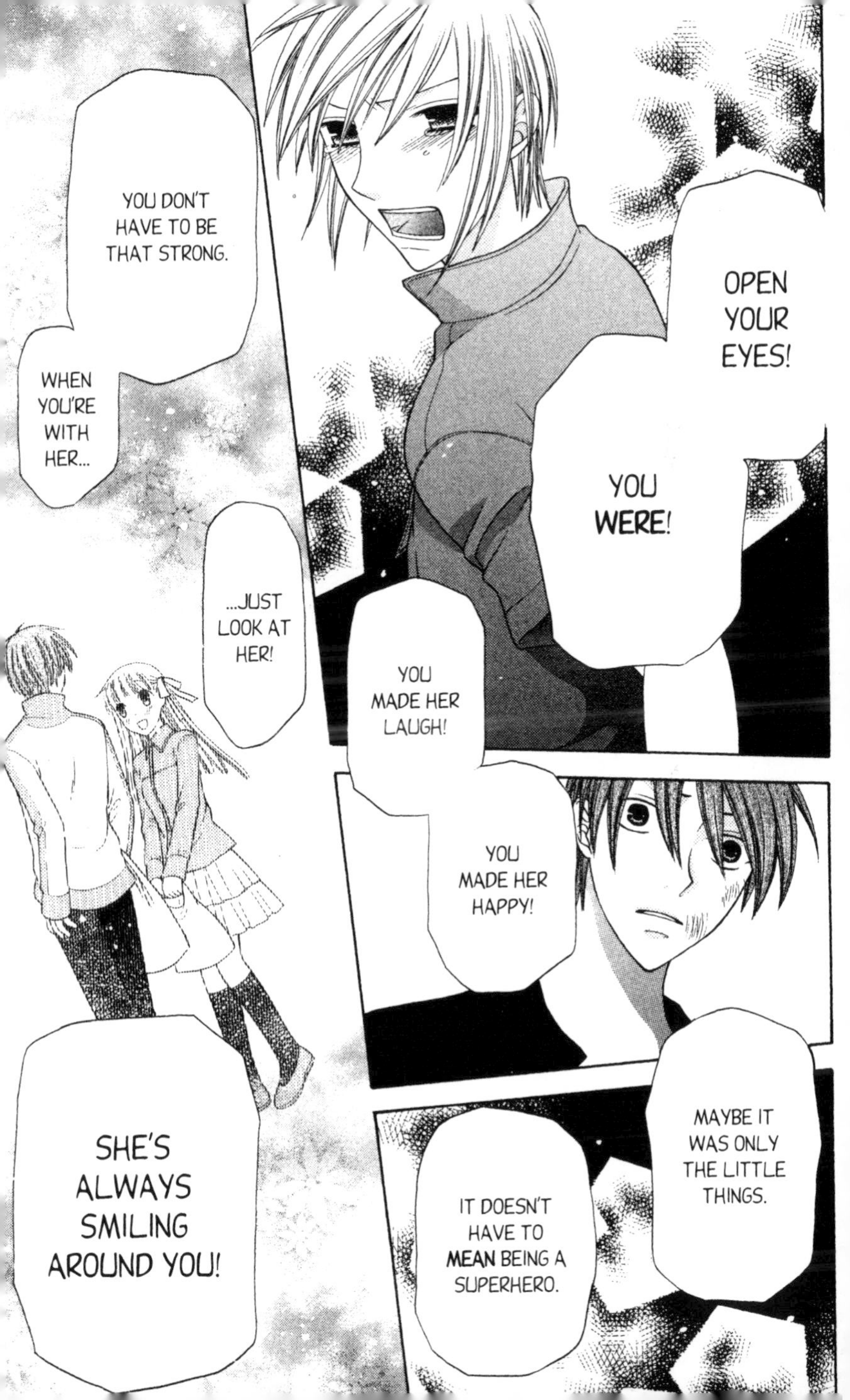
OPEN YOUR EYES!
YOU WERE!
YOU MADE HER LAUGH!
YOU MADE HER HAPPY!
MAYBE IT WAS ONLY THE LITTLE THINGS.
IT DOESN'T HAVE TO MEAN BEING A SUPERHERO.
YOU DON'T HAVE TO BE THAT STRONG.
WHEN YOU'RE WITH HER...
...JUST LOOK AT HER!
SHE'S ALWAYS SMILING AROUND YOU!

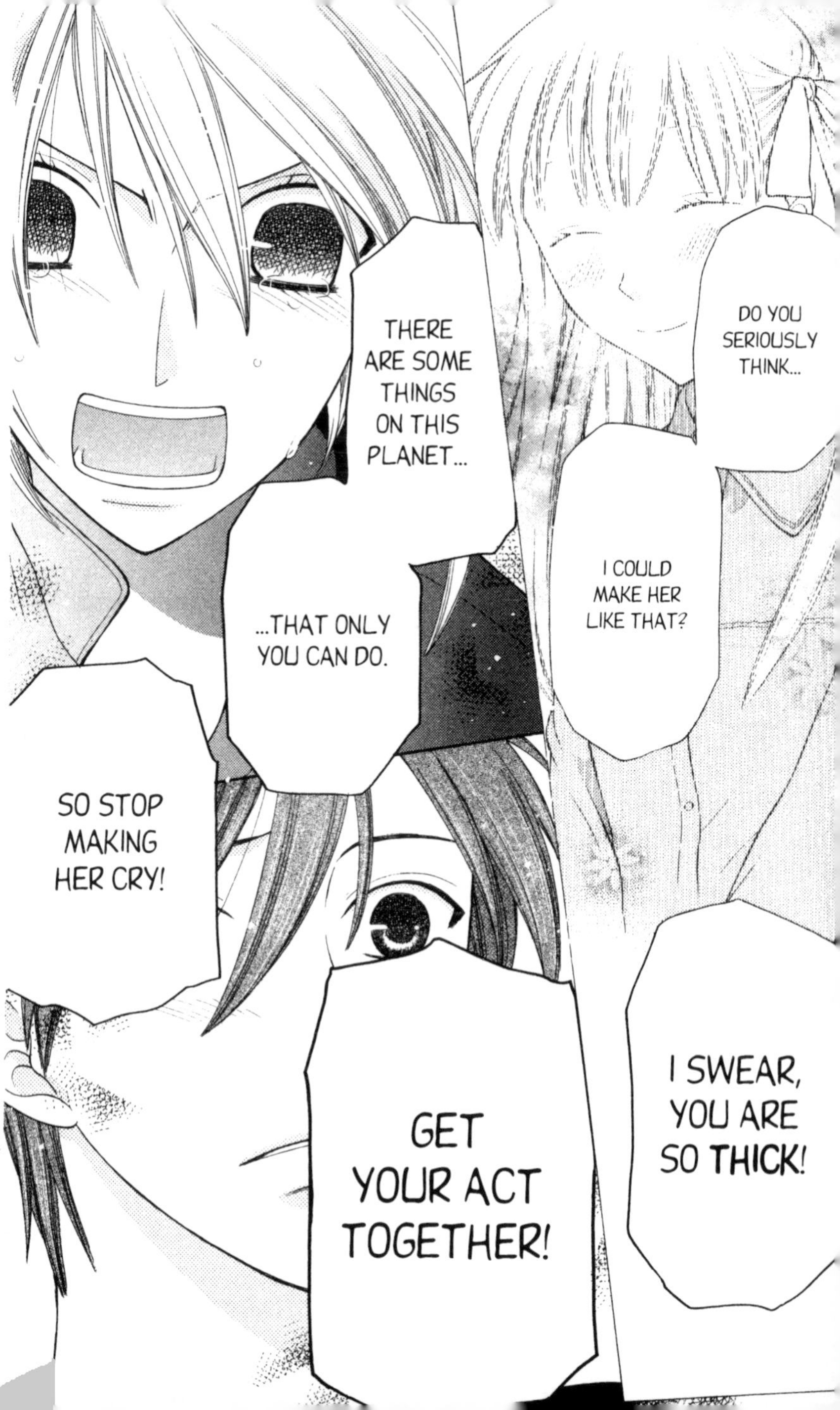
DO YOU SERIOUSLY THINK...
I COULD MAKE HER LIKE THAT?
I SWEAR, YOU ARE SO THICK!
THERE ARE SOME THINGS ON THIS PLANET...
...THAT ONLY YOU CAN DO.
GET YOUR ACT TOGETHER!
SO STOP MAKING HER CRY!

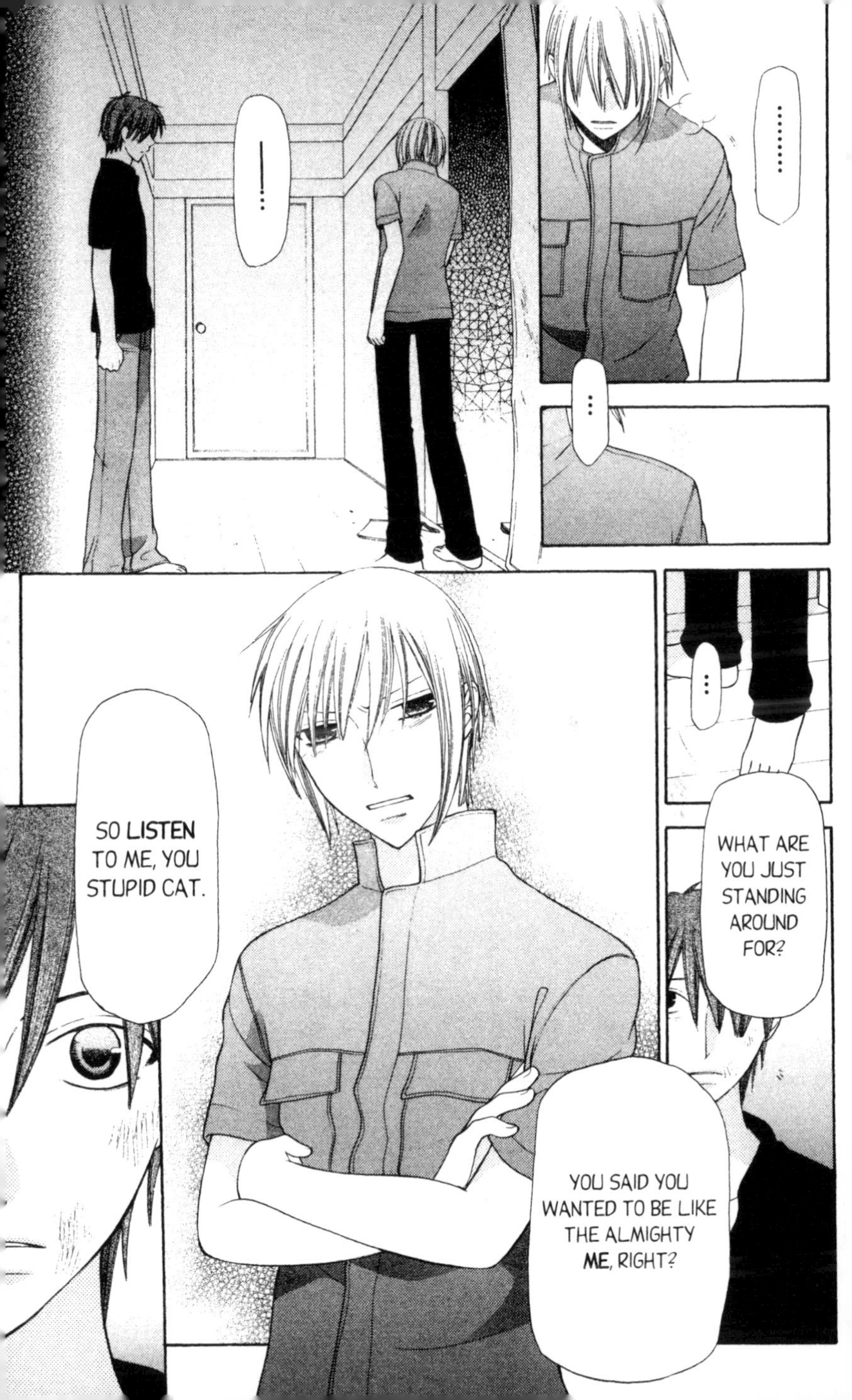
....
...
!...
...
WHAT ARE YOU JUST STANDING AROUND FOR?
YOU SAID YOU WANTED TO BE LIKE THE ALMIGHTY **ME**, RIGHT?
SO **LISTEN** TO ME, YOU STUPID CAT.

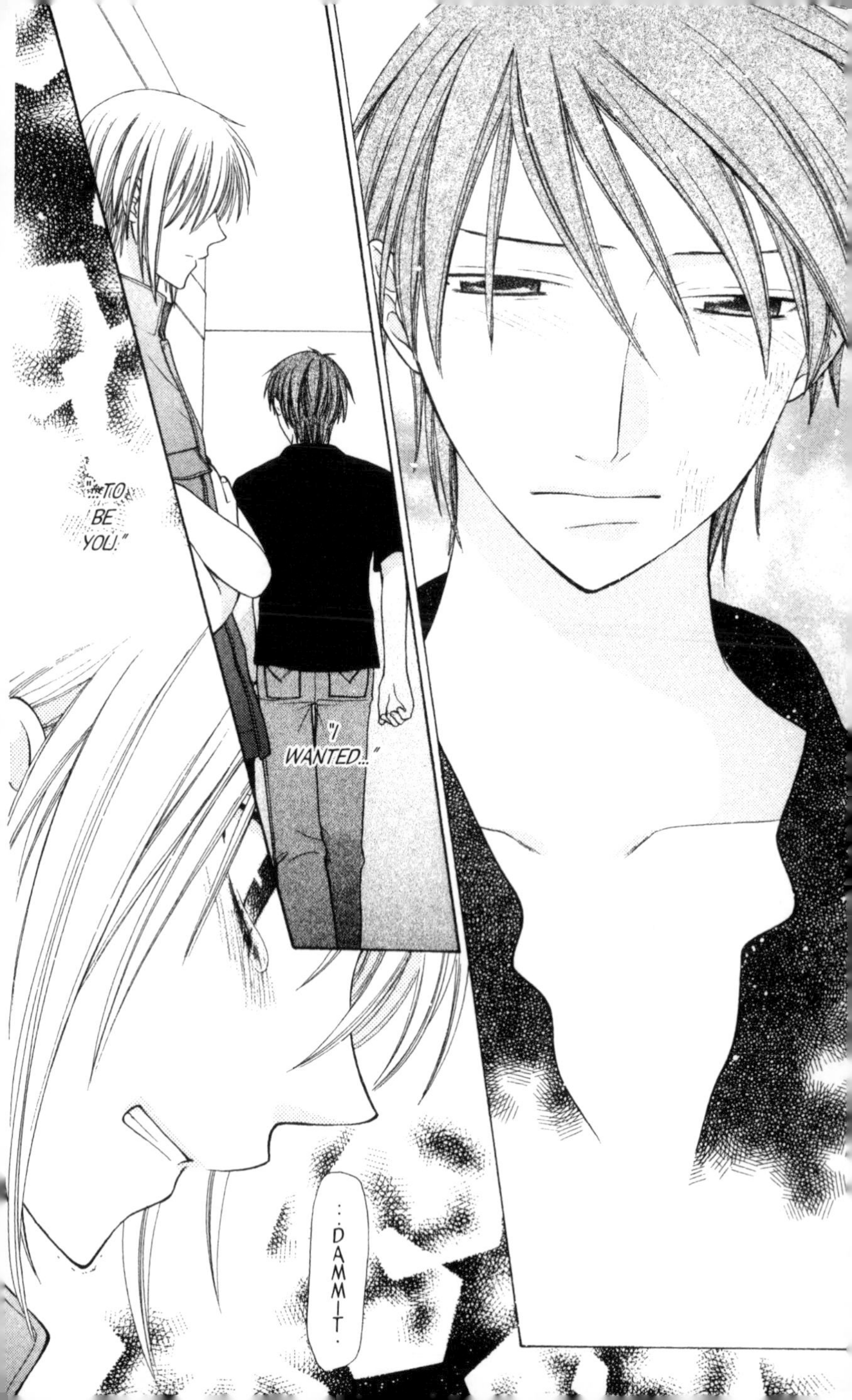
"I WANTED..."
"...TO BE YOU."
...DAMMIT.

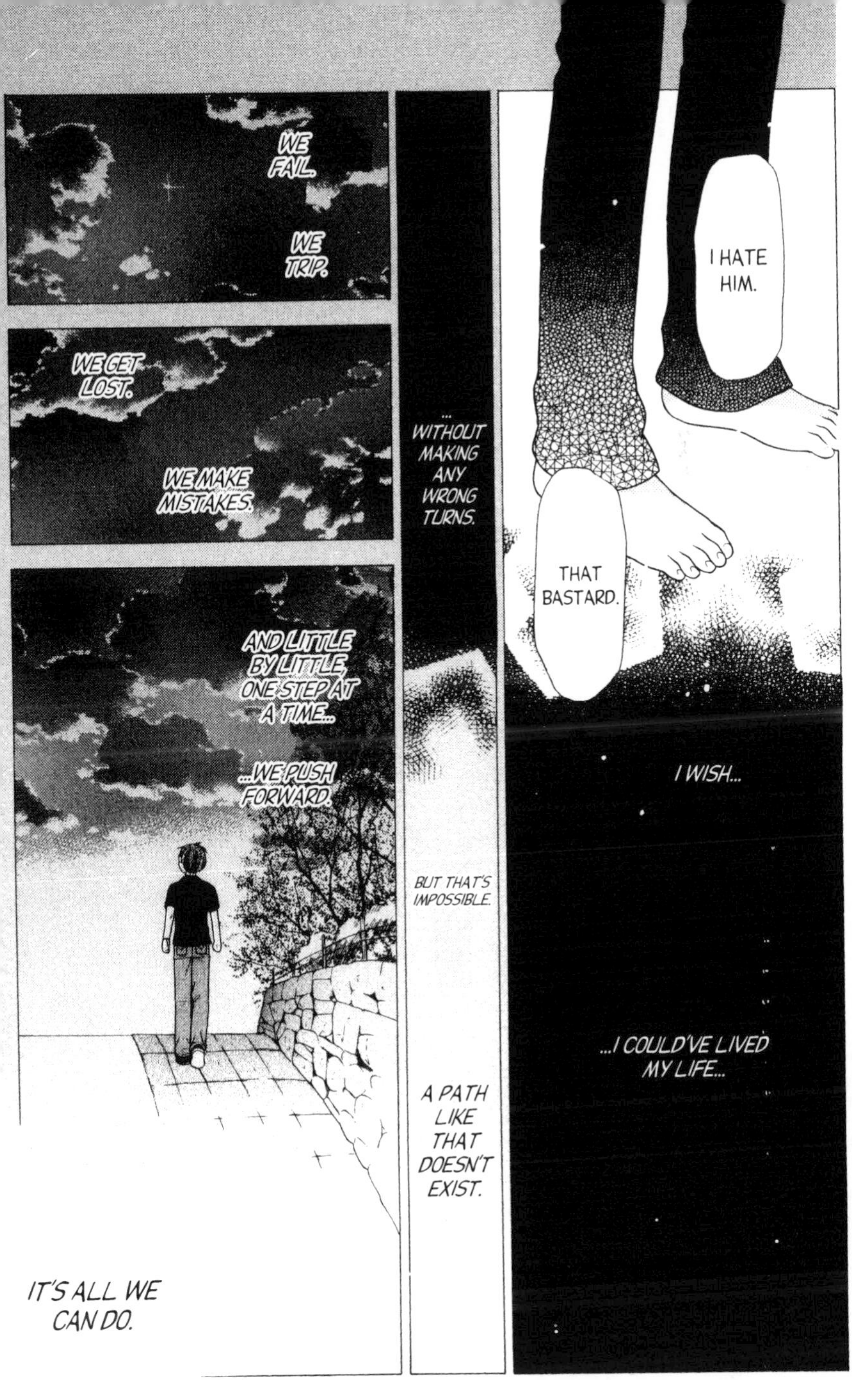
I HATE HIM.
THAT BASTARD.
I WISH...
...I COULD'VE LIVED MY LIFE...
...WITHOUT MAKING ANY WRONG TURNS.
BUT THAT'S IMPOSSIBLE.
A PATH LIKE THAT DOESN'T EXIST.
WE FAIL.
WE TRIP.
WE GET LOST.
WE MAKE MISTAKES.
AND LITTLE BY LITTLE, ONE STEP AT A TIME...
...WE PUSH FORWARD.
IT'S ALL WE CAN DO.

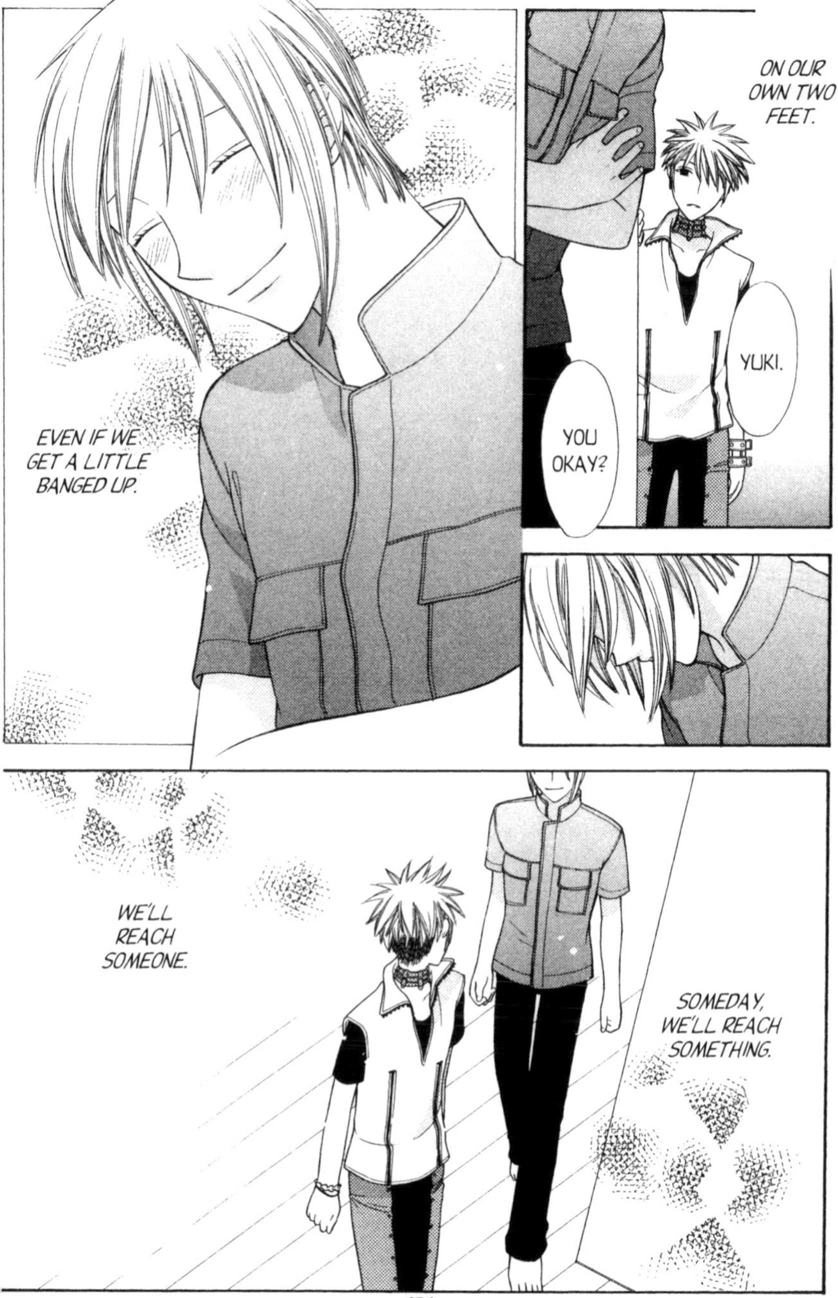
ON OUR OWN TWO FEET.
YUKI.
YOU OKAY?
EVEN IF WE GET A LITTLE BANGED UP.
SOMEDAY, WE'LL REACH SOMETHING.
WE'LL REACH SOMEONE.

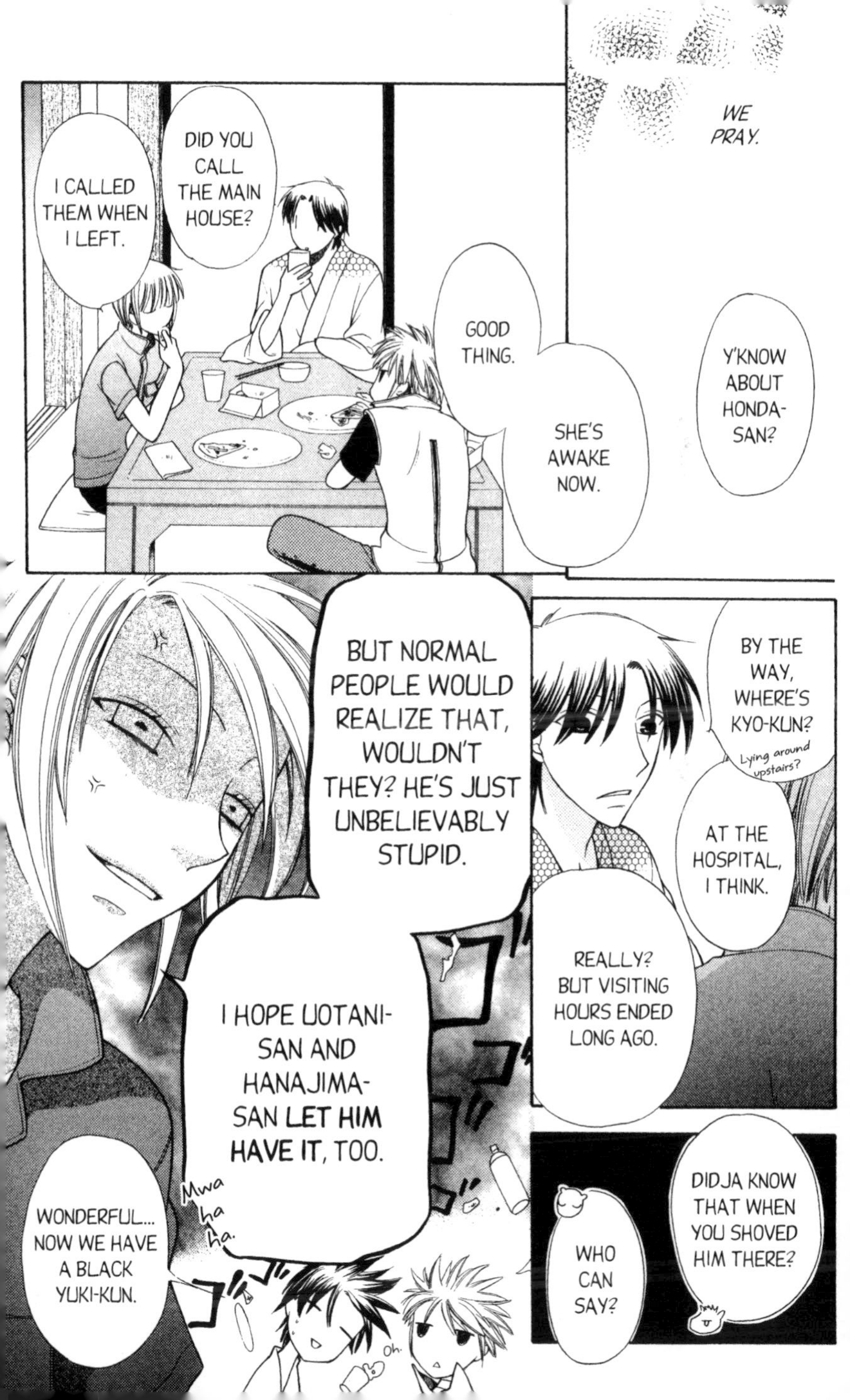
WE PRAY.
Y'KNOW ABOUT HONDA-SAN?
GOOD THING.
SHE'S AWAKE NOW.
DID YOU CALL THE MAIN HOUSE?
I CALLED THEM WHEN I LEFT.
BY THE WAY, WHERE'S KYO-KUN?
Lying around upstairs?
AT THE HOSPITAL, I THINK.
REALLY? BUT VISITING HOURS ENDED LONG AGO.
DIDJA KNOW THAT WHEN YOU SHOVED HIM THERE?
WHO CAN SAY?
BUT NORMAL PEOPLE WOULD REALIZE THAT, WOULDN'T THEY? HE'S JUST UNBELIEVABLY STUPID.
I HOPE UOTANI-SAN AND HANAJIMA-SAN **LET HIM HAVE IT**, TOO.
Mwa ha ha.
WONDERFUL... NOW WE HAVE A BLACK YUKI-KUN.
Oh.

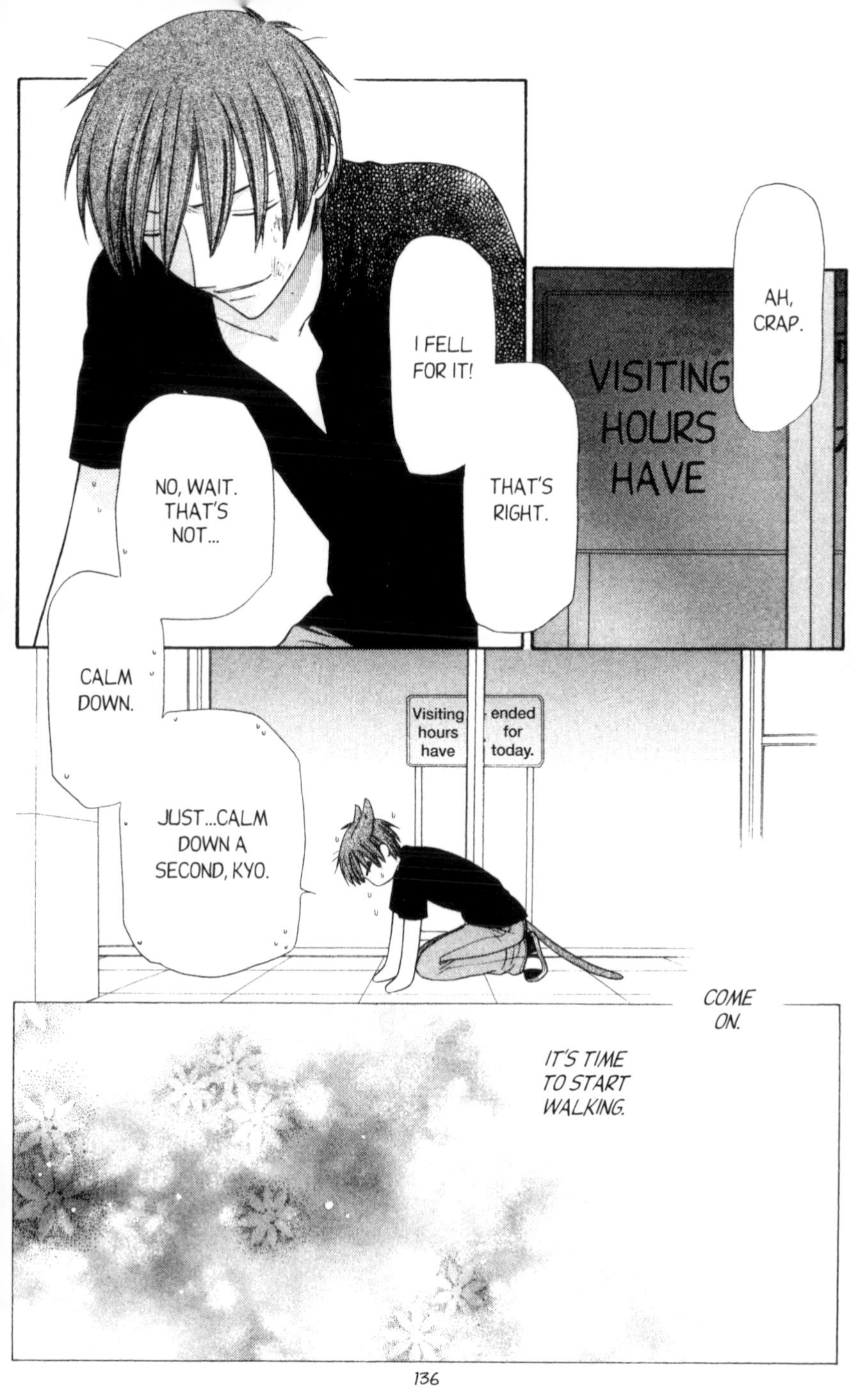
AH, CRAP.
VISITING HOURS HAVE
I FELL FOR IT!
THAT'S RIGHT.
NO, WAIT. THAT'S NOT...
CALM DOWN.
Visiting hours have ended for today.
JUST...CALM DOWN A SECOND, KYO.
COME ON.
IT'S TIME TO START WALKING.

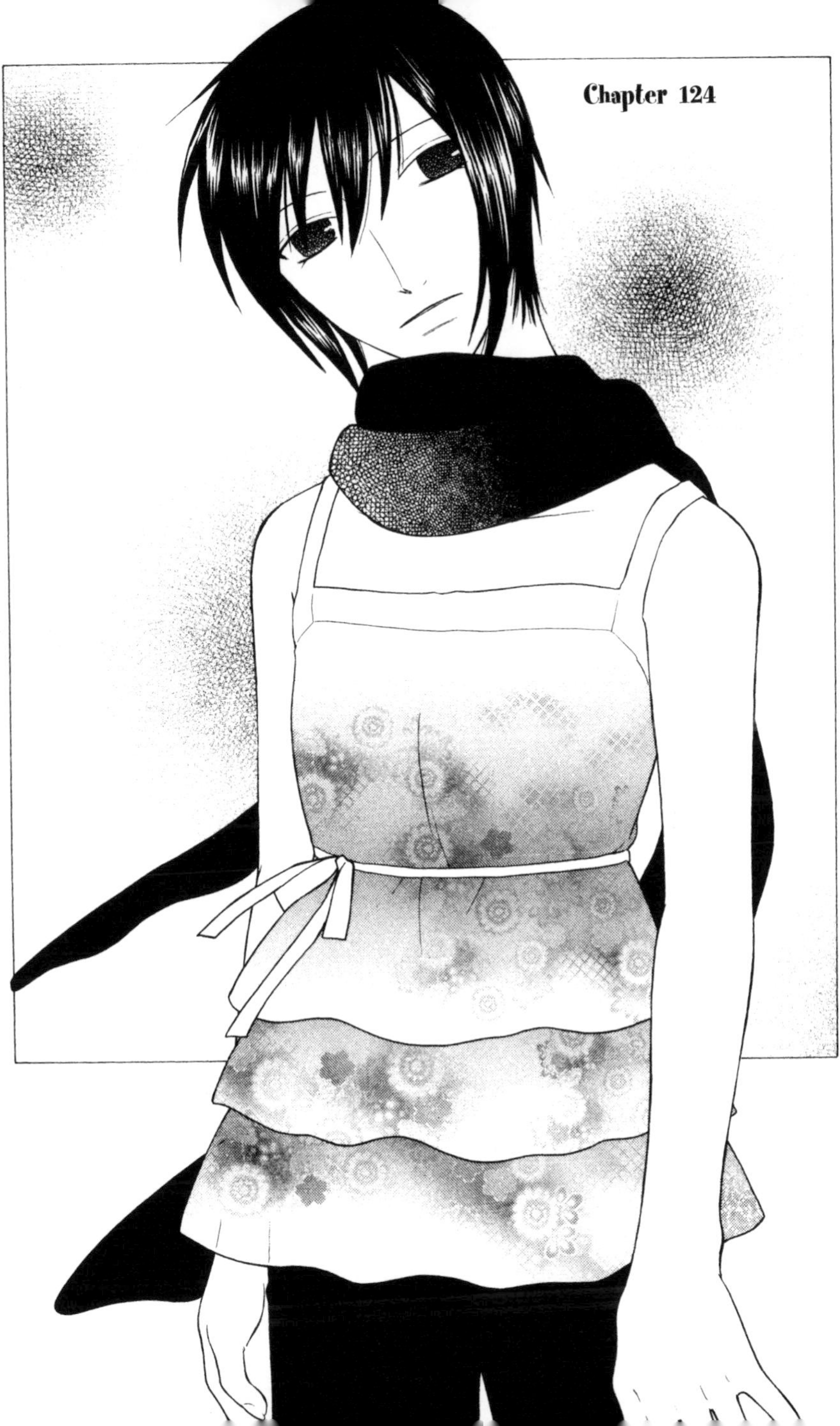
Chapter 124

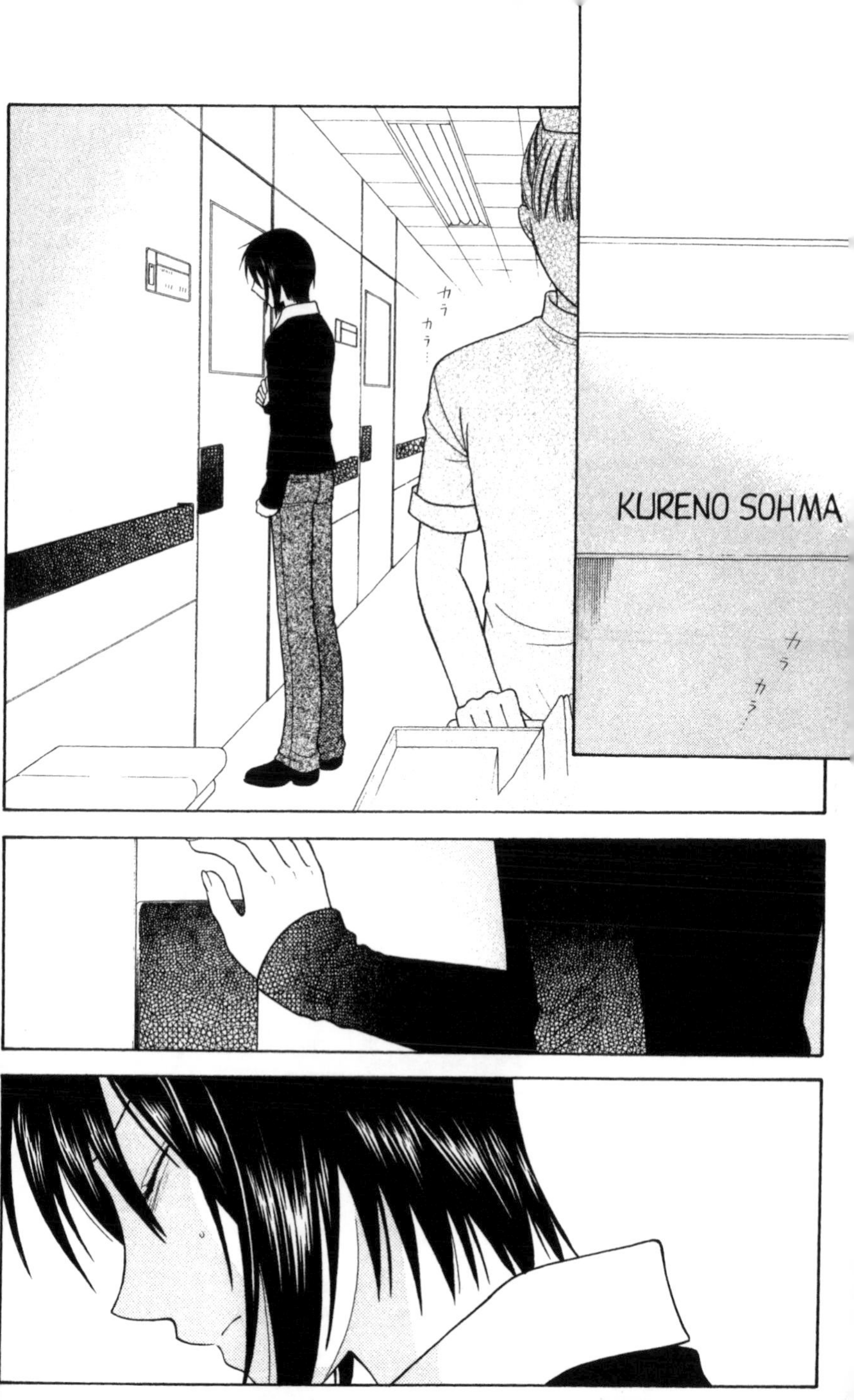
KURENO SOHMA
カラ カラ…
カラ カラ…

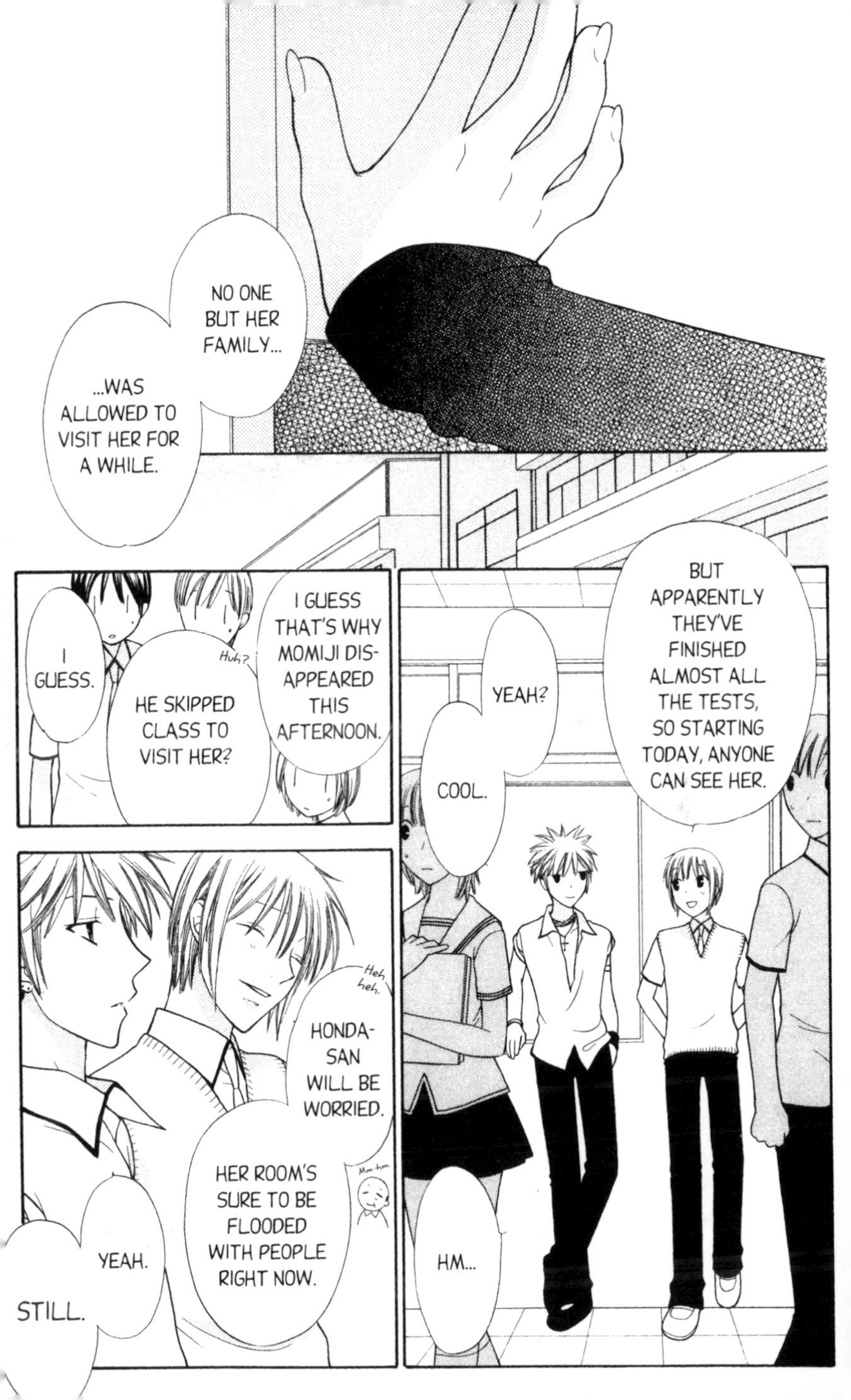
NO ONE BUT HER FAMILY...
...WAS ALLOWED TO VISIT HER FOR A WHILE.
BUT APPARENTLY THEY'VE FINISHED ALMOST ALL THE TESTS, SO STARTING TODAY, ANYONE CAN SEE HER.
YEAH?
COOL.
HM...
I GUESS THAT'S WHY MOMIJI DIS-APPEARED THIS AFTERNOON.
Huh?
HE SKIPPED CLASS TO VISIT HER?
I GUESS.
Heh heh.
HONDA-SAN WILL BE WORRIED.
HER ROOM'S SURE TO BE FLOODED WITH PEOPLE RIGHT NOW.
Mm-hm.
YEAH.
STILL.

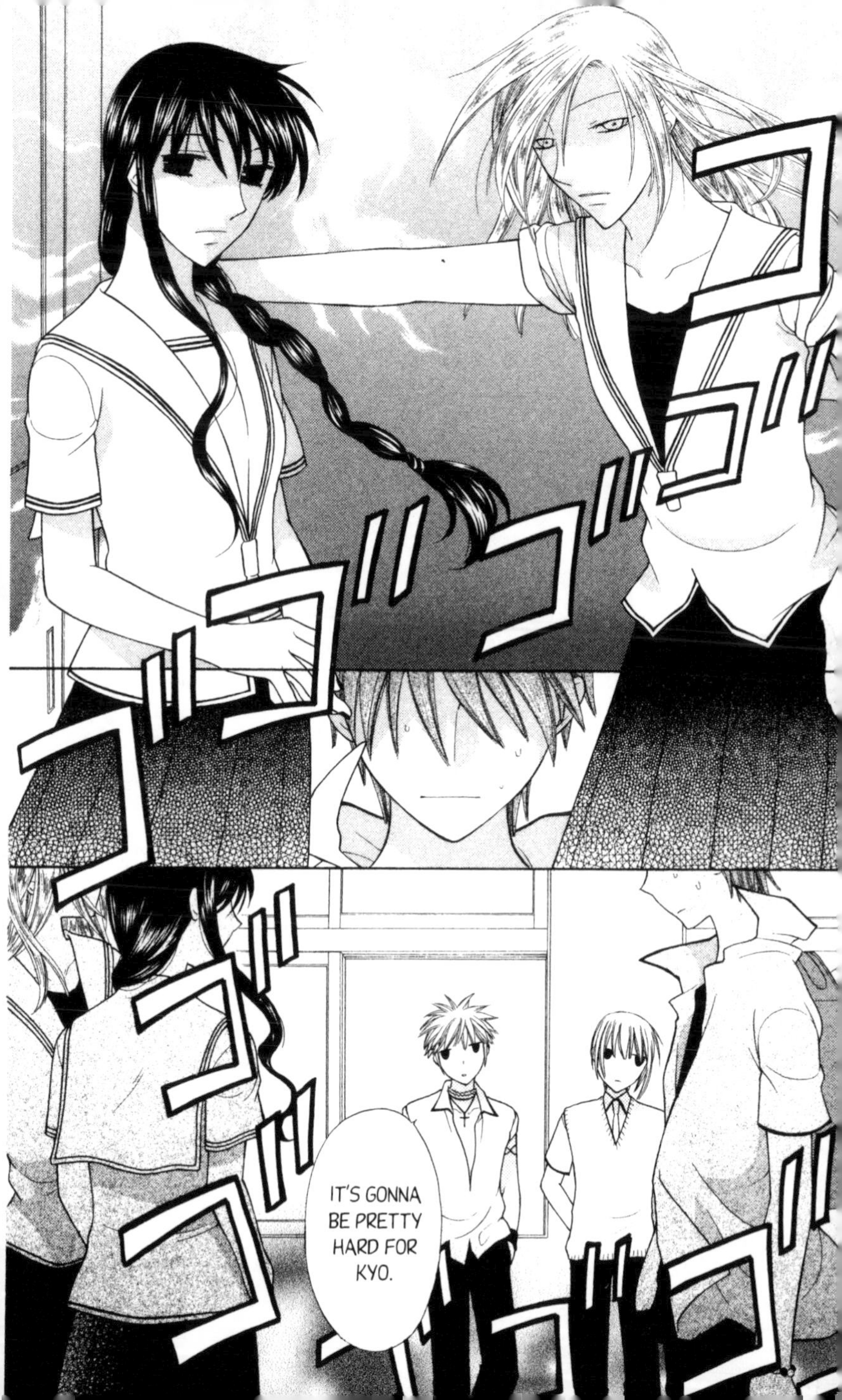
IT'S GONNA BE PRETTY HARD FOR KYO.

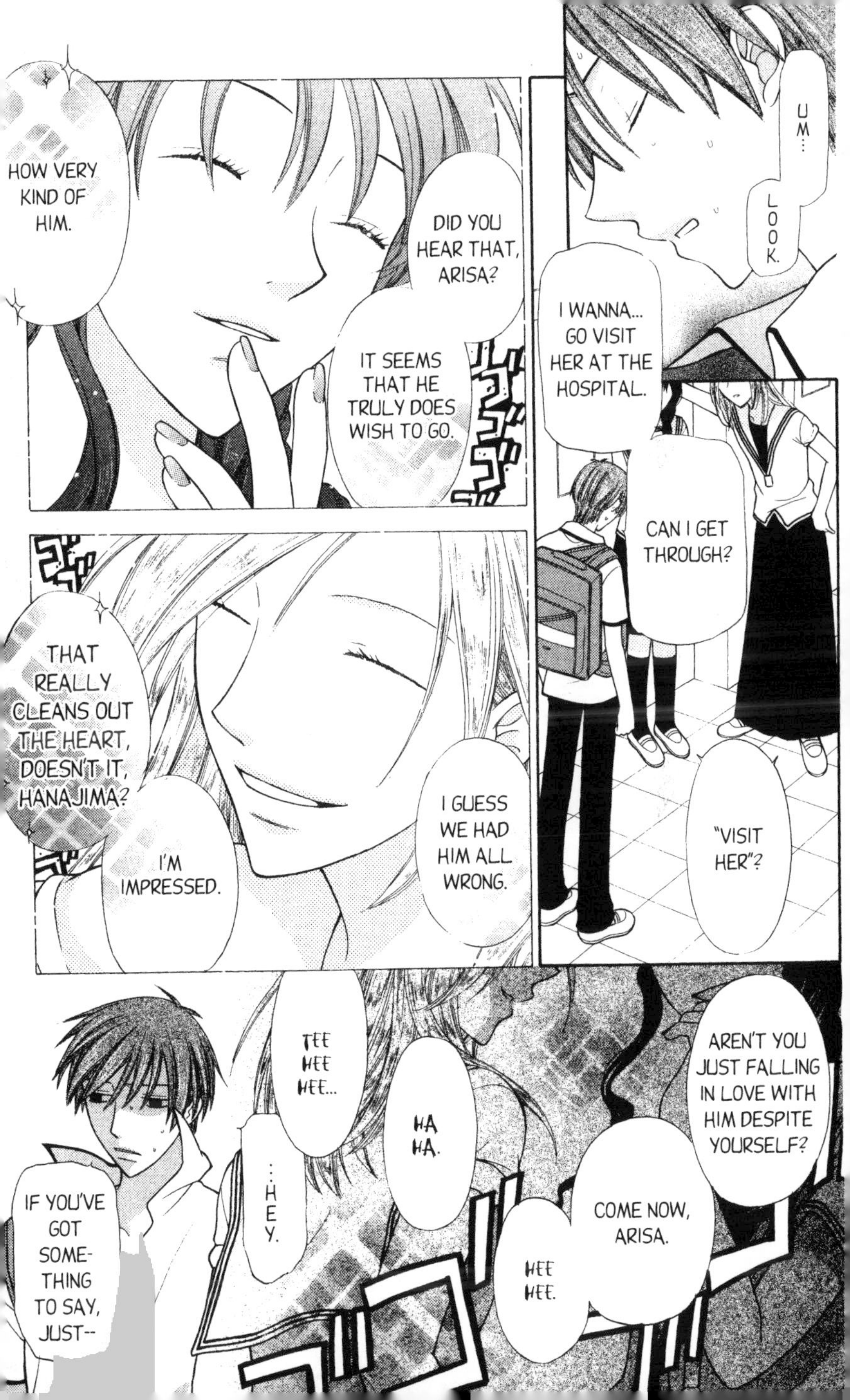
UM... LOOK.
I WANNA... GO VISIT HER AT THE HOSPITAL.
CAN I GET THROUGH?
"VISIT HER"?
DID YOU HEAR THAT, ARISA?
IT SEEMS THAT HE TRULY DOES WISH TO GO.
HOW VERY KIND OF HIM.
I GUESS WE HAD HIM ALL WRONG.
I'M IMPRESSED.
THAT REALLY CLEANS OUT THE HEART, DOESN'T IT, HANAJIMA?
AREN'T YOU JUST FALLING IN LOVE WITH HIM DESPITE YOURSELF?
COME NOW, ARISA.
HEE HEE.
HA HA.
TEE HEE HEE...
...HEY.
IF YOU'VE GOT SOME-THING TO SAY, JUST--

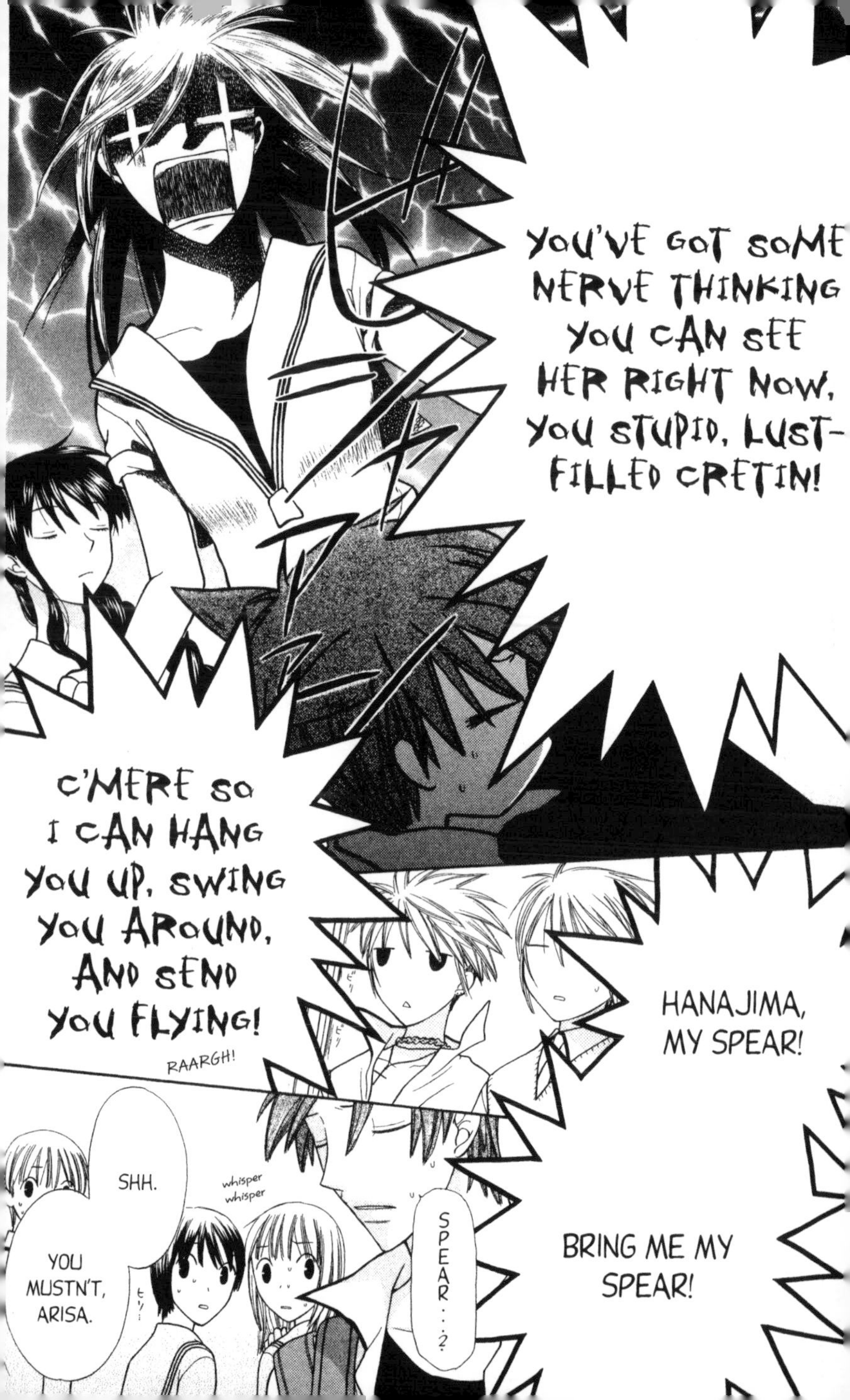
YOU'VE GOT SOME NERVE THINKING YOU CAN SEE HER RIGHT NOW, YOU STUPID, LUST-FILLED CRETIN!
C'MERE SO I CAN HANG YOU UP, SWING YOU AROUND, AND SEND YOU FLYING!
HANAJIMA, MY SPEAR!
RAARGH!
BRING ME MY SPEAR!
SPEAR...?
whisper whisper
SHH.
YOU MUSTN'T, ARISA.

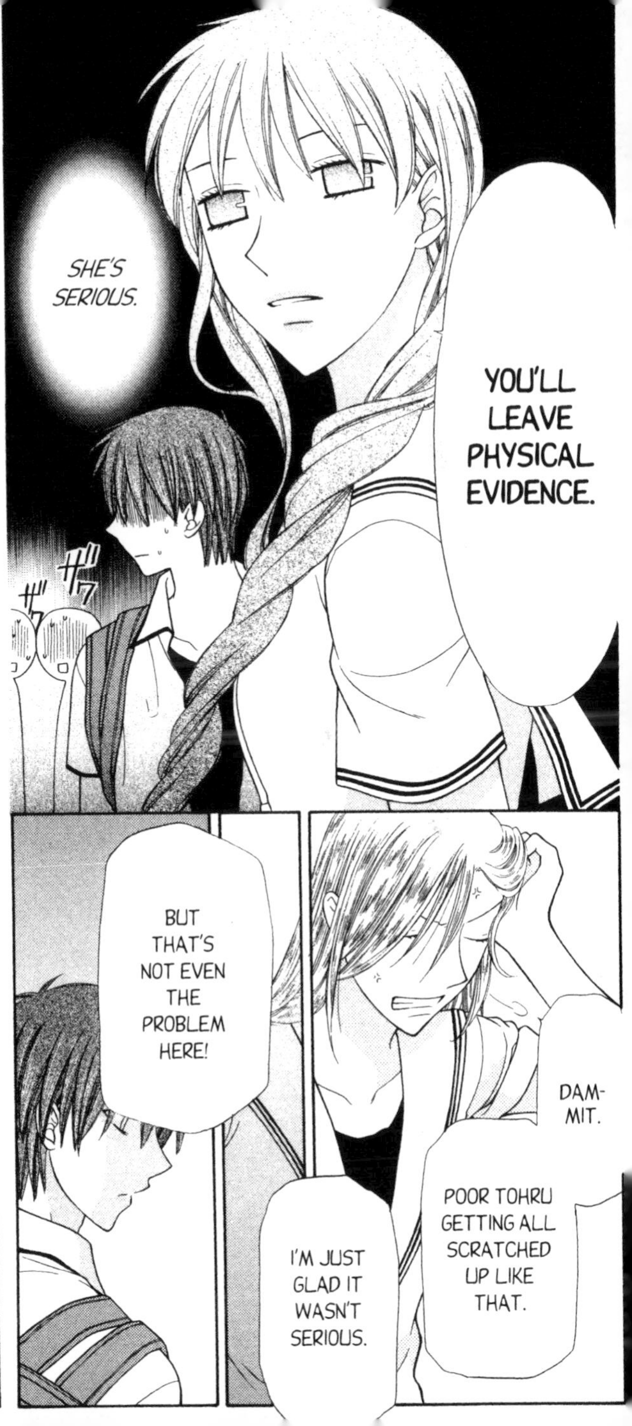
YOU'LL LEAVE PHYSICAL EVIDENCE.
SHE'S SERIOUS.
DAM-MIT.
POOR TOHRU GETTING ALL SCRATCHED UP LIKE THAT.
I'M JUST GLAD IT WASN'T SERIOUS.
BUT THAT'S NOT EVEN THE PROBLEM HERE!

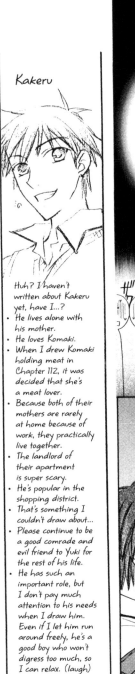

Kakeru

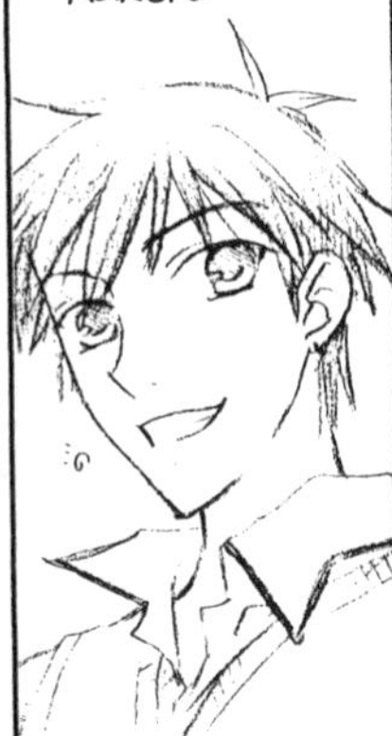

Huh? I haven't written about Kakeru yet, have I...?

- He lives alone with his mother.
- He loves Komaki.
- When I drew Komaki holding meat in Chapter 112, it was decided that she's a meat lover.
- Because both of their mothers are rarely at home because of work, they practically live together.
- The landlord of their apartment is super scary.
- He's popular in the shopping district.
- That's something I couldn't draw about...
- Please continue to be a good comrade and evil friend to Yuki for the rest of his life.
- He has such an important role, but I don't pay much attention to his needs when I draw him. Even if I let him run around freely, he's a good boy who won't digress too much, so I can relax. (laugh)

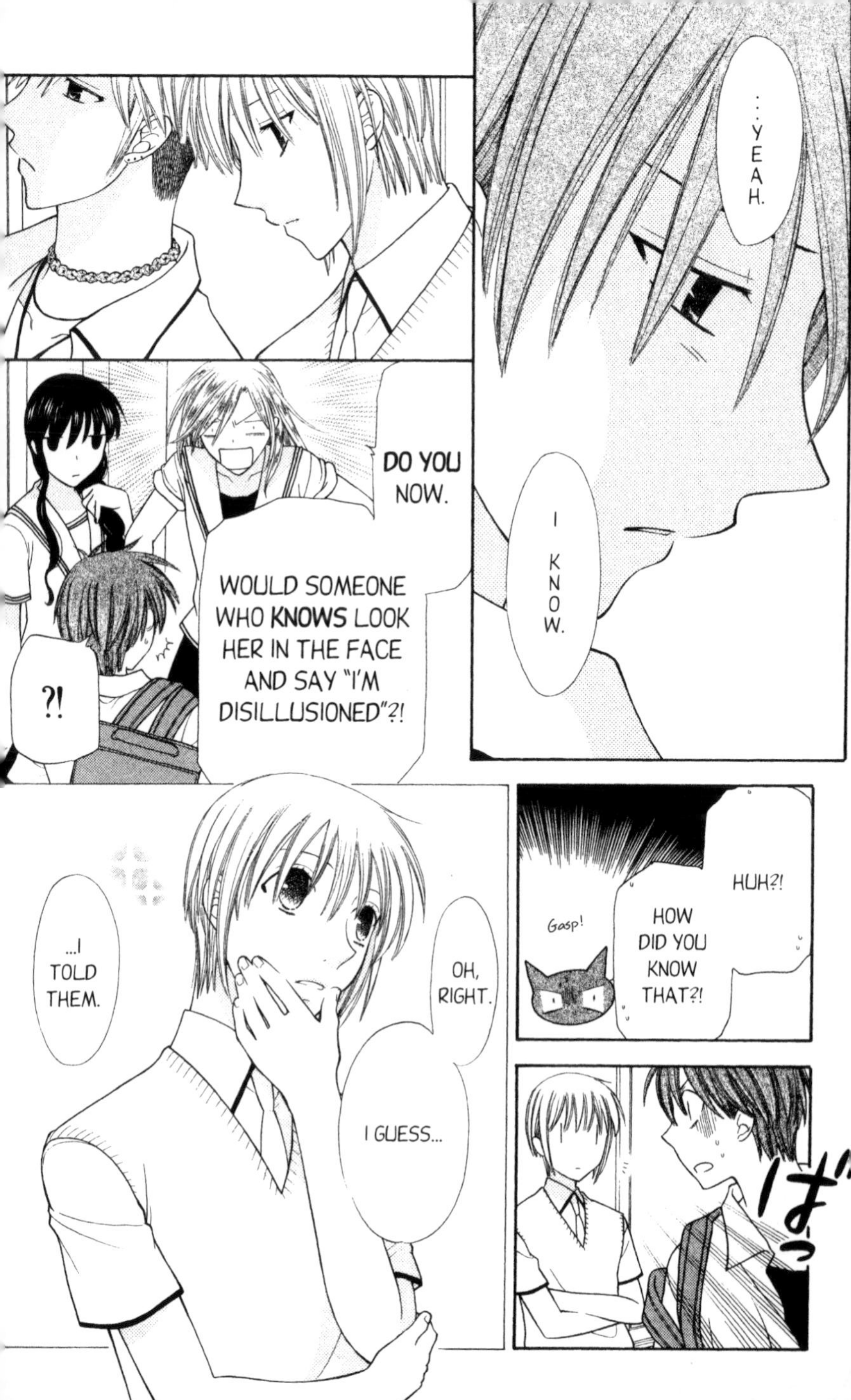
...YEAH.
I KNOW.
DO YOU NOW.
WOULD SOMEONE WHO KNOWS LOOK HER IN THE FACE AND SAY "I'M DISILLUSIONED"?!
?!
HUH?!
HOW DID YOU KNOW THAT?!
Gasp!
ばっ
OH, RIGHT.
I GUESS...
...I TOLD THEM.

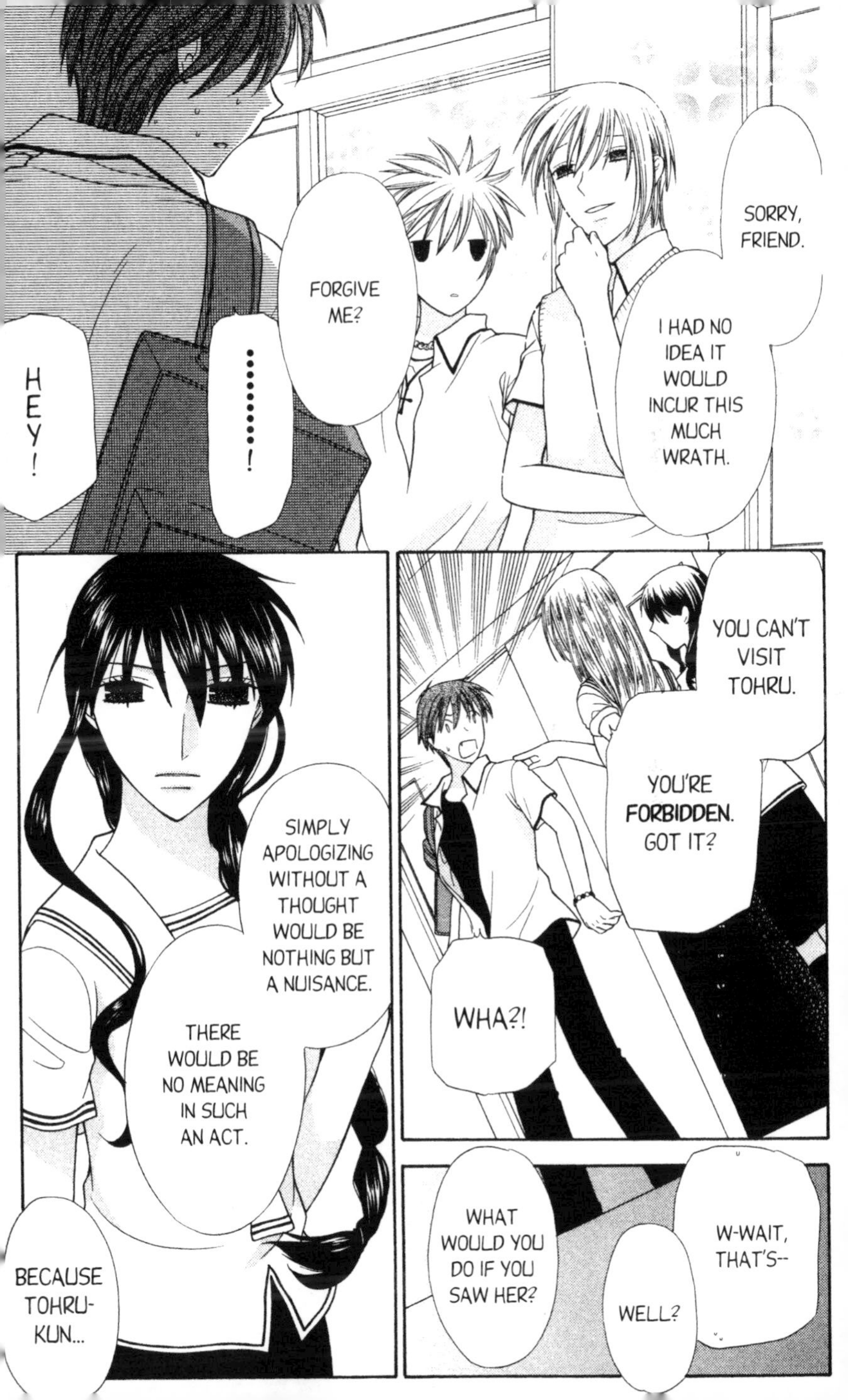
SORRY, FRIEND.
I HAD NO IDEA IT WOULD INCUR THIS MUCH WRATH.
FORGIVE ME?
..........!
HEY!
YOU CAN'T VISIT TOHRU.
YOU'RE **FORBIDDEN**. GOT IT?
WHA?!
W-WAIT, THAT'S--
WELL?
WHAT WOULD YOU DO IF YOU SAW HER?
SIMPLY APOLOGIZING WITHOUT A THOUGHT WOULD BE NOTHING BUT A NUISANCE.
THERE WOULD BE NO MEANING IN SUCH AN ACT.
BECAUSE TOHRU-KUN...

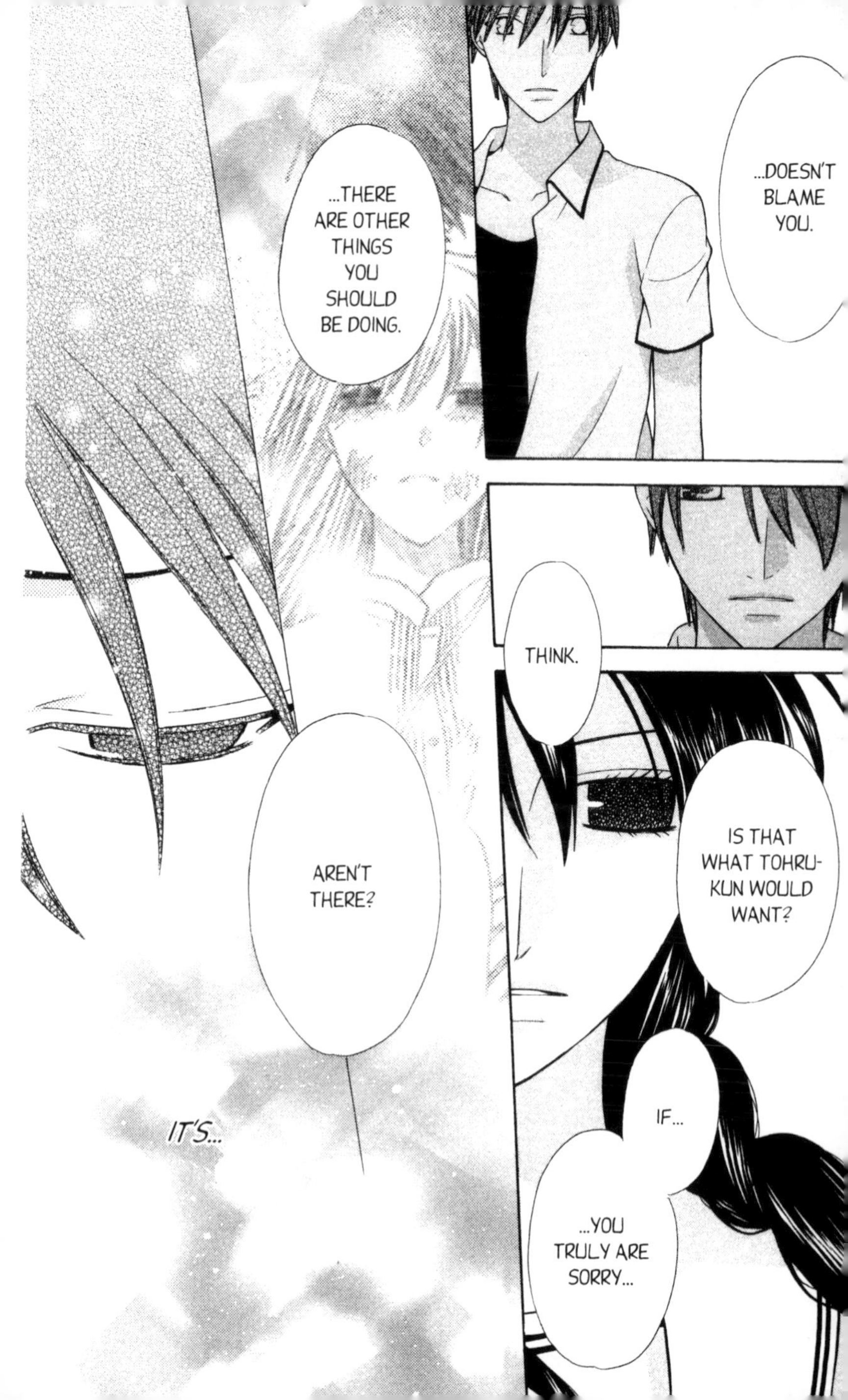
...DOESN'T BLAME YOU.
THINK.
IS THAT WHAT TOHRU-KUN WOULD WANT?
IF...
...YOU TRULY ARE SORRY...
...THERE ARE OTHER THINGS YOU SHOULD BE DOING.
AREN'T THERE?
IT'S...

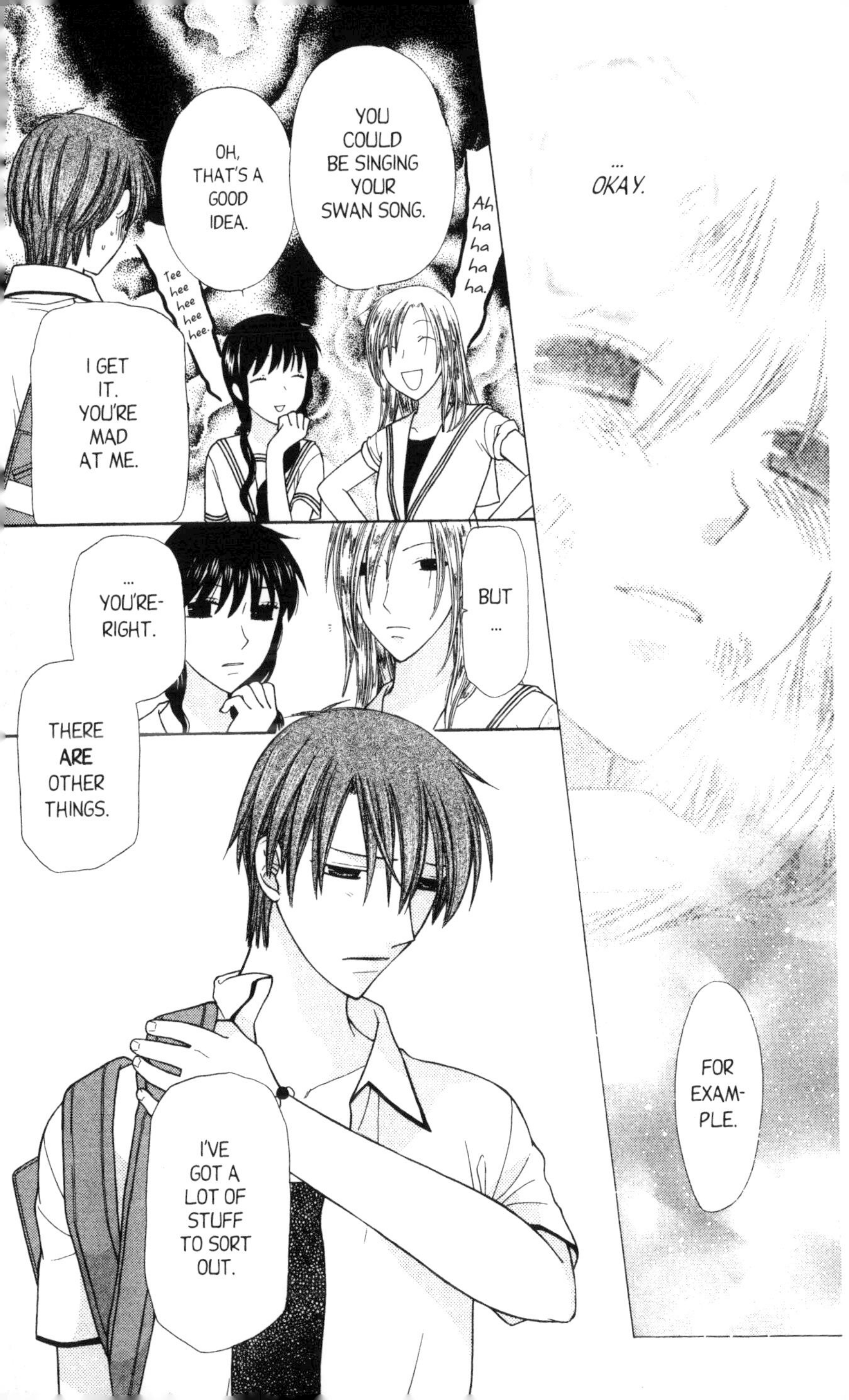

... OKAY.
FOR EXAMPLE.
YOU COULD BE SINGING YOUR SWAN SONG.
Ah ha ha ha ha.
OH, THAT'S A GOOD IDEA.
Tee hee hee hee hee.
I GET IT. YOU'RE MAD AT ME.
BUT ...
... YOU'RE-RIGHT.
THERE **ARE** OTHER THINGS.
I'VE GOT A LOT OF STUFF TO SORT OUT.

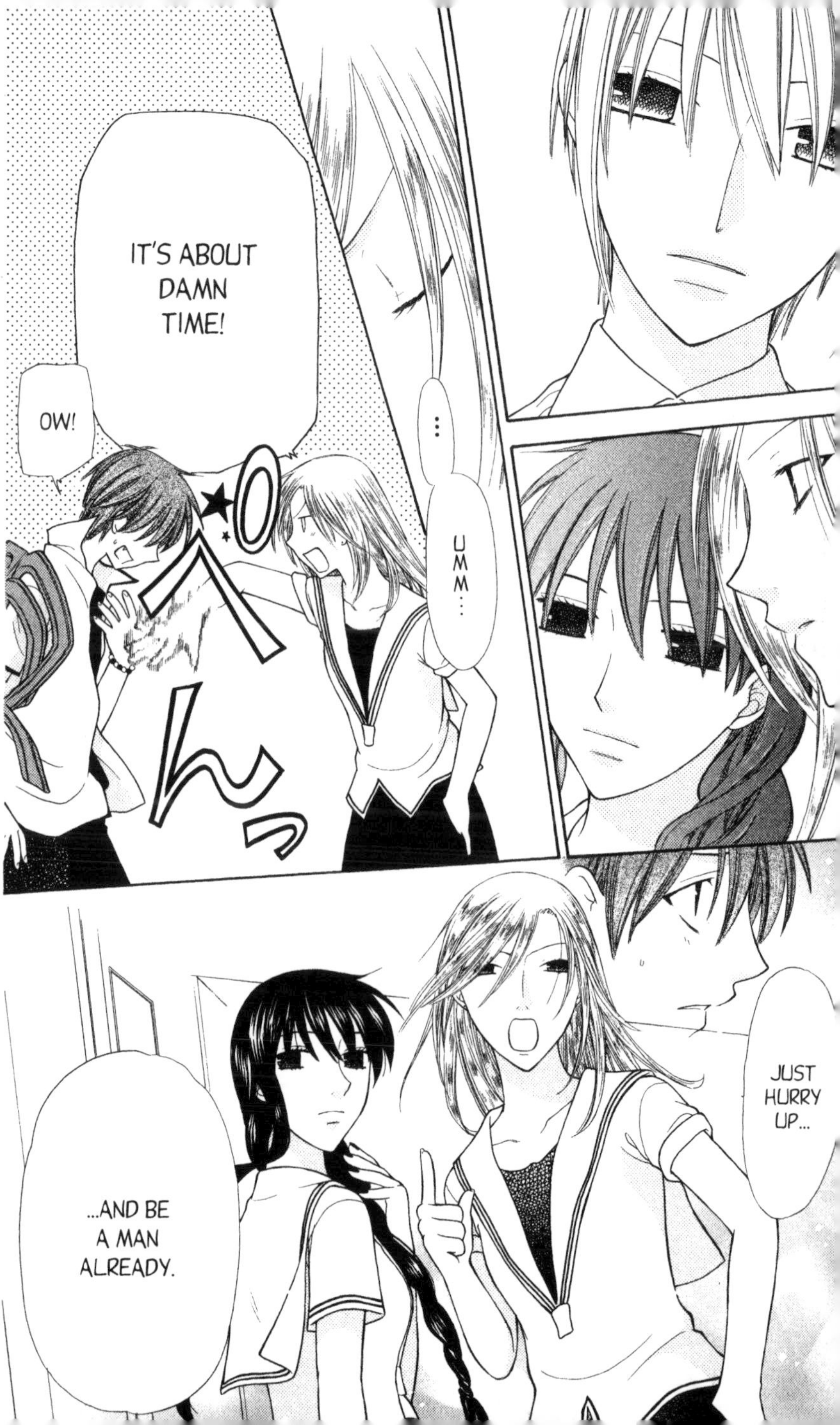
...
UMM...
IT'S ABOUT DAMN TIME!
OW!
JUST HURRY UP...
...AND BE A MAN ALREADY.

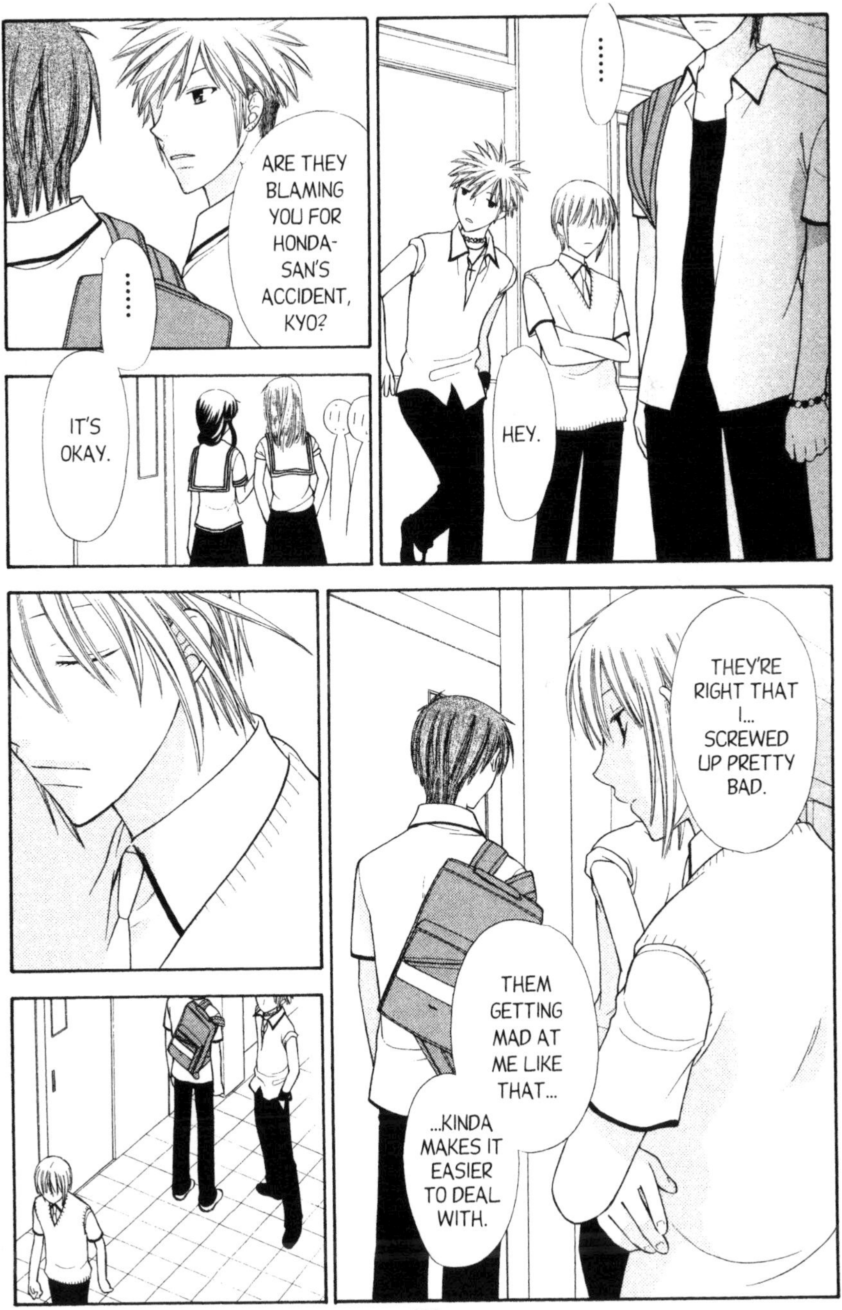
......
HEY.
ARE THEY BLAMING YOU FOR HONDA-SAN'S ACCIDENT, KYO?
......
IT'S OKAY.
THEY'RE RIGHT THAT I... SCREWED UP PRETTY BAD.
THEM GETTING MAD AT ME LIKE THAT...
...KINDA MAKES IT EASIER TO DEAL WITH.

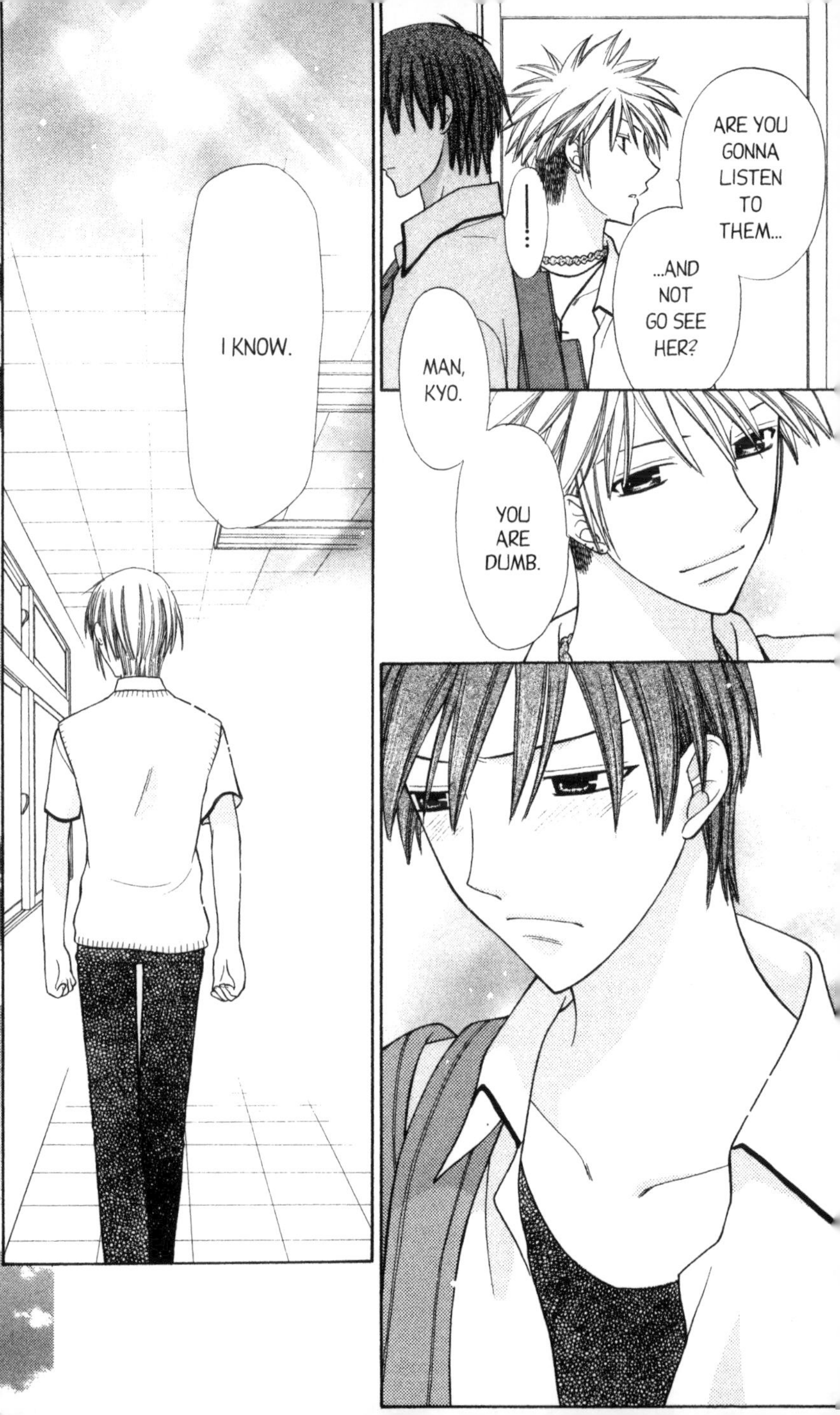
ARE YOU GONNA LISTEN TO THEM...
...AND NOT GO SEE HER?
!...
MAN, KYO.
YOU ARE DUMB.
I KNOW.

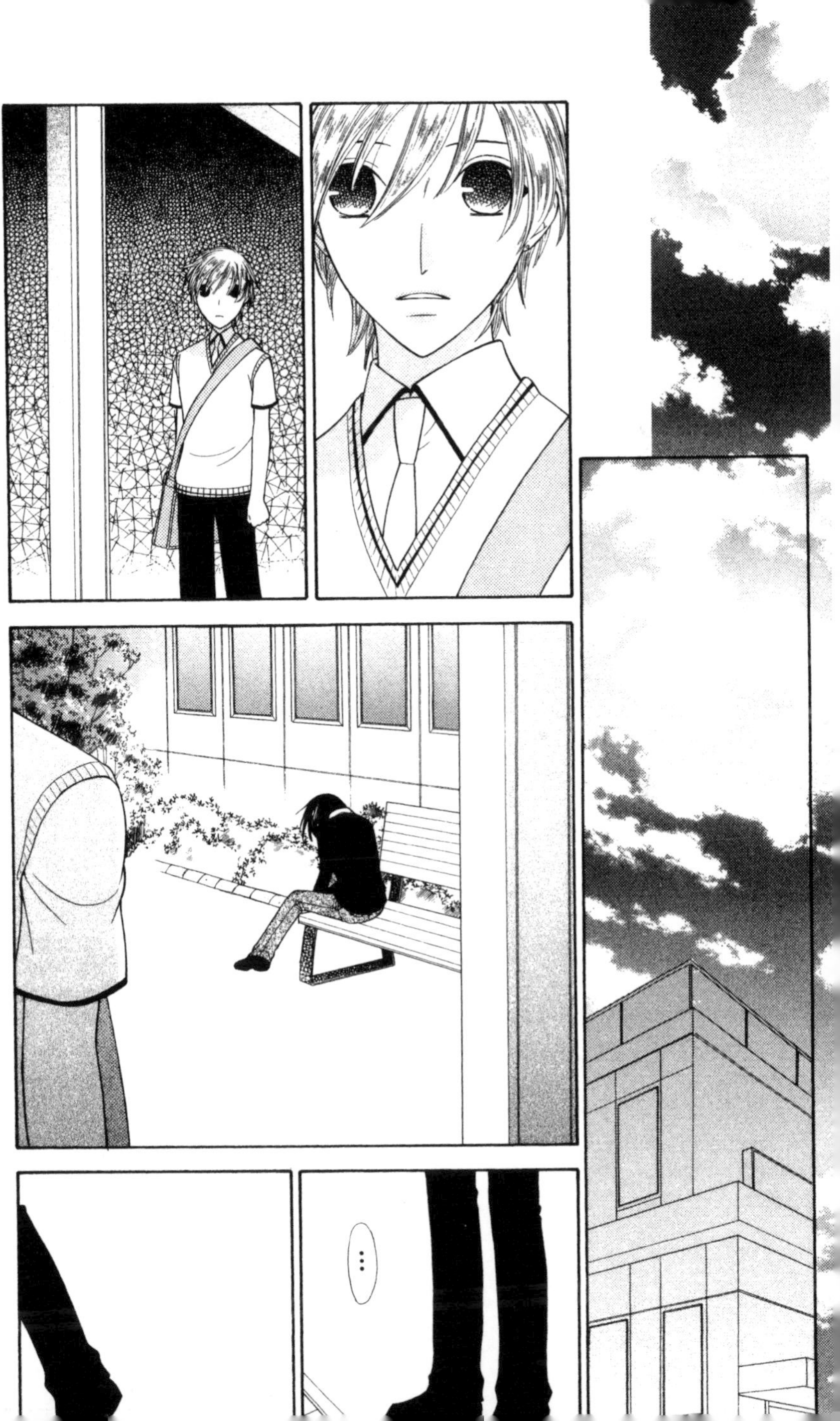
…

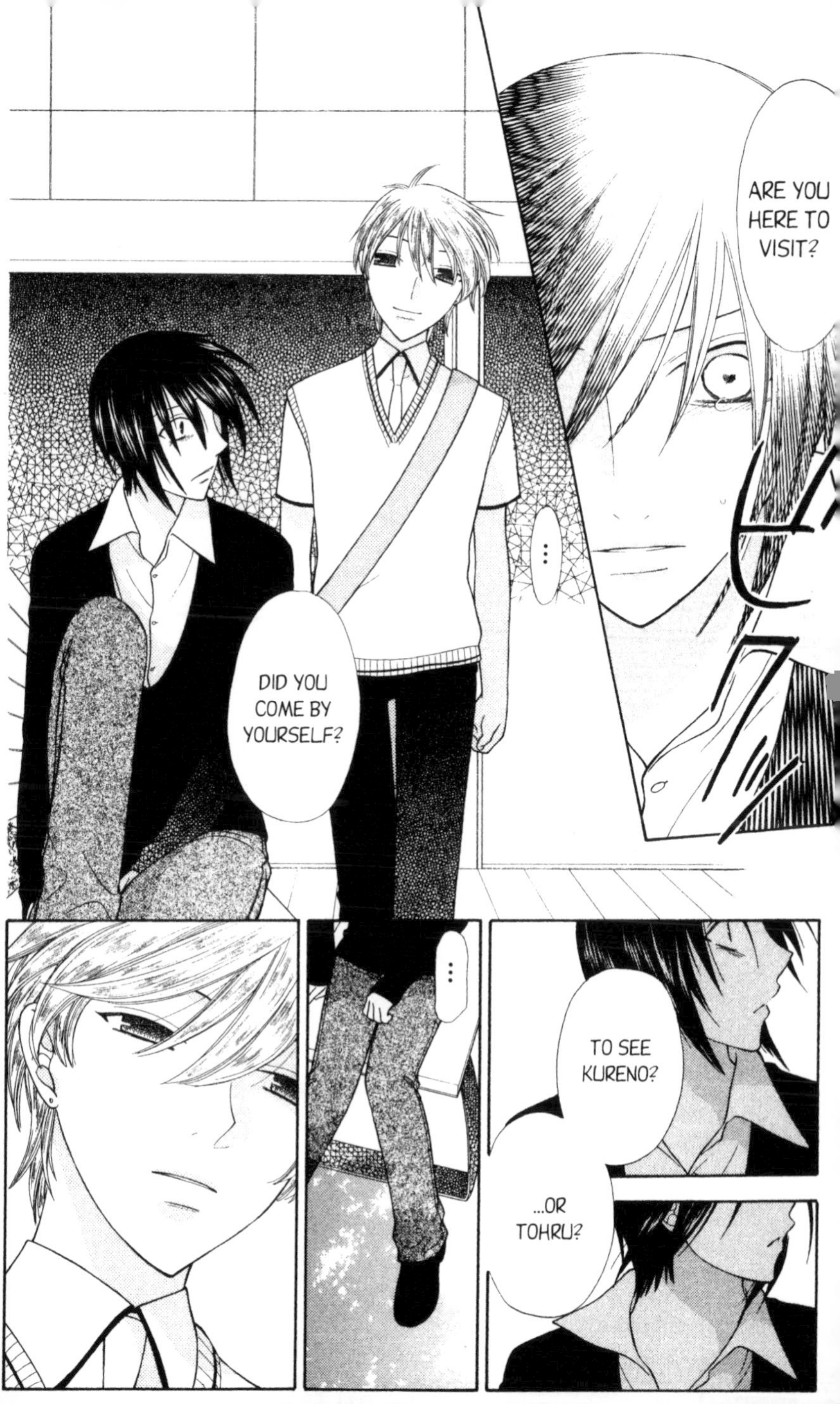
ARE YOU HERE TO VISIT?
...
DID YOU COME BY YOURSELF?
TO SEE KURENO?
...OR TOHRU?
...

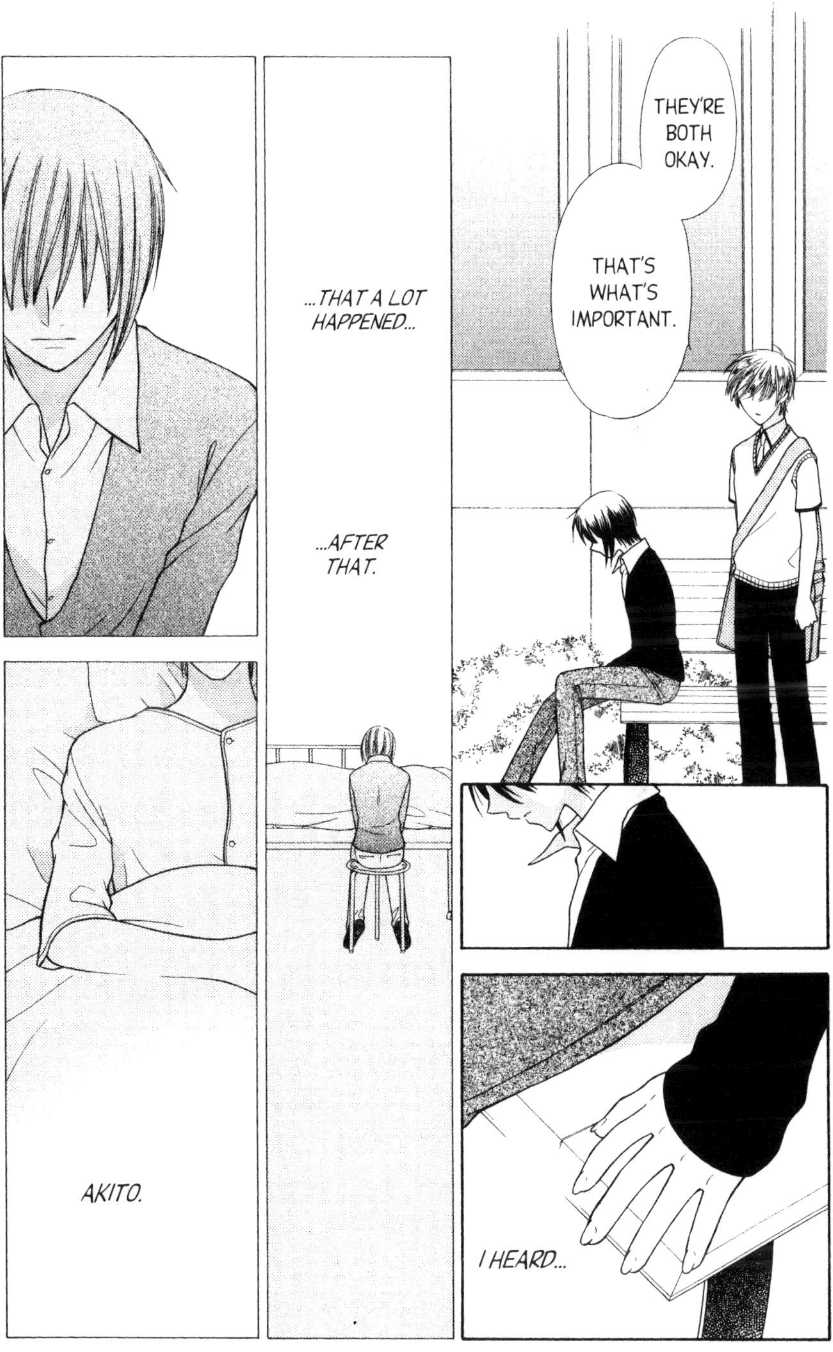
THEY'RE BOTH OKAY.
THAT'S WHAT'S IMPORTANT.
I HEARD...
...THAT A LOT HAPPENED...
...AFTER THAT.
AKITO.

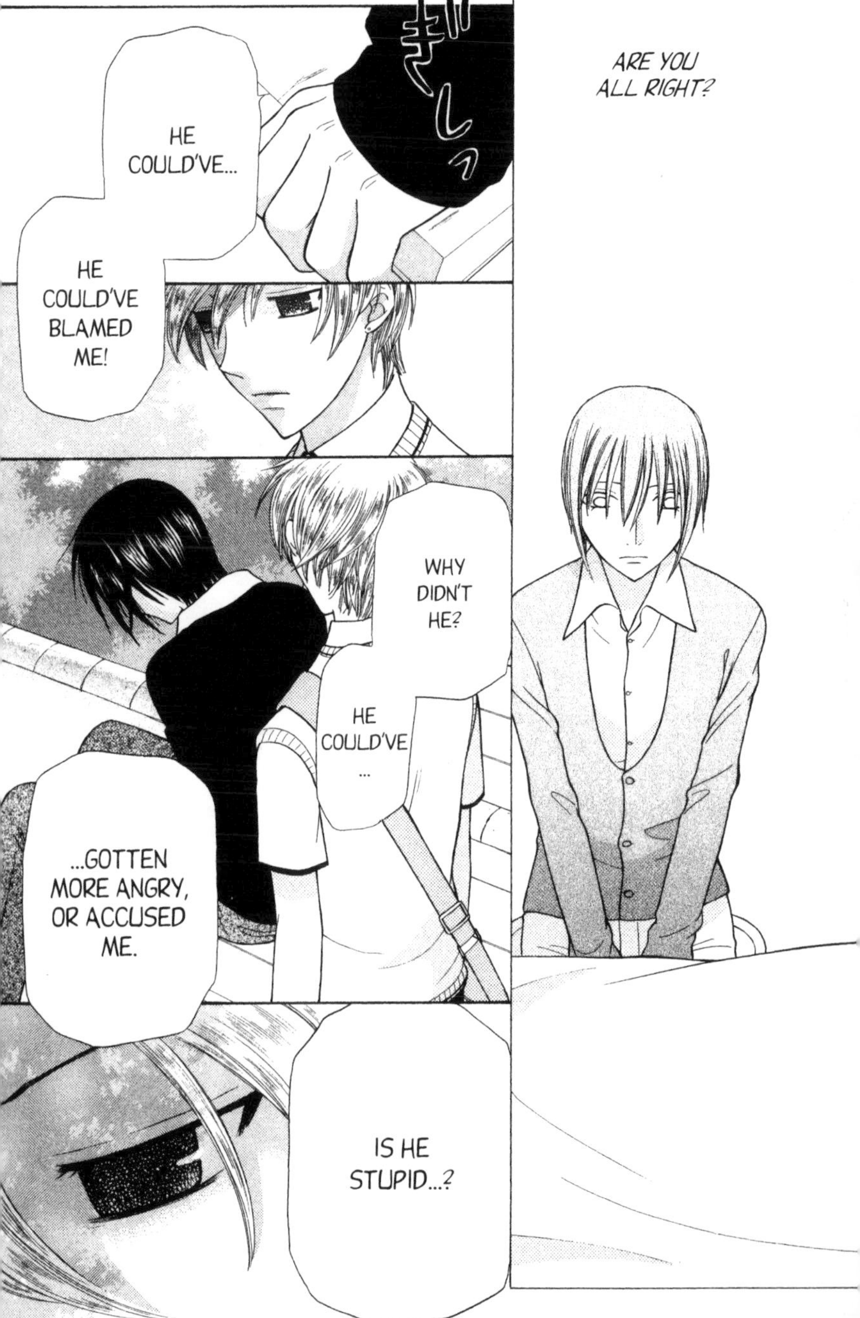
ARE YOU ALL RIGHT?
ぎしっ
HE COULD'VE...
HE COULD'VE BLAMED ME!
WHY DIDN'T HE?
HE COULD'VE ...
...GOTTEN MORE ANGRY, OR ACCUSED ME.
IS HE STUPID...?

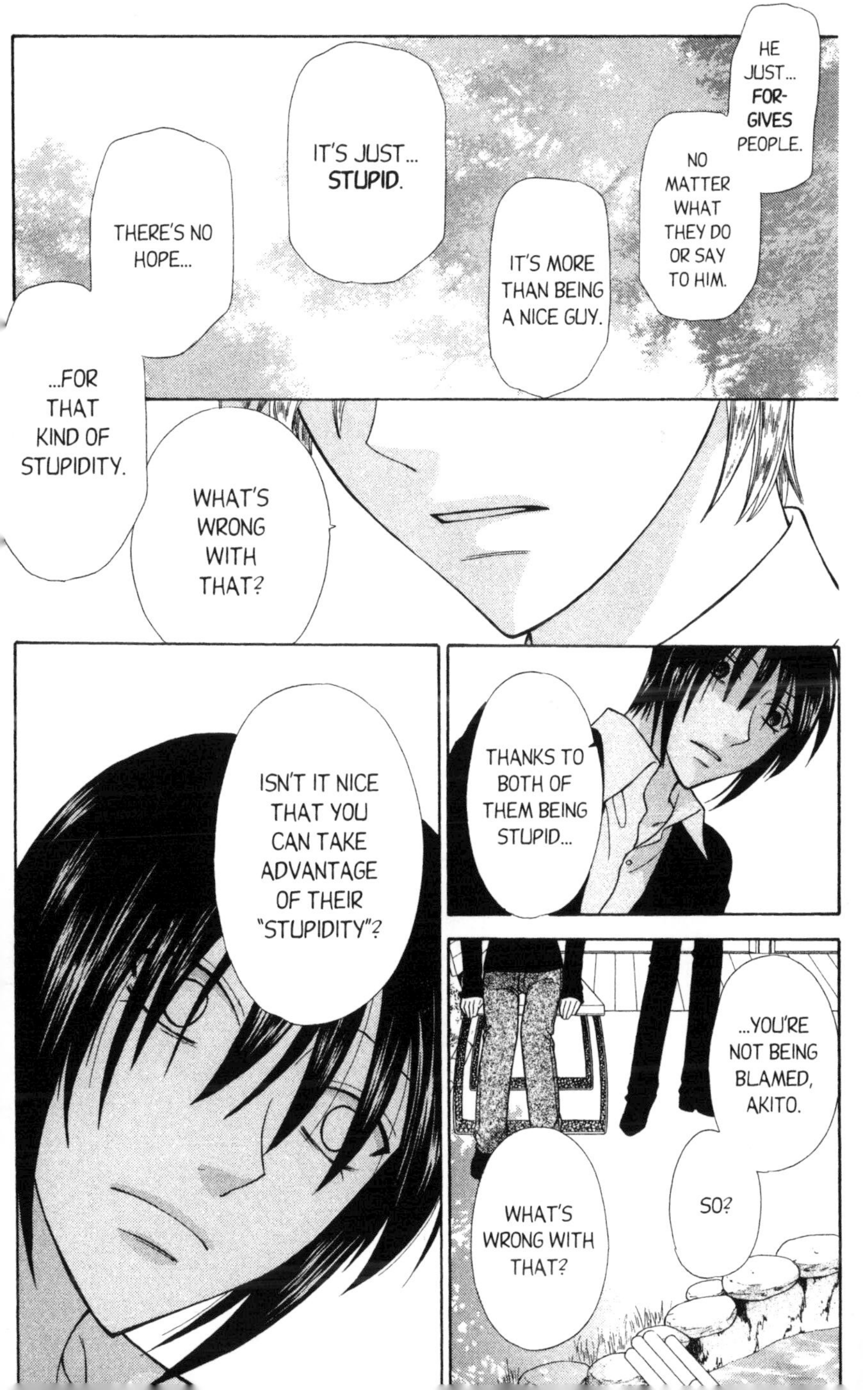
HE JUST... **FOR-GIVES** PEOPLE.
NO MATTER WHAT THEY DO OR SAY TO HIM.
IT'S MORE THAN BEING A NICE GUY.
IT'S JUST... **STUPID**.
THERE'S NO HOPE...
...FOR THAT KIND OF STUPIDITY.
WHAT'S WRONG WITH THAT?
THANKS TO BOTH OF THEM BEING STUPID...
...YOU'RE NOT BEING BLAMED, AKITO.
SO?
WHAT'S WRONG WITH THAT?
ISN'T IT NICE THAT YOU CAN TAKE ADVANTAGE OF THEIR "STUPIDITY"?

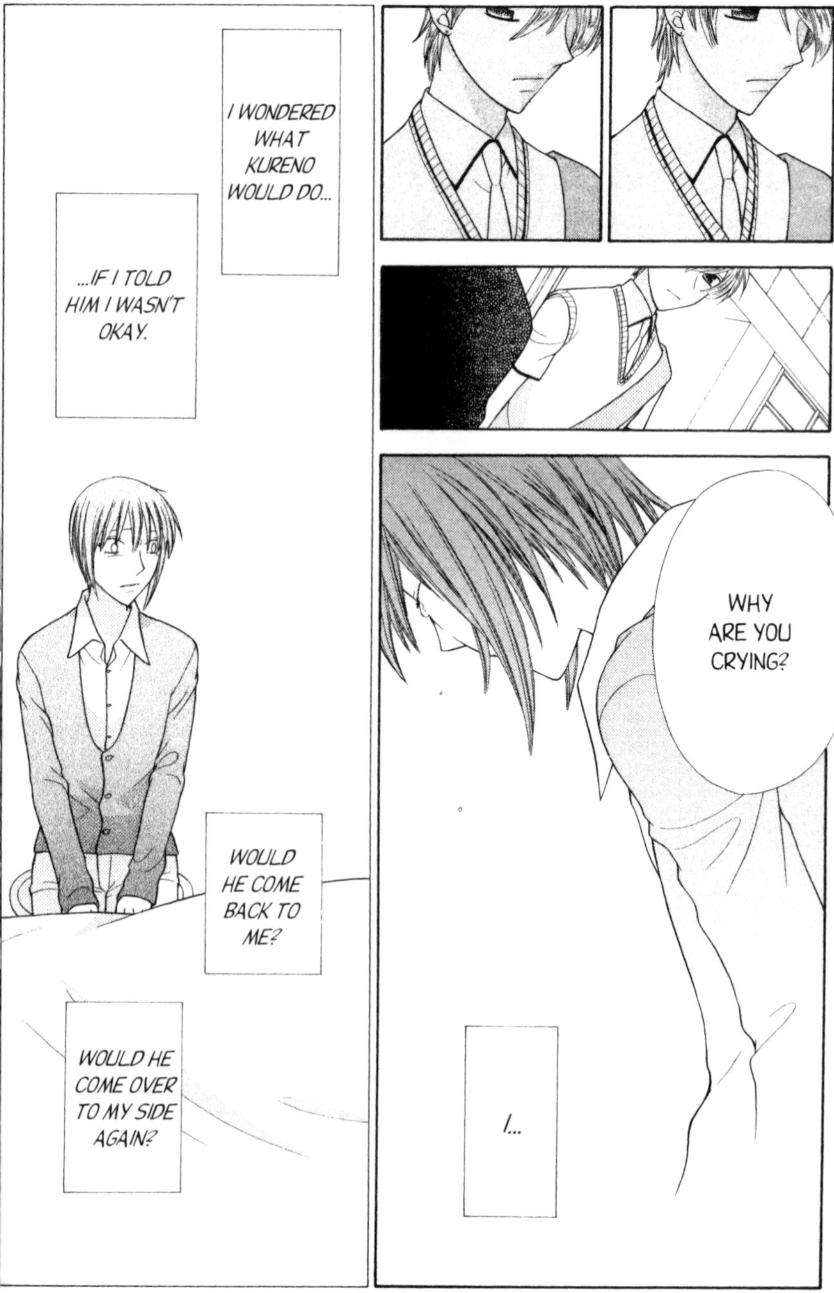
WHY ARE YOU CRYING?
I...
I WONDERED WHAT KURENO WOULD DO...
...IF I TOLD HIM I WASN'T OKAY.
WOULD HE COME BACK TO ME?
WOULD HE COME OVER TO MY SIDE AGAIN?

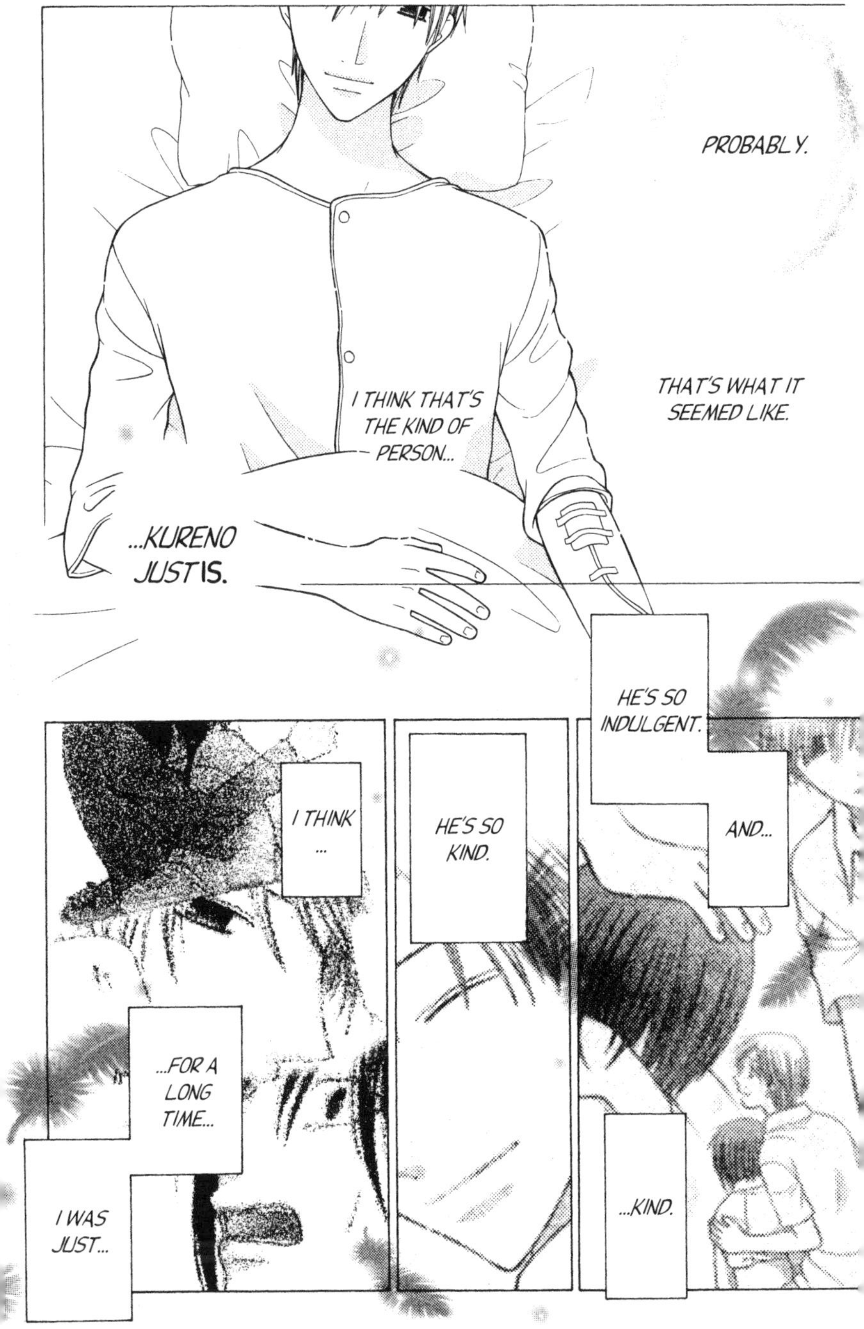
PROBABLY.
THAT'S WHAT IT SEEMED LIKE.
I THINK THAT'S THE KIND OF PERSON...
...KURENO JUST IS.
HE'S SO INDULGENT.
AND...
...KIND.
HE'S SO KIND.
I THINK ...
...FOR A LONG TIME...
I WAS JUST...

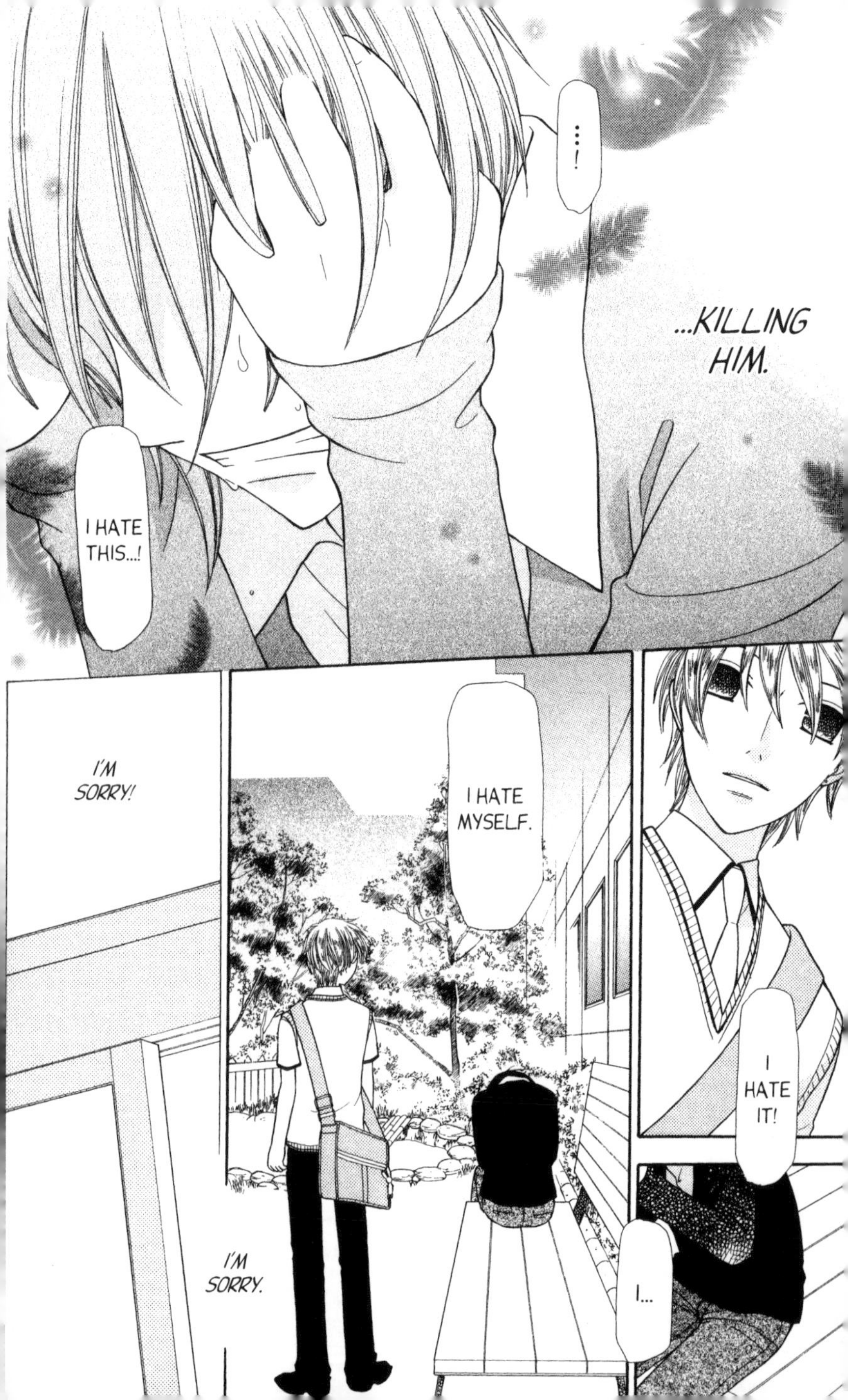
...!
...KILLING HIM.
I HATE THIS...!
I HATE IT!
I...
I HATE MYSELF.
I'M SORRY.
I'M SORRY!

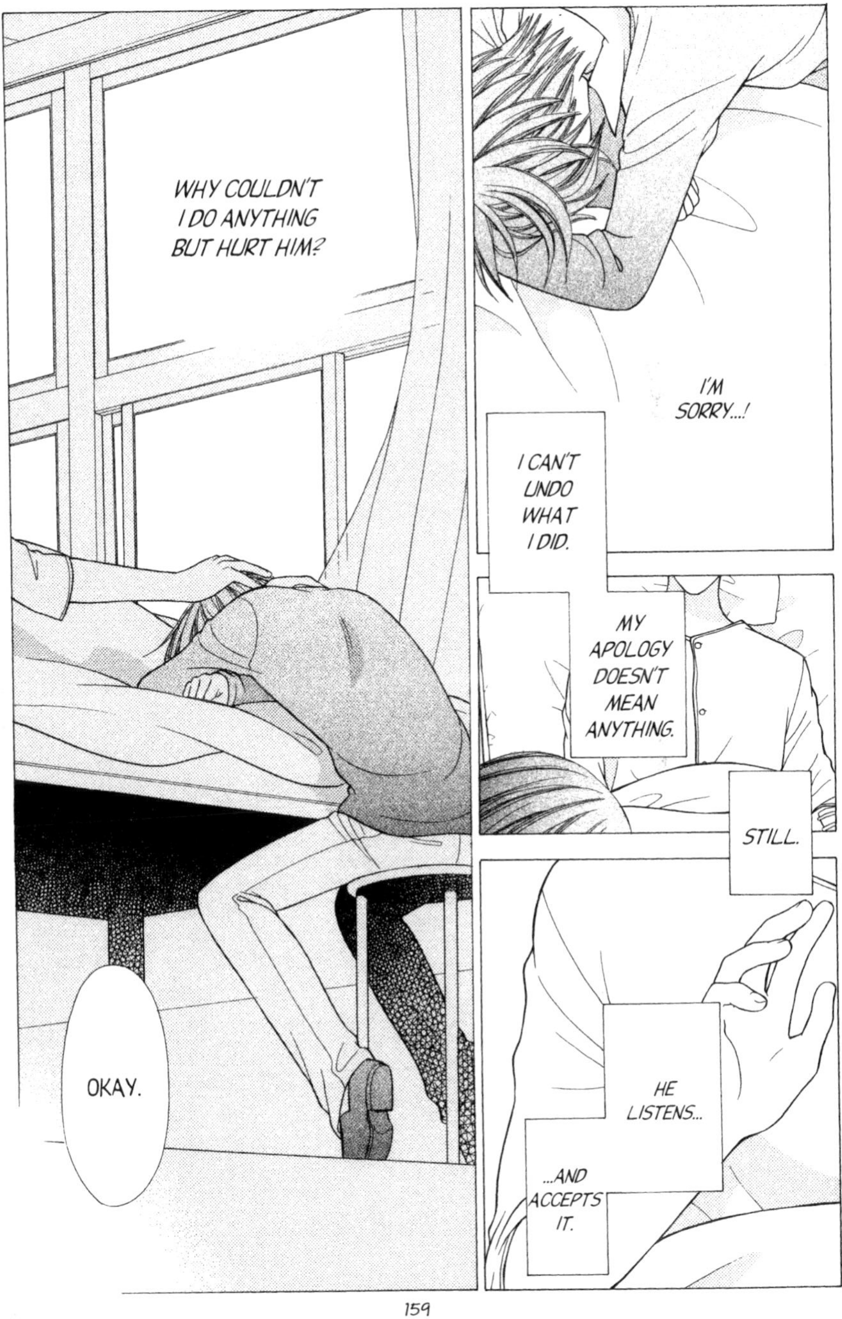
I'M SORRY...!
I CAN'T UNDO WHAT I DID.
MY APOLOGY DOESN'T MEAN ANYTHING.
STILL.
HE LISTENS...
...AND ACCEPTS IT.
WHY COULDN'T I DO ANYTHING BUT HURT HIM?
OKAY.

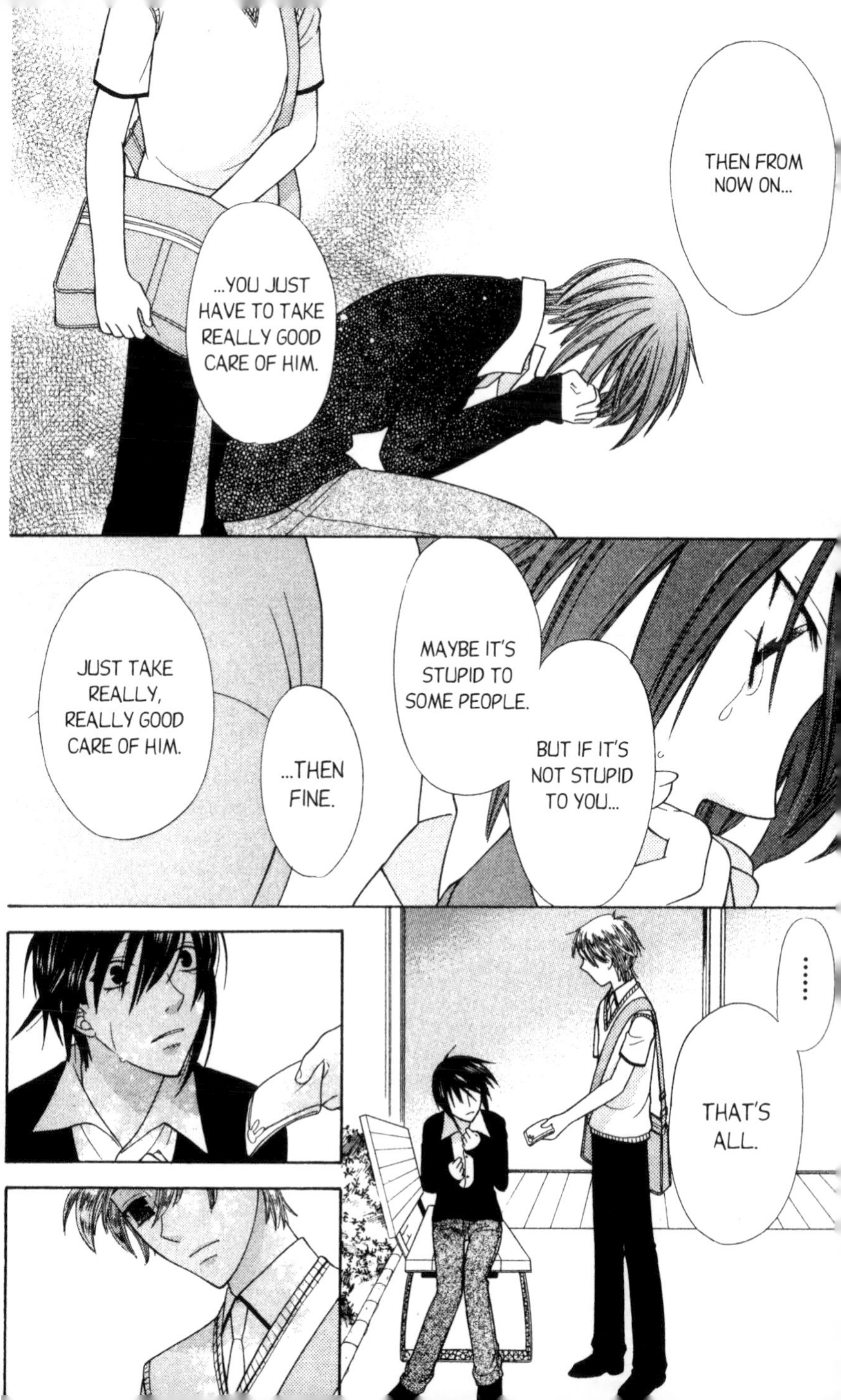
THEN FROM NOW ON...
...YOU JUST HAVE TO TAKE REALLY GOOD CARE OF HIM.
MAYBE IT'S STUPID TO SOME PEOPLE.
BUT IF IT'S NOT STUPID TO YOU...
...THEN FINE.
JUST TAKE REALLY, REALLY GOOD CARE OF HIM.
......
THAT'S ALL.

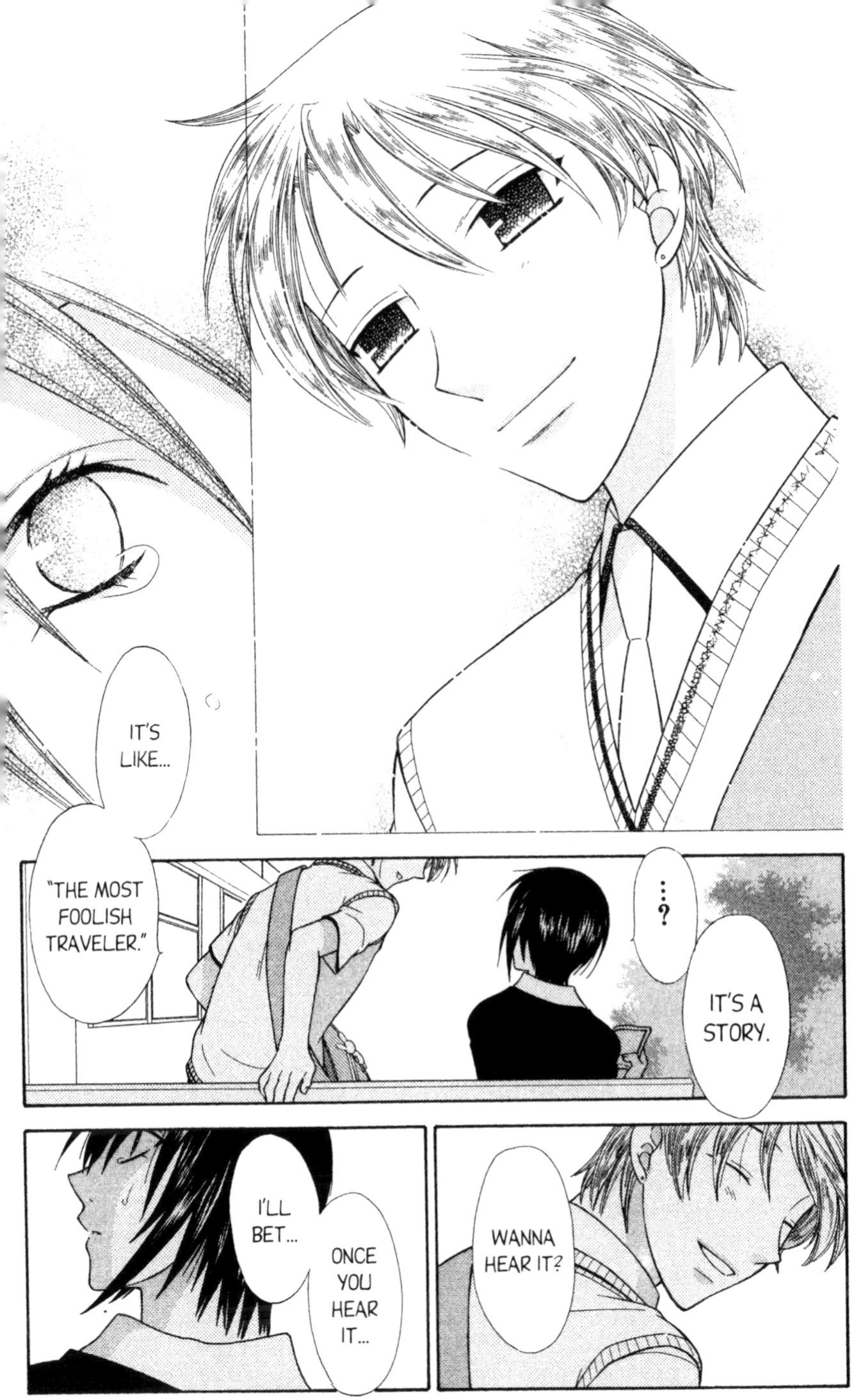
IT'S LIKE...
"THE MOST FOOLISH TRAVELER."
...?
IT'S A STORY.
WANNA HEAR IT?
I'LL BET...
ONCE YOU HEAR IT...

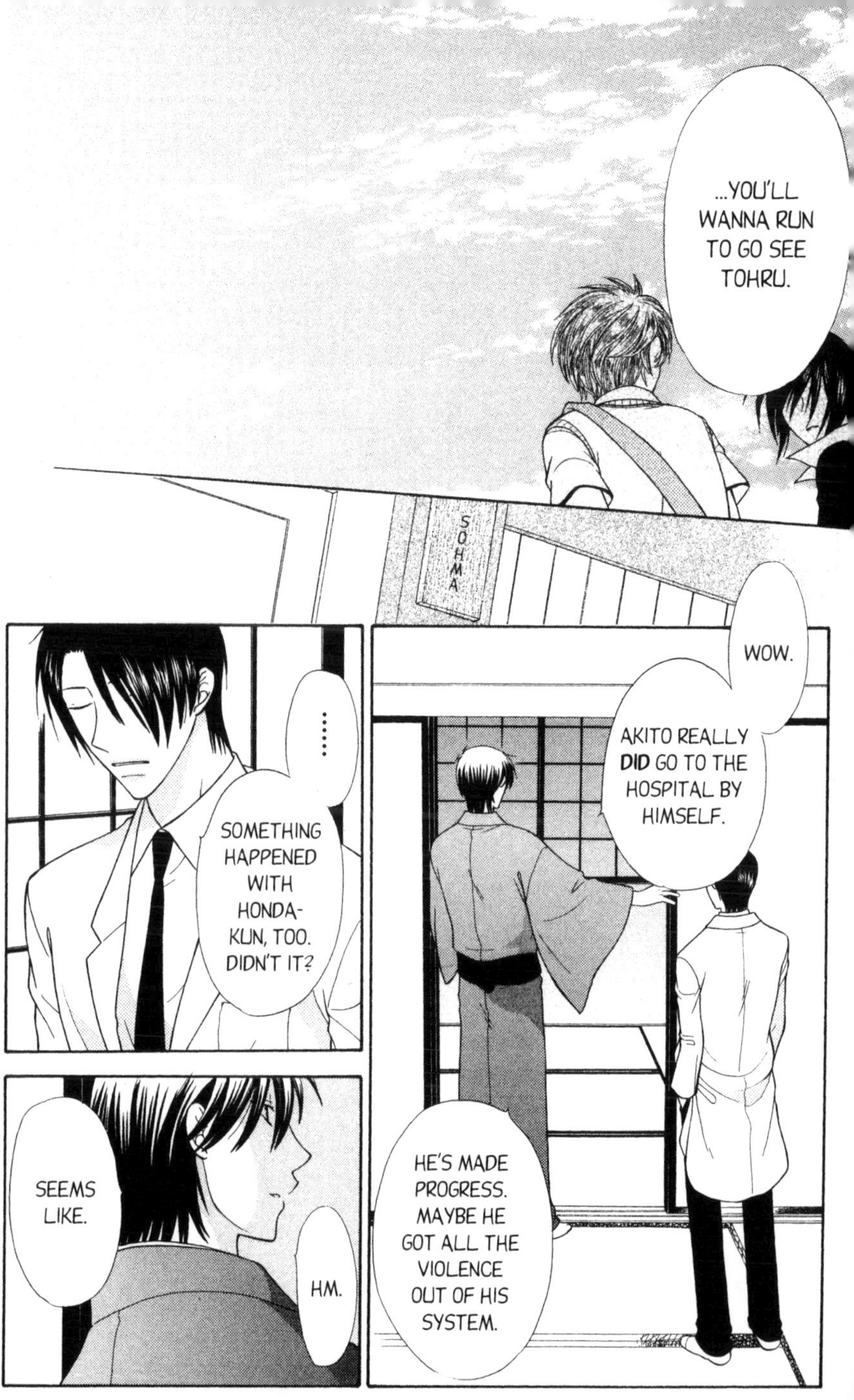
...YOU'LL WANNA RUN TO GO SEE TOHRU.
SOHMA
WOW.
AKITO REALLY **DID** GO TO THE HOSPITAL BY HIMSELF.
HE'S MADE PROGRESS. MAYBE HE GOT ALL THE VIOLENCE OUT OF HIS SYSTEM.
......
SOMETHING HAPPENED WITH HONDA-KUN, TOO. DIDN'T IT?
HM.
SEEMS LIKE.

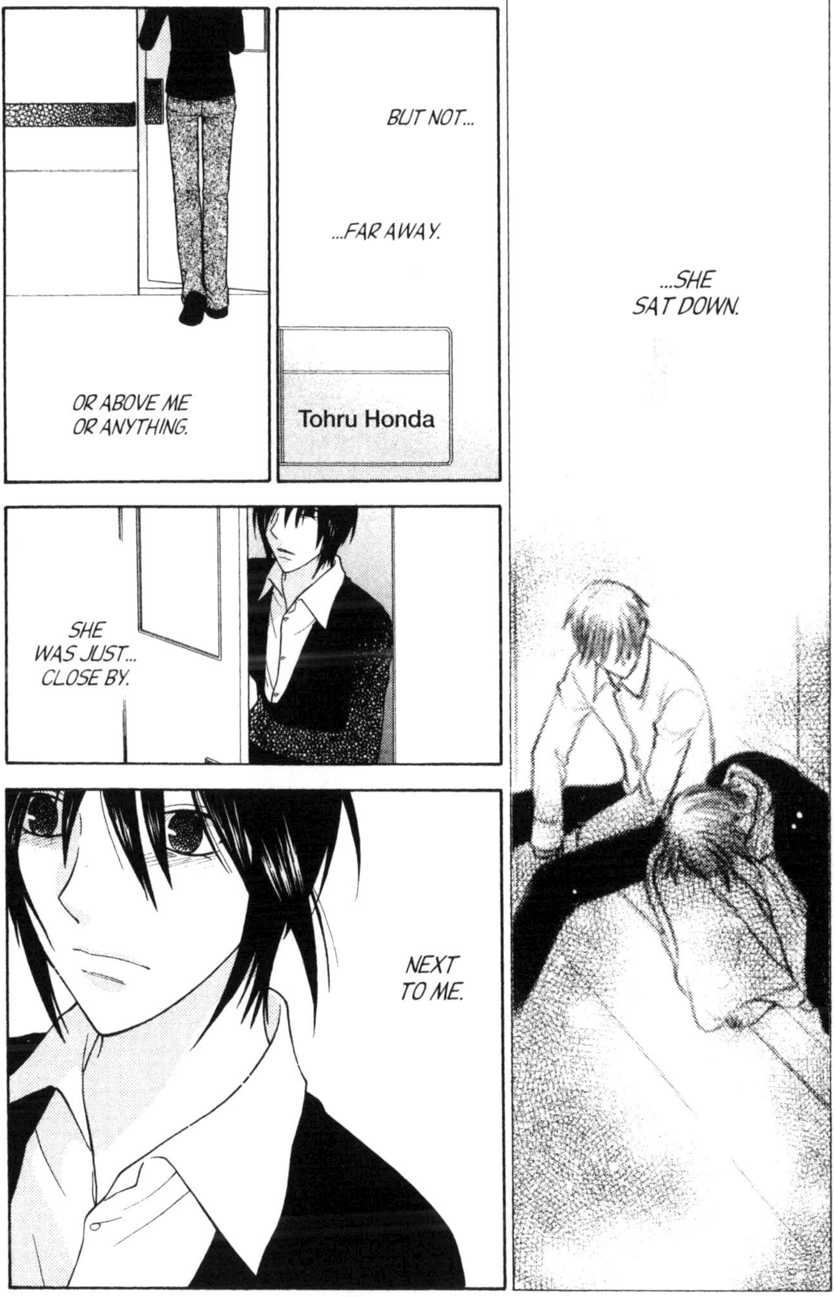
...SHE SAT DOWN.
BUT NOT...
...FAR AWAY.
Tohru Honda
OR ABOVE ME OR ANYTHING.
SHE WAS JUST... CLOSE BY.
NEXT TO ME.

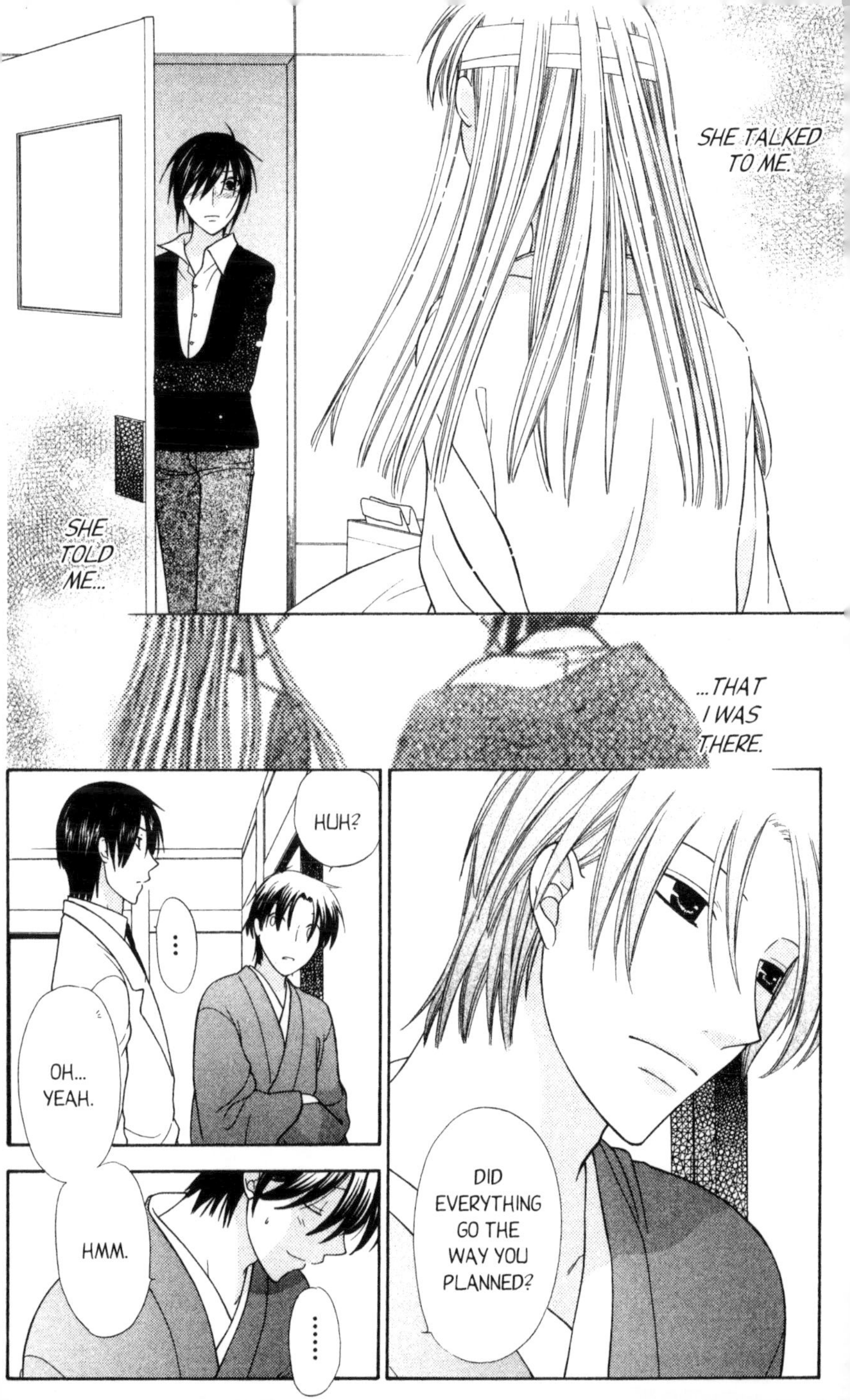
SHE TALKED TO ME.
SHE TOLD ME...
...THAT I WAS THERE.
DID EVERYTHING GO THE WAY YOU PLANNED?
HUH?
...
OH... YEAH.
HMM.
......

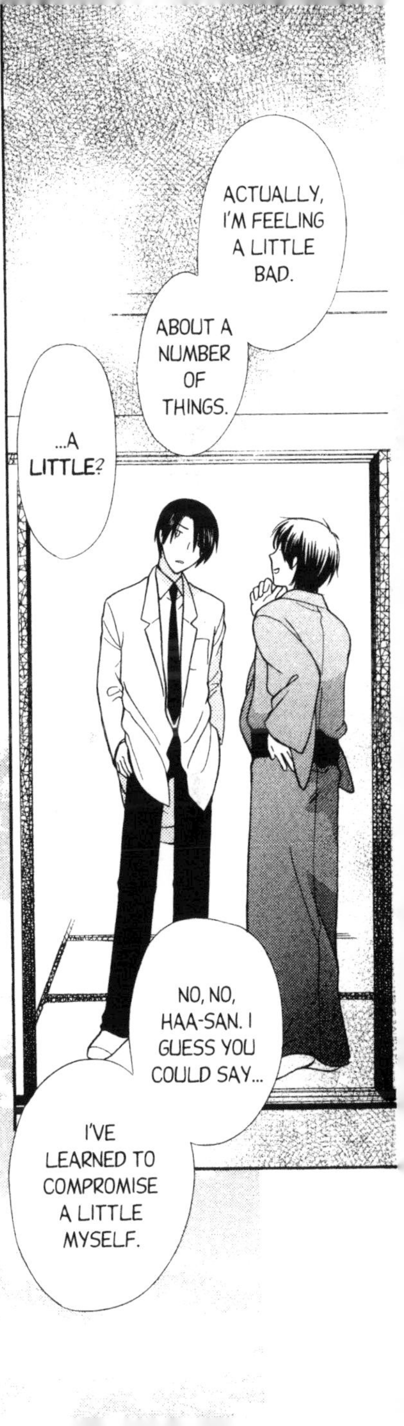
ACTUALLY, I'M FEELING A LITTLE BAD.
ABOUT A NUMBER OF THINGS.
...A LITTLE?
NO, NO, HAA-SAN. I GUESS YOU COULD SAY...
I'VE LEARNED TO COMPROMISE A LITTLE MYSELF.

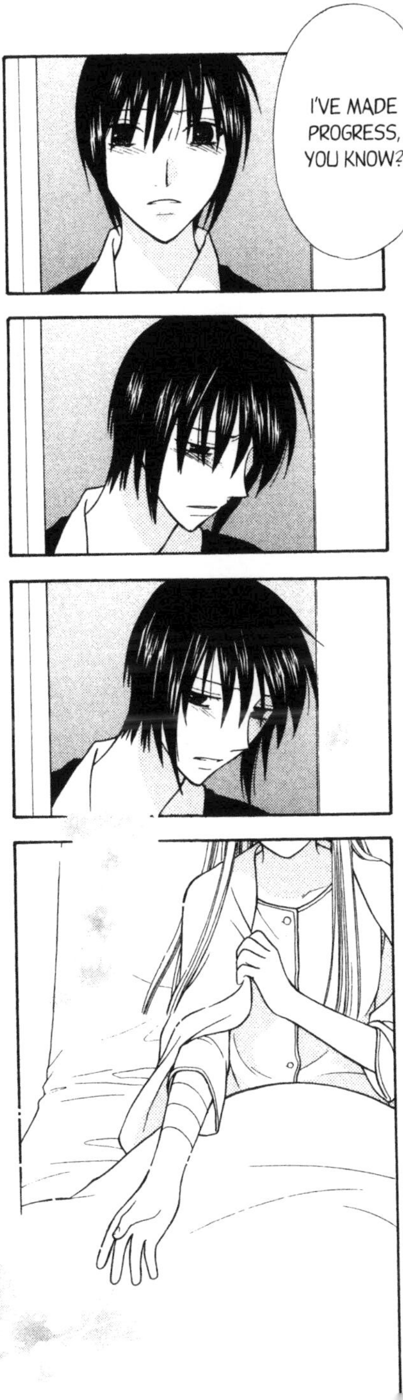
I'VE MADE PROGRESS, YOU KNOW?

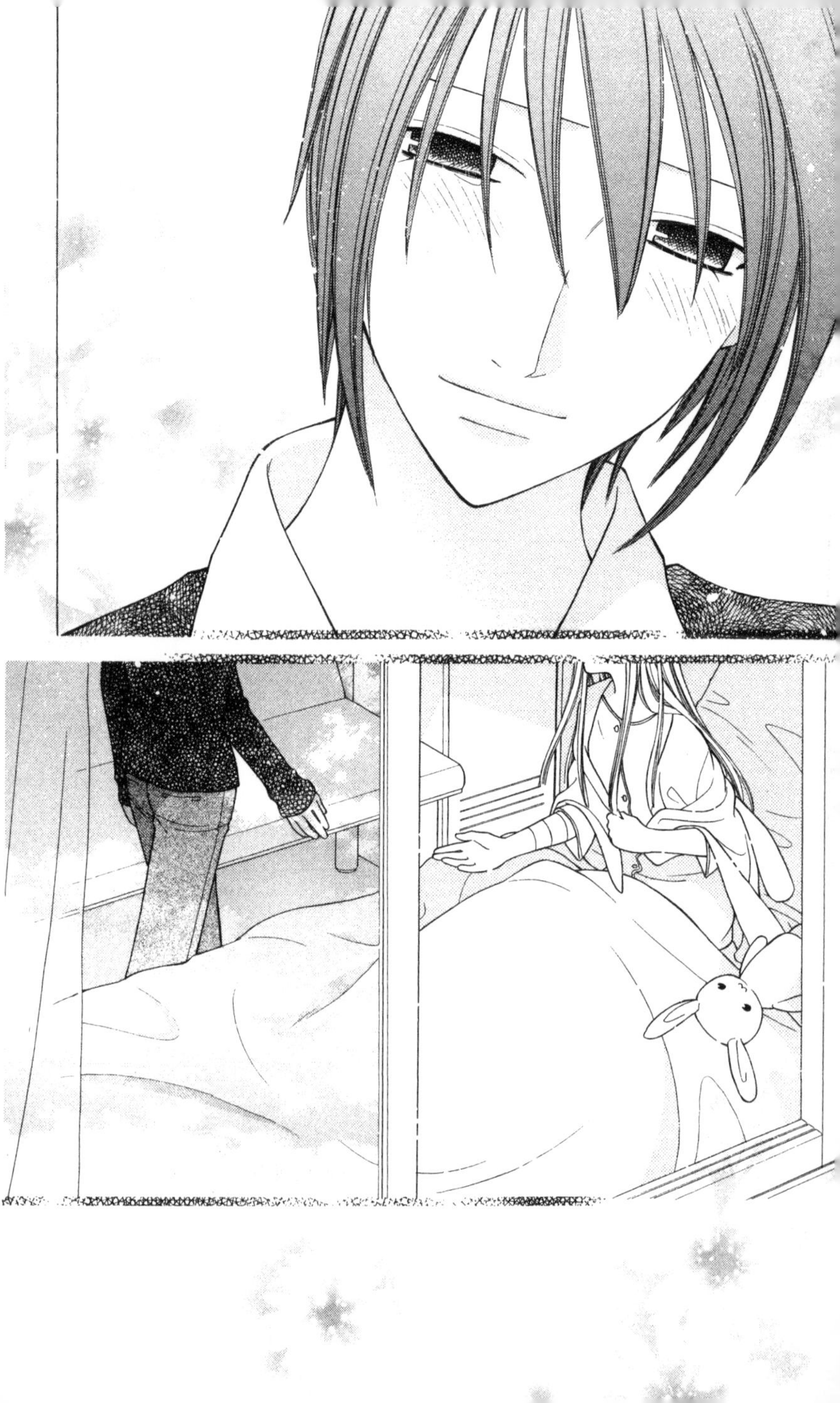

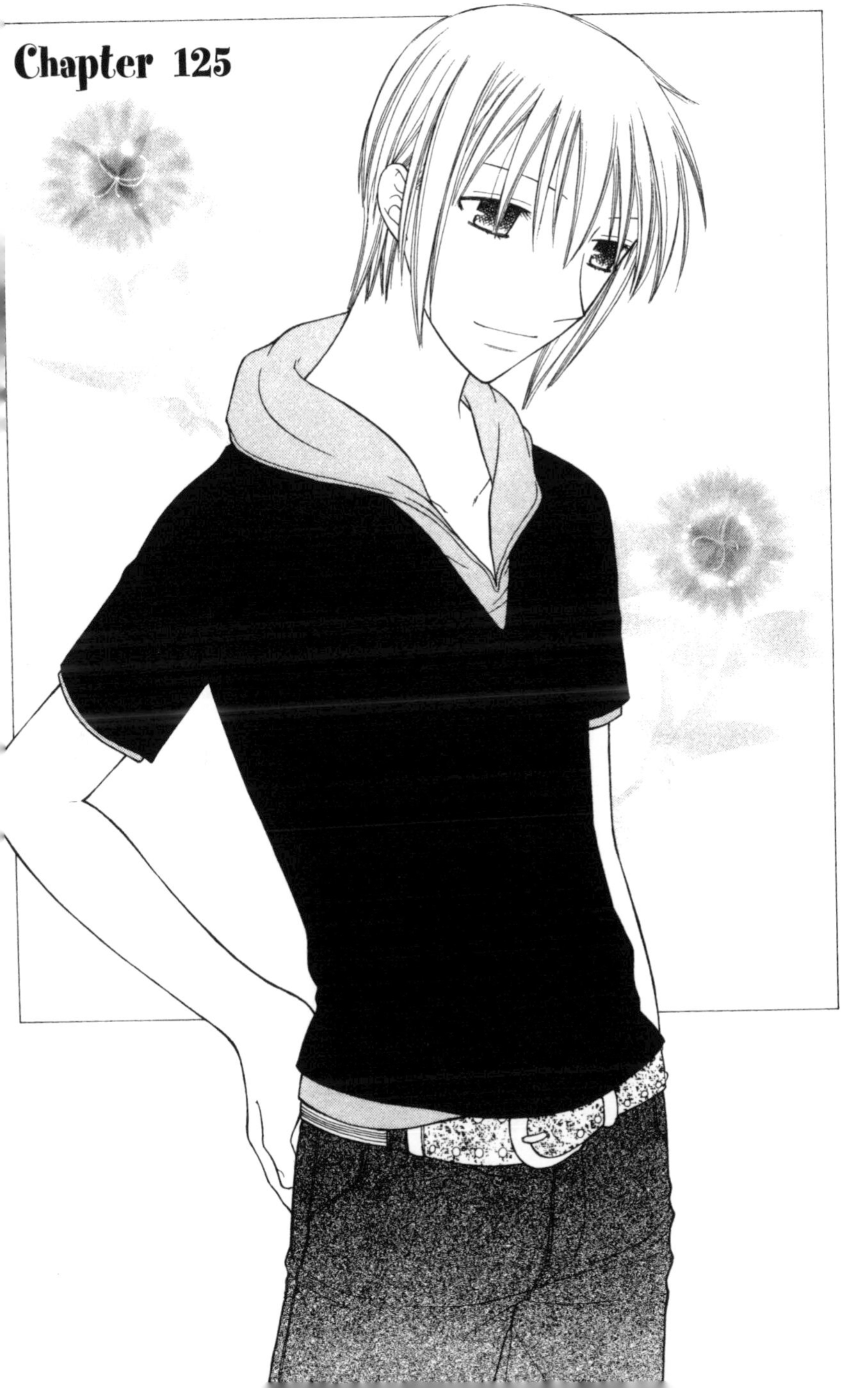
Chapter 125

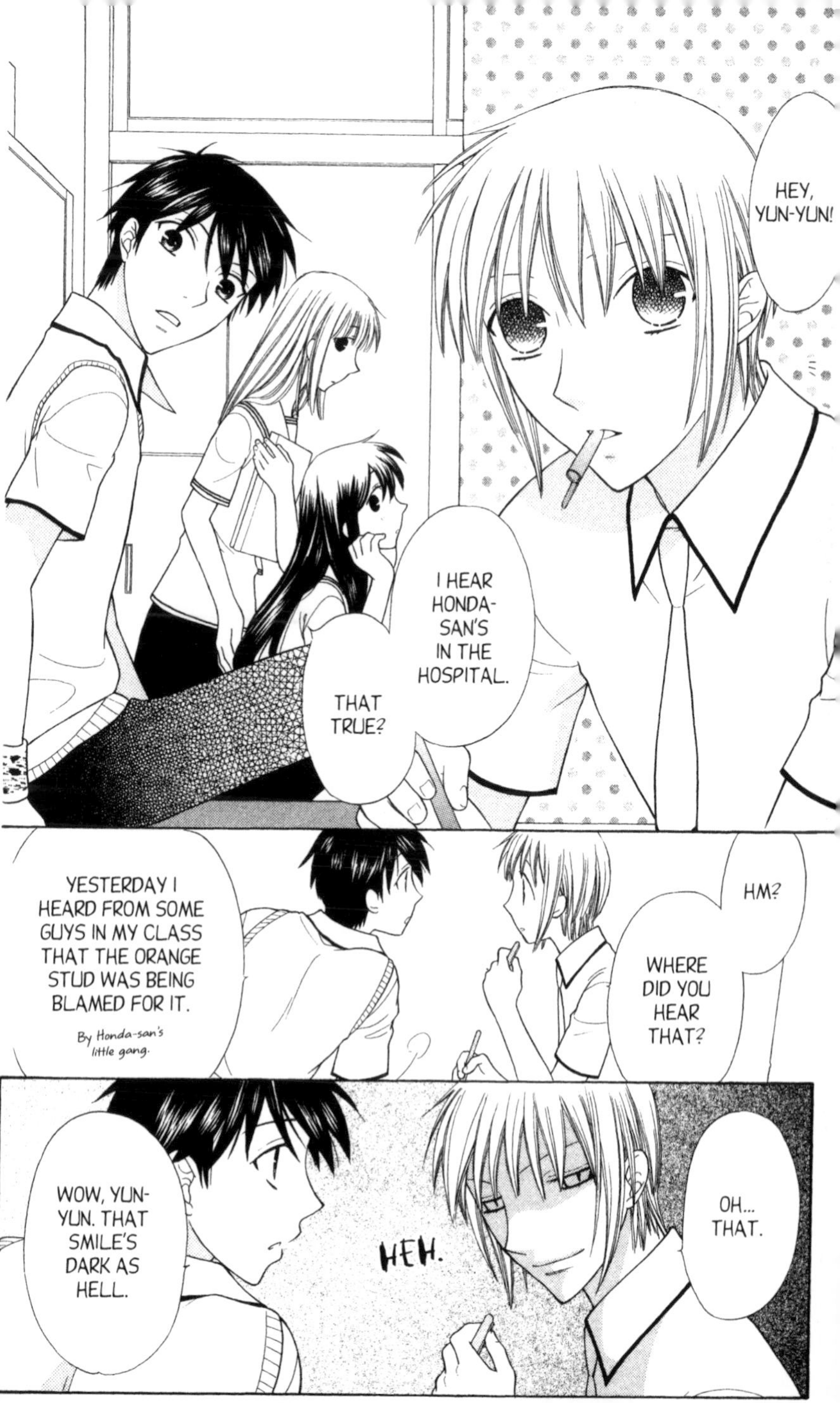
HEY, YUN-YUN!
I HEAR HONDA-SAN'S IN THE HOSPITAL.
THAT TRUE?
HM?
WHERE DID YOU HEAR THAT?
YESTERDAY I HEARD FROM SOME GUYS IN MY CLASS THAT THE ORANGE STUD WAS BEING BLAMED FOR IT.
By Honda-san's little gang.
OH... THAT.
HEH.
WOW, YUN-YUN. THAT SMILE'S DARK AS HELL.

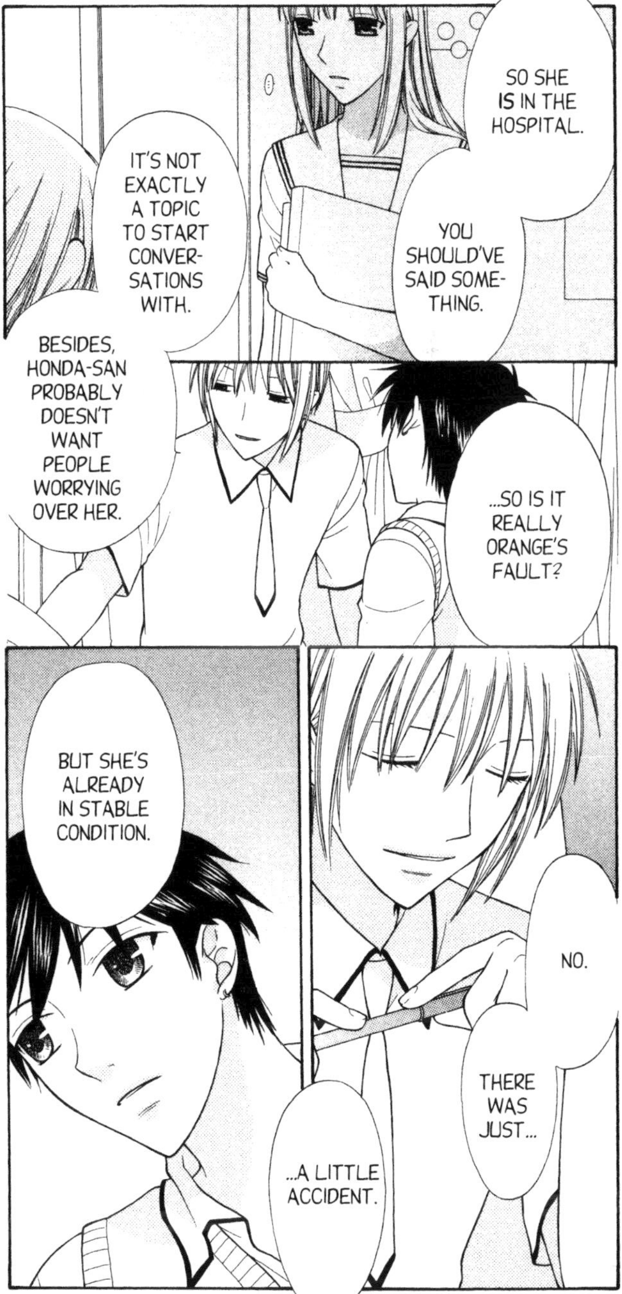
SO SHE IS IN THE HOSPITAL.
YOU SHOULD'VE SAID SOME-THING.
IT'S NOT EXACTLY A TOPIC TO START CONVER-SATIONS WITH.
BESIDES, HONDA-SAN PROBABLY DOESN'T WANT PEOPLE WORRYING OVER HER.
...SO IS IT REALLY ORANGE'S FAULT?
NO.
THERE WAS JUST...
...A LITTLE ACCIDENT.
BUT SHE'S ALREADY IN STABLE CONDITION.

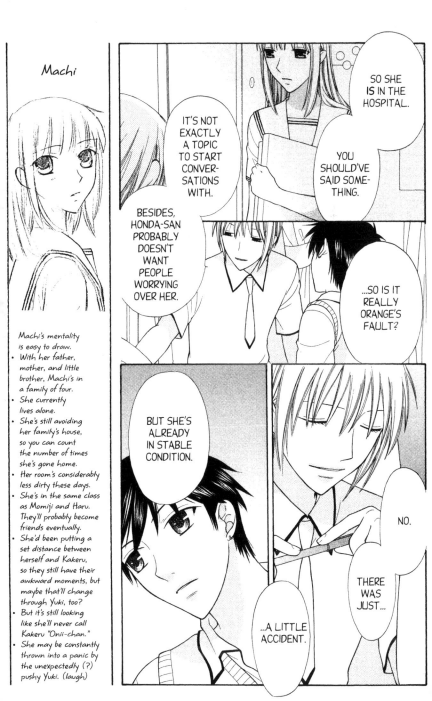

Machi

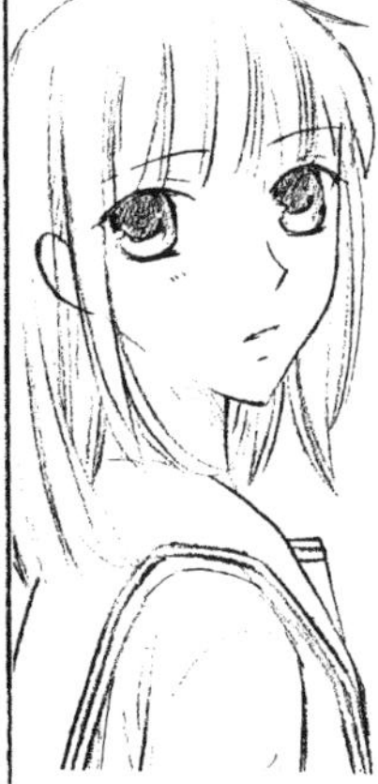

Machi's mentality is easy to draw.

- With her father, mother, and little brother, Machi's in a family of four.
- She currently lives alone.
- She's still avoiding her family's house, so you can count the number of times she's gone home.
- Her room's considerably less dirty these days.
- She's in the same class as Momiji and Haru. They'll probably become friends eventually.
- She'd been putting a set distance between herself and Kakeru, so they still have their awkward moments, but maybe that'll change through Yuki, too?
- But it's still looking like she'll never call Kakeru "Onii-chan."
- She may be constantly thrown into a panic by the unexpectedly (?) pushy Yuki. (laugh)

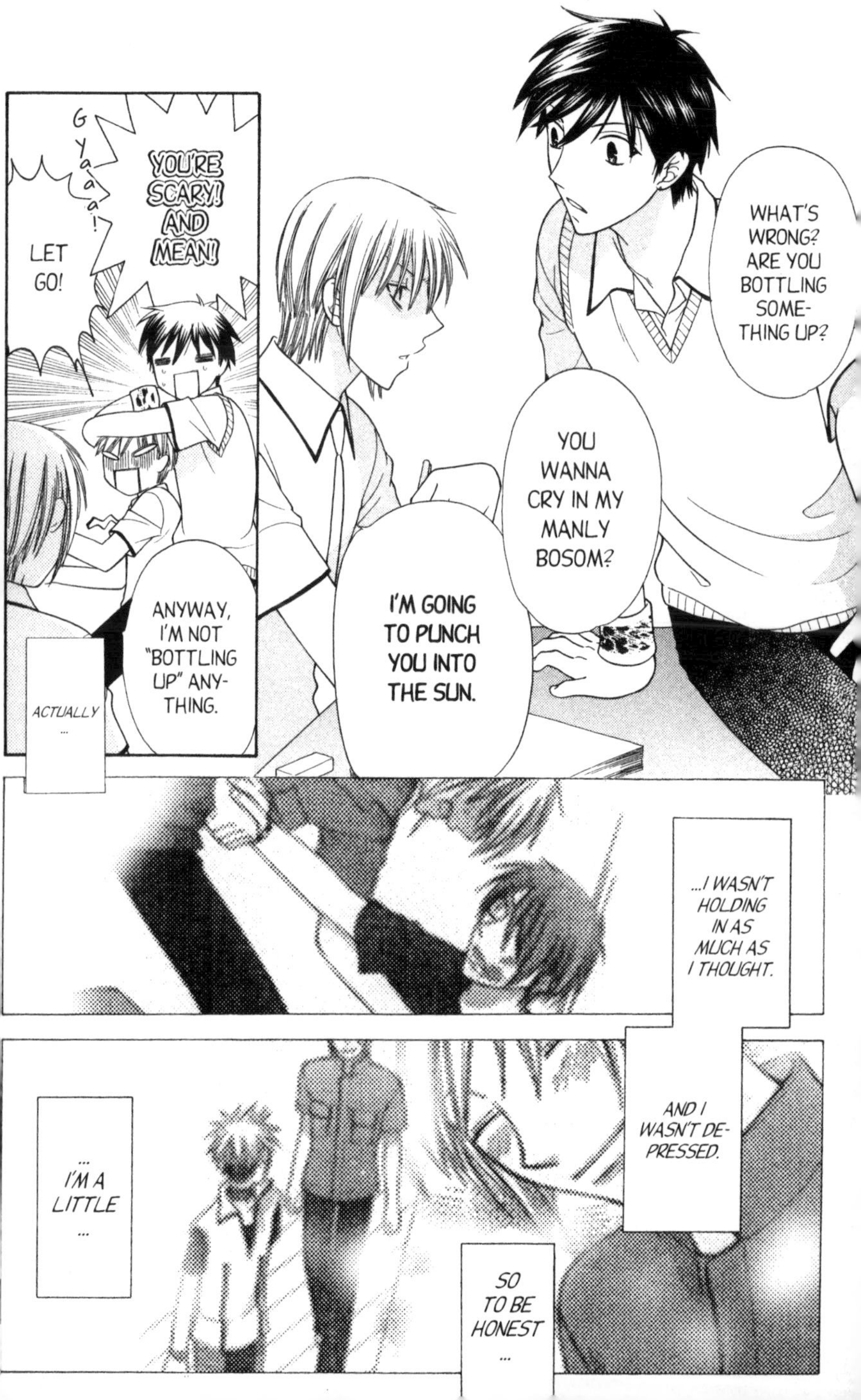
WHAT'S WRONG? ARE YOU BOTTLING SOMETHING UP?
YOU WANNA CRY IN MY MANLY BOSOM?
I'M GOING TO PUNCH YOU INTO THE SUN.
YOU'RE SCARY! AND MEAN!
Gyaaaa!
LET GO!
ANYWAY, I'M NOT "BOTTLING UP" ANYTHING.
ACTUALLY ...
...I WASN'T HOLDING IN AS MUCH AS I THOUGHT.
AND I WASN'T DEPRESSED.
SO TO BE HONEST ...
... I'M A LITTLE ...

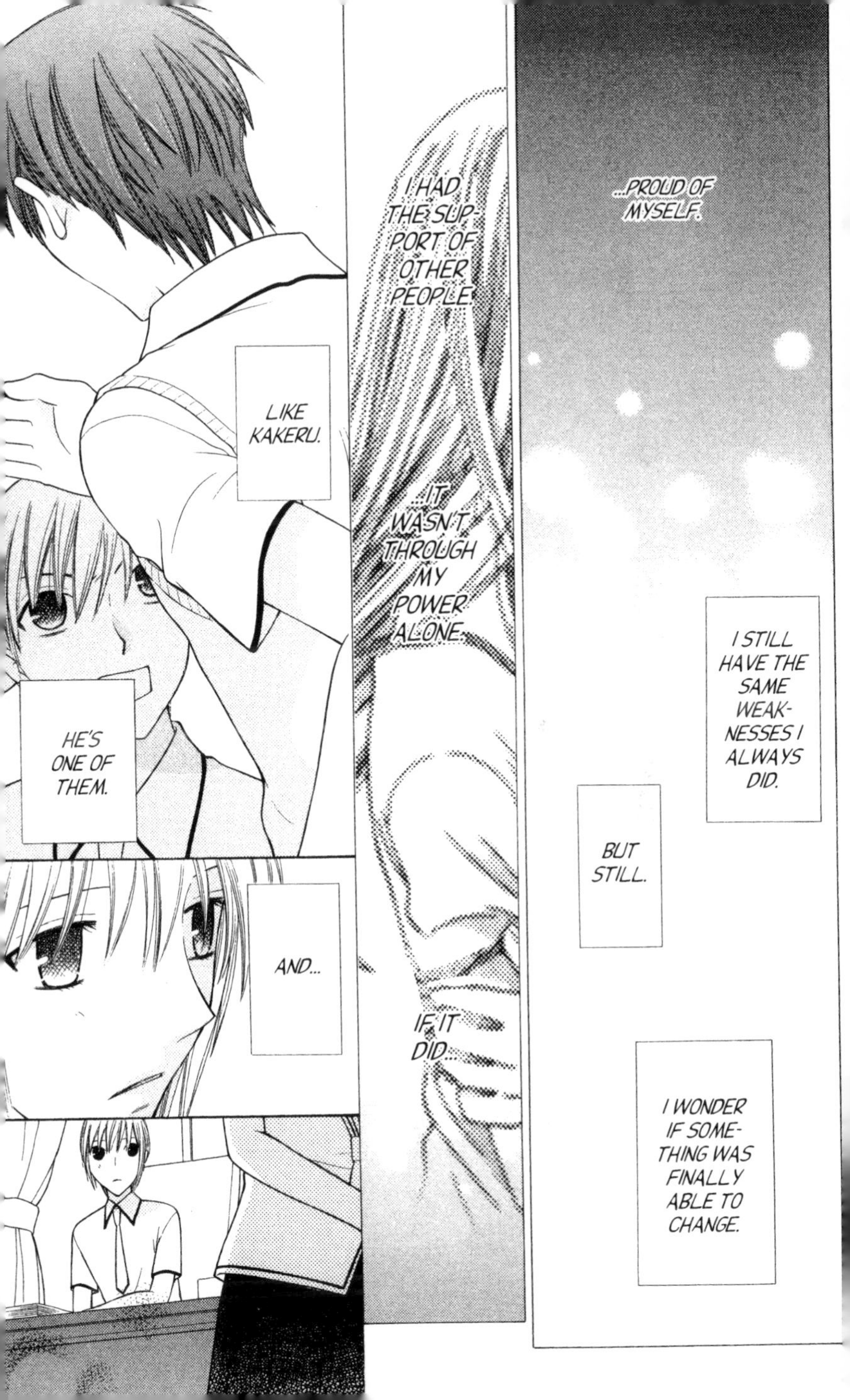
...PROUD OF MYSELF.
I STILL HAVE THE SAME WEAK-NESSES I ALWAYS DID.
BUT STILL.
I WONDER IF SOME-THING WAS FINALLY ABLE TO CHANGE.
I HAD THE SUP-PORT OF OTHER PEOPLE.
...IT WASN'T THROUGH MY POWER ALONE.
IF IT DID...
LIKE KAKERU.
HE'S ONE OF THEM.
AND...

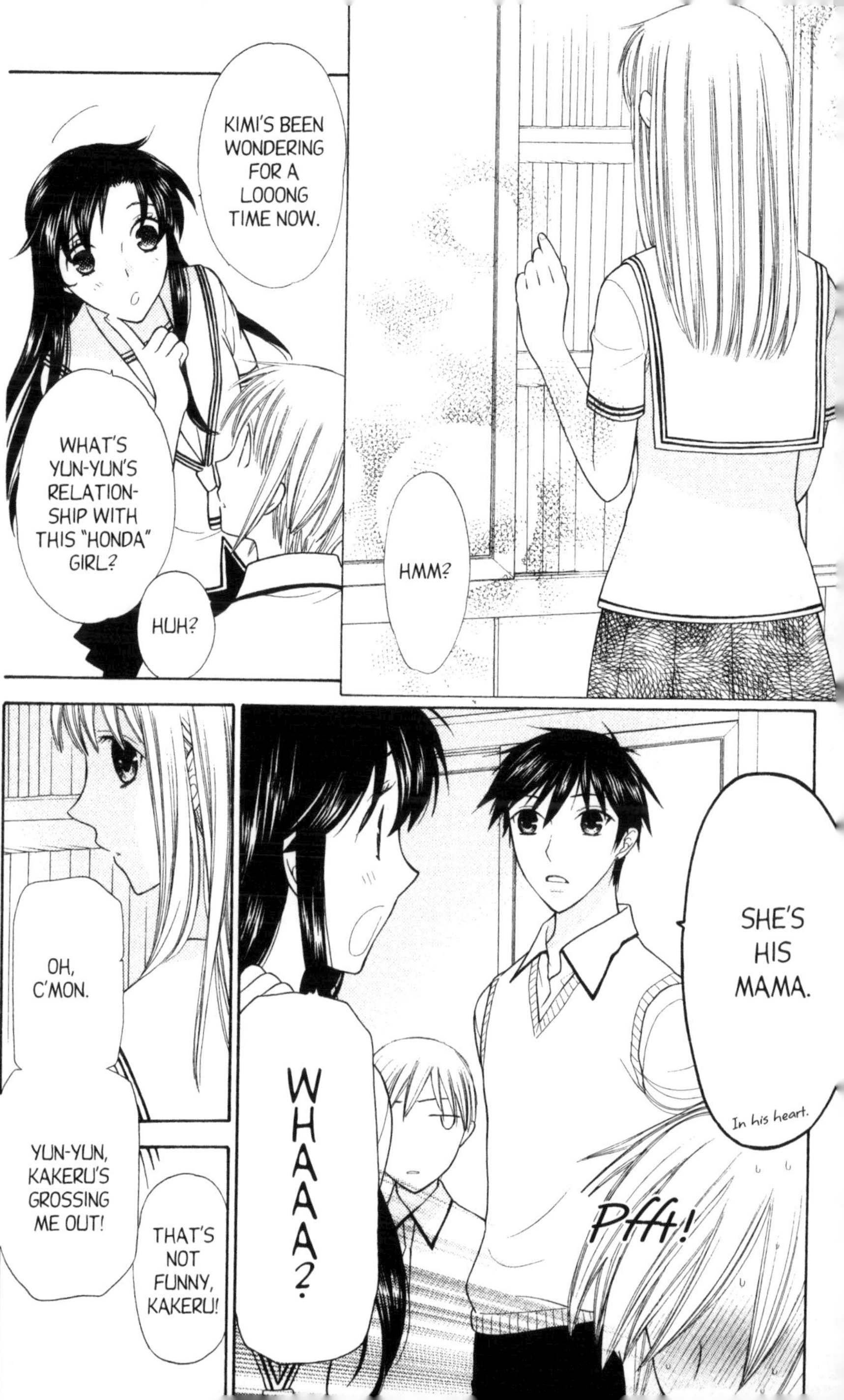
HMM?
KIMI'S BEEN WONDERING FOR A LOOONG TIME NOW.
WHAT'S YUN-YUN'S RELATIONSHIP WITH THIS "HONDA" GIRL?
HUH?
SHE'S HIS MAMA.
In his heart.
WHAAAA?
Pfft!
OH, C'MON.
THAT'S NOT FUNNY, KAKERU!
YUN-YUN, KAKERU'S GROSSING ME OUT!

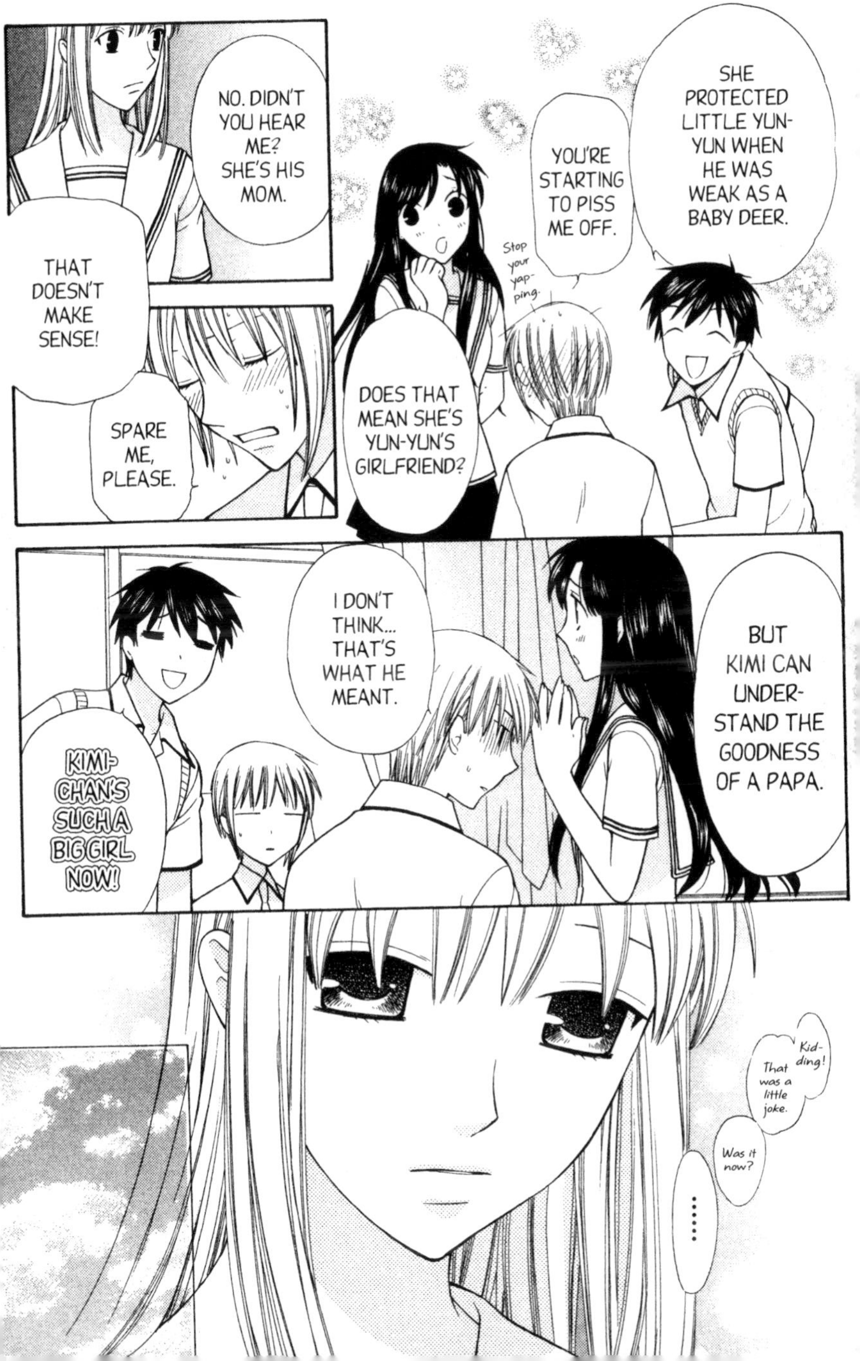
SHE PROTECTED LITTLE YUN-YUN WHEN HE WAS WEAK AS A BABY DEER.
YOU'RE STARTING TO PISS ME OFF.
Stop your yap-ping.
DOES THAT MEAN SHE'S YUN-YUN'S GIRLFRIEND?
NO. DIDN'T YOU HEAR ME? SHE'S HIS MOM.
THAT DOESN'T MAKE SENSE!
SPARE ME, PLEASE.
BUT KIMI CAN UNDER-STAND THE GOODNESS OF A PAPA.
I DON'T THINK... THAT'S WHAT HE MEANT.
KIMI-CHAN'S SUCH A BIG GIRL NOW!
Kid-ding! That was a little joke.
Was it now?
......

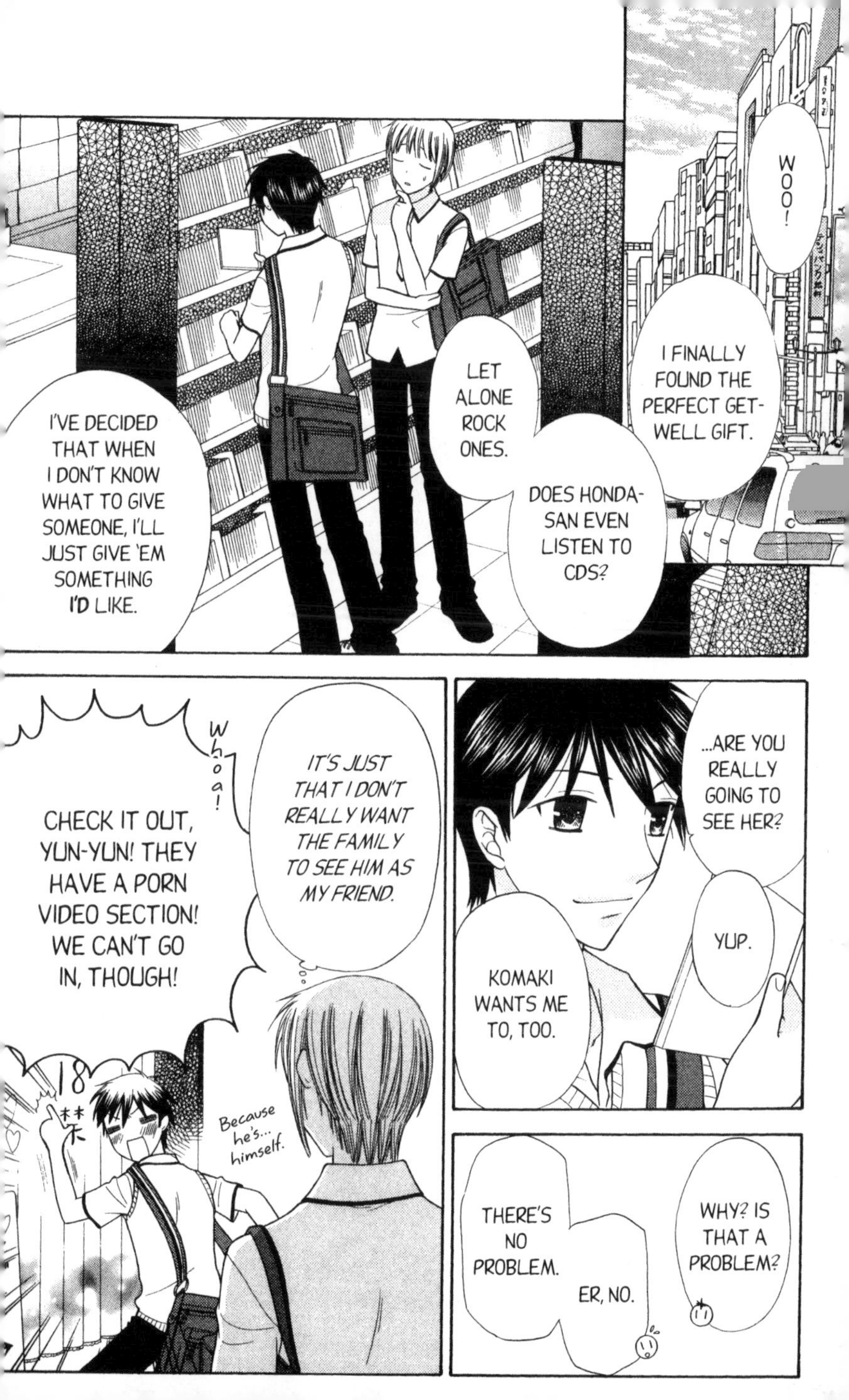
WOO!
I FINALLY FOUND THE PERFECT GET-WELL GIFT.
DOES HONDA-SAN EVEN LISTEN TO CDS?
LET ALONE ROCK ONES.
I'VE DECIDED THAT WHEN I DON'T KNOW WHAT TO GIVE SOMEONE, I'LL JUST GIVE 'EM SOMETHING **I'D** LIKE.
...ARE YOU REALLY GOING TO SEE HER?
YUP.
KOMAKI WANTS ME TO, TOO.
WHY? IS THAT A PROBLEM?
THERE'S NO PROBLEM.
ER, NO.
IT'S JUST THAT I DON'T REALLY WANT THE FAMILY TO SEE HIM AS MY FRIEND.
Whoa!
CHECK IT OUT, YUN-YUN! THEY HAVE A PORN VIDEO SECTION! WE CAN'T GO IN, THOUGH!
18 禁
Because he's... himself.

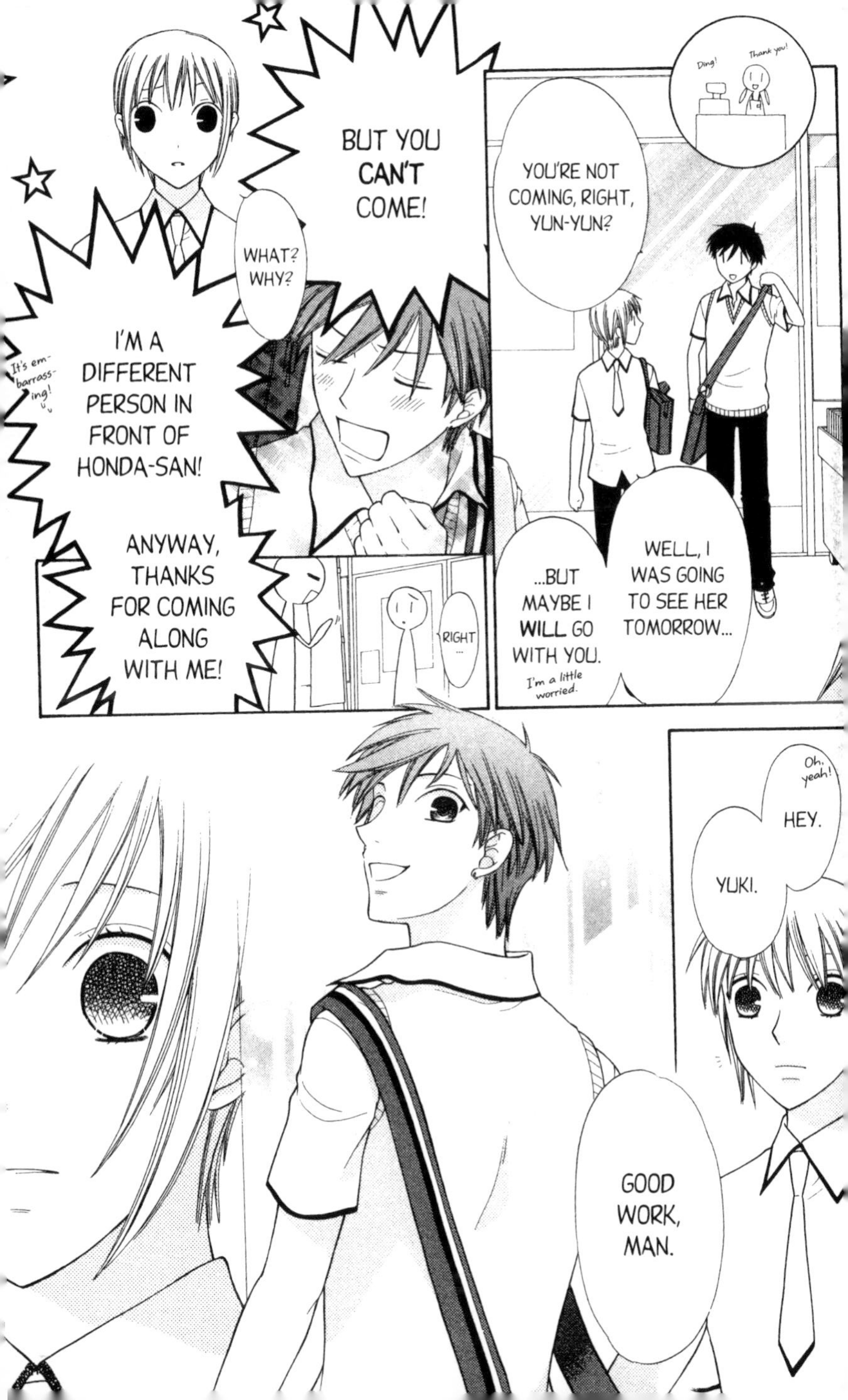
Ding!
Thank you!
YOU'RE NOT COMING, RIGHT, YUN-YUN?
WELL, I WAS GOING TO SEE HER TOMORROW...
...BUT MAYBE I WILL GO WITH YOU.
I'm a little worried.
BUT YOU CAN'T COME!
WHAT? WHY?
I'M A DIFFERENT PERSON IN FRONT OF HONDA-SAN!
It's embarrassing!
ANYWAY, THANKS FOR COMING ALONG WITH ME!
RIGHT...
Oh, yeah!
HEY.
YUKI.
GOOD WORK, MAN.

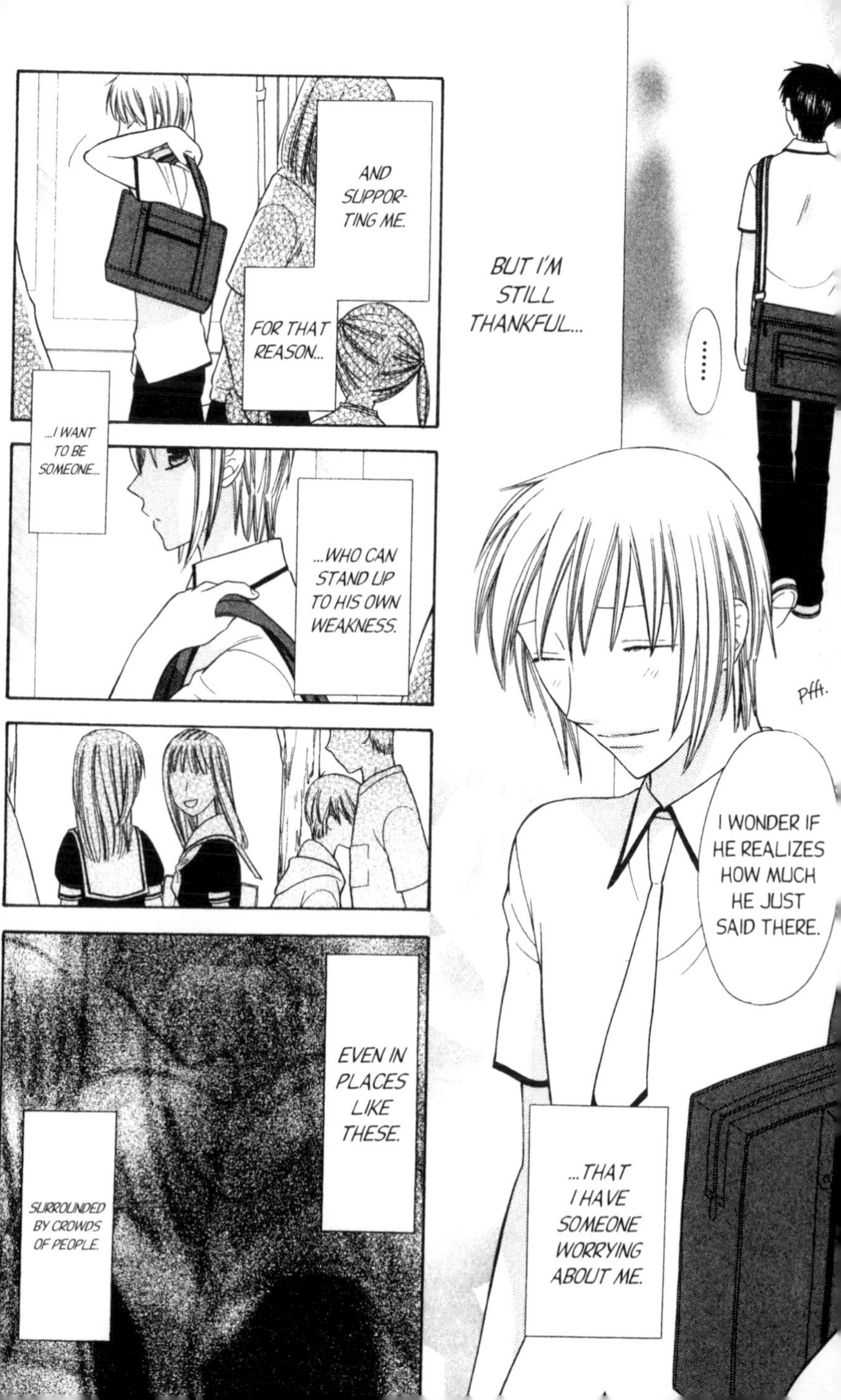
......
BUT I'M STILL THANKFUL...
pfft.
I WONDER IF HE REALIZES HOW MUCH HE JUST SAID THERE.
...THAT I HAVE SOMEONE WORRYING ABOUT ME.
AND SUPPOR-TING ME.
FOR THAT REASON...
...I WANT TO BE SOMEONE...
...WHO CAN STAND UP TO HIS OWN WEAKNESS.
EVEN IN PLACES LIKE THESE.
SURROUNDED BY CROWDS OF PEOPLE.

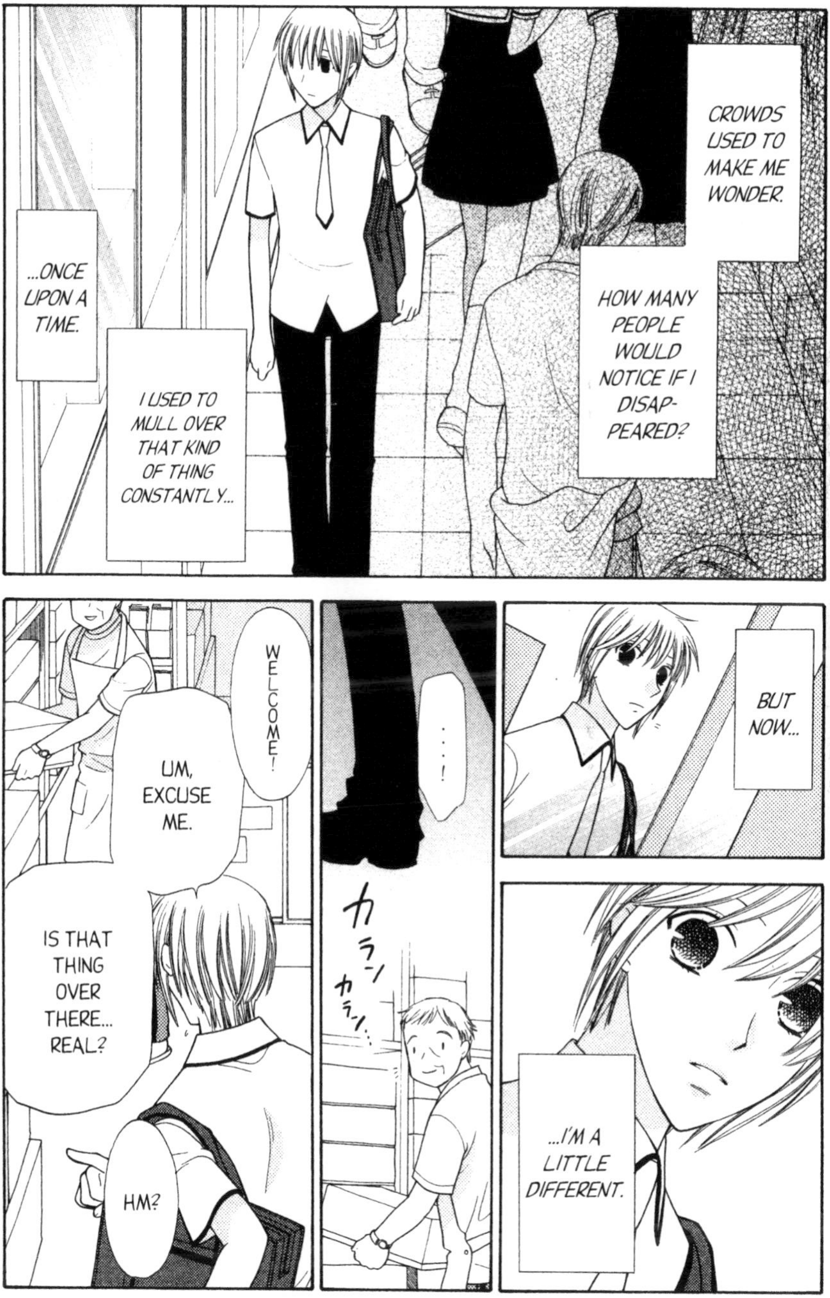
CROWDS USED TO MAKE ME WONDER.
HOW MANY PEOPLE WOULD NOTICE IF I DISAP-PEARED?
...ONCE UPON A TIME.
I USED TO MULL OVER THAT KIND OF THING CONSTANTLY...
BUT NOW...
...I'M A LITTLE DIFFERENT.
...!
カラン
カラン...
WELCOME!
UM, EXCUSE ME.
IS THAT THING OVER THERE... REAL?
HM?

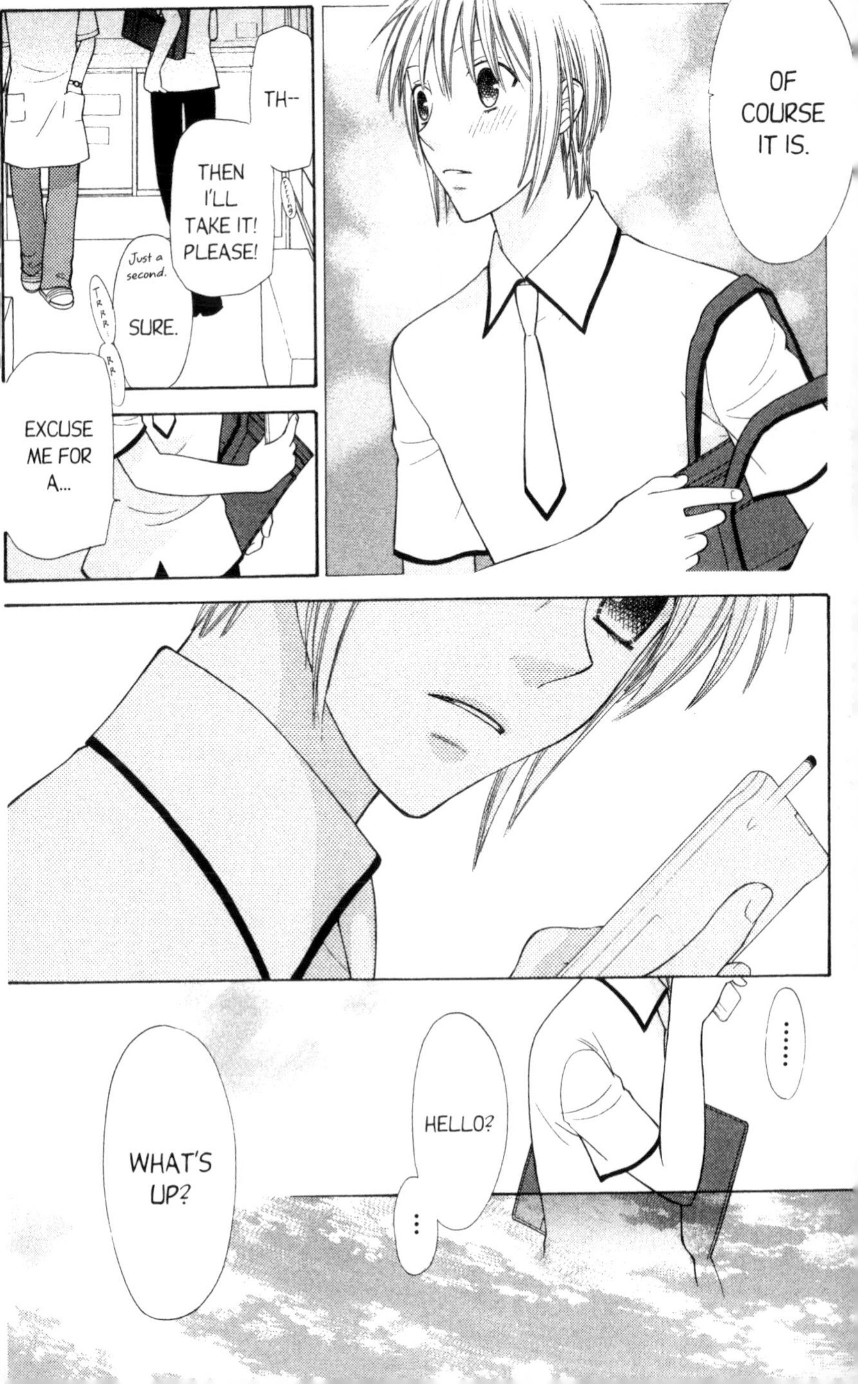
OF COURSE IT IS.
TH--
THEN I'LL TAKE IT! PLEASE!
Just a second.
SURE.
TRRR... RR...
EXCUSE ME FOR A...
......
HELLO?
...
WHAT'S UP?

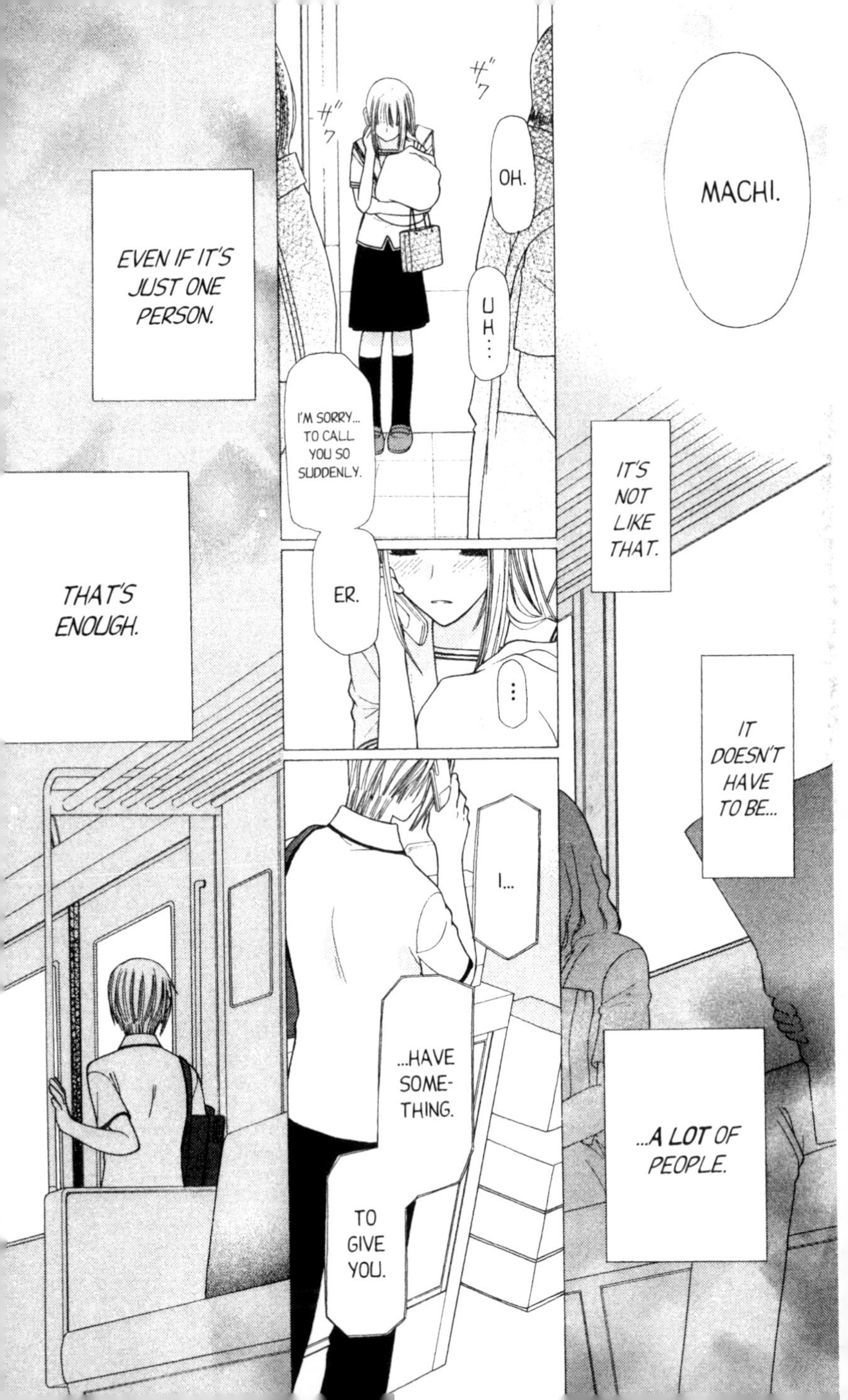
MACHI.
IT'S NOT LIKE THAT.
IT DOESN'T HAVE TO BE...
...A LOT OF PEOPLE.
OH.
UH...
I'M SORRY... TO CALL YOU SO SUDDENLY.
ER.
...
I...
...HAVE SOME-THING.
TO GIVE YOU.
EVEN IF IT'S JUST ONE PERSON.
THAT'S ENOUGH.

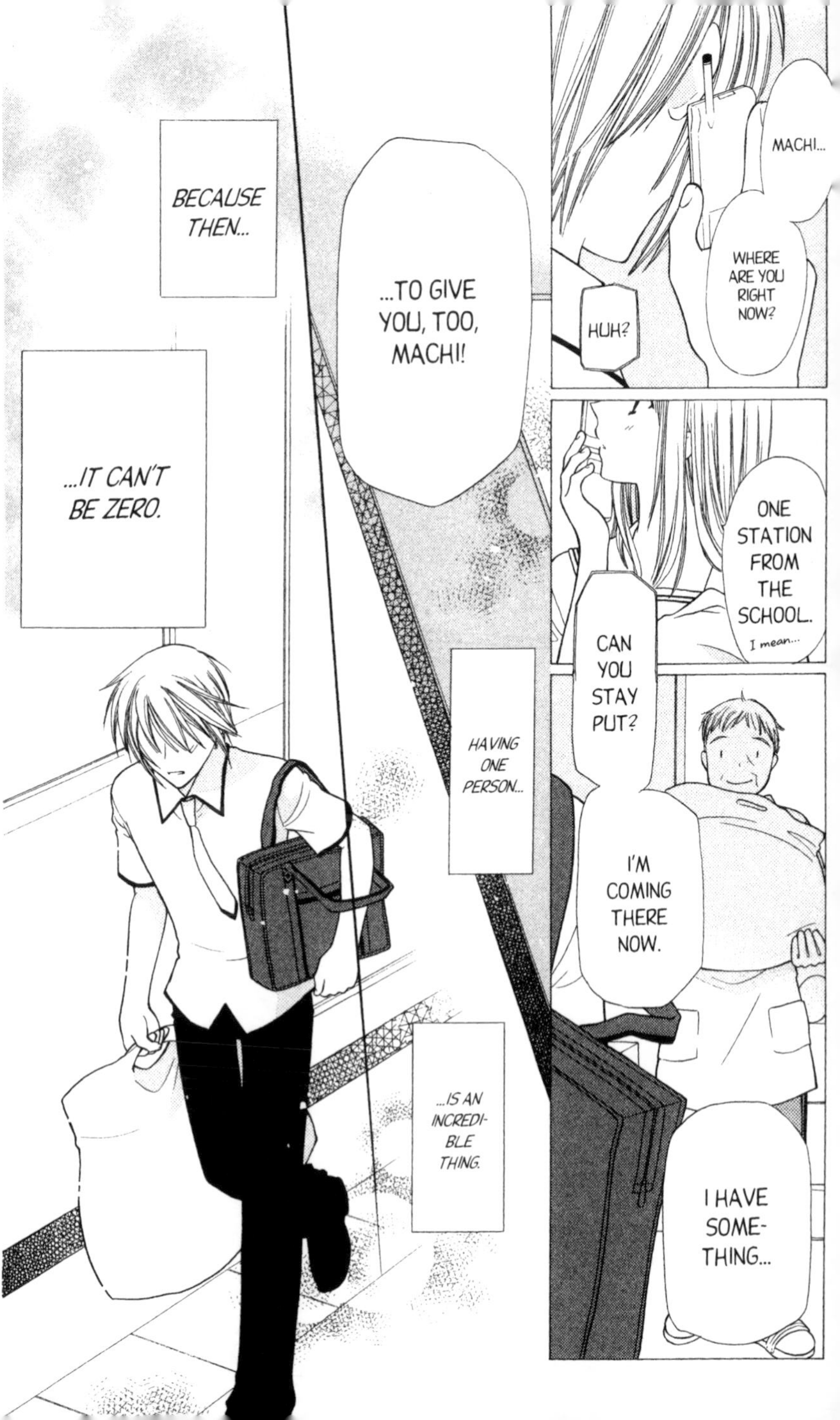
MACHI...
WHERE ARE YOU RIGHT NOW?
HUH?
ONE STATION FROM THE SCHOOL.
I mean...
CAN YOU STAY PUT?
I'M COMING THERE NOW.
I HAVE SOMETHING...
...TO GIVE YOU, TOO, MACHI!
HAVING ONE PERSON...
...IS AN INCREDIBLE THING.
BECAUSE THEN...
...IT CAN'T BE ZERO.

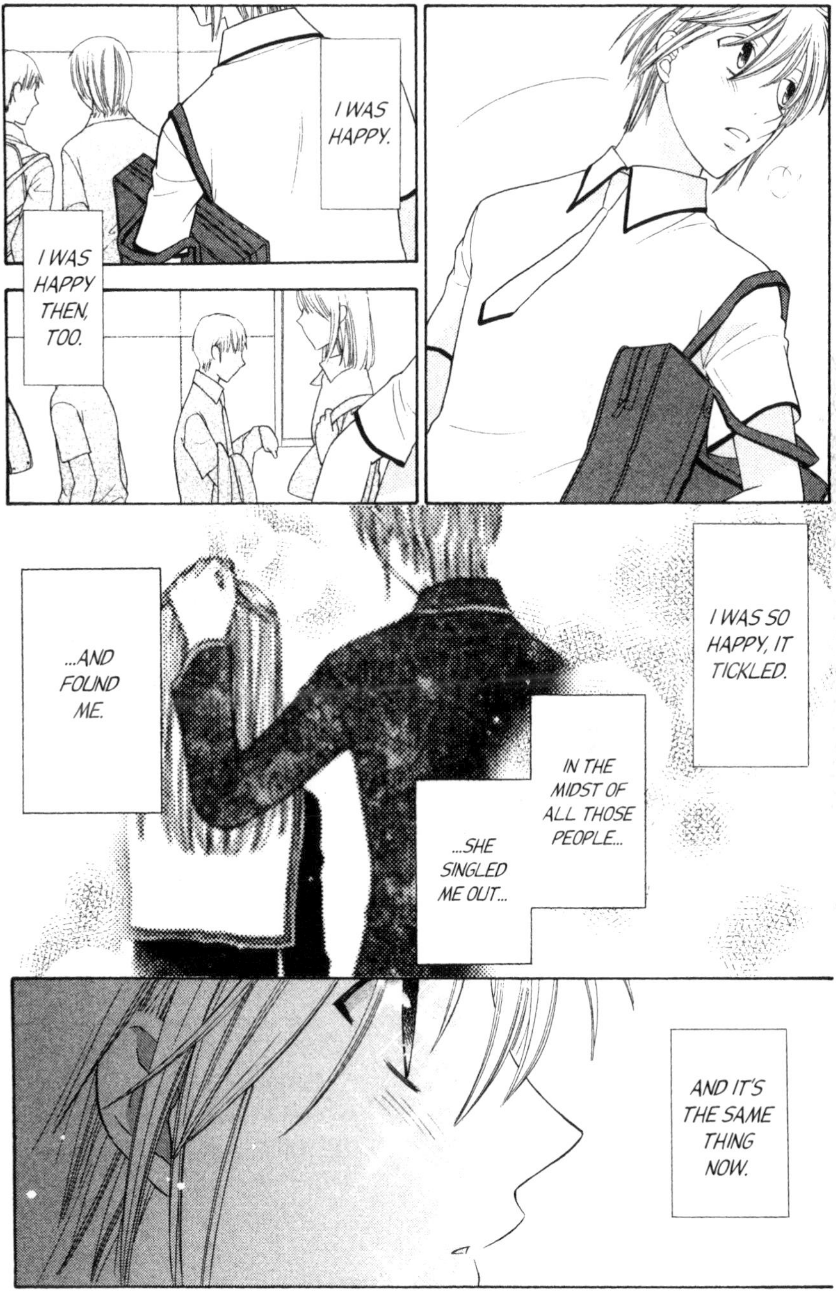
I WAS HAPPY.
I WAS HAPPY THEN, TOO.
I WAS SO HAPPY, IT TICKLED.
IN THE MIDST OF ALL THOSE PEOPLE...
...SHE SINGLED ME OUT...
...AND FOUND ME.
AND IT'S THE SAME THING NOW.

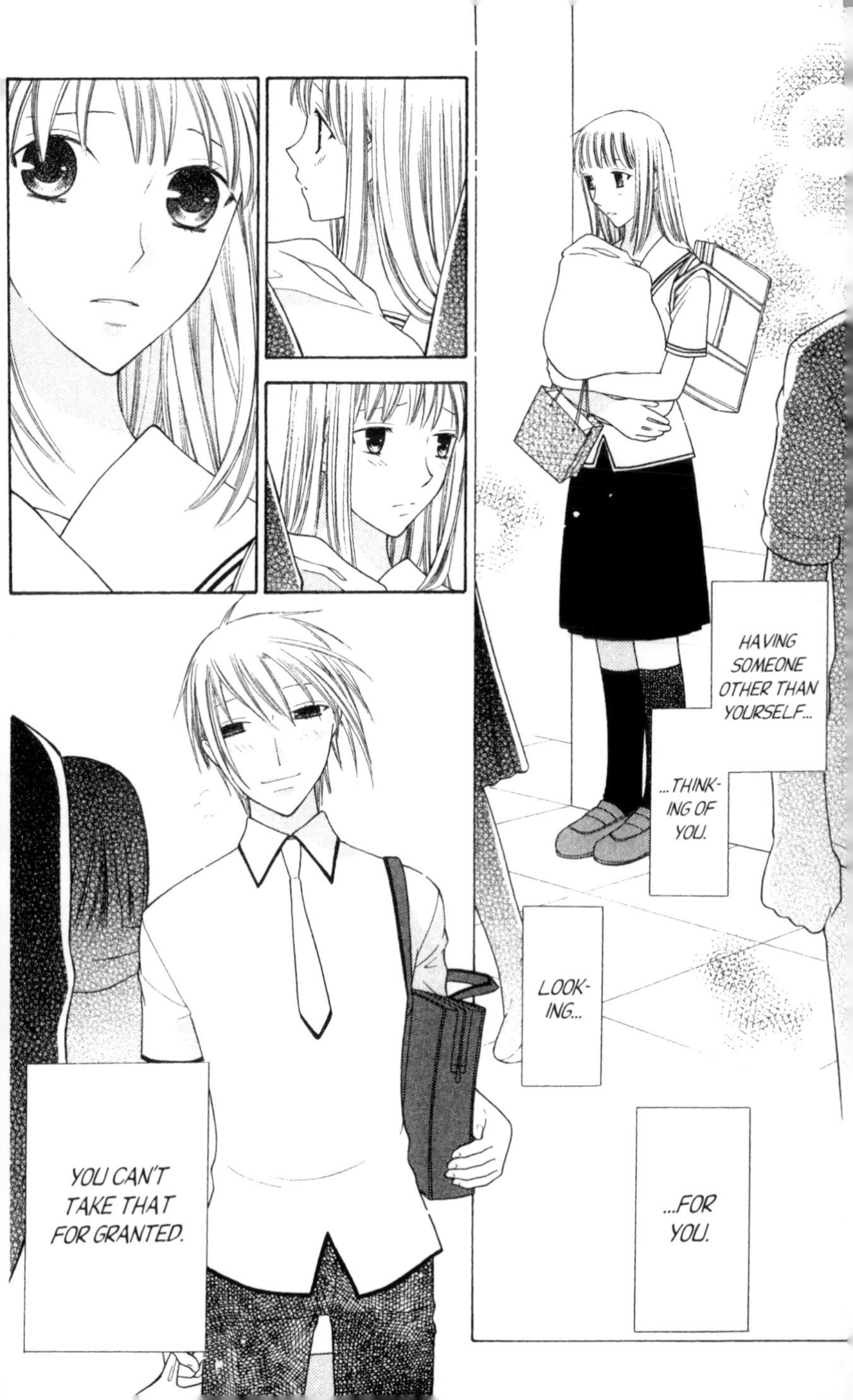
HAVING SOMEONE OTHER THAN YOURSELF...
...THINK-ING OF YOU.
LOOK-ING...
...FOR YOU.
YOU CAN'T TAKE THAT FOR GRANTED.

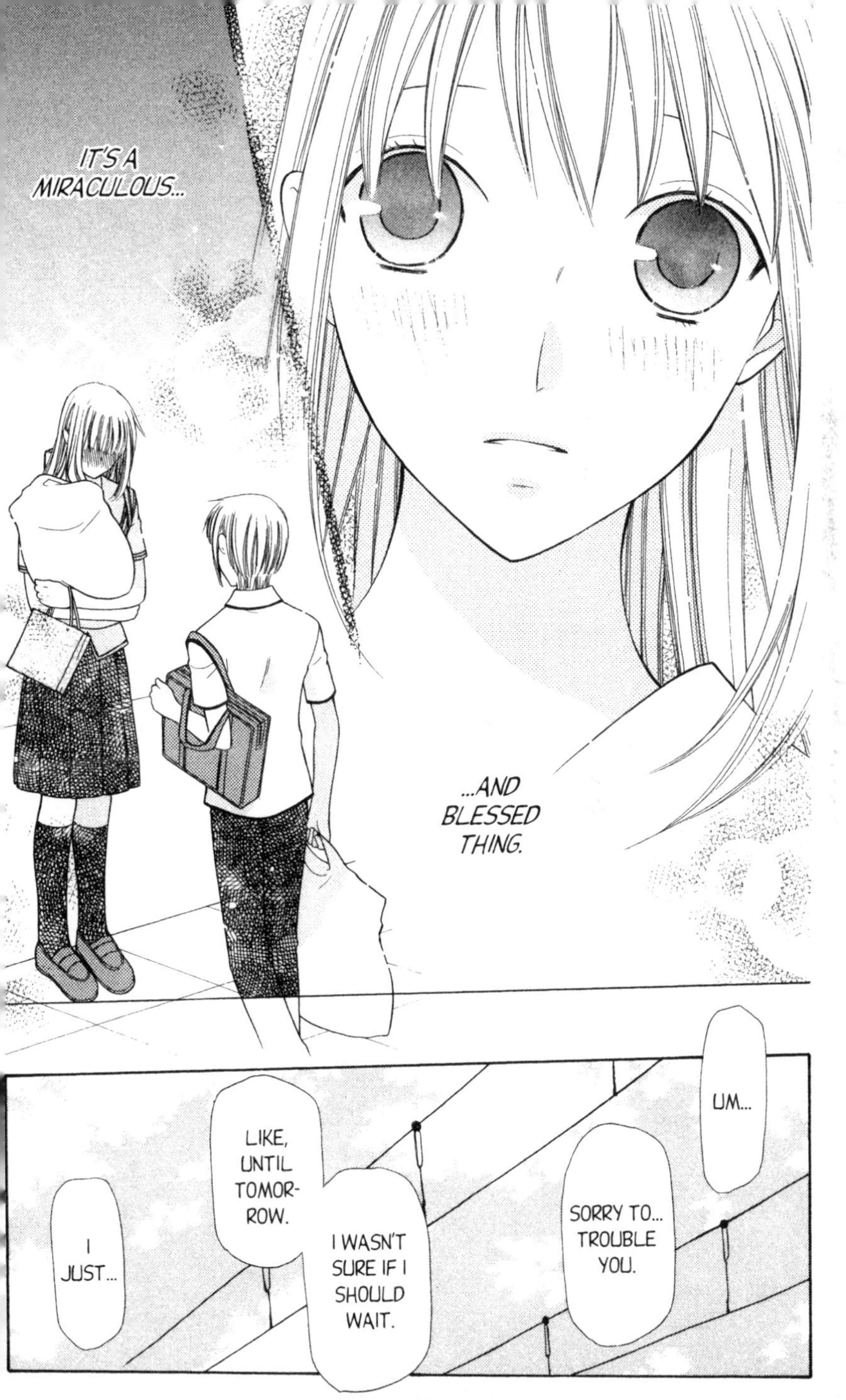
IT'S A MIRACULOUS...
...AND BLESSED THING.
UM...
SORRY TO... TROUBLE YOU.
I WASN'T SURE IF I SHOULD WAIT.
LIKE, UNTIL TOMOR-ROW.
I JUST...

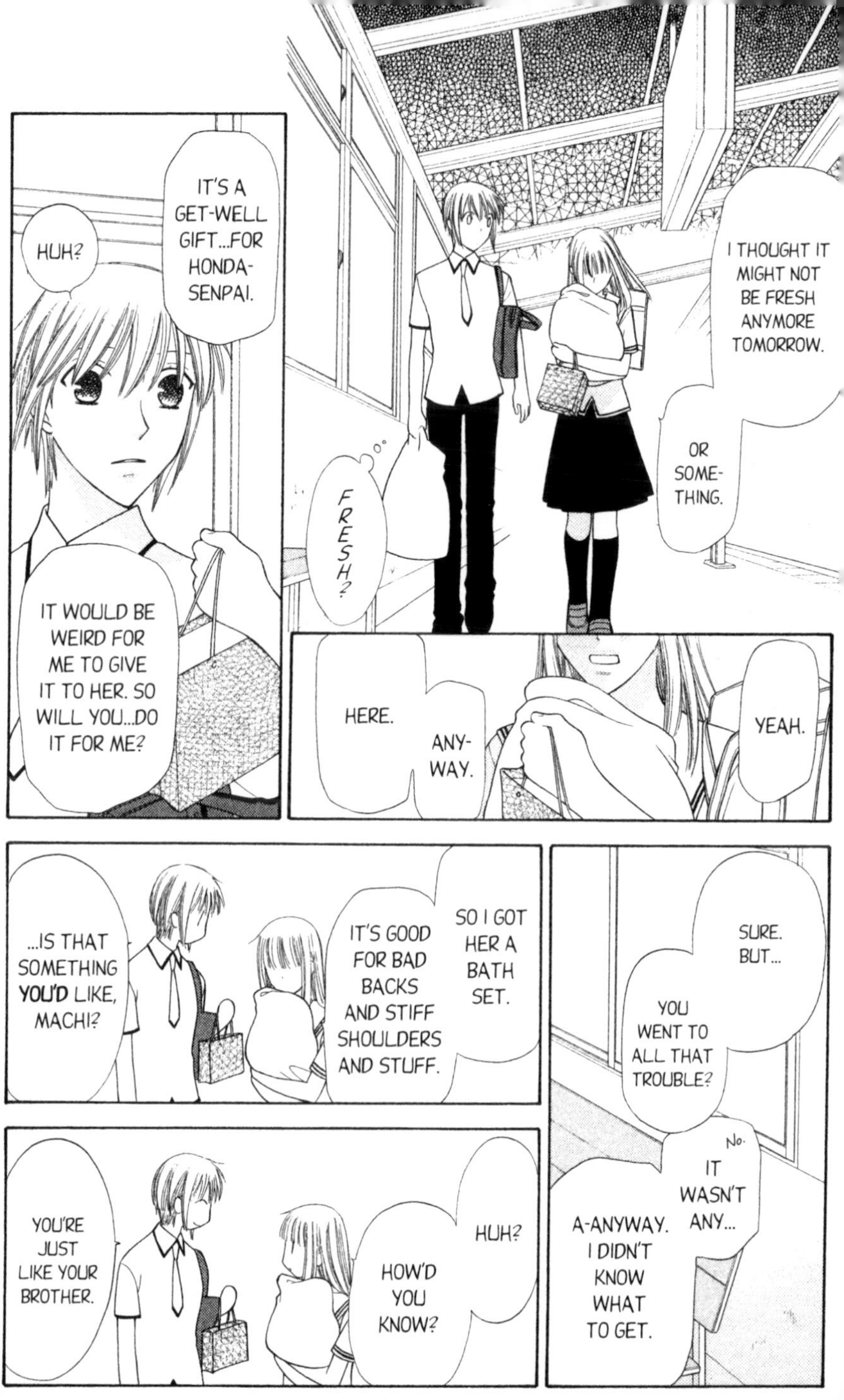
I THOUGHT IT MIGHT NOT BE FRESH ANYMORE TOMORROW.
OR SOMETHING.
FRESH?
YEAH.
ANYWAY.
HERE.
IT'S A GET-WELL GIFT...FOR HONDA-SENPAI.
HUH?
IT WOULD BE WEIRD FOR ME TO GIVE IT TO HER. SO WILL YOU...DO IT FOR ME?
SURE. BUT...
YOU WENT TO ALL THAT TROUBLE?
No.
IT WASN'T ANY...
A-ANYWAY. I DIDN'T KNOW WHAT TO GET.
SO I GOT HER A BATH SET.
IT'S GOOD FOR BAD BACKS AND STIFF SHOULDERS AND STUFF.
...IS THAT SOMETHING **YOU'D** LIKE, MACHI?
HUH?
HOW'D YOU KNOW?
YOU'RE JUST LIKE YOUR BROTHER.

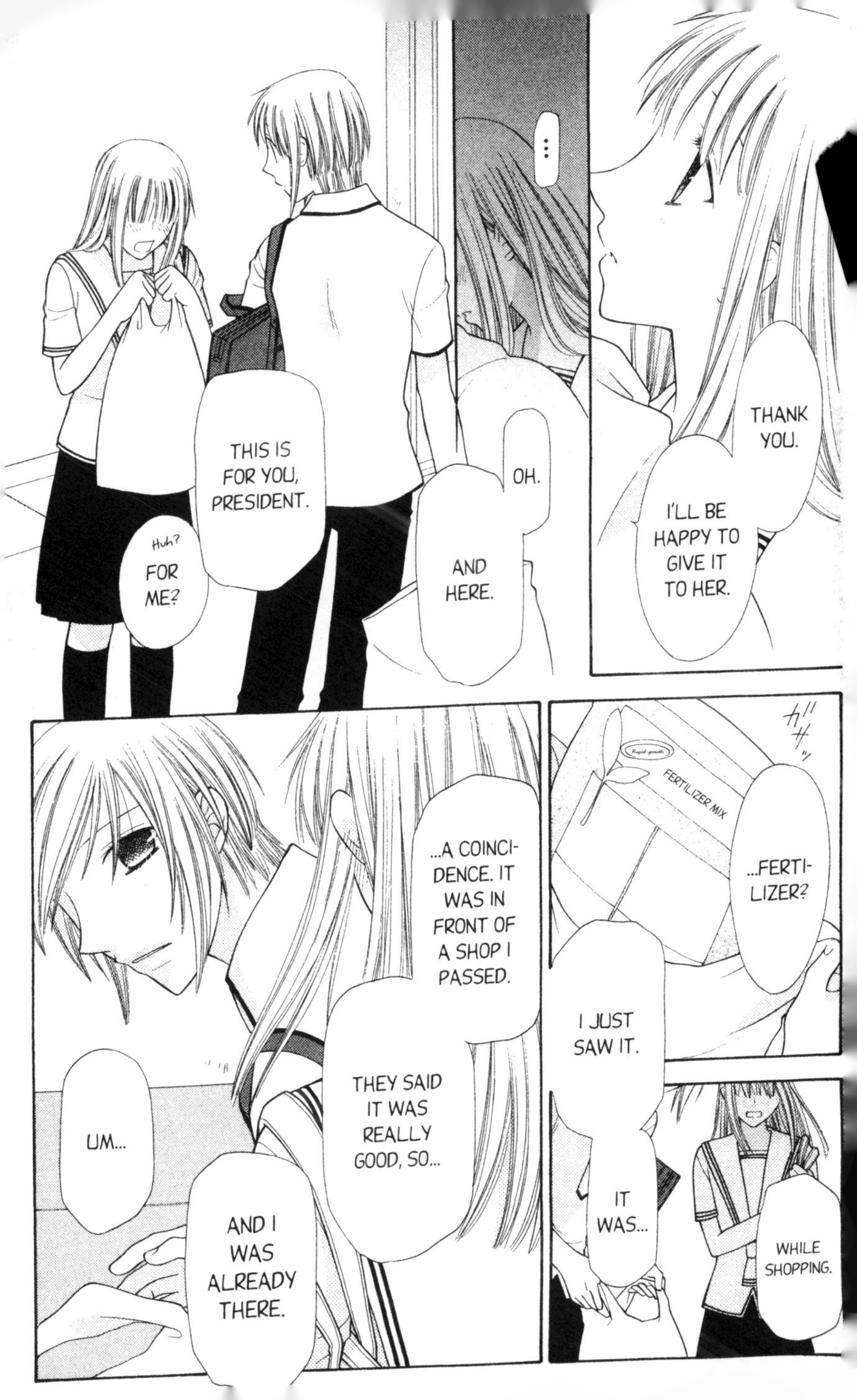
THANK YOU.
I'LL BE HAPPY TO GIVE IT TO HER.
...
OH.
AND HERE.
THIS IS FOR YOU, PRESIDENT.
Huh? FOR ME?
カサ
Rapid growth
FERTILIZER MIX
...FERTILIZER?
I JUST SAW IT.
IT WAS...
WHILE SHOPPING.
...A COINCIDENCE. IT WAS IN FRONT OF A SHOP I PASSED.
THEY SAID IT WAS REALLY GOOD, SO...
UM...
AND I WAS ALREADY THERE.

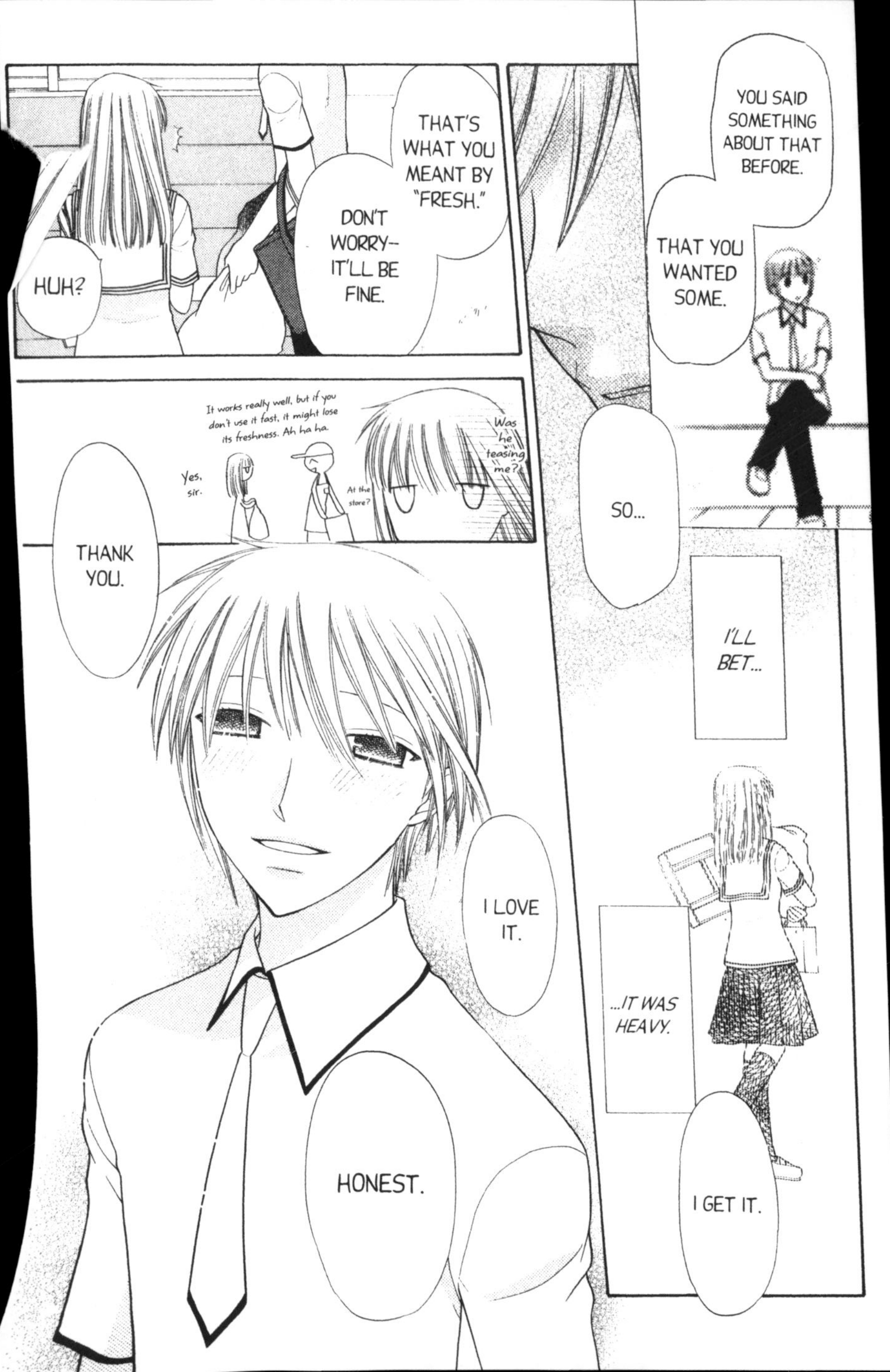
YOU SAID SOMETHING ABOUT THAT BEFORE.
THAT YOU WANTED SOME.
SO...
I'LL BET...
...IT WAS HEAVY.
I GET IT.
THAT'S WHAT YOU MEANT BY "FRESH."
DON'T WORRY-- IT'LL BE FINE.
HUH?
It works really well, but if you don't use it fast, it might lose its freshness. Ah ha ha.
At the store?
Yes, sir.
Was he teasing me?
THANK YOU.
I LOVE IT.
HONEST.

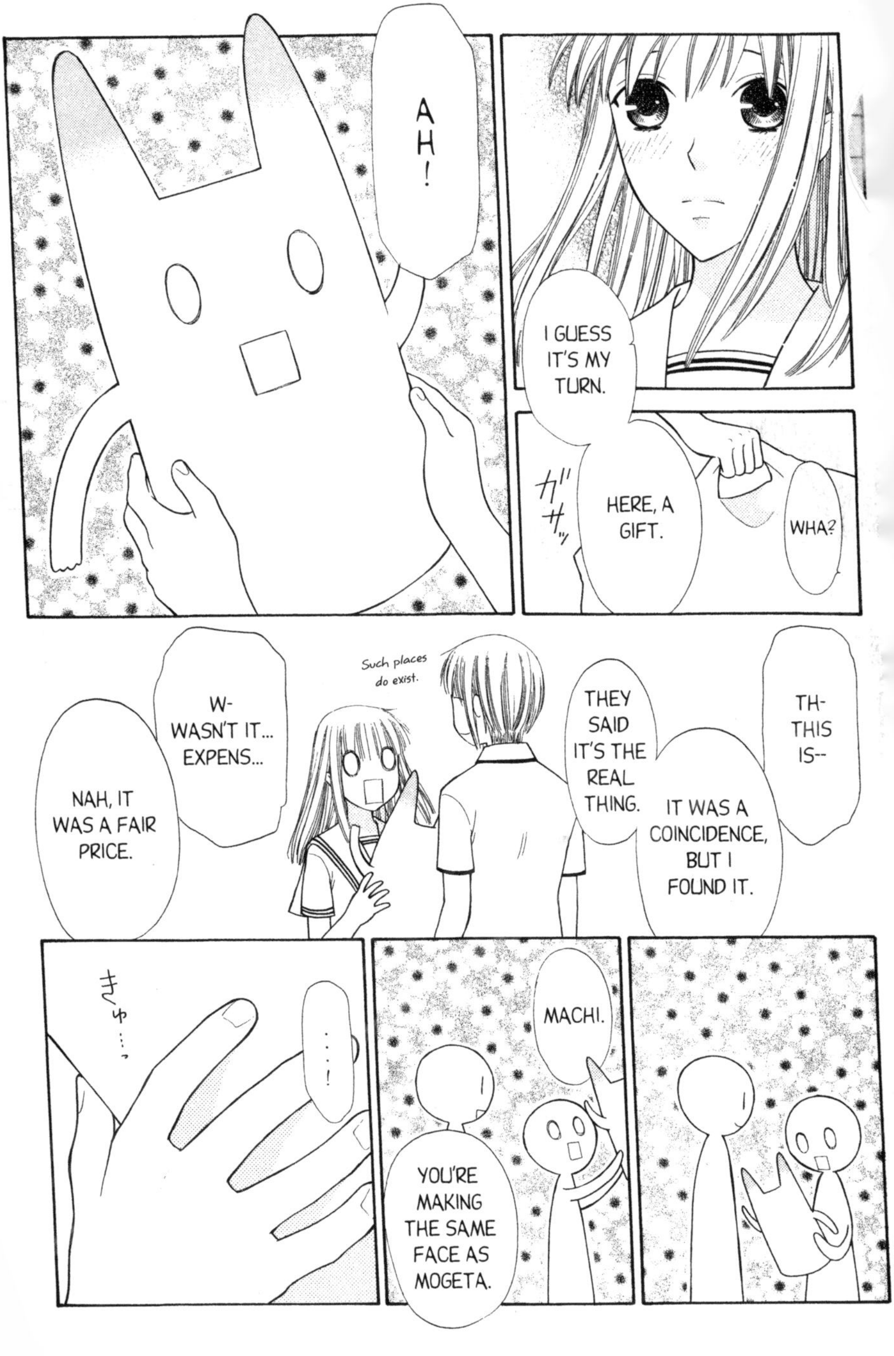
I GUESS IT'S MY TURN.
WHA?
HERE, A GIFT.
ガサッ
AH!
TH-THIS IS--
IT WAS A COINCIDENCE, BUT I FOUND IT.
THEY SAID IT'S THE REAL THING.
Such places do exist.
W-WASN'T IT... EXPENS...
NAH, IT WAS A FAIR PRICE.
MACHI.
YOU'RE MAKING THE SAME FACE AS MOGETA.
きゅ…っ
...!

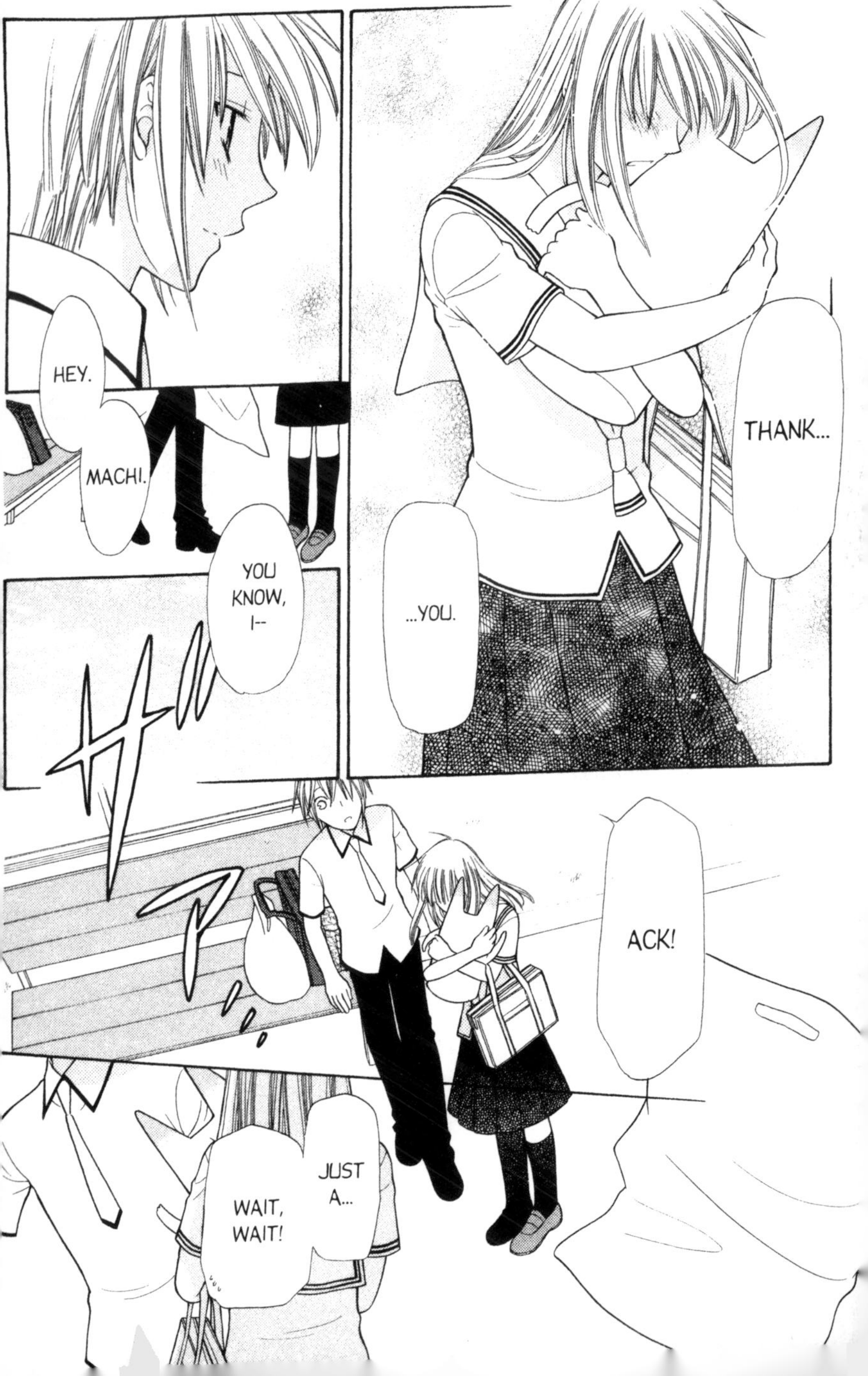
THANK...
...YOU.
HEY.
MACHI.
YOU KNOW, I--
ACK!
JUST A...
WAIT, WAIT!

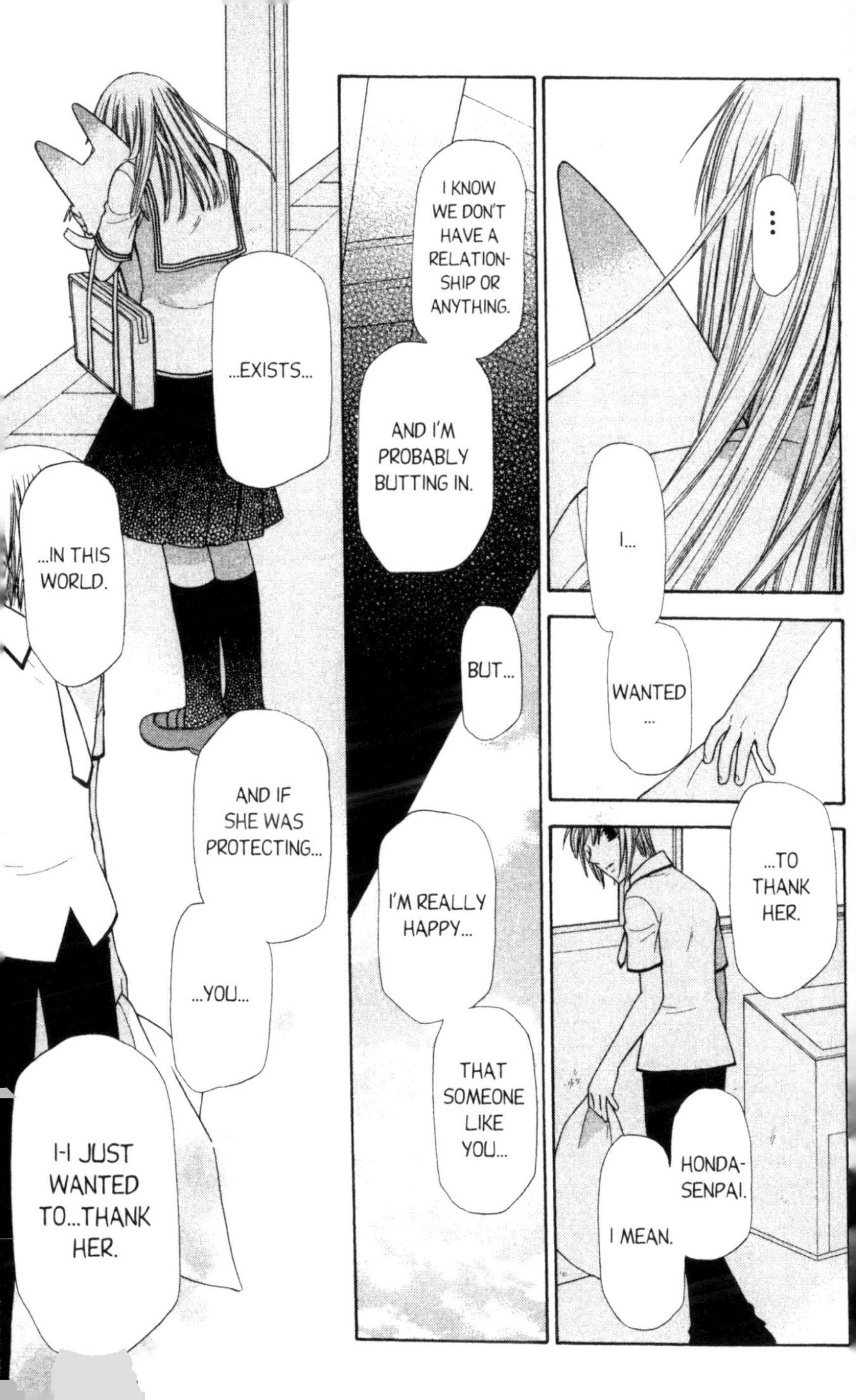
...
I...
WANTED ...
...TO THANK HER.
HONDA-SENPAI.
I MEAN.
I KNOW WE DON'T HAVE A RELATIONSHIP OR ANYTHING.
AND I'M PROBABLY BUTTING IN.
BUT...
I'M REALLY HAPPY...
THAT SOMEONE LIKE YOU...
...EXISTS...
...IN THIS WORLD.
AND IF SHE WAS PROTECTING...
...YOU...
I-I JUST WANTED TO...THANK HER.

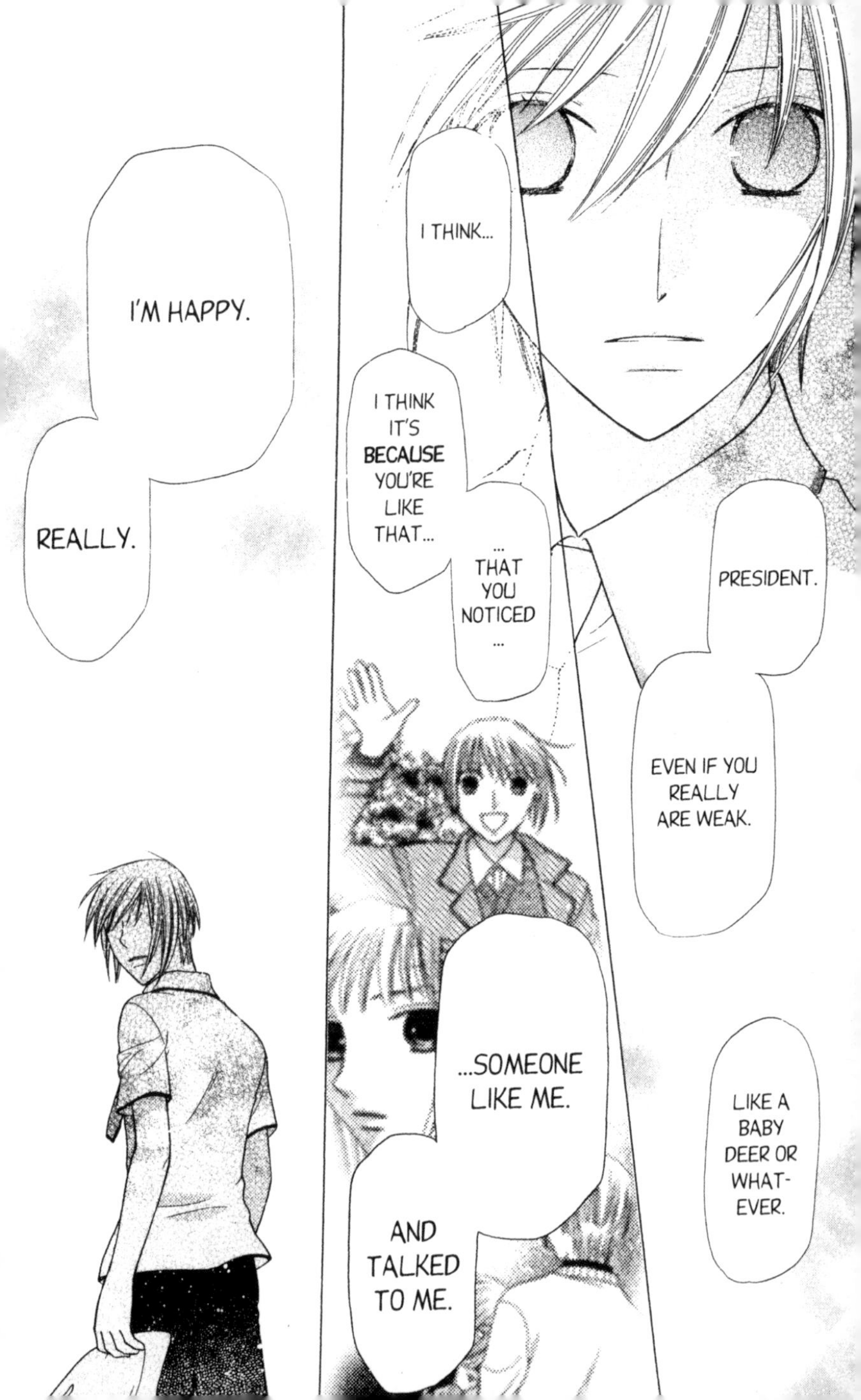
PRESIDENT.
EVEN IF YOU REALLY ARE WEAK.
LIKE A BABY DEER OR WHATEVER.
I THINK...
I THINK IT'S BECAUSE YOU'RE LIKE THAT...
...THAT YOU NOTICED...
...SOMEONE LIKE ME.
AND TALKED TO ME.
I'M HAPPY.
REALLY.

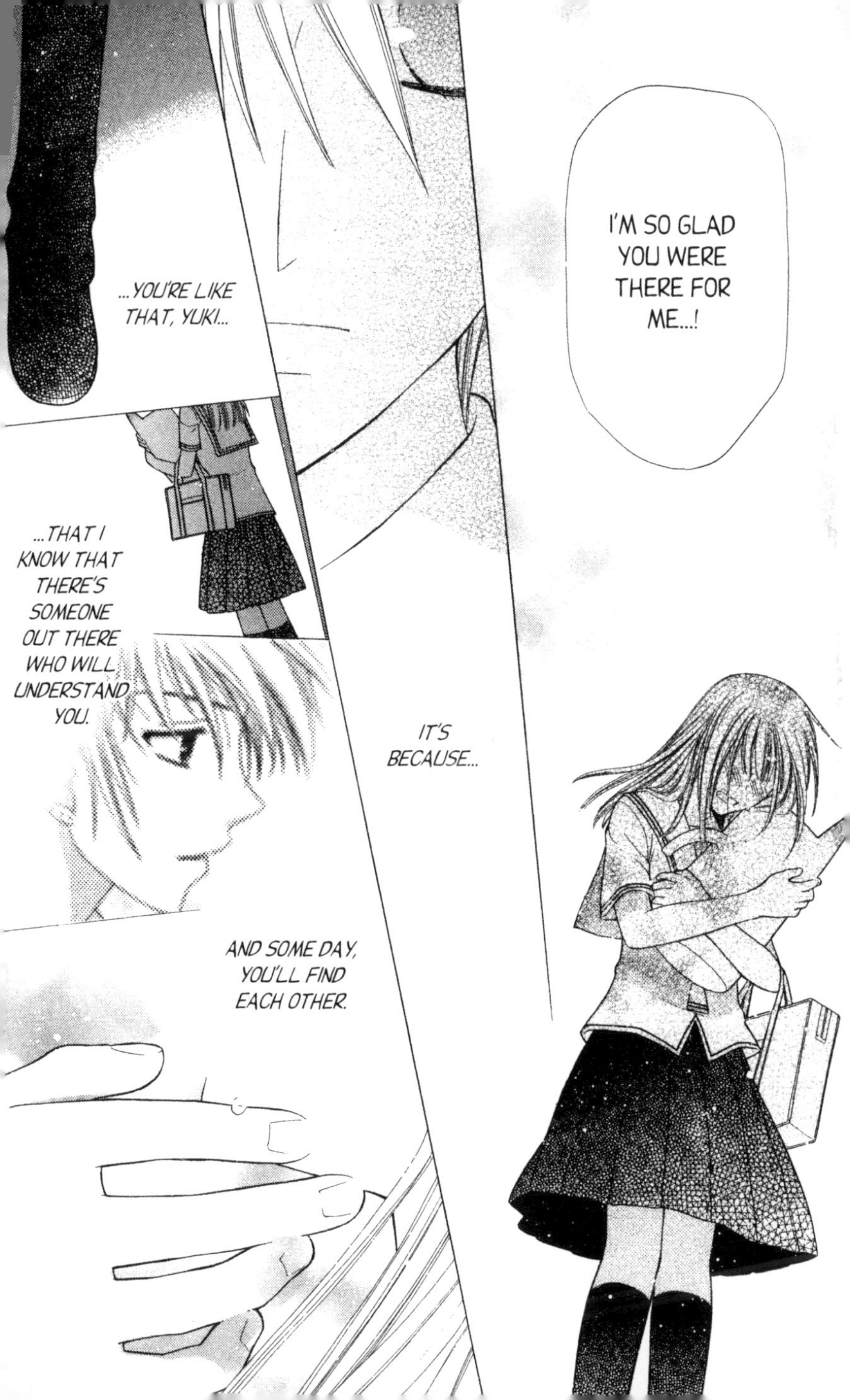
I'M SO GLAD YOU WERE THERE FOR ME...!
IT'S BECAUSE...
...YOU'RE LIKE THAT, YUKI...
...THAT I KNOW THAT THERE'S SOMEONE OUT THERE WHO WILL UNDERSTAND YOU.
AND SOME DAY, YOU'LL FIND EACH OTHER.

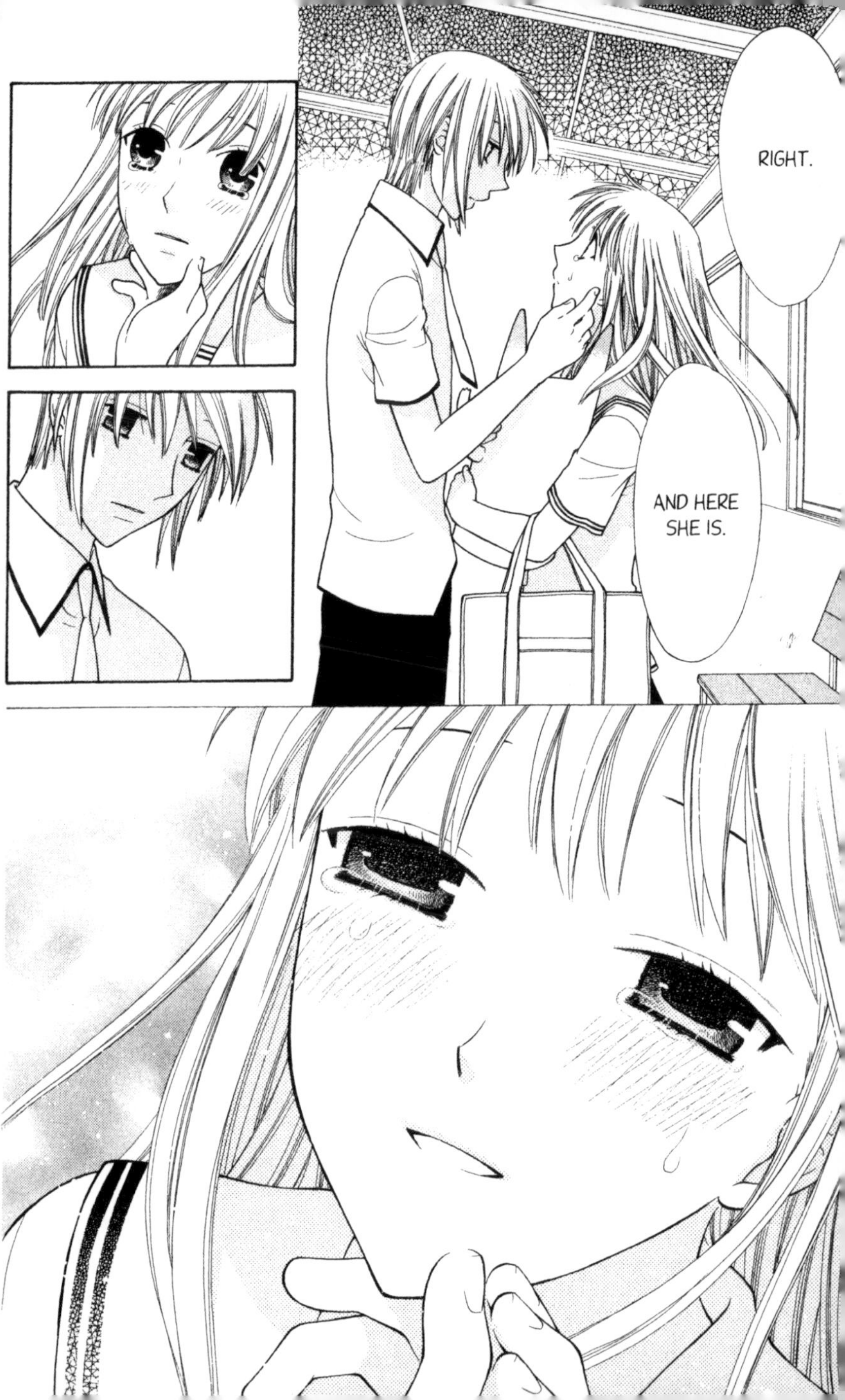
RIGHT.
AND HERE SHE IS.

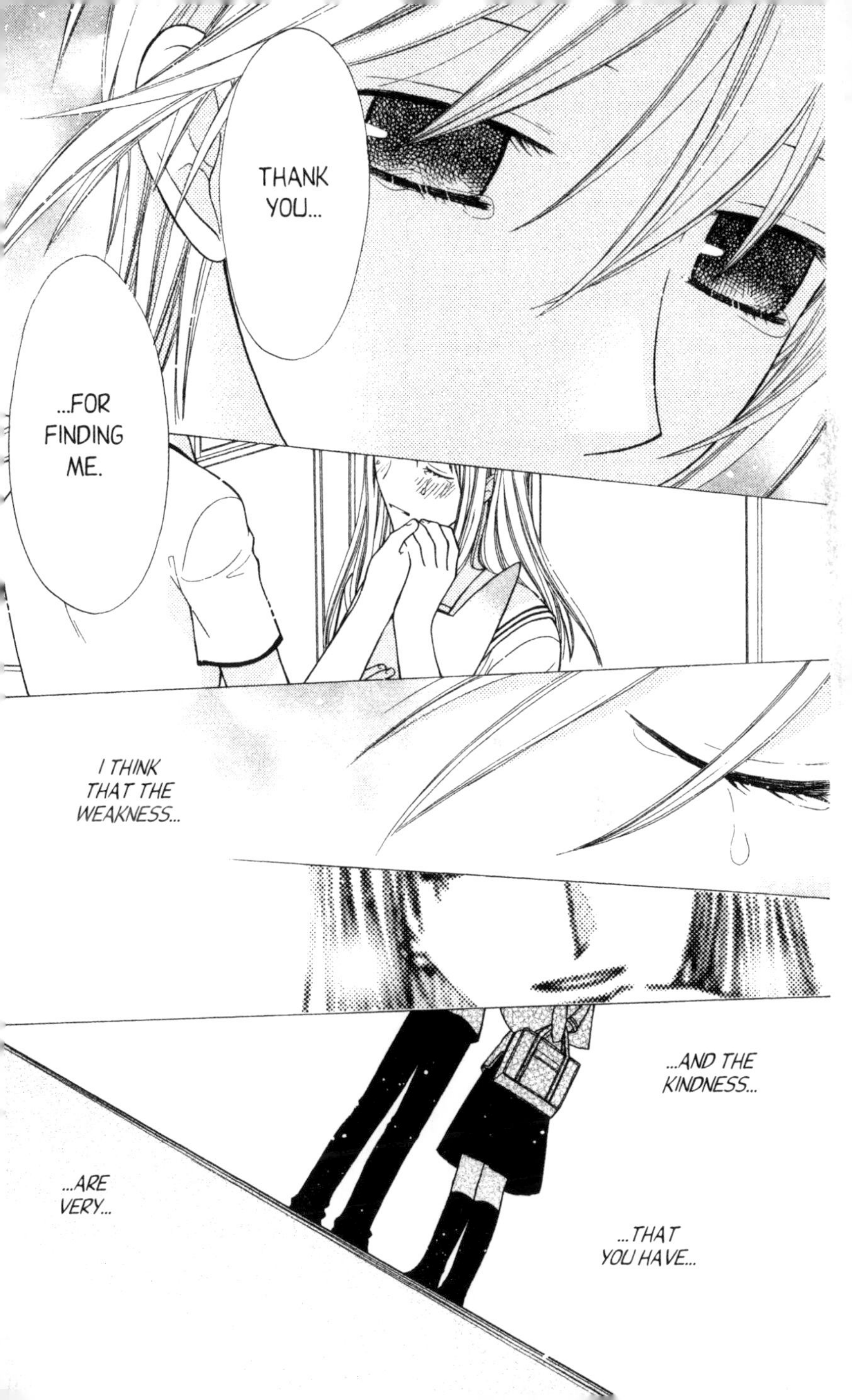
THANK YOU...
...FOR FINDING ME.
I THINK THAT THE WEAKNESS...
...AND THE KINDNESS...
...THAT YOU HAVE...
...ARE VERY...

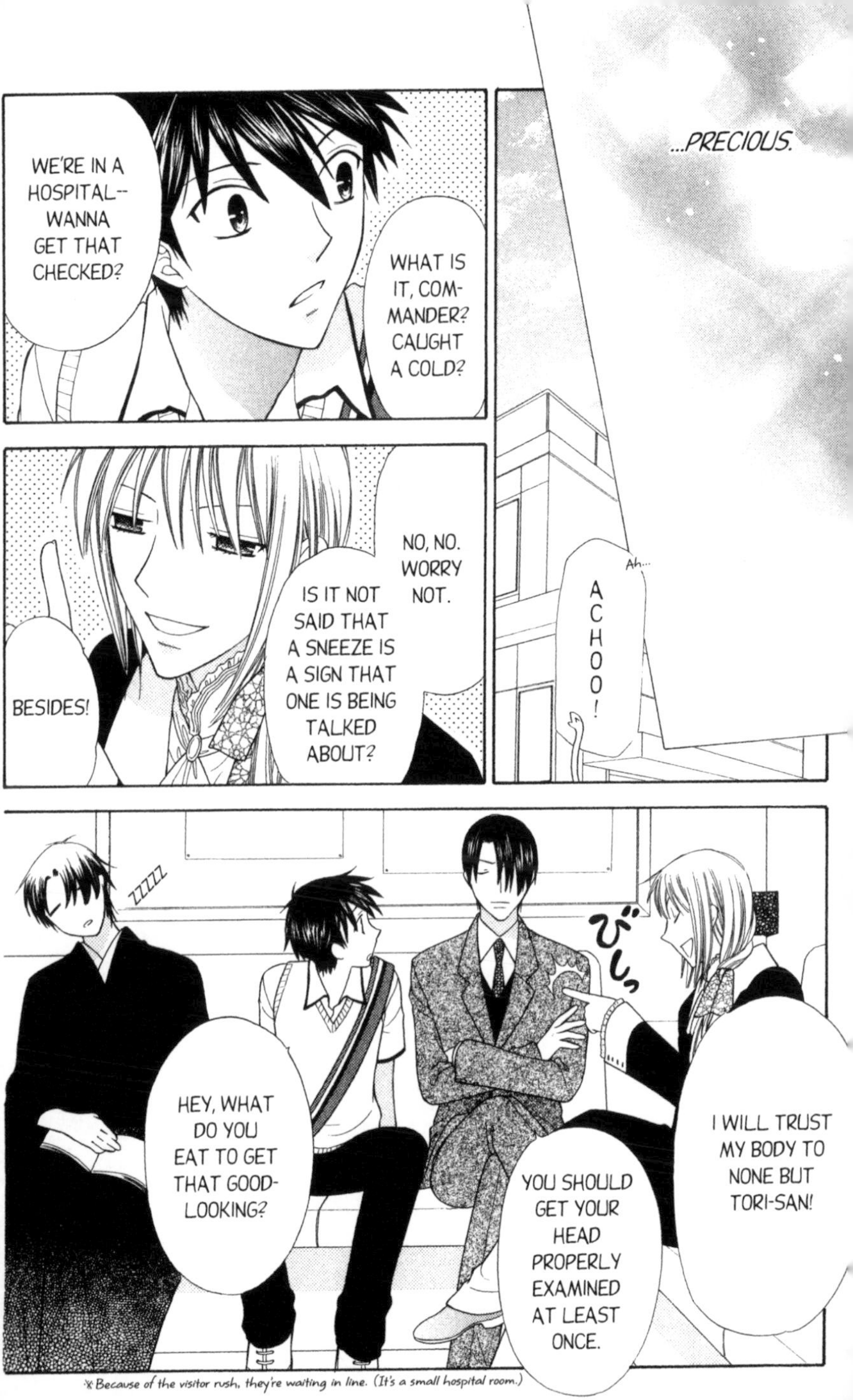
...PRECIOUS.
Ah...
ACHOO!
WHAT IS IT, COMMANDER? CAUGHT A COLD?
WE'RE IN A HOSPITAL-- WANNA GET THAT CHECKED?
NO, NO. WORRY NOT.
IS IT NOT SAID THAT A SNEEZE IS A SIGN THAT ONE IS BEING TALKED ABOUT?
BESIDES!
I WILL TRUST MY BODY TO NONE BUT TORI-SAN!
びしっ
YOU SHOULD GET YOUR HEAD PROPERLY EXAMINED AT LEAST ONCE.
HEY, WHAT DO YOU EAT TO GET THAT GOOD-LOOKING?
ZZZZZ

※Because of the visitor rush, they're waiting in line. (It's a small hospital room.)

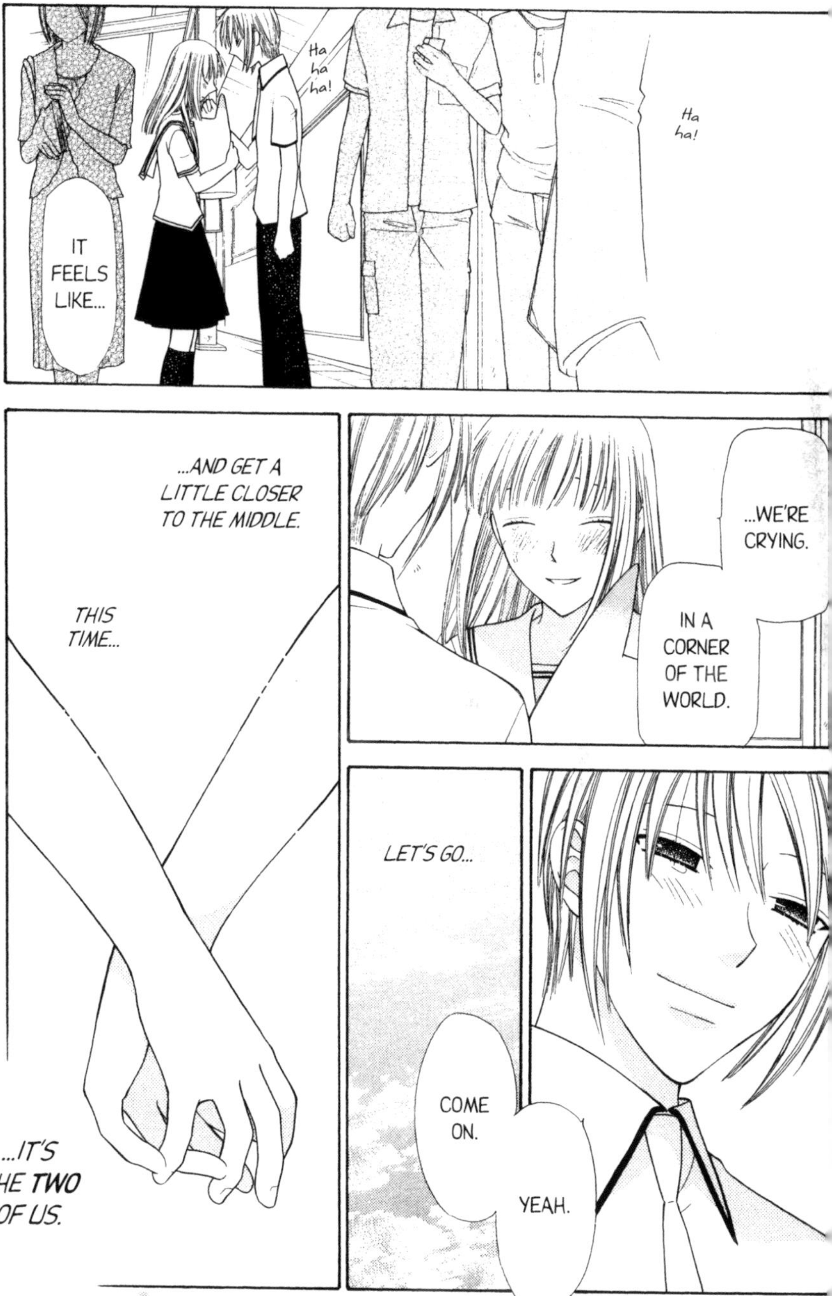
Ha ha!
Ha ha ha!
IT FEELS LIKE...
...WE'RE CRYING.
IN A CORNER OF THE WORLD.
COME ON.
YEAH.
LET'S GO...
...AND GET A LITTLE CLOSER TO THE MIDDLE.
THIS TIME...
...IT'S THE **TWO** OF US.

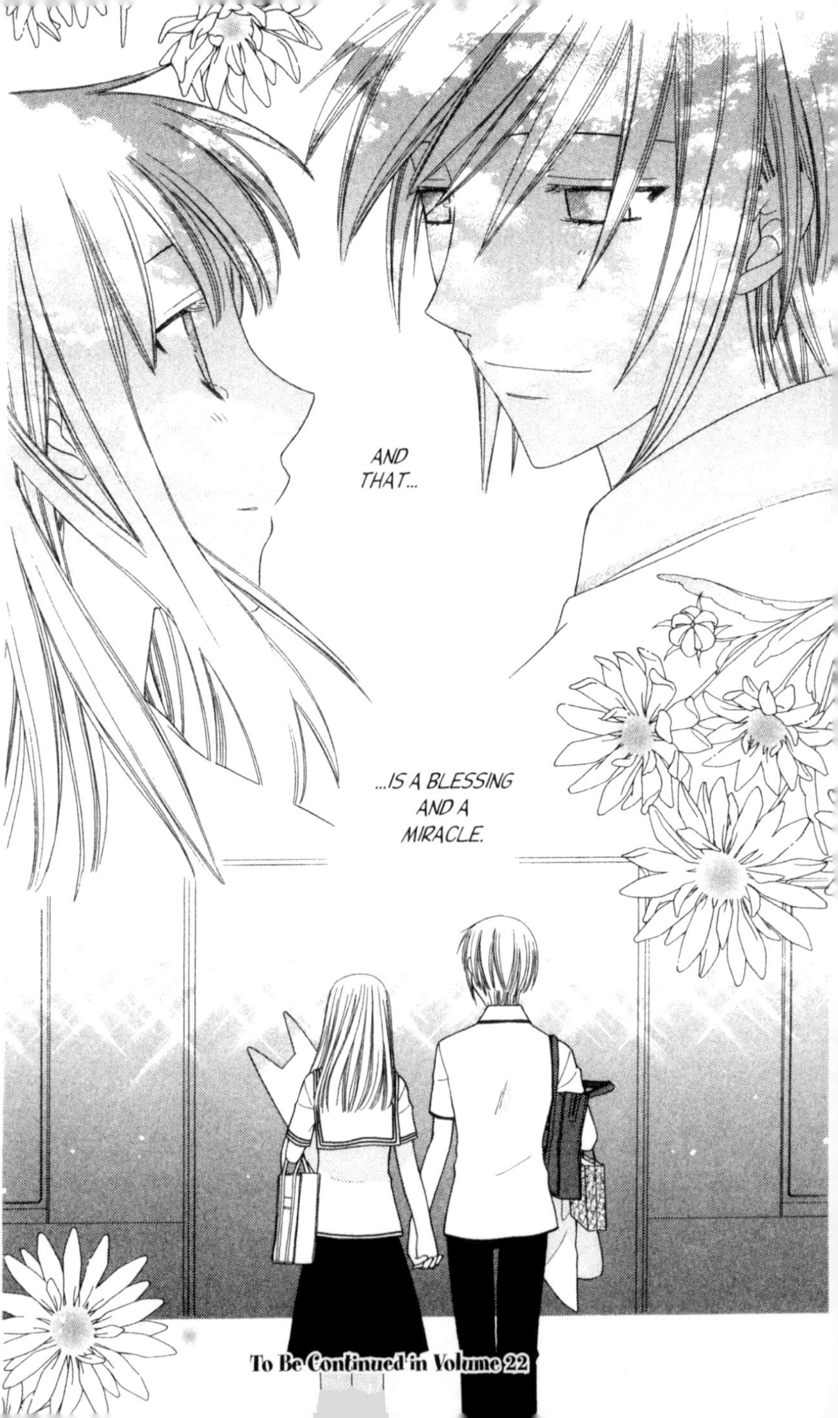
AND THAT...
...IS A BLESSING AND A MIRACLE.
To Be Continued in Volume 22

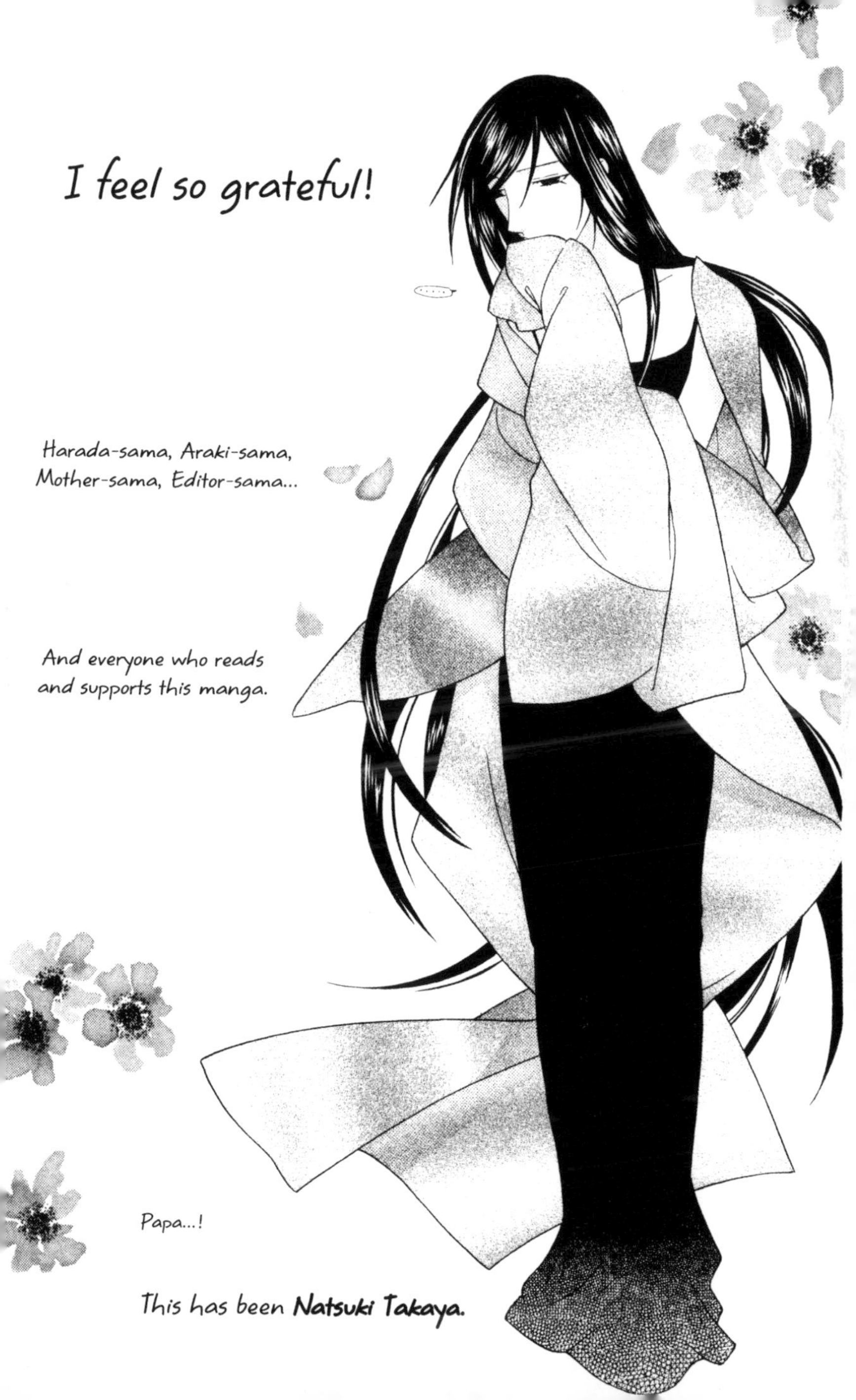
I feel so grateful!
.....
Harada-sama, Araki-sama, Mother-sama, Editor-sama...
And everyone who reads and supports this manga.
Papa...!
This has been Natsuki Takaya.

Next time in...

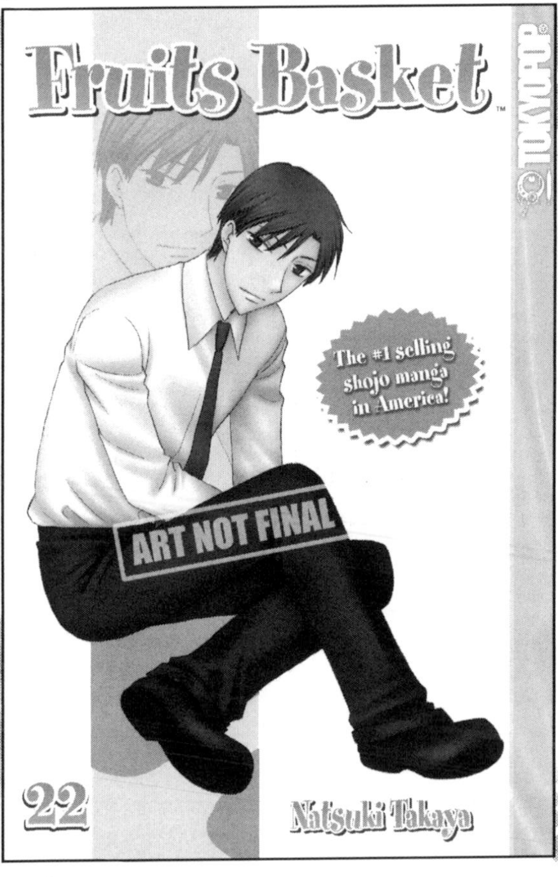
Fruits Basket
TOKYOPOP
The #1 selling shojo manga in America!
ART NOT FINAL
22
Natsuki Takaya

Crumbling Curse

Kyo finally makes the decision to stop running from his fears and confront his birth father. But how will he react to his father's pressure to accept an unwanted truth? Meanwhile, as Akito's control over the Sohma family slips away, will the last vestiges of her sanity and reason slip away as well?

Fruits Basket Volume 22
Available March 2009

Fans Basket

Welcome to another edition of Fans Basket! I'm taking over as editor for the series and the amount of mail we continue to get for Fruits Basket amazes me! Thanks so much to everyone for supporting Fruits Basket so strongly! Helping out for this section is our super awesome intern from upstate New York, Kaitlin Gallup! She worked very hard to sift through boxes of fan mail to pick out some great entries. Enjoy!

I'd also like to take this opportunity to thank Paul Morrisey, the longtime editor of Fruits Basket. Paul did an amazing job on the last dozen volumes of the series and he will be greatly missed. Matching his level of excellence will be a major challenge for us all. Thanks so much, Paul!

- Alexis Kirsch, Editor

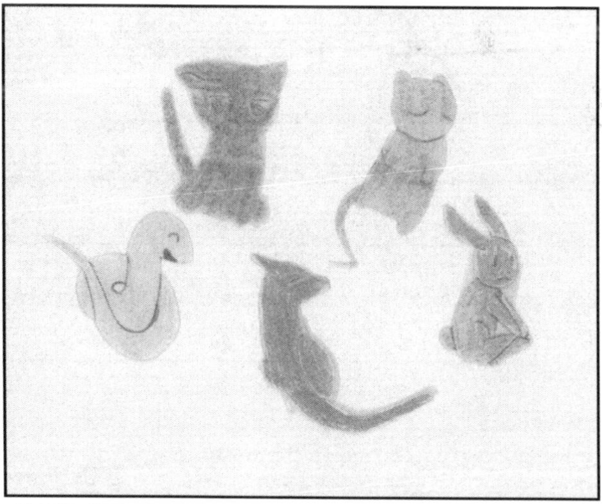

Catherine Schweitzer
Age 14
Tacoma, WA

All I could think of was "how cute!" I guess this answers your questions about your stickers, Catherine! Your artwork was great, but I just fell in love with the stickers, especially Momiji as a rabbit! Keep up the creativity and the good work!

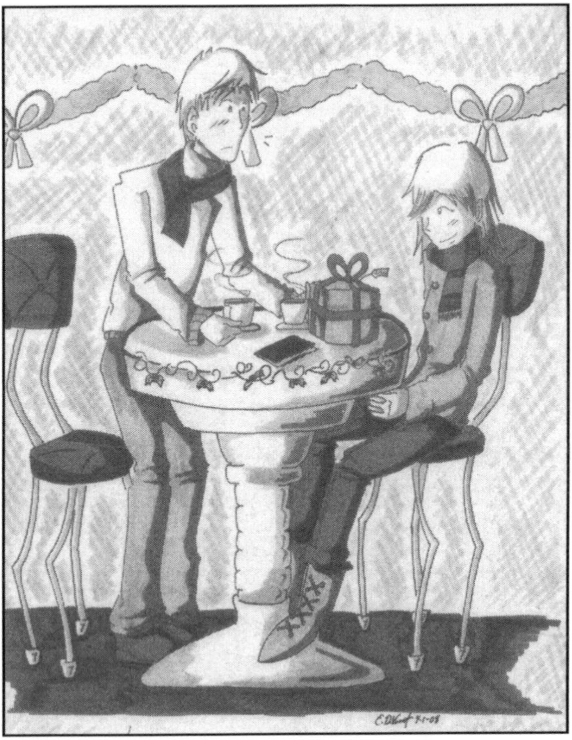

Emily DeVault
Age 15
Fairmont, WV

Emily's art was one of the first ones I picked up and it just blew me away. The way the shading was done really impressed me. I love the facial expressions, especially Arisa's, seeming just a little bit shy as Kureno gives her a Christmas present. Amazing!

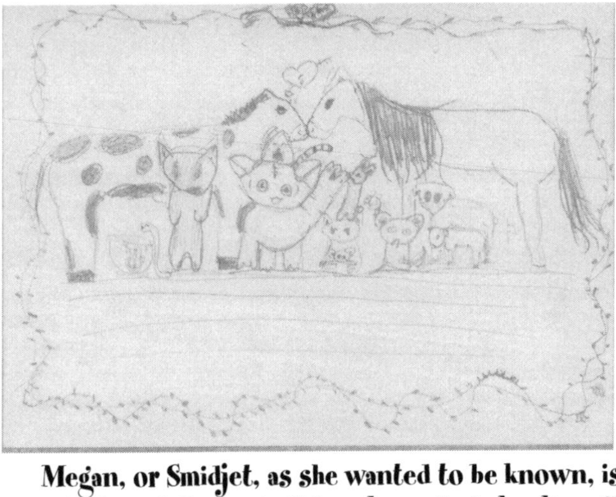

Megan Harp
Age 10
Stoke-on-trent UK

Megan, or Smidjet, as she wanted to be known, is not only our youngest contributor in this volume, but also lives the farthest away. I liked this picture, especially the different expressions on the animals, and I loved your letter. I daydream about Fruits Basket characters too!

"Ephemeral Promise" ~A Poem for Kagura and Kyo~

A child's promise is like the tears
That trail behind you as you walk
A child's promise is packed away
With the playthings in a box
A child's promise doesn't mean anything
Once childhood is passed

The words that are forgotten
The wish that fades away
A child's promise isn't worth much nowadays

The dreams that you grew out of
The innocent love of yesterday
A child's promise doesn't mean much anyway

Candice Crockett
Age 22
Cincinnati, Ohio

This poem is so beautiful, especially the imagery. Don't worry about not drawing well enough to turn in art, I can't draw or write beautiful poetry like this! Great job!

Natalie Wolfe
Age 14
Island Lake, IL

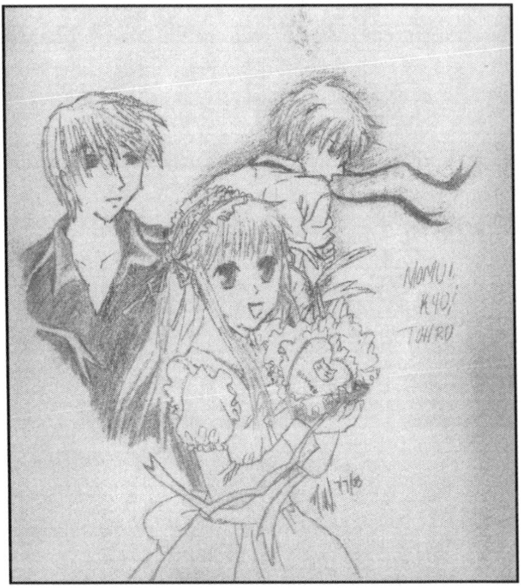
MOMIJI,
KYO,
TOHRU

Natalie is an example of how persistence pays off. And no payment necessary either! I love your depiction of a sad Momiji. He looks dark and depressed in the background, his back turned to the viewer. Definitely not the usual Momiji!

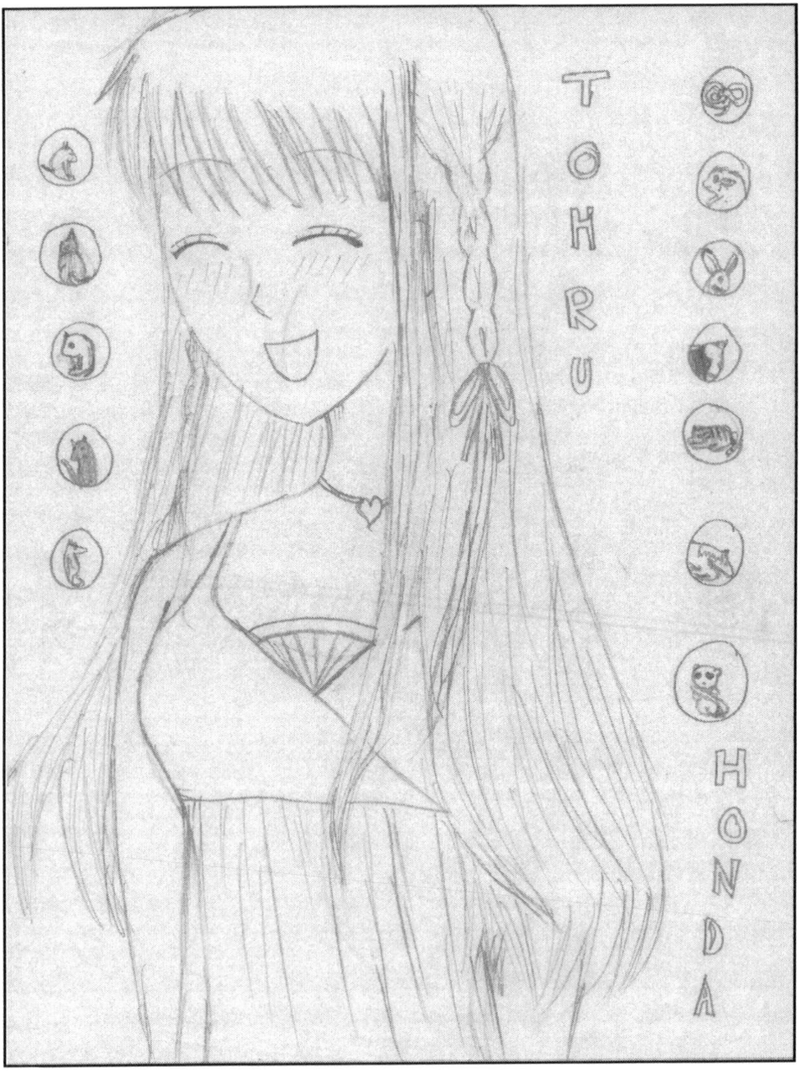
TOHRU
HONDA

Tatyana Mathis
Age 11
Willingboro, NJ

This seems almost like it could be a picture for a character profile. With a good drawing of Tohru, happy as usual, her name and the zodiac animals, the artwork really grabs you. The pictures of the zodiac animals really just complete the picture so well.

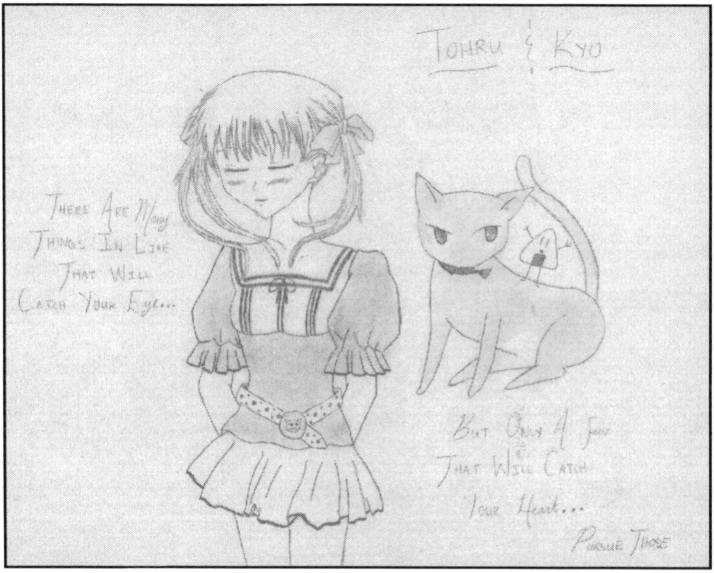
Tohru & Kyo
There Are Many Things In Life That Will Catch Your Eye...
But Only A Few That Will Catch Your Heart...
Pursue Those

Keisha Hanes
Age 13
Mississauga
Ontario, Canada

Tohru looks so cute here especially in this outfit and with Kyo and an onigiri next to her! I love the message most of all. It's such an important theme, to pursue the things you love, no matter what.

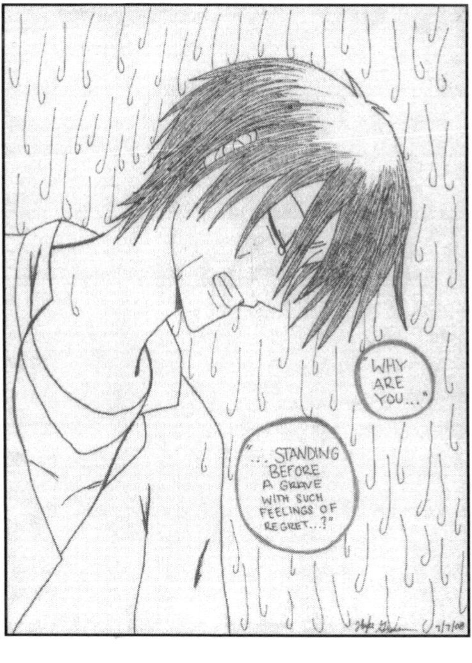
"WHY ARE YOU..."
"...STANDING BEFORE A GRAVE WITH SUCH FEELINGS OF REGRET...?"

Haylee Graham
Age 15
Chandler, AZ

This picture has such feeling behind it. Kyo's facial expression plus the rain and the tears make it very poignant. The quote is just the perfect touch.

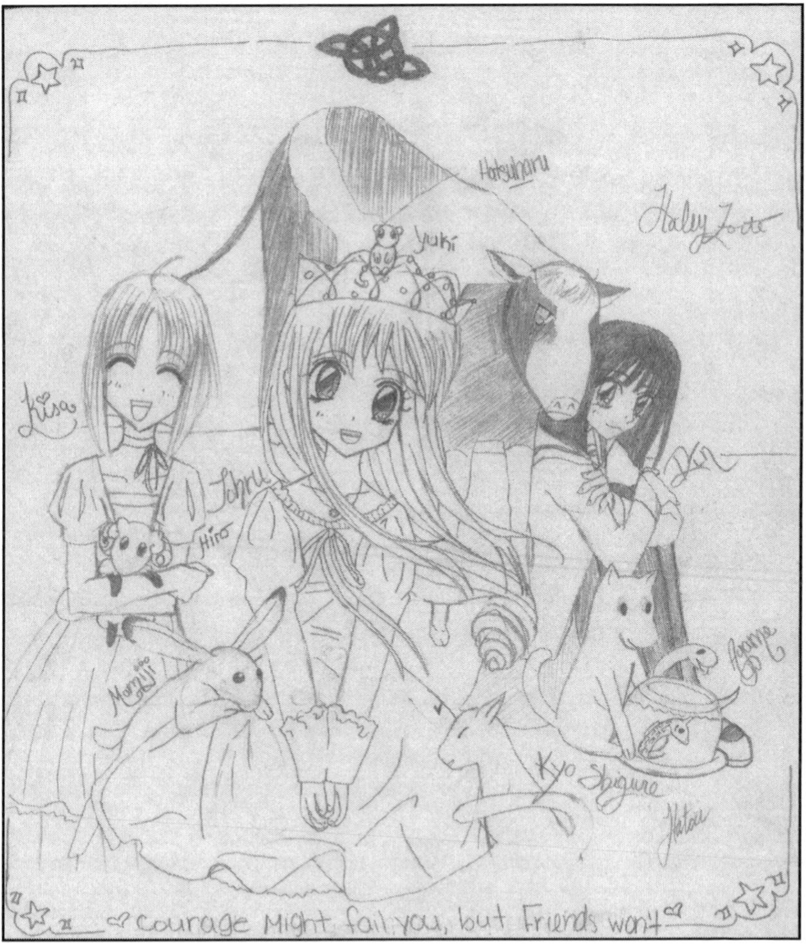
Hatsuharu
Haley Forte
Yuki
Kisa
Tohru
Hiro
Momiji
Kyo
Shigure
Hatori
courage Might fail you, but Friends won't

Haley Forté
Age 15
Rock Hill, SC

This is probably my favorite of the fanart I saw. The scene is set-up so well, with all the characters, their names (for anyone who doesn't already know them), a crown for Tohru, and even a border with a fancy Celtic symbol as well! The words written at the bottom are the perfect finishing touch with their message of friendship.

Do you want to share your love for *Fruits Basket* with fans around the world? "Fans Basket" is taking submissions of fan art, poetry, cosplay photos, or any other Furuba fun you'd like to share!

How to submit:

1) Send your work via regular mail (NOT e-mail) to:

"Fans Basket"
c/o TOKYOPOP
5900 Wilshire Blvd.
Suite 2000
Los Angeles, CA 90036

2) All work should be in black-and-white and no larger than 8.5" x 11". (And try not to fold it too many times!)

3) Anything you send will not be returned. If you want to keep your original, it's fine to send us a copy.

4) Please include your full name, age, city and state for us to print with your work. If you'd rather us use a pen name, please include that, too.

5) IMPORTANT: If you're under the age of 18, you must have your parent's permission in order for us to print your work. Any submissions without a signed note of parental consent cannot be used.

6) For full details, please check out our website: http://www.tokyopop.com/aboutus/fanart.php

Disclaimer: Anything you send to us becomes the exclusive property of TOKYOPOP Inc. and, as we said before, will not be returned to you. We will have the right to print, reproduce, distribute, or modify the artwork for use in future volumes of *Fruits Basket* or on the web royalty-free.

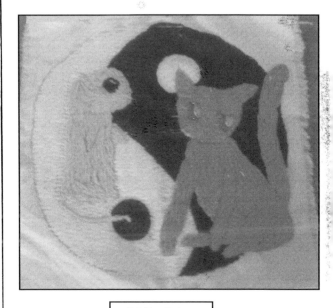

Kristina Keiner
Age 15
Owasso, OK

When I saw this picture, I was amazed. To be able to embroider something like this is incredible! Such a creative idea shows how great a fan you are.

Coming in December 2008

Phantom Dream™

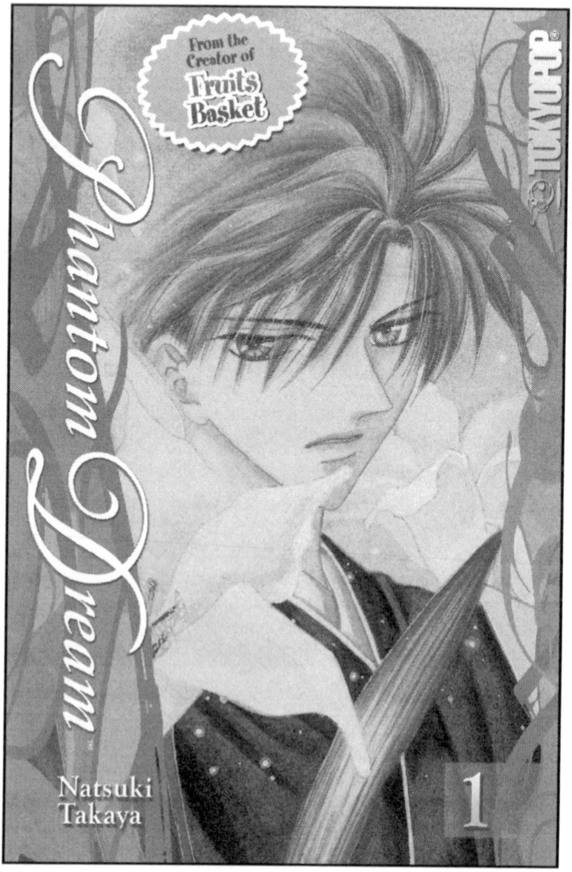
From the Creator of
Fruits Basket
TOKYOPOP
Phantom Dream
Natsuki Takaya
1

GENEIMUSOU by Natsuki Takaya

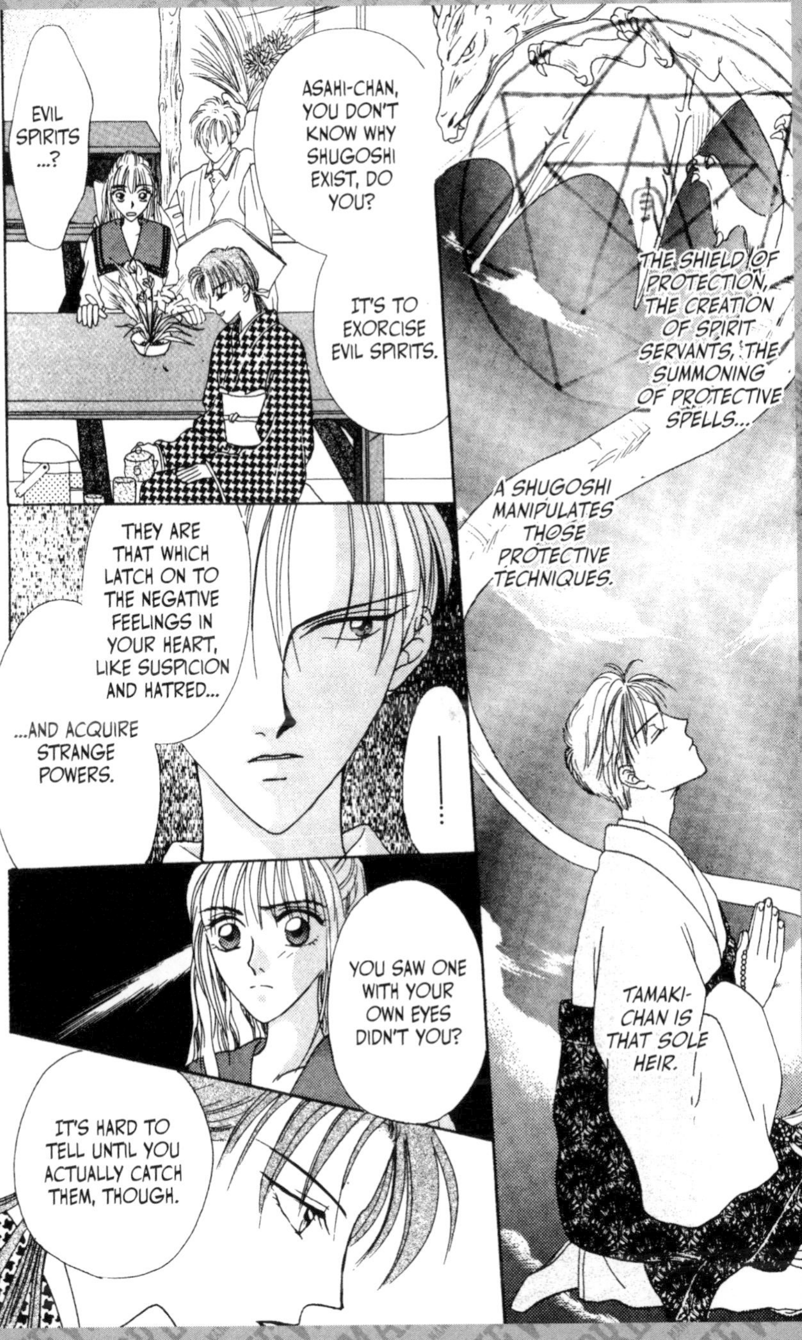
THE SHIELD OF PROTECTION, THE CREATION OF SPIRIT SERVANTS, THE SUMMONING OF PROTECTIVE SPELLS...
A SHUGOSHI MANIPULATES THOSE PROTECTIVE TECHNIQUES.
TAMAKI-CHAN IS THAT SOLE HEIR.
ASAHI-CHAN, YOU DON'T KNOW WHY SHUGOSHI EXIST, DO YOU?
IT'S TO EXORCISE EVIL SPIRITS.
EVIL SPIRITS ...?
THEY ARE THAT WHICH LATCH ON TO THE NEGATIVE FEELINGS IN YOUR HEART, LIKE SUSPICION AND HATRED...
......!
...AND ACQUIRE STRANGE POWERS.
YOU SAW ONE WITH YOUR OWN EYES DIDN'T YOU?
IT'S HARD TO TELL UNTIL YOU ACTUALLY CATCH THEM, THOUGH.

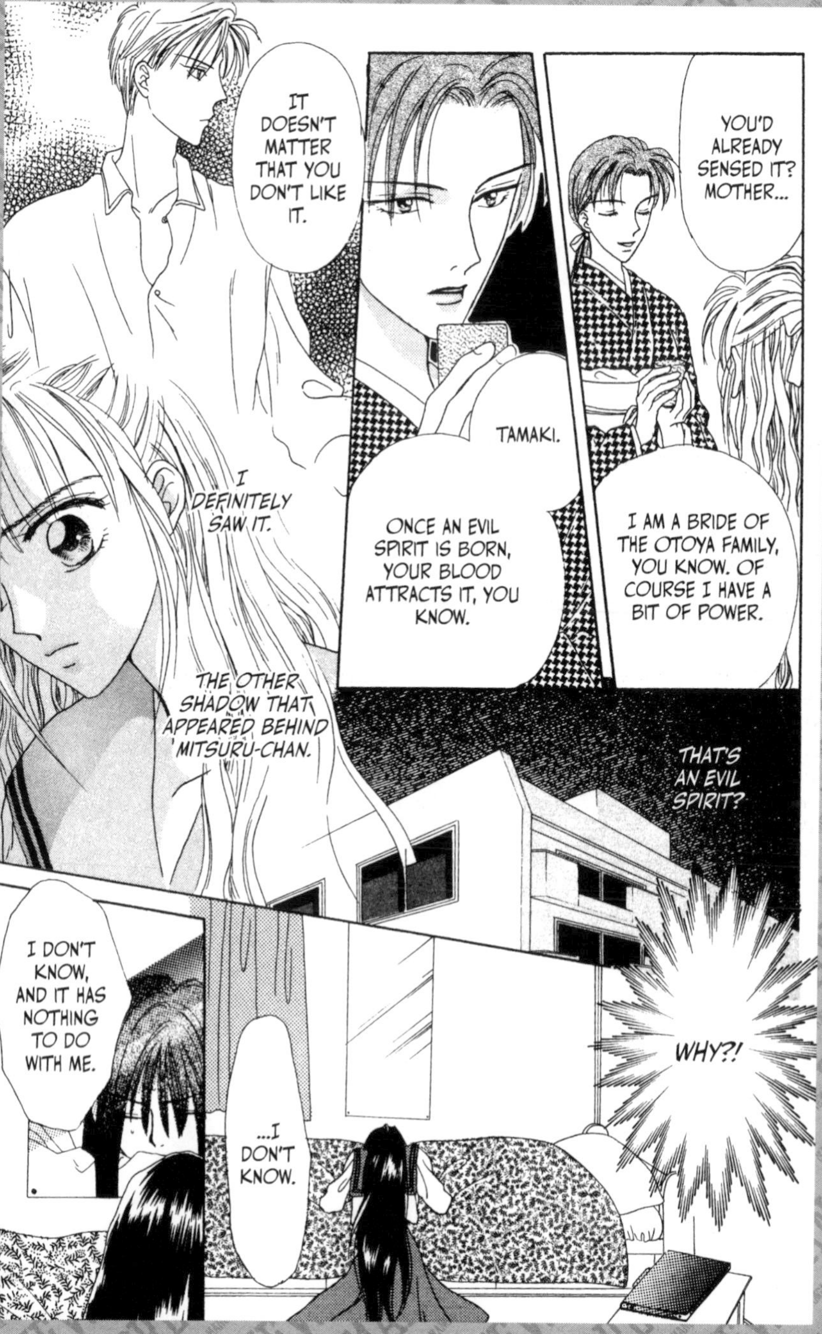
YOU'D ALREADY SENSED IT? MOTHER...
I AM A BRIDE OF THE OTOYA FAMILY, YOU KNOW. OF COURSE I HAVE A BIT OF POWER.
TAMAKI.
ONCE AN EVIL SPIRIT IS BORN, YOUR BLOOD ATTRACTS IT, YOU KNOW.
IT DOESN'T MATTER THAT YOU DON'T LIKE IT.
I DEFINITELY SAW IT.
THE OTHER SHADOW THAT APPEARED BEHIND MITSURU-CHAN.
THAT'S AN EVIL SPIRIT?
WHY?!
...I DON'T KNOW.
I DON'T KNOW, AND IT HAS NOTHING TO DO WITH ME.

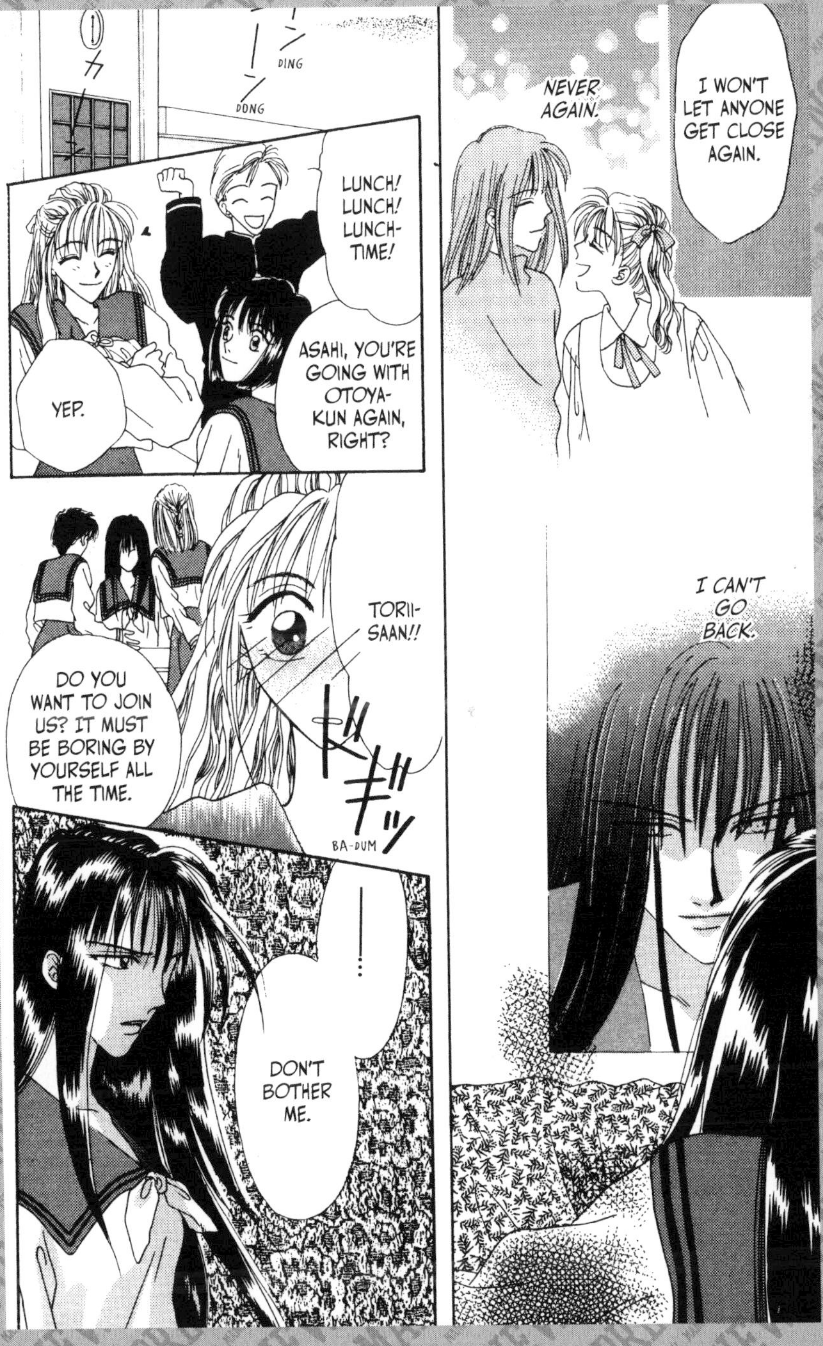
I WON'T LET ANYONE GET CLOSE AGAIN.
NEVER AGAIN.
I CAN'T GO BACK.
DING
DONG
LUNCH! LUNCH! LUNCH-TIME!
ASAHI, YOU'RE GOING WITH OTOYA-KUN AGAIN, RIGHT?
YEP.
TORII-SAAN!!
DO YOU WANT TO JOIN US? IT MUST BE BORING BY YOURSELF ALL THE TIME.
BA-DUM
......
DON'T BOTHER ME.

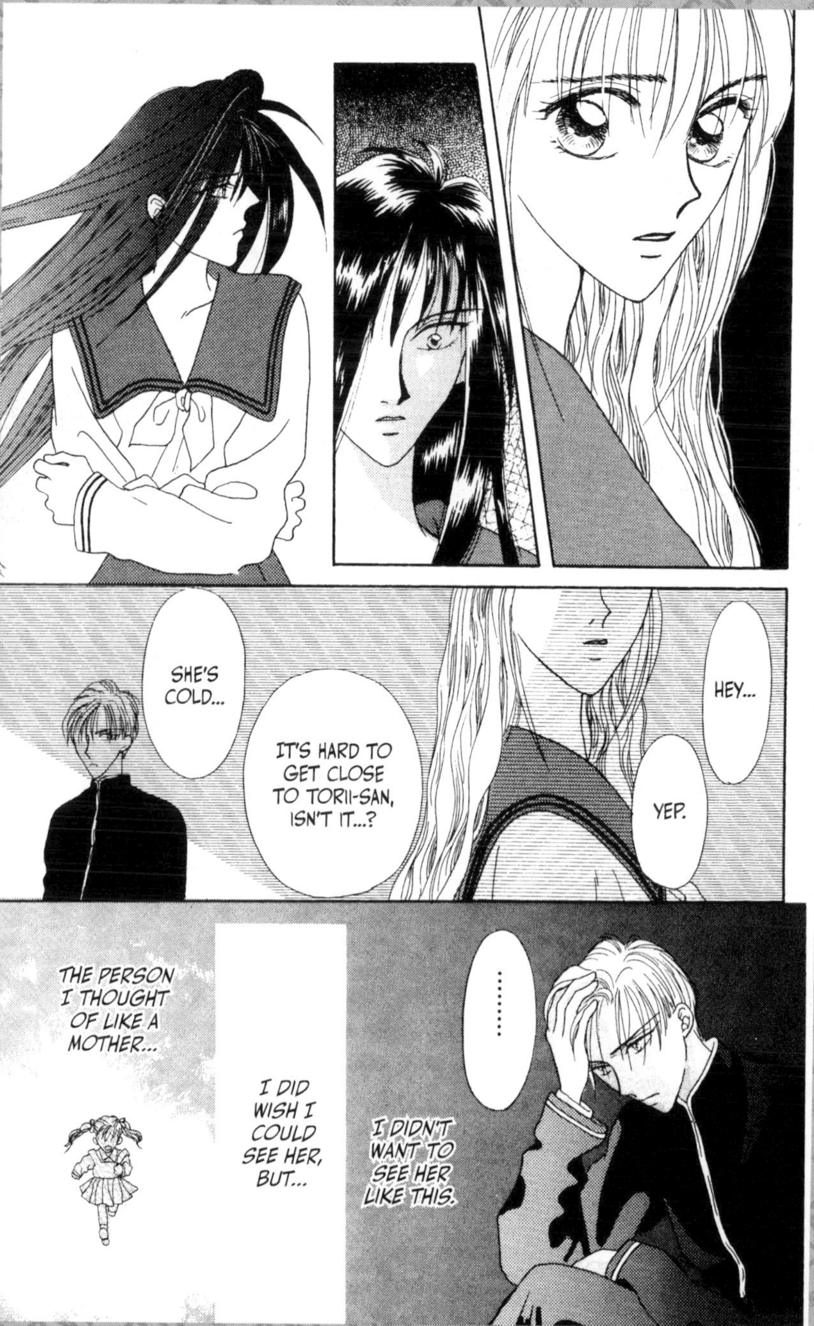
HEY...
YEP.
IT'S HARD TO GET CLOSE TO TORII-SAN, ISN'T IT...?
SHE'S COLD...
....
I DIDN'T WANT TO SEE HER LIKE THIS.
I DID WISH I COULD SEE HER, BUT...
THE PERSON I THOUGHT OF LIKE A MOTHER...

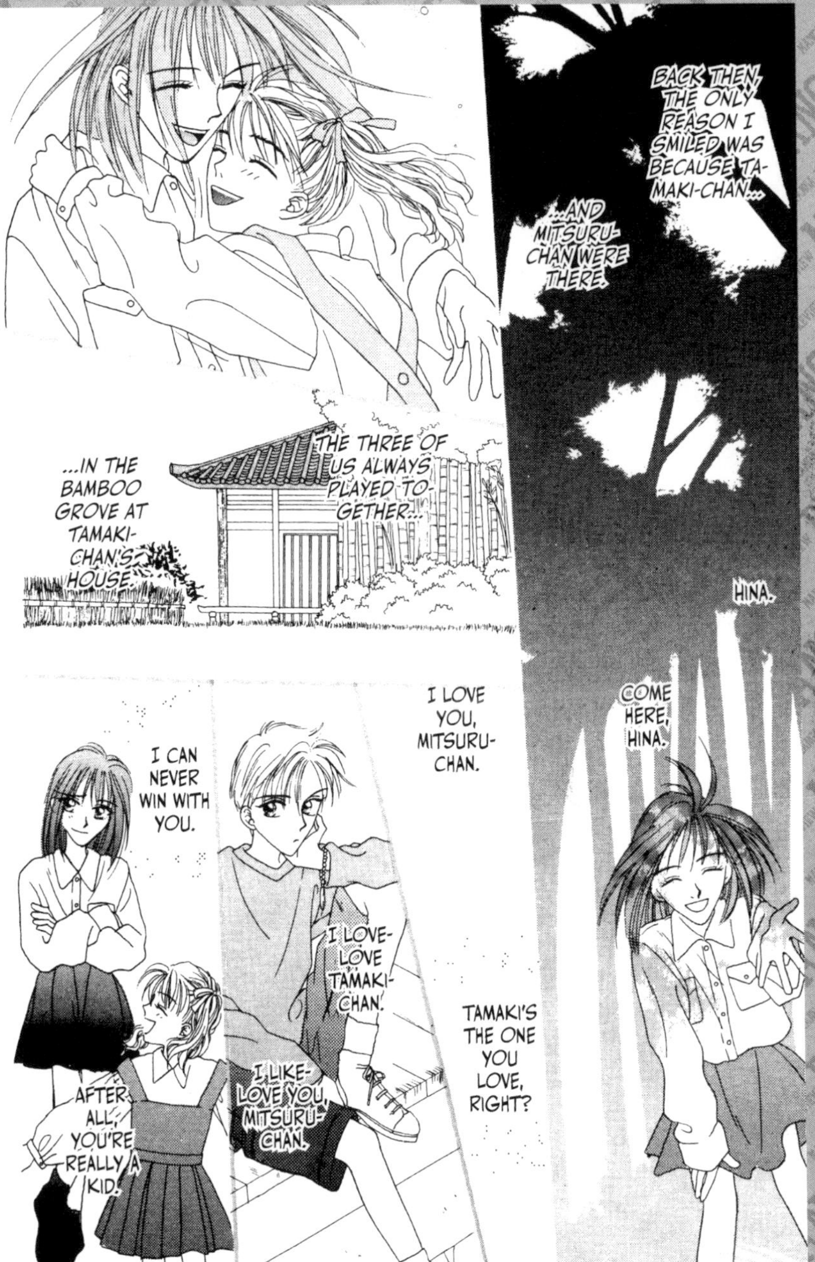
BACK THEN, THE ONLY REASON I SMILED WAS BECAUSE TA-MAKI-CHAN...
...AND MITSURU-CHAN WERE THERE.
HINA.
COME HERE, HINA.
THE THREE OF US ALWAYS PLAYED TO-GETHER...
...IN THE BAMBOO GROVE AT TAMAKI-CHAN'S HOUSE.
I LOVE YOU, MITSURU-CHAN.
TAMAKI'S THE ONE YOU LOVE, RIGHT?
I LOVE-LOVE TAMAKI-CHAN!
I LIKE-LOVE YOU, MITSURU-CHAN.
I CAN NEVER WIN WITH YOU.
AFTER ALL, YOU'RE REALLY A KID!

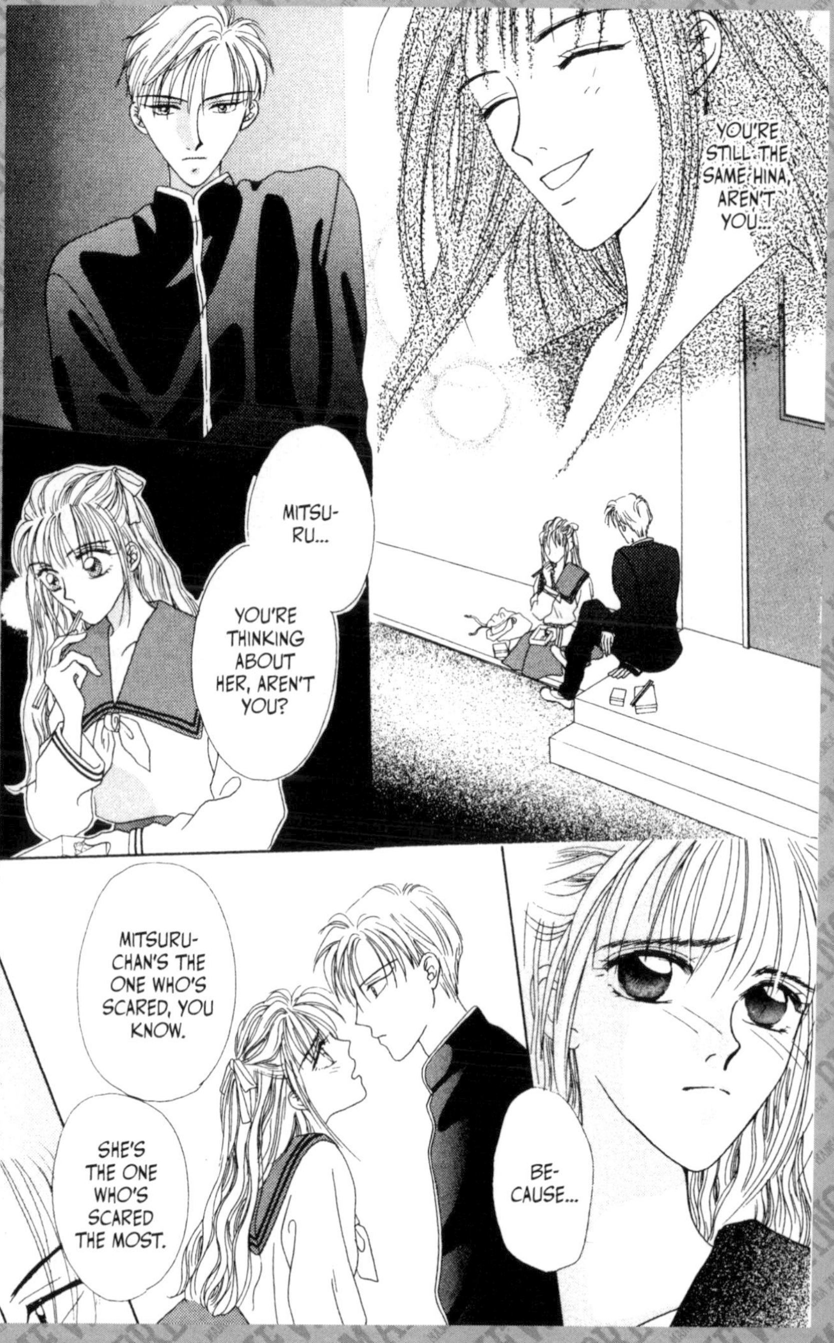
YOU'RE STILL THE SAME HINA, AREN'T YOU...
MITSU-RU...
YOU'RE THINKING ABOUT HER, AREN'T YOU?
BE-CAUSE...
MITSURU-CHAN'S THE ONE WHO'S SCARED, YOU KNOW.
SHE'S THE ONE WHO'S SCARED THE MOST.

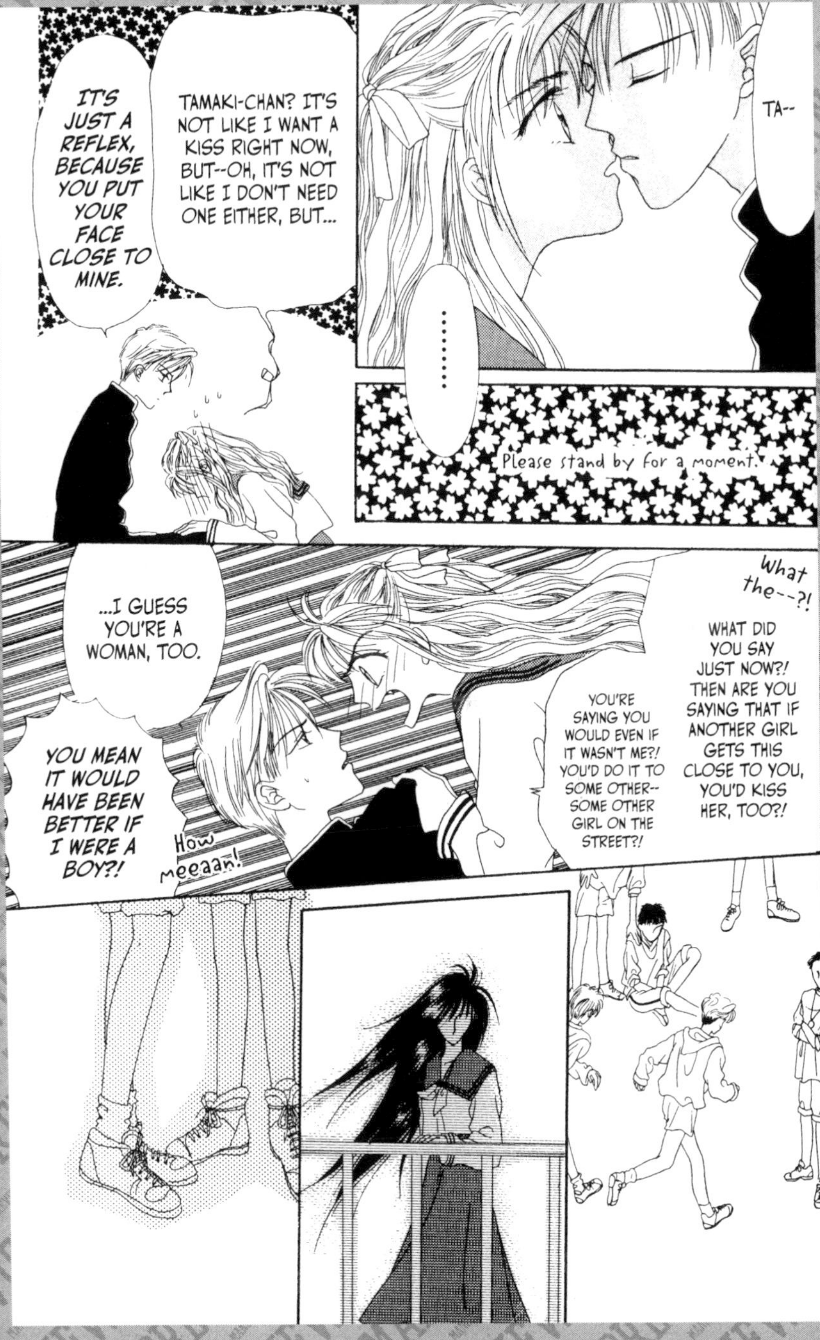
TA--
....
Please stand by for a moment.
TAMAKI-CHAN? IT'S NOT LIKE I WANT A KISS RIGHT NOW, BUT--OH, IT'S NOT LIKE I DON'T NEED ONE EITHER, BUT...
IT'S JUST A REFLEX, BECAUSE YOU PUT YOUR FACE CLOSE TO MINE.
What the--?!
WHAT DID YOU SAY JUST NOW?! THEN ARE YOU SAYING THAT IF ANOTHER GIRL GETS THIS CLOSE TO YOU, YOU'D KISS HER, TOO?!
YOU'RE SAYING YOU WOULD EVEN IF IT WASN'T ME?! YOU'D DO IT TO SOME OTHER-- SOME OTHER GIRL ON THE STREET?!
...I GUESS YOU'RE A WOMAN, TOO.
YOU MEAN IT WOULD HAVE BEEN BETTER IF I WERE A BOY?!
How meeaan!

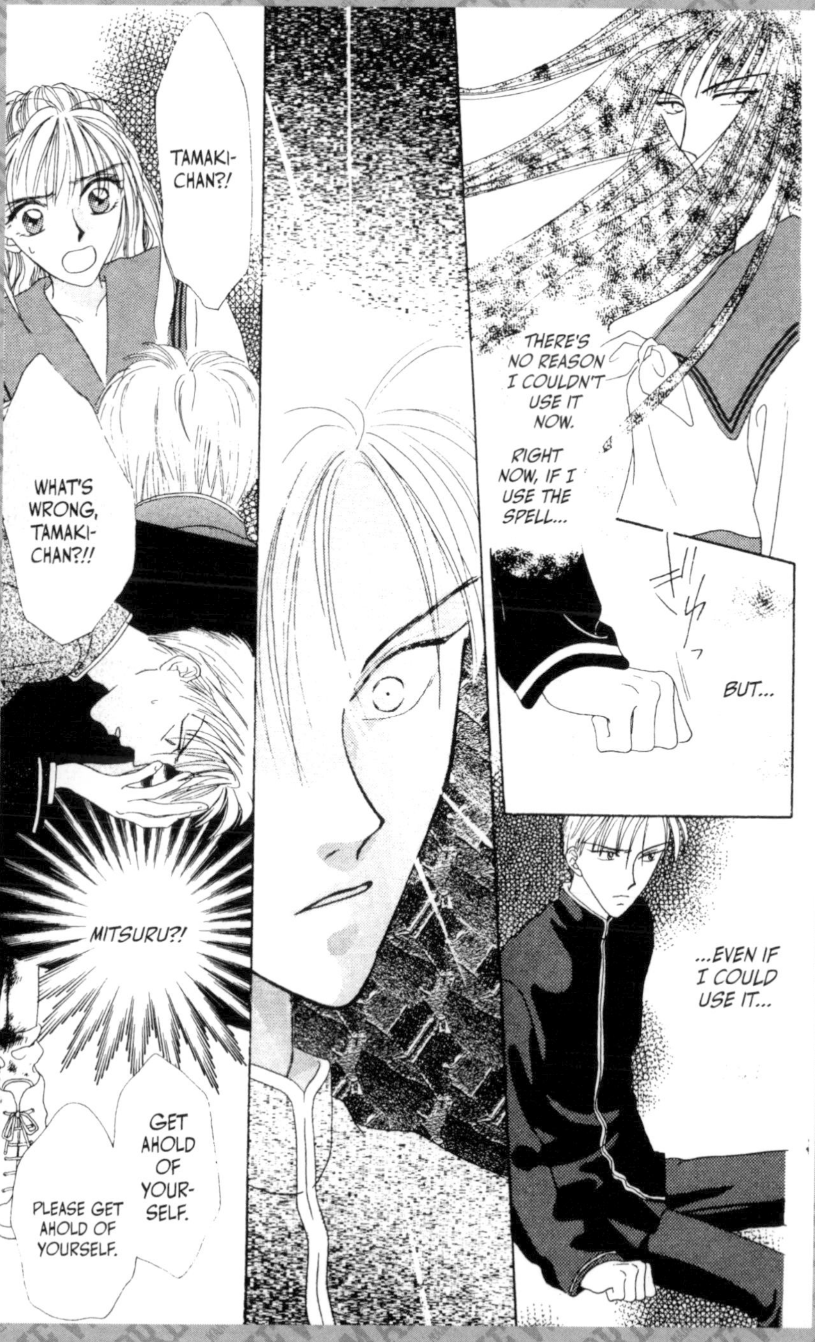
THERE'S NO REASON I COULDN'T USE IT NOW.
RIGHT NOW, IF I USE THE SPELL...
ぎゅっ
BUT...
...EVEN IF I COULD USE IT...
TAMAKI-CHAN?!
WHAT'S WRONG, TAMAKI-CHAN?!!
MITSURU?!
GET AHOLD OF YOURSELF.
PLEASE GET AHOLD OF YOURSELF.

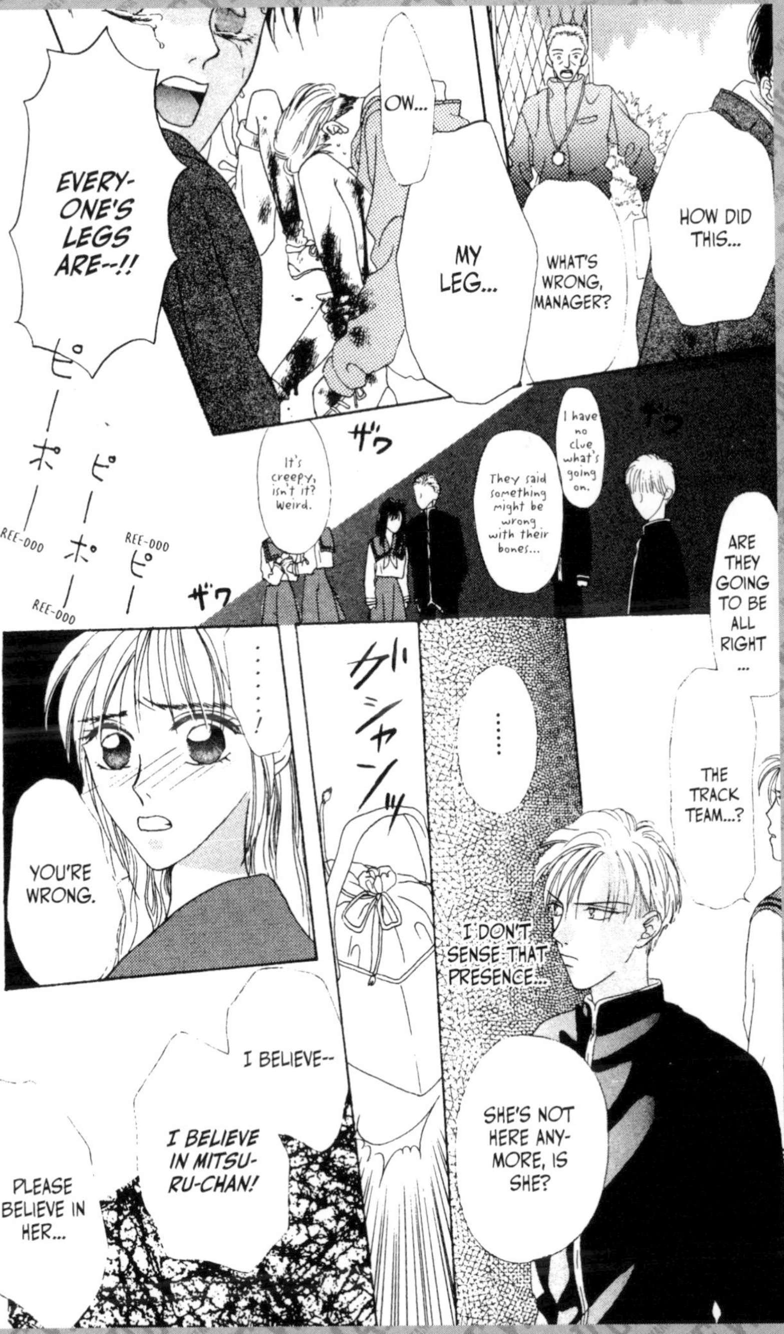
HOW DID THIS...
WHAT'S WRONG, MANAGER?
MY LEG...
OW...
EVERY-ONE'S LEGS ARE--!!
ピーポーピーポーピー
REE-OOO REE-OOO REE-OOO
ザワ
ARE THEY GOING TO BE ALL RIGHT...
ザワ
I have no clue what's going on.
They said something might be wrong with their bones...
It's creepy, isn't it? Weird.
ザワ
THE TRACK TEAM...?
......
I DON'T SENSE THAT PRESENCE...
SHE'S NOT HERE ANY-MORE, IS SHE?
ガシャンッ
......!
YOU'RE WRONG.
I BELIEVE--
I BELIEVE IN MITSU-RU-CHAN!
PLEASE BELIEVE IN HER...

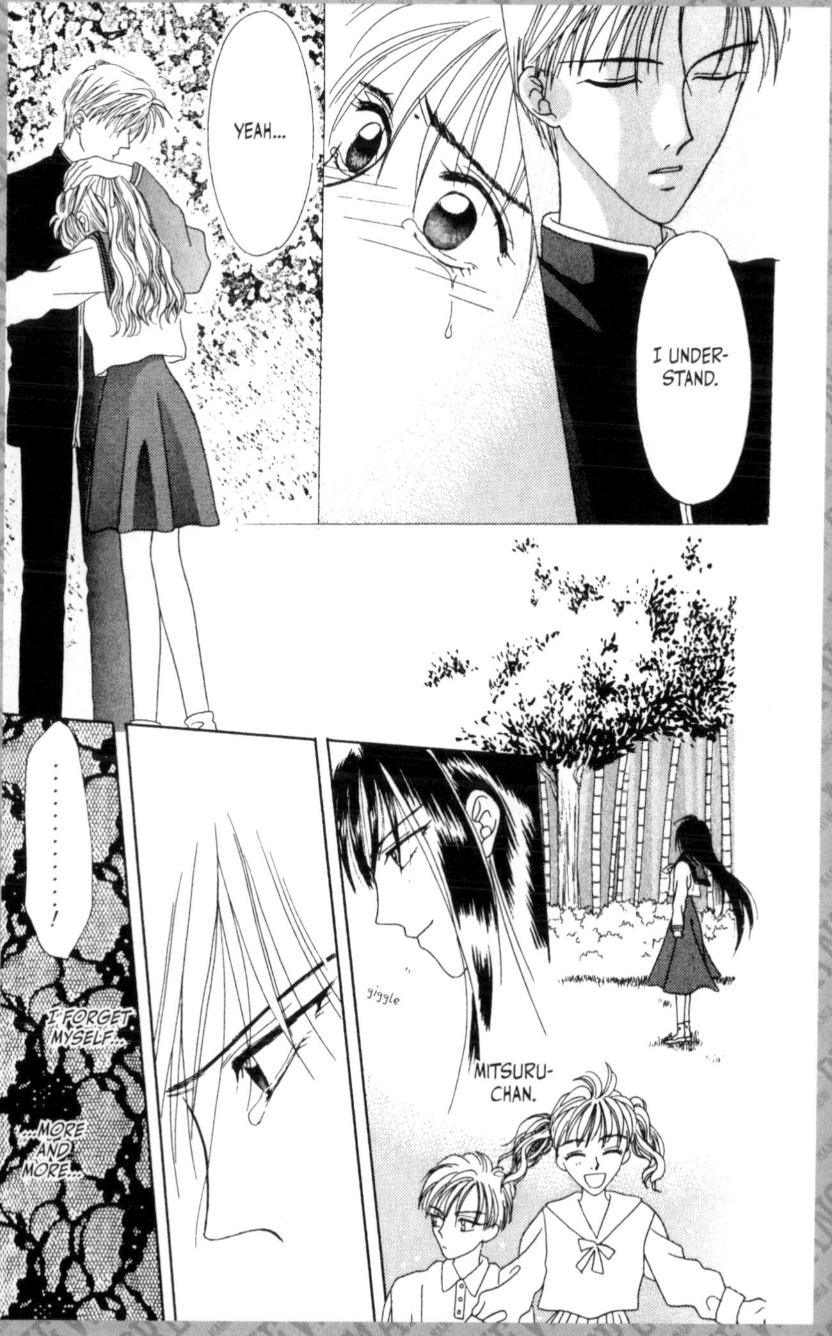
I UNDER-STAND.
YEAH...
MITSURU-CHAN.
giggle
......!
I FORGET MYSELF...
...MORE AND MORE...

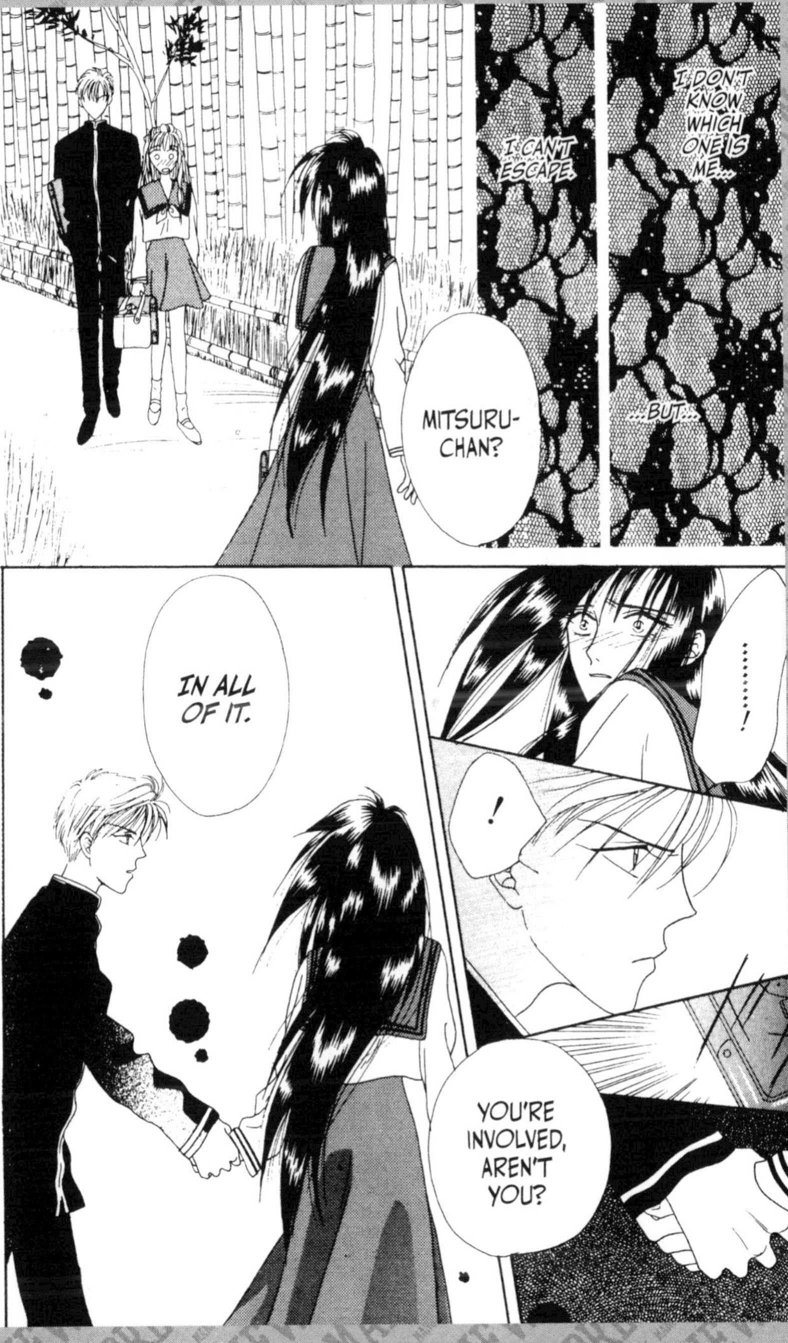

I DON'T KNOW WHICH ONE IS ME...
...BUT...
I CAN'T ESCAPE.
MITSURU-CHAN?
......!
!
YOU'RE INVOLVED, AREN'T YOU?
IN ALL OF IT.

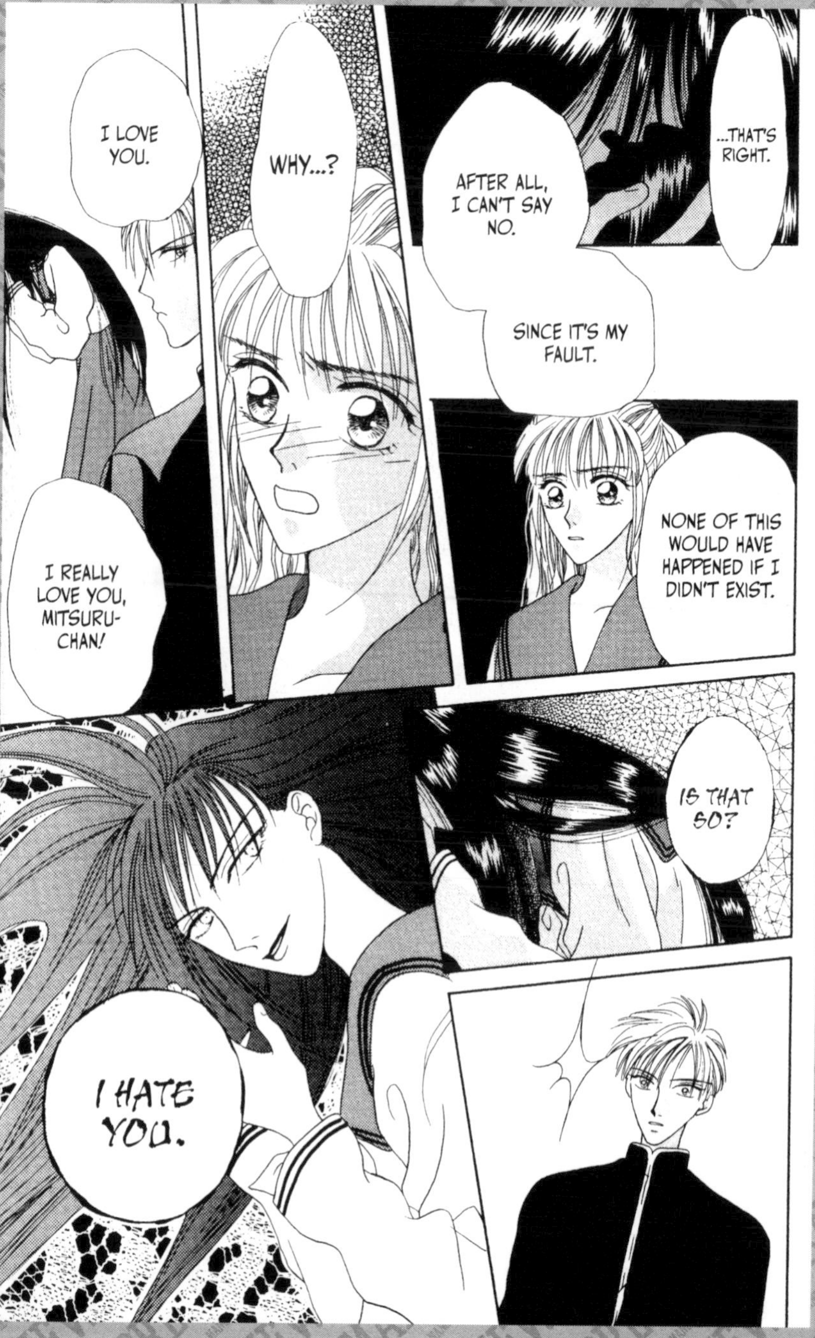
...THAT'S RIGHT.
AFTER ALL, I CAN'T SAY NO.
SINCE IT'S MY FAULT.
NONE OF THIS WOULD HAVE HAPPENED IF I DIDN'T EXIST.
WHY...?
I LOVE YOU.
I REALLY LOVE YOU, MITSURU-CHAN!
IS THAT SO?
I HATE YOU.

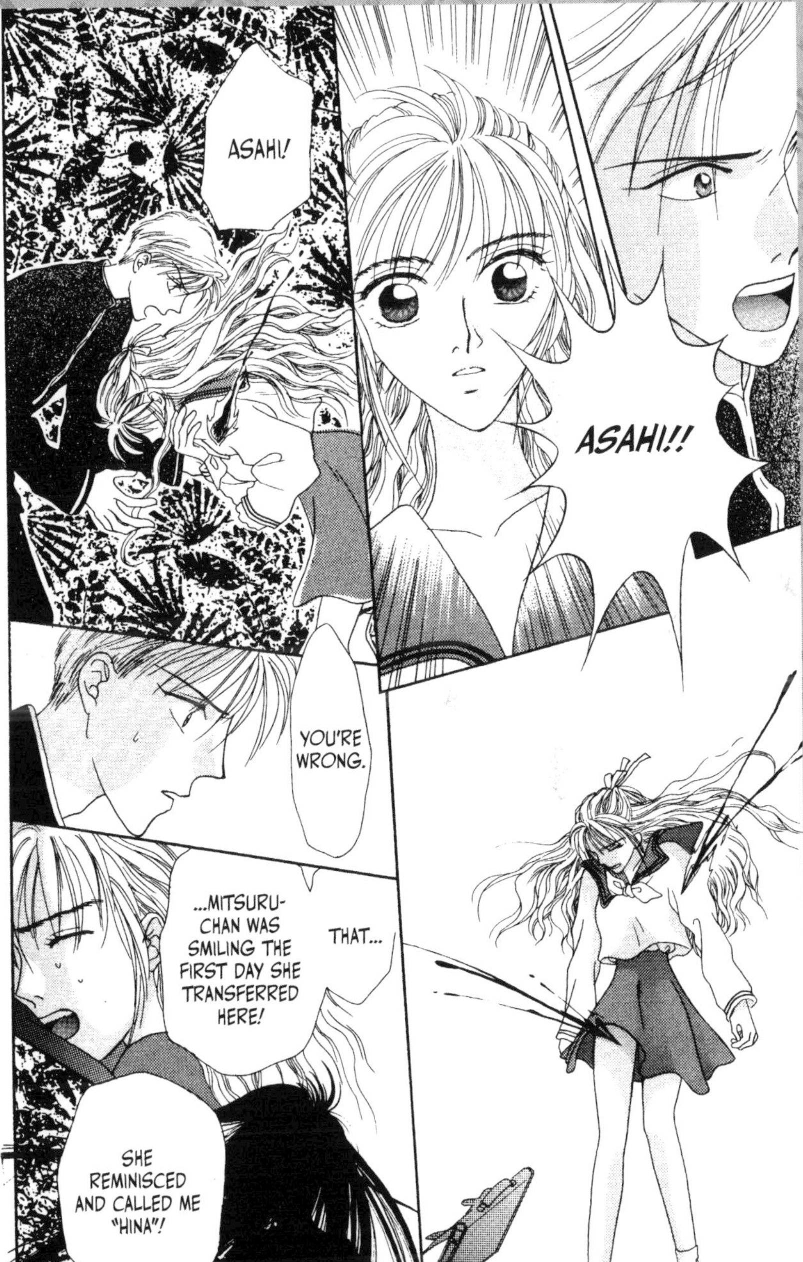
ASAHI!!
ASAHI!
YOU'RE WRONG.
THAT...
...MITSURU-CHAN WAS SMILING THE FIRST DAY SHE TRANSFERRED HERE!
SHE REMINISCED AND CALLED ME "HINA"!

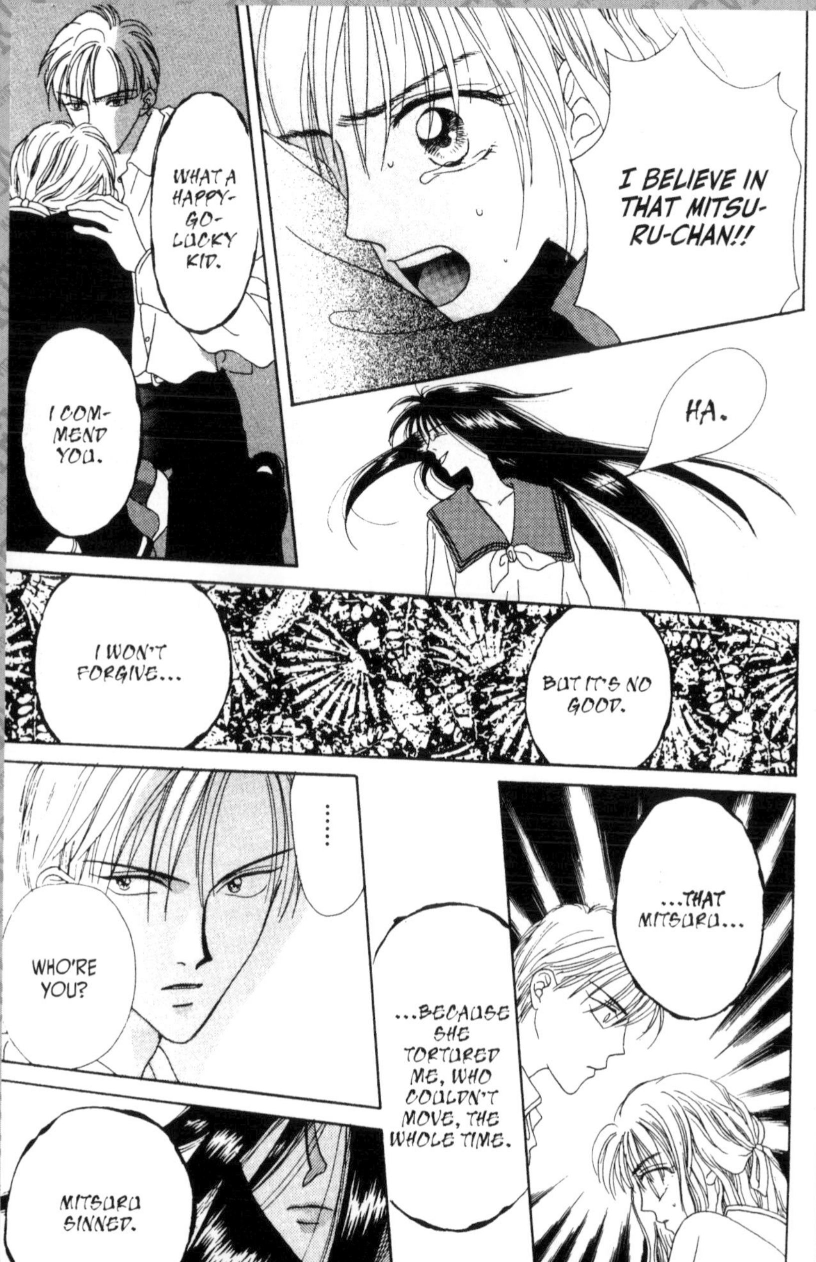
I BELIEVE IN THAT MITSU-RU-CHAN!!
HA.
WHAT A HAPPY-GO-LUCKY KID.
I COM-MEND YOU.
BUT IT'S NO GOOD.
I WON'T FORGIVE...
...THAT MITSURU...
...BECAUSE SHE TORTURED ME, WHO COULDN'T MOVE, THE WHOLE TIME.
......
WHO'RE YOU?
MITSURU SINNED.

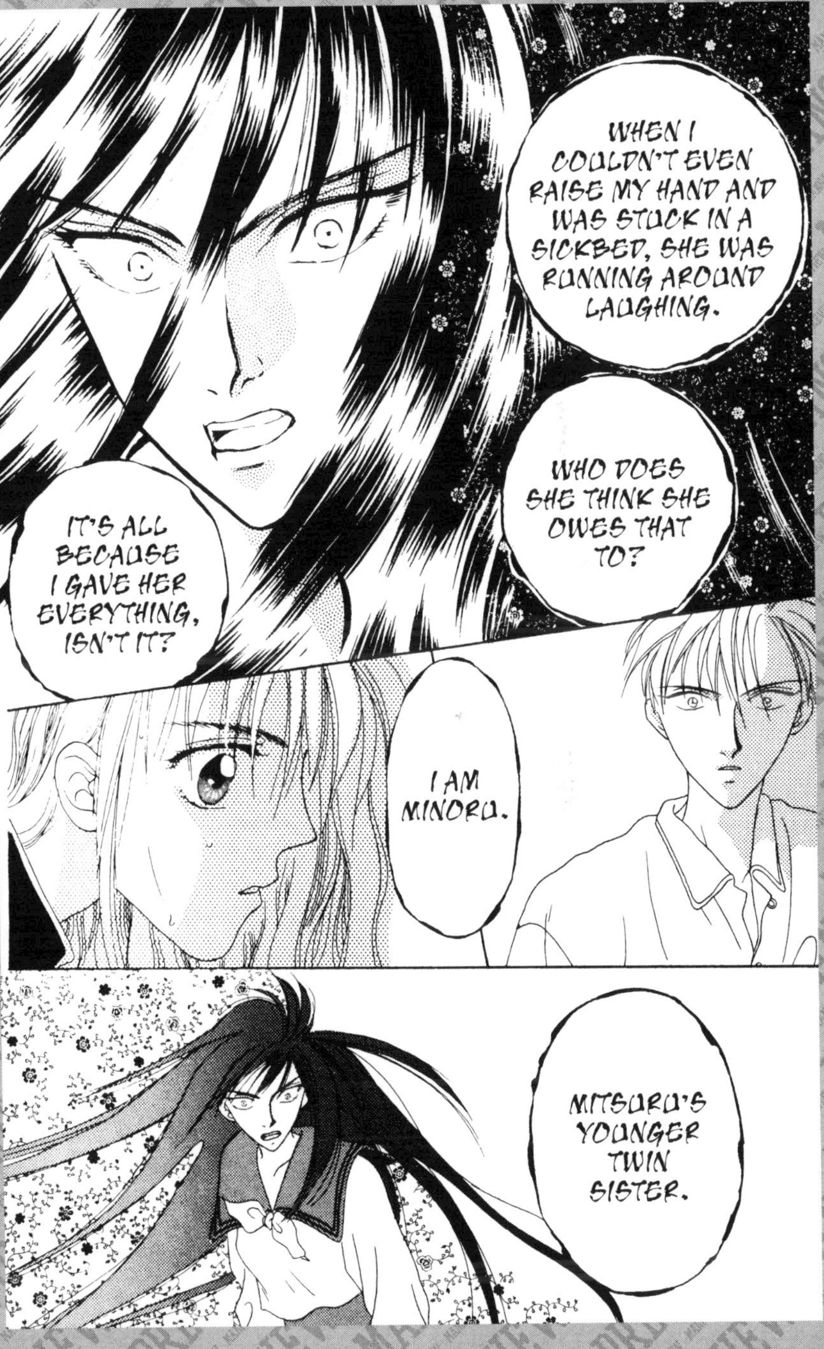
WHEN I COULDN'T EVEN RAISE MY HAND AND WAS STUCK IN A SICKBED, SHE WAS RUNNING AROUND LAUGHING.
WHO DOES SHE THINK SHE OWES THAT TO?
IT'S ALL BECAUSE I GAVE HER EVERYTHING, ISN'T IT?
I AM MINORU.
MITSURU'S YOUNGER TWIN SISTER.

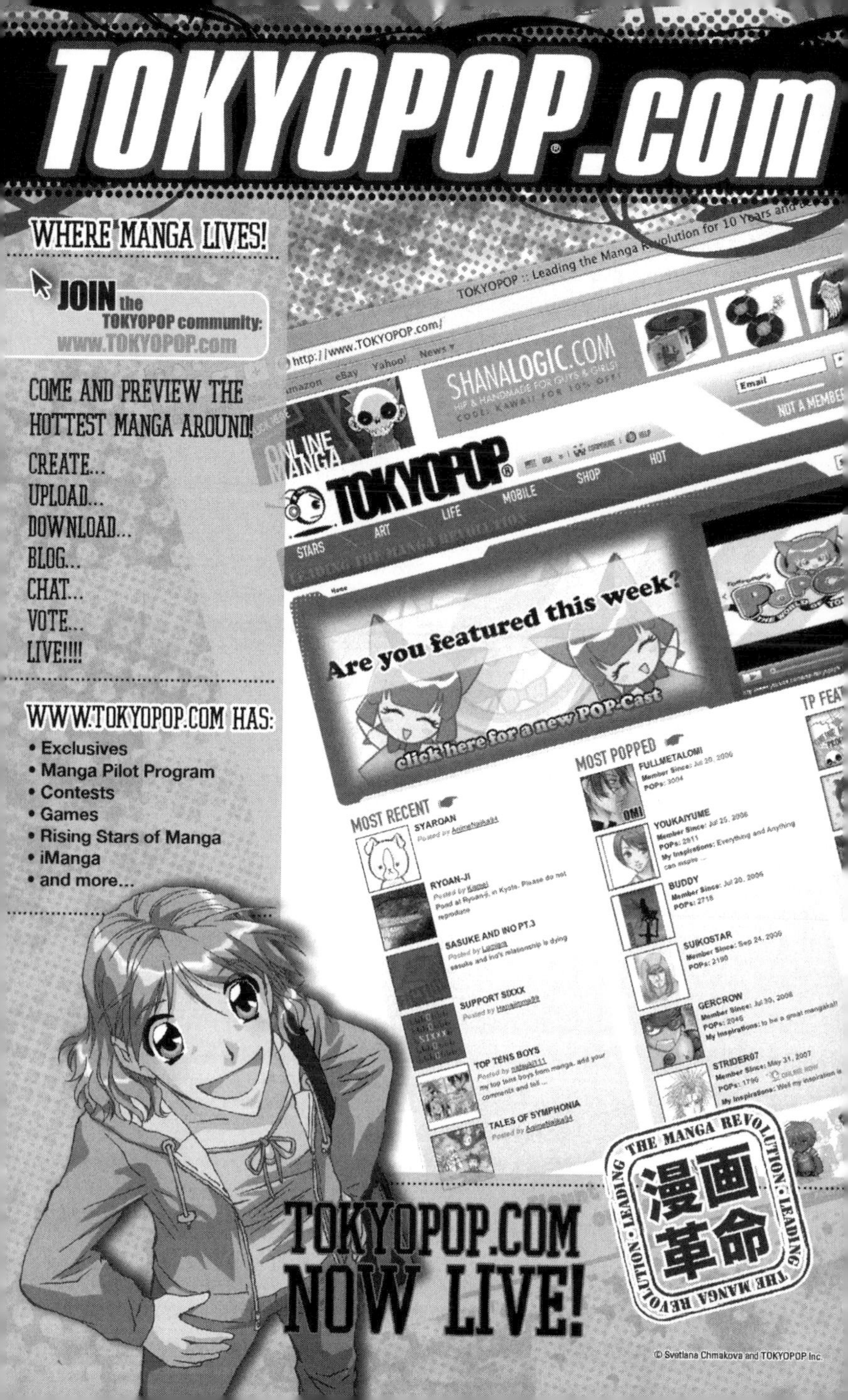
TOKYOPOP®.com
WHERE MANGA LIVES!
JOIN the TOKYOPOP community: www.TOKYOPOP.com
COME AND PREVIEW THE HOTTEST MANGA AROUND!
CREATE...
UPLOAD...
DOWNLOAD...
BLOG...
CHAT...
VOTE...
LIVE!!!!
WWW.TOKYOPOP.COM HAS:
• Exclusives
• Manga Pilot Program
• Contests
• Games
• Rising Stars of Manga
• iManga
• and more...
TOKYOPOP :: Leading the Manga Revolution for 10 Years and
http://www.TOKYOPOP.com/
SHANALOGIC.COM
TOKYOPOP®
STARS
ART
LIFE
MOBILE
SHOP
HOT
Are you featured this week?
click here for a new POP-Cast
MOST RECENT
MOST POPPED
SYAROAN
RYOAN-JI
SASUKE AND INO PT.3
SUPPORT SIXXX
TOP TENS BOYS
TALES OF SYMPHONIA
FULLMETALOMI
YOUKAIYUME
BUDDY
SUIKOSTAR
GERCROW
STRIDER07
TOKYOPOP.COM NOW LIVE!
THE MANGA REVOLUTION • LEADING THE MANGA REVOLUTION • LEADING
漫画革命
© Svetlana Chmakova and TOKYOPOP Inc.

STOP!

This is the back of the book.
You wouldn't want to spoil a great ending!

This book is printed "manga-style," in the authentic Japanese right-to-left format. Since none of the artwork has been flipped or altered, readers get to experience the story just as the creator intended. You've been asking for it, so TOKYOPOP® delivered: authentic, hot-off-the-press, and far more fun!

DIRECTIONS

If this is your first time reading manga-style, here's a quick guide to help you understand how it works.

It's easy... just start in the top right panel and follow the numbers. Have fun, and look for more 100% authentic manga from TOKYOPOP®!